Weird Georgia

Weird Georgia

Close Encounters, Strange Creatures, and Unexplained Phenomena

JIM MILES

CUMBERLAND HOUSE
NASHVILLE, TENNESSEE

WEIRD GEORGIA
PUBLISHED BY CUMBERLAND HOUSE PUBLISHING, INC.
431 Harding Industrial Drive
Nashville, Tennessee 37211

Cover design by Unlikely Suburban Design, Nashville, Tennessee
Text design by Mike Towle

Library of Congress Cataloging-in-Publication Data

Miles, Jim.
  Weird Georgia : close encounters, strange creatures, and unexplained phenomena / Jim Miles.
      p.   cm.
  Includes index.
  ISBN 1-58182-138-7 (pbk.)
  1. Human-alien encounters—Georgia. 2. Unidentified flying objects—Sightings and encounters—Georgia. I. Title.
  BF2050.M56 2000
  001.94'09758—dc21   00-057069

2 3 4 5 6 7 8 9—07 06 05

Contents

Acknowledgments

This book was many years in the making and originated from hundreds of sources. For nearly thirty years I have been a plague to librarians and curators across the state. I am indebted to all of them. Most acceded to my requests with little more than a smile and an occasional slight smirk. Special thanks are extended to the Washington Street Library in Macon, particularly the well-stocked and staffed genealogical section, whose employees were deceived into thinking I was writing another respectable Civil War book; the Mercer University library, which I have been intellectually plundering for decades; and the University of Georgia library—their Georgia newspaper collection on microfilm is a treasure.

I traveled thousands of miles across Georgia in search of the strange and unusual, often accompanied by my wife, Earline, and son, Paul(daughter Melanie was too smart to indulge me, but she's young yet).

My childhood interest was fueled by the books of Coral and Frank Lorenzo, founders of the Aerial Phenomenon Research Organization (APRO, whose ranks I joined while in junior high), Jacques Vallee, and John Keel, and the less-respectable books of Frank Edwards, Herald T. Wilkins, and the various pseudonyms of Brad Steiger. The TV show *The Invaders* also fueled my flying saucer fantasies.

My thanks extend to a group of magazines (and, yes, a few tabloids) that published nearly a hundred of my UFO-weirdness articles during the late 1970s and early 1980s. This was before I turned to more legitimate journalistic pursuits (Civil War books featured by the History Book Club). The best-paying market, with a considerate editor, was Saga's *UFO Report*, followed by *True UFOs*, where the kind and desperate editor often ran two or three of my articles in one issue—only one attributed to me—*Beyond Reality*, and *Argosy UFO*, which published my first UFO article and then folded (I like to think there was no relationship between the two events). Then there were the tabloids—one was the *Midnight Globe*—the others I have banished from memory.

The only enduring magazine is *Fate*, then digest-sized and published by Curtis and Mary Fuller, true legends in weirdness. They published my more respectable material and even required intelligent rewriting. They are gone now, but it's still a damn good magazine.

The madmen now deemed prophets include Jacques Vallee, a French scientist who approached UFOs from a scientific perspective before realizing the flaws of that notion. *Passport to Magnolia* is required reading for the weird initiate. The dean of strangeness is John Keel, whose *Mothman Prophesies* is holy writ. He understood early that UFOs were not extraterrestrial spacecraft and that there is an underlying connection between all manner of paranormal events.

A second mention, this one a kudo, goes to the founding father of Fortean science, Charles Fort, who spent decades scouring publications from around the world for the weirdness that filled his speculative classics *Book of the Damned, Lo!*, and *Strange Talents*. Several organizations, active to varying degrees, continue his work today, as does William Corliss with his Sourcebook Project.

I also owe a debt to John Thompson and all the researchers at the International Society for UFO Research (ISUR) and Mutual UFO Network (MUFON) GA, the pioneers of the Georgia Swamp Ape Research Center, and Ann Davis and her Altamaha-ha work.

I am eternally thankful to my parents, Ray and Eddie Lee Miles, not only for refraining from killing me during my youth, but for indulging my interests no matter how odd, and to Earline, my long-suffering Southern Baptist wife, who has resisted the urge to throw my work into the fire (a Sequoyah reference).

I must thank my Alabama grandmothers, Cleo Miles and Minnie Davis, who have passed to the next world, and my aunt, Flora Craven, for sharing our weird family heritage with me.

I am thankful for my Protestant upbringing, which led me to approach these subjects with caution. My family, teachers, and comrades instilled a healthy skepticism toward human behavior and extraordinary events while maintaining a relatively open mind. My profession—teaching—left me summers, long holidays, and weekends to be filled with extensive traveling and research.

Thanks to my immediate family for not being embarrassed by my unusual interests, and to readers who will hopefully enter into this work with open minds and a healthy sense of humor.

Most importantly, I am forever appreciative to all the unique people who, despite danger of ridicule, shared with me and others their stories, however bizarre.

There were times when I felt the rules of the weird netherlands were conspiring against the completion of this learned tome. Chapter 3, "UFOs: The Clash of '73," was abducted twice by electronic demons and written from scratch three times. The "Ancient Mysteries" chapter only vanished like the Roanoke settlers once. The computer gods also once dismembered this section. Now I feel assured that the entities that don't want their secrets spilled have been vanquished.

Introduction

Did ancient silver crosses excavated from Indian mounds originate with European colonials or ancient space visitors? Are artifacts stored at Brenau University, in Gainesville, frauds or authentic messages left behind from the lost English colony at Roanoke? Was the metallic object found in a LaGrange flower bed actually engraved with Minoan characters, and did a stone discovered at Fort Benning contain a Phoenician inscription? Did ancient inhabitants of Etowah and Ocmulgee incorporate astronomical calendars into their earthworks? And who were the giants uncovered from prehistoric burial mounds? Why do long-dead Indians wail in the predawn at Macon's Ocmulgee Mounds, and what invisible guardians once ejected trash thrown into an ancient ceremonial circle in Habersham County?

Bigfoot creatures and things even stranger have been reported across Georgia. Even a giant water serpent has been observed by four hundred people in the Altamaha River. Big phantom cats and bizarre unions of tigers and lions reportedly have prowled the countryside. Giant dinosaur-era birds supposedly have been seen flapping their great wings on several occasions.

Close encounters of the first, second, third, and fourth kinds have occurred across the state since the 1940s, and those came long after a wave of "airship" sightings were reported at the turn of the century. In one highly regarded case, a woman in Henry County came across an alien work crew busily probing a highway. Police have chased UFOs, and the air force has dispatched planes to investigate unidentified radar images over Georgia. The only president to report a UFO sighting was native son Jimmy Carter, and recently declassified CIA, FBI, and air force documents reveal that in 1955 Georgia senator Richard B. Russell, chairman of the powerful Armed Forces Committee, witnessed two UFOs while touring the Soviet Union. Some researchers have alleged that a UFO that crashed in rural Heard County in 1977 was recovered in a secret government operation.

Mysterious atmospheric booms have no apparent cause. Phantom screamers haunt skyscrapers. Elusive hummers torment homeowners. Schools, factories, offices, neighborhoods, and even a Marta passenger train succumb to inexplicable odors, sometimes permeating entire counties and sickening hundreds.

Odd things occasionally fall from Georgia skies: seeds in Savannah, fifty thousand birds in Warner Robins, an endless string in Elberton, "angel hair" from Savannah to Atlanta, a fiery tornado in Americus, alligators in Bulloch County, two fireballs under apparent intelligent control near Griffin, and several icebergs.

The most intriguing case of spontaneous human combustion on record occurred in Savannah, where the victim survived to tell the tale. The Atlanta area twice was plagued by a mysterious arsonist who torched dozens of cars but was never seen.

Georgia's unique people are not to be ignored. Lulu Hurst, "the Electric Girl," astounded audiences with her superhuman abilities over a century ago. People traveled from many states to consult seer Mayhayley Lancaster, whose testimony influenced one of Georgia's most famous court trials. Lonnie Taylor miraculously healed more than thirty-five thousand afflicted people. A woman was brought back from the dead after fifteen minutes as a congregation prayed. Images of Jesus have appeared on a Columbus tree, a giant billboard, a communion cloth, and the side of a rural house.

Zell Miller changed travel plans to Europe on a hunch, just before terrorist attacks erupted, and a college student suddenly chose a different flight—her original flight fell from the sky over Lockerbee, Scotland. Ben Fortson, Georgia's long-term and beloved secretary of state, had a premonition of his death hours before it occurred. So did several Union soldiers fighting in Georgia during the Civil War.

For two weeks in October 1872, a house in Appling County was the most haunted structure in the world, and one day in 1987 a house in Atlanta *bled*. Reportedly, a pillar in Augusta is still cursed. In Adairsville the spirits of two unknown Confederate soldiers, killed and buried in 1864, transmitted their identities through a table-tapping seance. The evidence convinced the federal government to provide tombstones. Did a hellhound dog the Allman Brothers, a triangle of doom down Otis Redding, and can REM's Michael Stipe predict earthquakes?

Ghost trains, complete with lights and sounds, rumble along a half dozen rail lines, and more than one spectral conductor searches the tracks for his missing head.

Nature is a weird thing. Not every event is governed by its laws. At certain places cars roll uphill and stop going downhill. Lightning strikes leave patterns of vegetation on humans. Caves blow, then suck. Lakes fill, then empty of their own accord. Meteors, traditional and glazed, fall, and an extinct comet left us with celestial acne. There are years when winter never comes, and sometimes no light accompanies the day. Rainfall has been confined to a tightly restricted area and has been known to piddle from a cloudless sky for long periods of time. We have great cracks in the ground and bald mountains from which the sounds of an eternal bowling game seem to emanate. Tourists flock to limestone sinks, giant stones, and rock cities.

The accounts of these and many other phenomena contained in *Weird Georgia* are factual, not rehashed folklore. Each story is supported by reputable evidence. Although the tales are told in a straightforward manner, a healthy dose of skepticism and occasional humor are available to help us hold on to reality. This is a book for readers with open minds, and true believers in various phenomena will find abundant material presented nowhere else.

I have spent thirty years exploring the backwoods of Georgia. I have pored over hundreds of books about Georgia history, many collections of yellowed newspaper clippings, and newspapers, magazines, and journals beyond counting, for any mention of curious occurrences in Georgia. Very few of these stories have received publicity, which makes them fresh and fascinating.

There are many legitimate mysteries in Georgia, but you can't accept everything that is presented as fact. Several false cases are exposed here, such as the monkeyman from Mars and the crosses from Atlantis. Note also that many "explanations" for our bizarre occurrences often don't hold water.

This book concerns Fortean science, named for Charles Fort, who, during the earliest decades of the twentieth century, scoured libraries for strange events, including UFOs, odd occurrences in nature, and out-of-place artifacts. His groundbreaking *Book of the Damned* opened with the line, "A procession of the damned." It is a procession chronicled here for Georgia. Enjoy.

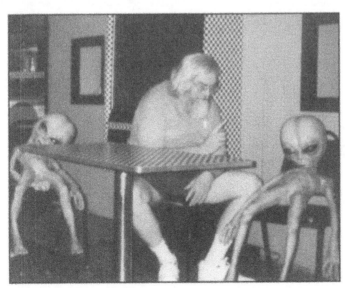

The author and two of his new friends at Roswell, New Mexico, enjoy a lively discussion.

1

The Early History of Georgia UFOs

ATLANTA ENTERS THE AIRSHIP AGE

UFOs have always been with us but in different guises that have happened to match the next logical advancement of human transportation. This age-old phenomena mutates as society develops. The "phantom airship" phenomenon of the nineteenth century started in California (where else?) in mid-November 1896. The craft were frequently spotted as the phenomenon moved east until spring 1897. Thousands of people saw them in at least eighteen states and Canada. Consternation accompanied the airships wherever they appeared, generating extensive press coverage and public speculation, but the ships left no physical evidence. They were the "flying saucers" of the turn of the twentieth century.

What were the airships? They appeared to be rigid, steerable, cigar-shaped dirigibles propelled by steam or primitive internal-combustion engines. Their inhabitants, frequently seen and occasionally heard to speak English, often with a foreign accent, were ostensibly human. No investigator could ever pinpoint their construction or base sites. The airships were elusive, and there is even an alleged Roswell-like "crash" site of one in Texas, the disposal of its occupants a continuing controversy. Several "abductions" were also attributed to the phenomenon.

On or around April 15, 1897, a Chattanooga newspaper described an incident in which several "presumably truthful" citizens averred they "came upon the vessel resting on a spur of a mountain near this city. Two men were at work on it and explained that they had been compelled to return to earth because the machinery was out of order. One of the men said that his name was 'Prof. Charles Davidson.' He is alleged to have said that the vessel left Sacramento a month ago and had been sailing all over the country."

Georgia's most prominent airship sighting occurred at 1:00 A.M. on June 7, 1897. It was seen primarily in the northern part of Atlanta, and then departed to the northeast, crossing the Southern Railway line beyond

1

Ponce de Leon Avenue. The craft was witnessed by what the *Atlanta Journal* described as "a number of well-known citizens." They said it presented "a most novel and striking sight."

The object, which flew gracefully over the city at an estimated height of one mile and a speed of ten miles per hour, was in clear sight for some time. The craft's "outlines were distinctly visible" and was described as the size of a streetcar, "brilliantly lighted as with electricity," the newspaper accounts continued. It had "the appearance of the upper-deck saloon of an ocean steamer when seen at a great distance on the sea at night."

"Worse than the Air Ship" proclaimed the *Journal* on June 14. It reported that "a strange-looking figure which resembled a woman with long flowing hair was seen by a few of our citizens a few evenings ago, flying through the air three or four hundred feet over the Litchfield Hotel" at Acworth.

Throughout that June many Atlantans rose between three and four in the morning to scan the northeastern skies for the appearance of what some considered a skyship and others a natural phenomenon. According to the June 14 *Atlanta Constitution*, E. P. Chamberlin believed "the strange, luminous body is an enormous meteor falling through the immensity of space toward the earth's surface. The object," he said, "has appeared nearer and nearer every time he has seen it." The fact that it appeared each day at the same time lends some credence to the object being a celestial body, but a meteor that size would have been another dinosaur killer. Others thought it was "nothing more than a small patch of clouds glowing in the first beams of the rising sun."

Farmer Jim Nelson swore he saw the "mysterious air traveler" which was "descending straight to the earth with great rapidity," a maneuver that made his hair stand on end in fear. It paused momentarily several hundred feet above the ground, then started moving away at the speed of a train. Such antics are commonly attributed to modern UFOs.

Another Atlanta witness, presumably tongue in cheek, reported seeing three men on an aerial vessel singing "Nearer My God to Thee" (shades of *Titanic*) and distributing temperance literature (Carrie Nation in space).

The good citizens of Georgia were not misinterpreting natural phenomenon, a fact proven around 8:00 P.M. on June 21, 1897, when a dazzling meteor flashed through the skies. The meteor passed from east to west at about twenty-five degrees above the horizon with "electric brilliancy," the *Eatonton Messenger* stated. The object "left a train of sparks like a gorgeous rock. Probably no larger nor more beautiful meteor was ever seen." The celestial light show was viewed for several seconds southeast of Hartwell, where it was described as "a huge ball of fire . . . as large as an infant's head."

The next Southern airship appeared over Chattanooga at 9:00 A.M. on January 12, 1910, and returned on the following two days. Thousands of citizens saw the craft, dubbed the "Chattanooga Chugger" and described as a large white cigar, cruise repeatedly through the skies at thirty miles per hour. Witnesses heard a faint chugging sound and saw flickering blue flames along its length. On the twelfth the device disappeared over the mountains to the west. A similar object was spotted over Huntsville, Alabama, fifteen minutes and seventy-five miles later. This craft, assuming it was the same one and assuming it was bound by earthly restrictions, had really poured on the speed (three hundred miles per hour? Do the math). On January 13 the ship departed to the south, presumably entering Georgia airspace, the direction from which it appeared for its final twenty-minute cruise above the city on January 14. It again left in the direction of Georgia across Missionary Ridge.

THE 1940s

SOMEWHERE IN GEORGIA

The next phase of the UFO phenomenon was "foo fighters"—balls of light that combat and transport pilots reported observing in the air war over Europe and Japan during World War II. Georgia escaped their attention, but the outbreak of war brought a traditional UFO incident to the state seven years before the modern UFO era started.

Four respectable citizens made the sighting in early December 1941. They were a Lieutenant Nad, Mrs. Walter Hanson, and two other officers from Camp Hahn, California. According to Mrs. Hanson, who later reported the incident to the National Investigating Committee on Aerial Phenomenon (NICAP), the four were "somewhere in Georgia" one night when they ran out of gas. While one officer, Lieutenant Turnbull, hitched to the nearest gas station, the other three watched the stars. After a while, Mrs. Hanson related, "I suddenly spotted what I thought was a star begin to move. I watched it several minutes before I could bring myself to mention it."

"It went in circles, counterclockwise, which was especially baffling," she continued. "It made these circles so quickly it was hard to believe our own eyes. Suddenly, it stopped dead again and just as quickly took off obliquely, upward and out of sight."

Mrs. Hanson emphasized that all of the witnesses were college graduates, and "we knew a little of the principles of physics. Nothing we could possibly think of would answer our questions."

IN THE BEGINNING

The modern UFO age began on June 24, 1947, when pilot Kenneth Arnold, flying above the Cascade Mountains in the Pacific Northwest, saw a group of unidentified flying objects shaped like discs, or saucers, which instantly earned the phenomenon the moniker "flying saucers." Saucer fever instantly swept the nation.

Georgia officially entered the "flying saucer" age on the evening of July 9, 1947, when two Macon residents phoned in sightings to the *Telegraph*. At 8:30 a woman on Edgewood Avenue saw a "giant purple disc whirling over Porter Stadium." The UFO was described as "twice the size of a large beach umbrella." It was high in the air, fast, and shone like the sun.

The second report originated at 10:30 from a man on Broadway who saw a green disc with whirling lights.

THE MODERN ERA: CHILES-WHITTED, A CLASSIC CASE

The moon was bright and visibility was excellent, broken only by scattered clouds, as Capt. Clarence S. Chiles and his copilot John B. Whitted flew their normal passenger-plane route from Houston. They had taken off at 8:30 P.M., July 23, 1948, bound for Atlanta via New Orleans. At 2:45 A.M. on July 24 an extraordinary event occurred between Montgomery and Atlanta.

"It was a moonlit night with some clouds," Chiles reported, "and we were flying along on the regular airway (at an altitude of five thousand feet), when we saw ahead and slightly above and to our right what appeared to be a tremendous jet of flame."

Chiles spotted it first, a dull red glow that "approached with incredible swiftness." He tapped Whitted on the arm and pointed it out.

The pilots looked at each other and asked, "What in the world is that?"

"It flashed down, and we veered to the left and it veered to its left, and passed us about seven hundred feet to our right and about seven hundred feet above us," Chiles told reporters.

"Then, as if the pilot had seen us and wanted to avoid us, it pulled up with a tremendous burst of flame out of its rear and zoomed up into the clouds. Its prop-wash or jet-wash rocked our DC-9."

After the object disappeared, "we must have sat there for five minutes without saying a word, we were so speechless," Chiles said.

The pilots had sufficient time for a detailed look at the craft, which was described as enormous in size, one hundred feet long and thirty feet in diameter. That was twice the diameter of the B-29s Whitted had piloted over Japan three years earlier, only this aircraft had no wings. It did have a double deck—Whitted saw two rows of square windows, six windows to a row, but it was traveling too fast to tell if there were occupants. "You could see right through the windows and out the other side," he said. An intensely bright light, described as being "brilliant as a magnesium flare," was visible through the windows. The UFO was so brightly lighted that the pilots suffered "lightning blindness" and were forced to turn up their instrument

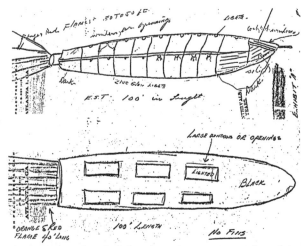

*A giant jet aircraft rocked the pilots of a passenger airliner flying
from Montgomery to Atlanta in 1948. Personnel at Robins Air
Force Base saw a similar craft at the same time. The pilots
made this sketch of what they saw. (USAF Archives)*

panel lights in the cockpit. The giant rocket aircraft was moving at a speed
estimated at between five and seven hundred miles an hour. Chiles and
Whitted noticed beneath the ship an intense dark blue fluorescent glow
extending the length of the object. They also saw a projecting pole, like a
radar probe, jutting from the front. The DC-9 had been flying northeast
while the craft whizzed past to the southwest.

"It was a manmade thing," both concluded.

Chiles and Whitted radioed a report of the sighting, which was forwarded to the Civil Aviation Administration, Maxwell Field at Montgomery, and Lawson Field at Fort Benning. The sighting had taken place
twenty miles southwest of Montgomery. When the pilots landed in
Atlanta, they were swarmed by newspaper and radio reporters and related
their story to universal incredulity.

The men, veteran combat and airline pilots, had seen meteors before
and were certain this object was not natural in origin. As Whitted said, "I
saw some strange things over Japan, but I never saw anything like that."

Only one of twenty passengers, Clarence L. McKelvie of Ohio, a managing editor for the *American Education Press*, had been awake, but he confirmed the sighting, calling it a "strange, eerie streak of light, very intense."

The phenomenon had apparently passed through Georgia ahead of
Chiles and Whitted. At about the same time as the airliner incident, a
ground maintenance crew chief at Robins Air Force Base, located at

Warner Robins, twelve miles south of Macon and two hundred miles from the initial sighting, spotted a huge wingless craft racing across the base toward the west at five hundred miles per hour. Similar objects were also reported over Washington, Indiana, Virginia, and the Netherlands.

On the following day two fox hunters near Covington reported "an unusually bright light—as bright as a moon—which sped away to the west at about 3:00 A.M. The men, J. V. Morris and Lindsay Fall, were near Snapping Shoals on the Yellow River when they spotted the craft, which remained in view for several seconds. It could have been the same craft.

On the night of July 26, a "ball of fire" trailing a flaming tail was seen by over a dozen people from various areas of Atlanta at two different times, 9:00 P.M. and 9:45 P.M. The UFO, near the horizon, traveled from west to east.

An attendant at the Atlanta Naval Air Station first spotted the object near Stone Mountain. It resembled a falling star until it climbed, then turned sharply away from the city. The "bluish stream of light" was fast and high, he said, and did not resemble a jet plane at night. It returned nearly an hour later.

"I was brushing my hair," said Atlantan Betty Strickland, when a "big light bulb with a tail of red fire" passed over the trees outside her window.

A "reddish-white ball of fire about the size of a cantaloupe with a tail on it" was spotted downtown by Mr. and Mrs. Richard P. Sellers. The fast but low-flying UFO would disappear behind buildings then reappear several seconds later.

The Bo Carroll family of Doraville observed a "big ball of fire with a red tail" as they drove home. It flew more than thirty degrees across the sky before disappearing beyond the horizon. Chamblee resident Harold Shaw, with his wife and four others, witnessed a "green light with a short tail" that "moved across the sky rapidly." The tail was silver. All witnesses reported the object was silent, and they could not distinguish any definite form besides a small, shapeless fireball.

The U.S. Weather Service in Atlanta received several calls, but could offer no atmospheric explanation for the phenomenon.

At the same time, a UFO variously described as a rocket ship, ball of fire, and streak of light was seen by many witnesses over downtown Augusta. After fielding several reports, *Augusta Chronicle* city editor John Battle peered out his window and saw the object, which he pointed out to other employees. The newspaper reported a wingless mystery plane described by one woman as "a double fuselage, one on top of the other, with flame shooting out the rear." The Weather Bureau there also received calls but had no answer.

6

The UFOs that returned to Atlanta on the following night, July 27, were described as stationary "jet dirigible" planes emitting long blue flames, and balls of fire. The object seen by one twelve-year-old reminded him of "a man riding a horse." It was suggested that a giant searchlight in Lakewood Park caused the sights by flashing on clouds.

"No, that's not it," said a woman. "I know a burning plane when I see it, and it's up there right now—burning but not falling."

Macon residents reported not rockets but blue blazes. They were said to be blue, red, white, and silver balls of fire trailing three- to four-foot-long flames. Seen at various times, they traveled at low altitudes and rapid speeds.

In early September 1949, an Elberton newspaper noted that upstanding citizens putting out milk bottles before retiring for the night had watched with "awe as a strange disc-shaped light (swept) across the sky from east to west before striking the ground nearby with a dull thud."

Also in 1949, a Valdosta woman reported "a red flying saucer standing still."

THE 1950s

THE BLUE BOOK ERA

The U.S. government sponsored several early programs to study UFOs, but its primary effort originated in 1952 when Edward J. Ruppert, an air force officer, headed Project Blue Book. The program stumbled along for nearly twenty years, closing down in 1969 with the statement that UFOs posed no serious threat to national security. More than twelve thousand sighting reports had been investigated, and most of them were closed as identified, even if the reputed causes often seriously strained believability. However, the air force admitted that 585 cases remained unidentified, including several from Georgia. Those sightings, which we might consider USAF Approved, Prime Grade, are designated by their case numbers.

CASE NO. 868

It was 10:00 P.M. on January 12, 1951, when 2nd Lt. A. C. Hale, stationed at Fort Benning, spotted a light with a fan-shaped wake that hovered without movement for twenty minutes, then instantly accelerated and raced out of sight.

WHAT THE PILOT SAW

Project Blue Book dismissed a number of credible cases for little reason. The files, now preserved in the National Archives, confirm a significant encounter by an air force pilot with a disc-shaped craft over Dearing on June 9, 1951. Lt. George H. Kinmon Jr., a World War II combat veteran, departed Lawson Air Force Base at 11:40 P.M. in an F-51. He soon encountered a UFO described as "completely round and spinning in a clockwise direction" which made a head-on pass at his fighter. According to quotes from an air force intelligence document: "Object described as flat on top and bottom and appearing from a front view to have rounded edges and slightly beveled . . . No vapor trails or exhaust or visible system of propulsion. Described as traveling at tremendous speed . . . Pilot had leveled off at eighty-five-hundred-feet altitude on a course of 247 degrees . . . object dived from the sun in front and under the plane and continued to barrel-roll around the plane for a period of ten minutes, when it disappeared under the plane . . . object was three hundred to four hundred feet from plane and appeared to be ten to fifteen feet in diameter. Pilot states he felt disturbance in the air described as a 'bump' when object passed under plane . . . Pilot considered by associates to be highly reliable, of mature judgment and a creditable observer. Pilot notified tower, Robins AFB, by radio and contacted flight service at Maxwell AFB . . . Pilot unable to take photo due to camera malfunction."

That incident sounds like a young, hotshot alien pilot had just received his UFO pilot's license and was hot-dogging it. Diving from the sun is a classic fighter pilot trick, the barrel rolling was grandstanding, and the camera malfunction a typical UFO encounter characteristic. The alien pilot probably buzzed his home base on return and received a severe dressing-down from Fleetlord Atvar.

SHADES OF THE DAY THE EARTH STOOD STILL

Across the Savannah River in South Carolina is the top secret Savannah River Atomic Energy Plant. For decades nuclear-weapons-grade material was manufactured there. A number of UFOs were seen over the area, some from the Georgia side. The best documented sighting occurred at 10:00 A.M. on July 19, 1952, when a hundred engineers, scientists, and technicians were gathered outside for a ceremony. John A. Anderson reported that most of the distinguished attendees saw a glowing green glob about one-fifth the size of a full moon that darted around the sky at great speed and altitude. The scientists were impressed by the "phenomenal maneuverability" of the object, which abruptly changed direction many times. After a two-minute show, the UFO disappeared "at apparently tremendous velocity." Many early ufologists (yes, that's a legitimate term describing those who study the phenomenon) believed extraterrestrial spacecraft were attracted to earth by our atomic explosions and monitored our weapons programs. Perhaps they did.

On July 21, 1952, the commander of Dobbins Air Force Base in Marietta revealed that a mysterious object had registered on base radar. It had achieved the respectable speed of twelve hundred miles per hour and flown at an altitude of fifty thousand feet.

On August 28 Atlanta police officers, including patrolmen M. J. Spears and A. L. Elsbery, watched a UFO that changed colors and occasionally shot out a red-flamed tail. It was a lively thing, frequently ascending and descending and turning several flips.

Continuing UFO reports induced the media to speculate on the origin of the UFOs. Popular theories included American or Soviet experimental planes or rockets, or saucers from some extraterrestrial source. Dr. W. A. Calder, director of the Bradley Observatory at Agnes Scott College in Decatur, advanced his own theory, saying "that the saucers are of earthly origin . . . The government can do many things with only a few people knowing about it," giving the government more credit than it deserves, "and I've seen a couple of things I can't explain myself," the astronomer admitted.

CASE NO. 2022

The metropolitan Atlanta area had a rash of UFO sightings on the night of September 1, 1952. At 9:43 in Atlanta, Mrs. William Davis and nine others watched a lighted object, bright as the evening star, fly up and down for a lengthy period. At 10:30 in Marietta, twenty-five people, including a former artillery officer, observed a red, white, and blue-green object spin and shoot out sparks for fifteen minutes. Also in Marietta at the same time, a man with binoculars watched two large objects, shaped like spinning tops and colored red, blue, and green, fly together through the sky for thirty minutes, leaving a sparkling trail.

Either there were a number of different UFOs in the sky or the witnesses had markedly different perspectives, because just twenty minutes later, again in Marietta, a former World War II tail gunner spotted two large, white, disc-shaped craft flying in trail formation. They left green vapor trails before merging and flying away at a rapid speed.

CASE NO. 2100

Two weeks later, at 7:30 P.M. on September 16, three air force officers and two civilians at Robins Air Force Base watched two white lights fly side by side through the air for fifteen minutes at an estimated one hundred miles per hour.

CASE NO. 2200

The best officially approved UFO sighting from Georgia occurred six weeks later, at 7:40 P.M. on October 31, 1952. The witness was Lt. Col. Charles

Smith Jr., who commanded the 9325th Squadron based at Gainesville. After the sighting he wrote a detailed account for the intelligence office at Robins. Perhaps with justification, Project Blue Book gave special credence to observations by trained military personnel.

Smith was driving north on GA 85 four miles south of Fayetteville at sixty-five miles per hour when "a strange object was seen flying overhead." The orange, blimp-shaped object was at treetop level and approaching. Smith "immediately thought of falling aircraft" and attempted to stop before he was beneath the ship. He failed and the UFO sailed directly over his car at a slow speed. The craft was silent, and so was Smith's radio, which ceased operating until the object passed.

The air force officer scrambled out of his car for a better view of the UFO, which he thought was five hundred feet above him. The night sky was clear and the moon and stars very bright, giving him enough light to make a detailed examination of the object. Smith believed it was eighty feet long, twenty feet wide, and twenty feet thick. It was dull orange along the centerline, and brighter near the outer edges. The color of the UFO "seemed to blend in with that of the moon," he noted, but was still visible. The great ship emitted no flames, sparks, or light beams.

After passing directly overhead for twenty seconds, the nose of the object pointed up and began a "forty-five-degree climb, steadily increasing its speed and angle of climb until it disappeared" to the east. "The speed was tremendous and the object disappeared in approximately thirty to forty seconds," Smith concluded.

A week later UFOs were seen over Georgia and the Savannah River Atomic Energy Plant. Similar objects were seen over Mobile, Alabama (my hometown), for several consecutive nights. "They're all nuts!" the intelligence officer at Brookley Air Force Base declared when he received the first reports. After three of his subordinates had spotted the UFO and a radar crew called to report that it registered on their screen, the officer walked outside and saw it visually, then watched the return on the radar scope. He became a believer.

Dr. J. M. Valentine, a researcher of weird things whose primary claim to fame was coauthoring a book about the Bermuda Triangle with Charles Berlitz, witnessed two UFOs in southeastern Georgia. The first appeared at 2:00 A.M. on December 6, 1952, between Fargo and Douglas. It was a "dark-core, tunnel-like vortex" which he thought was "a stream of neutron emission indicating atomic fusion" capable of building "up a magnetic field which would power the UFO at incredible speeds." Later, a UFO shaped like a hat with a wide brim and shining light from the bottom and top was seen at 3:00 A.M. on U.S. 441 just south of Pearson, near the Okefenokee

Swamp. Hovering above trees one hundred feet away, it was luminescent and "pulsating with a bluish light."

CASE NO. 2365

One month later an unidentified object was again spotted in Georgia skies, and again by trusted military personnel. As a sky object hovered above Albany on January 28, 1953, radar operators painted one stationary target on their screen for twenty minutes.

Another impressive pilot encounter with a UFO occurred on that same evening. An air force pilot took off in an F-86 for a routine flight from Moody Air Force Base in Valdosta northwest to Lawson Field at Fort Benning, where he would turn east to Robins Air Force Base and return home. Hours after he landed, Edward Ruppert, head of Blue Book, was taping the pilot's experience.

At 9:15 the pilot glanced down at the lights of Albany. When he looked up at the sky again he noticed an unusually bright white light in his ten o'clock position. He scrutinized it for several minutes, deciding that it was either an airplane, so far away that he could not see the red and green lights on its wing tips, or a star. However, neither explanation accounted for its circular shape.

The pilot was simply accumulating flight hours, so he decided to kill some time attempting to close on the object, which is, after all, what fighter jocks do. He checked his oxygen supply and started a climb from his six-thousand-foot cruising altitude to thirty thousand feet. Four minutes later he had gotten above the object, which had changed position in relation to the stars, indicating it was not a celestial body. It was probably an airplane, he concluded at that point.

To further close with the target, the pilot next descended. This tactic was obviously working because the light grew larger, but then the white light started changing colors, to red, then back to white, and repeating the cycle every two seconds. He also realized that it had changed shape from circular to a perfect triangle, then it split into two triangles, one above the other. Then it vanished. "It was just like someone turning off a light—" he stated, "it's there, then it's gone."

The pilot told Ruppert that despite his experience, he "just couldn't swallow those stories" about flying saucers. He wrote the episode off as a case of vertigo and considered himself lucky to be alone—at least there were no witnesses to his actions.

Near Lawson Field the pilot checked his gauges and found that his maneuvers had consumed an alarming amount of fuel. At that point he elected to return immediately to Valdosta. He called the ground radar operator to report the change and the operator immediately interrupted him to ask if he had seen an unusual light in the sky. The operator had watched the entire aerial ballet on radar. When the UFO first appeared on the screen it was apparently moving too slowly to be an aircraft. As the F-86 climbed it had indeed started to close with the UFO, but the mysterious object sped up just enough to stay ahead of the jet. After two or three minutes the UFO raced out of range at an incredibly high speed.

This incident, a UFO sighted by a reliable air force pilot and tracked on radar by air force personnel, remains one of the most credible ever reported over Georgia.

MONKEY MEN FROM MARS

Sixteen days before I was born, in the predawn darkness of July 8, 1953, Cobb County policeman Sherley (don't call me *Shirley*) Brown and his part-ner were patrolling Bankhead Highway near Leland. Seeing a decrepit pickup truck sitting in the middle of the road and three young men gathered around a figure lying on the pavement and waving for their attention, they stopped to investigate. Stretched out on the highway was a gangly, two-foot-long humanoid corpse. The creature had two arms and two legs, but no hair.

"They told us they had run up on this little red spacecraft in the middle of the highway," Brown related recently. "They said they saw three of these little men come running to the ship and jump on it. One of them didn't make it before the spaceship took off, and they ran over it. There were scorched circles on the pavement where the ship had been."

The story sounded solid. Just one night earlier a number of Atlanta-area residents had watched a large, multicolored, cone-shaped UFO maneuver slowly across the sky.

"They weren't drunk," Brown continued. "They acted scared, about how you'd be if you'd run up on a space alien."

The story, flashed to news agencies within hours, alarmed the world. Atlanta newspapers and TV and radio stations were hounded by news agencies far and wide for the latest information. Two air force investigators packed for an emergency research trip.

The three men who killed the creature, barbers Edward Watters and Tom Wilson, and butcher Arnold "Buddy" Payne, were between nineteen and twenty-eight years old and shared an apartment. While they went home with the alien corpse, Officer Brown returned to headquarters. There several Austell residents called in to report having seen the mini-UFO that had left one of its crewthings behind.

"I went in and tried to explain what we'd found to the chief," Brown said, "but he wasn't interested in it. So I went home and went to bed, and about an hour later I got a phone call.

"It was the chief, and he wanted to know what was going on. The newspapers and some intelligence fellow from the air force were all over him."

The Killer Bs (two barbers and a butcher) spread word of their discovery and called the *Atlanta Constitution* later in the day. A skeptical reporter asked the men to cart the carcass to his office, which they did. There a veterinarian said it "looked like something out of this world."

Several hours later Herman Jones, founder and director of the State Crime Lab, took the odd being to an anatomy professor at Emory University. They shortly pronounced the alien to be a hairless, de-tailed monkey.

BUBBLES? OR ASPCA ALERT

After sticking to their story for several hours, the team caved and admitted it was a hoax formulated over a card game and masterminded by Watters. The three men purchased a monkey at an Atlanta pet shop and overdosed it with chloroform at their apartment. The barbers initially claimed to have shaved the poor creature, then said they had used a depilatory, which may have made them traitors to their trade. No one accepted responsibility for de-tailing the poor animal.

The hoaxsters had finished their scenario just five minutes before the policemen arrived.

"They had taken a blowtorch and burned those circles in the highway," Brown related, "and they had shaved that monkey.

"I should have known it wasn't real, (but) it was just so realistic. I did believe it. It was almost impossible not to believe."

The trio achieved their fifteen minutes of fame and were featured in *Life* magazine.

"Everybody was angry" at the men, Brown remembered. "It got pretty hot there for a while."

Watters accepted responsibility for the incident and paid a forty-dollar fine for obstructing a highway. He moved out of Atlanta two months later.

"How would you like to be known as the Monkey Man?" Watters asked. "It got to be a big joke, you know. But jokes can go too far. They ran it into the ground, calling me Monkey Man and laughing at me."

For more than forty years the creature has resided in a jar of formaldehyde in Decatur at the GBI's State Crime Lab headquarters. Some true believers swear this was a cover-up for the real alien found that night in Georgia.

CASE NO. 2983

At 7:35 P.M. on April 26, 1954, four residents of Athens, a C. Cartey and Mr. and Mrs. H. Hopkins and their daughter, were awed by an observation of fifteen to twenty UFOs that flew from south to north in a V formation.

AN ASTRONOMER SIGHTS DINNER PLATES AND SKY LIGHTS

Noted astronomer Percy Wilkins was flying between Charleston, West Virginia, and Atlanta on June 11, 1954, on a two-engine Convair. Near Atlanta at 10:45 A.M. he glanced out his window and spied two brass-colored, radiant ovoids, each about fifty feet in diameter with thin edges, which darted in and out of cumulus clouds several miles from the plane. After landing, Wilkins described the incident to reporters:

"They looked exactly like polished metal dinner plates reflecting the sunlight as they flipped and banked around inside the clouds. Presently a third object came slowly out of a huge cloud, remaining motionless in the shadow of the cloud and therefore darker than the others. Presently it zipped away and plunged into another cloud mass. After about two minutes, the first two did the same maneuver and I did not see them again."

Just nine days later a group of Maconites, including an official from Robins Air Force Base and another federal employee, observed a cluster of spectacular sky lights. While standing on Mary Drive about 9:00 P.M. on June 20, they watched the "brilliant white light" as it hung in the sky for twenty-five minutes before fading away beyond the horizon.

Mrs. W. E. Tyler first thought it was Venus, but then she "noticed the rays of light were extremely long." Believing it could be an optical illusion, she moved to another part of her yard and saw that "it was a brilliant white light, and it was really moving so gradually you could hardly tell it. The thing glowed and the rays would lengthen. It was almost indescribable." The best guess from the Weather Bureau was an extremely unusual appearance of the Aurora Borealis, the Northern Lights, which rarely appear this far south.

1955: IT WAS A VERY GOOD YEAR—OUR FIRST ALIENS

In this book we encounter big hairy bipeds, generally called bigfoot and various types of alien humanoids. Throw in one example of each and stir vigorously, and you have one of the strangest episodes in Georgia's weird history.

Mrs. Margaret Symmonds, fifty-two, and her husband, Wesley, of Coverdale, Ohio, left Cincinnati at 7:30 A.M. on July 2, 1955, in their brand-new Oldsmobile. They drove all day and into the night, stopping at regular intervals and sharing the driving duties while one slept in the back seat. At 3:30 A.M. on July 3 Wesley was asleep and Margaret was behind the wheel, piloting through Henry County a few miles south of Stockton on U.S. 129.

"I was not drinking or groggy from driving," Mrs. Symmonds emphasized later. "My head was clear," and she was chewing gum to help her stay alert. It was a clear, moonlit night and visibility on the generally straight two-lane highway was excellent.

Mrs. Symmonds described the landscape as "desolate . . . devoid of houses or sign of human habitation." The highway was lined with scrub brush and low trees. It was a location where "anything might happen, and there would be no one within miles to know it," she stated.

ALIENS WITHOUT CONVEYANCE

Margaret was driving sixty miles per hour on the isolated road when her high beams "shone on four objects that I first thought were animals—maybe hogs or something." Cautiously, she reduced her speed to about forty. When Margaret drew closer she saw that the objects were four small humanoids, each measuring three and a half to four feet in height. Their legs appeared to be short for their size, but their arms, apparently devoid of elbows, seemed long for their proportions. She could see little of their bodies because they all wore long "gray-greenish capes." On their heads were slouchlike hats turned down all around the rim.

The nearest figure, standing in her lane, apparently detected the car's approach. It stepped out of the way and looked directly at Margaret. "I was terrified," she related, but managed to note considerable details of the creature. The head seemed normal in size, but rounded. The eyes "were big, like saucers, and they reflected a reddish light." She saw no pupils. "The nose was long—real long, and pointed," she continued, making it sound like a classic witch. The mouth was small, with no visible lips.

For some reason, perhaps fright from being startled, the creature had its arms raised over its head. "The hands had claws on them, real long claws," she noted, but she did not count the number of claws nor notice if there were thumbs. The skin was dark colored and "very rough or coarse," but she could not determine if it was scaly.

Mrs. Symmonds was unfamiliar with the fabric of the cape and hat, and saw no buttons or other fastening devices on the long cape.

D.O.T. NIGHT CREW

The figure to the left of the one who stepped aside was bent over, its arms in a "hanging position," and both hands were holding what looked like a straight stick, as if it were about to dig in the center of the road or "poking at the road." Its back was to Mrs. Symmonds, and she thought its "shoulders were very square and seemed unusually strong-looking" for the size of the body.

The other two figures, standing in a cluster with the one holding the stick, had their backs to the Symmonds's car. None of the three moved, "didn't move a muscle" in the estimated thirty seconds it took for the vehicle to pass. Mrs. Symmonds heard no sounds nor smelled anything unusual during the experience.

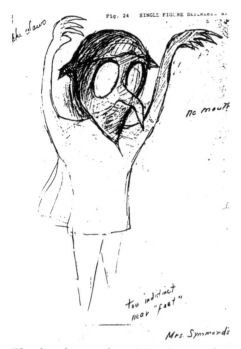

The alien that was facing Mrs. Symmonds had clawed hands, large eyes, and a hooked nose. UFO researcher Leonard Stringfield made this sketch based on his interview with Symmonds. (Courtesy of Center for UFO Studies)

When she realized what she had encountered, Symmonds screamed, swerved onto the right shoulder of the road, and accelerated rapidly upon regaining the pavement. "I passed close enough to reach out and touch them," she said, three or four feet. Wesley woke up but did not see anything. "He wanted to go back and see what it was," Margaret said, "but I was afraid," "terrified," she added later, and continued driving south at a fast rate of speed.

Although no UFO was reported by the Symmonds or any local residents, the large, glowing eyes, clawed hands, and diminutive size match the descriptions of a number of reported aliens seen at UFO landing sites, at least before popular science fiction decreed that all aliens had to be of the "Grey" variety. Their clothing corresponded to a recent troubling phenomenon named the Shadows (see chapter 7).

"It does sound like a strange story when you tell it," Mrs. Symmonds said. "But it isn't when you see it."

After reaching Florida, Mrs. Symmonds revealed the experience to a close friend, Mrs. Bart Mangini, who advised her not to describe the encounter to others. However, upon returning to Ohio a month later, she read news accounts about one of the most fantastic UFO-alien encounters in history. A small "army" of aliens besieged a family in Hopkinsville, Kentucky, for an entire night, surviving point-blank rifle fire and returning for more.

The reports motivated Mrs. Symmonds to call the *Cincinnati Post* and tell her story to reporter Charles Doctor. She then visited their office to approve a sketch of the aliens and have her photograph taken. The story ran on August 23. On September 5 she made a deposition to Calvin W. Prem, an assistant prosecuting attorney for Hamilton County, Ohio, who notarized the document.

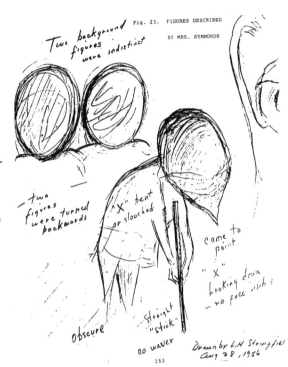

Fig. 23. FIGURES DESCRIBED BY MRS. SYMMONDS

The four aliens Mrs. Symmonds encountered were apparently probing the roadway. (Courtesy of Center for UFO Studies)

A year later, on August 28, 1956, two highly respected UFO researchers, Leonard Stringfield and Ted Bloecher, visited the Symmonds. Margaret cleared up several misrepresentations reported in news accounts, recalled a few additional details, and advised Stringfield as he sketched more accurate representations of the creatures. The researchers reported that Mrs. Symmonds gave a "clear and detailed account" of the episode and found her "straightforward and cooperative" with no indications that she was lying or elaborating on the story.

This tale was fantastic by itself, but it was actually the end of a wave of weirdness that swept across Georgia that summer from Lincolnton in the northeast to Edison in the southwest. Earlier a short, hairy wildman ran amuck in southwestern Georgia, and a phantom panther raced around the northeastern part of the state. For details, see chapter 4.

Senator Richard Russell and the Russian UFO

In 1985 the U. S Government declassified twelve formerly top-secret CIA, air force, and FBI files that detailed a dramatic UFO sighting made thirty years earlier in the USSR by Georgia senator Richard B. Russell, one of the most important legislators in the U.S. Congress.

Russell was on a fact-finding mission in the Trans-Caucasian region of the Soviet Union. At 7:10 P.M. on October 4, 1955, his train was ten minutes out of Atjaty, bound for Adzbijabul along the Caspian Sea, traveling at twenty-five to thirty miles per hour. The area was a bare plain with no hills, vegetation, or buildings in sight. It was nearly dusk when Russell, feeling ill, left his traveling companions, Lt. Col. E. U. Hathaway, a U.S. Army staff officer assigned to the Senate Armed Forces Committee and acting as his aide, and Ruben Efron, a committee consultant and interpreter, and went to his private sleeping compartment. He had extinguished the light and laid down when he noted a greenish-yellow ball rising rapidly outside the window. Russell ran into the adjoining compartment and blurted out, according to one participant, "I saw it! I just saw a flying saucer!" When the lights were doused, the two assistants were disappointed to see nothing in the clear, darkening skies.

"Where?" they asked skeptically.

"I just saw it coming up over there," Russell said, and pointed. "Here it is coming again!"

Suddenly, a second glowing yellow ball sped into the sky a minute after the first. It was initially seen at an altitude of seven thousand to eight thousand feet, while the original object had been higher when Russell spotted it. The shape of the UFO was difficult to distinguish, and its size was also indeterminate due to a lack of reference points. The three witnesses thought it to be the size of a small rocket, although no jet trail was visible. Believed to be one to two miles distant, the object ascended smoothly, almost vertically, into the sky, and seemed to be rotating. Then, moving from south to north, it greatly increased speed in level flight and disappeared over the train. One of the witnesses ran across to the other side of the car and looked out a window for another glimpse of the object, but it had vanished. Two searchlights about a mile away were aimed very low, perhaps for use as ground illumination, and did not appear to be focused on the UFO or following it. The sighting was over in less than ten seconds.

Five minutes later a guard entered the compartment and closed the window curtains, cryptically stating, "It's better this way."

When the incident was over Russell said, "We saw a flying saucer. I wanted you boys to see it so that I would have witnesses." At that moment all agreed that what they had observed was not a conventional aircraft.

At 9:45 P.M. on October 12 Russell and his party reached the American Embassy in Prague, Czechoslovakia, via rail from Kiev. There U.S. Air Force attaché Thomas S. Ryan, a lieutenant colonel in the air force, debriefed all but Russell. When Hathaway confided that he needed to report an extremely important matter, "something you may not believe, but something that we've been told by your people (the U.S.A.F.) doesn't exist," Ryan advised him to wait until the following morning when they could speak in a secure facility.

SUPPLEMENT TO AF FORM 112

~~ING AGENCY~~ US AIR ATTACHE	REPORT NO. IR 193-55	PAGE 4	OF 9	PAGES

first flying object and recognized it as something drastically different rushing in to get Mr. Efron and Col. Hathaway to see it. Col. Hathaway stated that he got to the window with the Senator in time to see the first while Mr. Efron said that he got only a short glimpse of the first due to crowding. However all three saw the second disc and all agreed that they saw the same round, disc shaped aircraft which was the same as the first.)

11. "The take-off area was about one mile away, maybe a little further." (Searchlights were located in the same area.)

12. "There were two lights towards the inside of the disc which remained stationary as the outer surface went around." (Both agreed firmly on this point.) "The lights sat near the top of the disc." (If a line representing the diameter of the disc were divided into three segments, the lights would have been located at the two points of division between the middle segment and the two outside segments ie. see sketch drawn with aid of Mr Efron:

RELATIVE POSITION OF 2 LIGHTS

13. "The aircraft was circular." "The aircraft was round." "It resembled a flying saucer." "It seemed to be the shape of a discus, round and circular revolving clockwise or to the right." (It was definitely round or at least circular in the eyes of these two observers, containing no protrusions or "sticks" or bulges. No estimate could be obtained from either observer re thickness or diameter.

14. " There was no noticeable color" (It was stated that dusk prevented any color impressions.)

15. "After reaching 2000 meters, it whipped off at a great speed from our left to our right, or towards the north from the south." (Speed differential was very noticeable between ascent and level flight speed.)

16. "We could see the take-off on the horizon to our left or south of our train."

17. "Outer part revolved slowly to right." (There seemed to be a different impression of the disc's movement while climbing and after assuming level flight, with the terms "revolving slowly" used for the climb and the term "whirring" for the cruising flight.

18. "The disc rose in the same position as it was in when it sped away." The flying attitude of the flying disc was said to resemble a discus in flight.)

USAIRA COMMENT: I believe that further debriefing of all three US observers in a more relaxed atmosphere and with more time would produce much more valuable technical details than the hurried interview above.

This is part of a formerly top secret report from the air force, FBI, and CIA that related the UFO seen by Senator Russell and his staff.

At 9:00 A.M. the following morning Hathaway and Efron were interviewed in the presence of Ryan and Col. Thomas Dooley, U.S. Army attaché. Hathaway started by saying, "I doubt if you're going to believe this, but we all saw it. We've been told for years that there isn't such a thing, but all of us saw it." The debriefing lasted an hour as the witnesses talked and made sketches of the things they had seen back in the USSR, including the UFO.

Ryan described the witnesses as "three highly reliable United States citizens" who were "firmly convinced that they saw a genuine flying saucer." Ryan believed the sighting was "remarkable and lends credence to many 'saucer reports.' "

The CIA later interviewed all three witnesses, including Senator Russell. The incident was deemed important enough to brief John Foster Dulles, the U.S. secretary of state, on October 18, 1955, during an executive session.

Russell's party had been advised to travel by train whenever possible so they could view more of the countryside. They kept comprehensive notes and made sketches of every military asset they could observe. Besides the UFO, the party returned with descriptions of forty-two jet fighters of a type not seen before, a long train of flatcars bearing landing craft, radar sites, helicopters, and railroad facilities.

There remains a curious unresolved detail involving the part of the journey where the UFO was sighted. The three Americans had attempted to fly to their next destination, but were informed that there were no regularly scheduled flights between those two points. However, they learned afterward that a number of flights were made every day, which suggests, but certainly does not prove, that the Soviets wanted them to observe the phenomenon. It might be significant to note that during their tour the team passed several airbases, and no attempts were made by the Soviets to conceal them from the Americans.

The importance of the guard/porter drawing the curtains is also disputed. Some maintained it was normal procedure for traveling at night with the interior lights on, and that on this occasion the trainman was tardy in performing this duty and was apologizing for the oversight. The witnesses were divided over whether the porter was concerned about the lapse or was aware of the UFOs.

However, the air attaché concluded: "The behavior of the trainmen was such as to indicate that the U.S. passengers had seen something they were not supposed to see." One of the top secret reports advised keeping the incident from the Russians to prevent restrictions on the travel of Americans in the future.

The released documents are partially censured, poorly reproduced from thirty-year-old typed pages, and originated from three separate government agencies. From these accounts it is sometimes difficult to accurately determine what each of the three witnesses said about the appearance of the UFO. Also bear in mind that the UFO was seen briefly, in motion and in the dark. Their descriptions of the object are similar, but the details described in the debriefings often disagree, which is quite common in UFO sightings. People interpret the same phenomenon differently.

There were no prominent protrusions or bulges on the craft, although one saw stubby wings and another a slight dome on top. Color could not be determined because of darkness, but the witnesses suggested a yellowish-green color, or just dark and shadowy. There was a discrepancy regarding the number, two to four; color, white, green, and red; and placement of lights and whether they or the UFO rotated. Other disagreements focused on the size of the UFO, a small rocket, one-third the size of the nearby searchlight, and the size of a U.S. jet fighter, and changes in trajectory. The UFO was variously described in shape as round, a ball, circular, a discus, or a flying saucer; a squat, darkened, round or square object; or an equilateral triangle with the point to the rear. All witnesses described its speed as very fast: a "tremendous speed . . . much faster than a jet," said one.

Efron noted no noise or exhaust, but the other two saw flames or sparks. One thought a glow moved slowly around the perimeter in a clockwise motion, "giving the appearance of a pinwheel." No sound was heard, although train noises would have obscured most sounds, except perhaps a jet engine.

After hearing the evidence, Herbert Scoville, associate director of Scientific Intelligence, concluded that the object sighted was an aircraft "in a dive followed by a sharp pull-up in such a way that nothing was seen until the exhaust was visible to the observer," which seems an unusual maneuver for a jet plane flying close to the ground at night. It was also suggested that the plane was making a mock strafing run on the train. The possibility of the object being a vertical takeoff airplane was mentioned, but the report also noted that nothing "supports the theory that the Russians have developed saucer-like, or unconventional aircraft." Scoville thought the objects "climbed surprisingly rapidly" for jets.

There was no evidence of a military air base in the region, and the CIA considered it "most unlikely that experimental flying would be conducted" in the region, or that two experimental aircraft would be operated at the same time in such close proximity. The spooks also stated that it "seems inconsistent that the Soviets, if they have such an object in service, would continue their large development and production programs on conventional type aircraft." Remember that Russell and company had returned with information about a newly developed Soviet jet plane. Further, the rotation or spiraling of the craft "does not fit" with a vertical-takeoff aircraft. Most experts dismissed the notion that the UFOs were Soviet machines.

This declassified collection of top secret reports were revealed through inquiries sponsored by Dr. Bruce Maccabee, a navy physicist, and his organization, the Fund for UFO Research, by using the Freedom of Information Act. Maccabee felt the case was important because "one of the most powerful U.S. senators witnessed and reported a UFO." The case was "unique because the CIA took the sighting seriously." Noting that the case received absolutely no publicity at the time, Maccabee thought the witnesses "were no doubt advised not to talk" about it. He called the documents "startling new evidence that UFOs exist."

The FBI seemed to agree, for a memo from the Bureau, dated November 4, 1955, stated that Hathaway's testimony "would support existence of a flying saucer."

Another recently declassified document indicates that Senator Russell had a previous interest in UFOs. The following letter was found in the Secretary of the Air Force, Office of Information UFO File:

United States Senate
Committee on Armed Services

February 21, 1952

Honorable Thomas K. Finletter,
Secretary of the Air Force
Washington, D.C.

Dear Mr. Secretary:

Members of the Committee on Armed Services have expressed a desire to be informed of air force evaluation of recent news articles concerning the observation of "flying saucers" by combat airmen in the Far East.

I would appreciate you furnishing for the use of the committee an official report of these observations together with your evaluation thereof and such other information as you deem pertinent to this inquiry.

Sincerely,

Richard B. Russell (signed)

Perhaps future documents released under the Freedom of Information Act will reveal the secretary's response. Several public figures with impeccable reputations have reported UFOs—Jimmy Carter several years before his presidency and several governors and congressmen—but few had the reputation of Richard Brevard Russell Jr., whose father became chief justice of the Georgia Supreme Court. Russell received his law degree in 1918 from the University of Georgia, then served a year in the naval reserve. He spent ten years in the Georgia General Assembly, where he became Speaker of the House, and was sworn in at age thirty-four by his father as Georgia's youngest governor. He was elected to fill a term in the U.S. Senate in 1932 and won six straight terms, eventually becoming chairman of the armed services committee, a position he held from 1951 until 1969. He was one of the most influential senators during a number of world-shaping events—the Great Depression, World War II, the Cold War, the Cuban Missile Crisis, and Vietnam—encompassing four decades of dramatic history. Russell sat on the Warren Commission, which investigated JFK's assassination. He was Georgia's most powerful politician of the twentieth century, a confidant of presidents, and a major power broker in the Senate. Russell died in office on January 21, 1971, fourteen years before his UFO sighting was made public.

ALIEN TELEGRAPHIC MESSAGES AND CIGARS

Strange things were afoot, or rather aloft, in November 1957. On November 3 a giant orange-red disc attacked Itaipu Fortress in Brazil, sending two soldiers to the hospital with burns and heat strokes. Among the numerous witnesses was a doctor. On November 4 two teams of military policemen at White Sands Proving Grounds, New Mexico, where the first atomic bomb had been exploded twelve years earlier, spotted bright, egg-shaped objects one hundred yards in diameter hovering over the installation. On the following night a "red ball" was seen hanging above the Atomic Energy Commission's plant near Augusta, on the South Carolina side of the Savannah River.

"It could be a tiny red light about three blocks away or a gigantic thing at a great distance," said skeptical Louis Harris, executive news editor of the *Augusta Chronicle*, who observed a "constant red light" from the newspaper building in downtown Augusta.

At the same time crewmen aboard the Coast Guard cutter *Sebago* in the Gulf of Mexico spotted "a brilliant white light" that buzzed above the waves at tremendous speeds. The ship's radar tracked the UFO for twenty-seven minutes. Huge, brightly lighted cigar- and oval-shaped objects were witnessed by reliable citizens in Tennessee and Wisconsin.

A related phenomenon, a mysterious radio signal which was detected across the country, perplexed government officials and shortwave operators. The broadcast, heard near the frequency of the new Russian satellite *Muttnik* (*Sputnik II*) was on 20.003 megacycles; *Muttnik* was broadcasting on 20.005. Initially rated a classified secret, the mysterious signal was soon declassified on November 8.

Atlantan Ronnie Burch first noticed the pattern of one long note of low pitch and two shorter beeps at 6:59 on the evening of November 5. Later that night it changed to three equal beeps. At ten-minute intervals

Military personnel at Robins Air Force Base in Warner Robins sighted a number of UFOs during the 1940s and 1950s, and several were labeled "Unknown" by the official air force investigation program.

a signal that he thought was a series of numbers disrupted the original beeps. Attempts to decode this new series were unsuccessful. Two other shortwave operators in Atlanta, Bill Duggan and Tomby Giglio, confirmed his observations.

The scene then turned to a bizarre "contactee" story from Nebraska, where Reinhold Schmidt claimed he drove up on a silver, blimp-shaped craft one hundred feet long, thirty feet wide, and fourteen feet high, sitting on the ground. His car was immobilized, as was he upon approaching the ship. Schmidt was eventually allowed into the object, which was transparent from the inside, as five apparent humans, albeit with German accents, "floated" around the craft repairing a mechanical problem. After twenty minutes he was released.

UFOs returned to Atlanta skies on November 8, when at 2:30 P.M. a housewife hanging out clothes saw a cigar-shaped object flying southwest to northeast. That morning Charlie E. McKinley, a carrier for the *Atlanta Constitution*, witnessed a fiery ball crossing the sky at Lakewood.

A dispatcher at a truck terminal in Atlanta reported that three different truckers, independent of each other but all driving from Macon to Atlanta between 1:00 and 1:30 A.M., sighted a red, egg-shaped ball the size of the moon sitting on the road. The object disappeared as each driver approached it.

At Tifton in south Georgia three teenagers, Mike Henderson, Reggie Gunn, and Bobby Fullerton, saw a fiery "missile" as they drove out of town early that morning on a hunting trip. Colored like a blue gas flame, it traveled at great speed from north to south.

CASE NO. 5419

A silver, cigar-shaped UFO was spotted, again at Robins Air Force Base, at 10:07 A.M. on November 26, 1957, by eight workers, including three control tower operators, one of them a weatherman. After eight minutes of continuous observation, the object suddenly vanished.

DOWN ON THE FARM

Two years later, in mid-November 1959, the Bud and Dorsey Nally family, which lived west of Rydal in Bartow County, had been working at their dairy barn at 5:45 P.M. when they spotted a silver UFO the size of the moon flying toward the northeast. It was in sight for five to eight minutes, and turned a flaming red color before disappearing. At least ten people reported seeing the object. It was no mirage, argued Dorsey, "because too many people were craning their necks skyward, watching beside me."

At 10:30 one night in 1959 a long-distance telephone operator was driving on Fairground Street near Lawrence Street close to downtown Marietta when she caught sight of a giant egg-shaped UFO the size of a football field passing directly overhead at three to four hundred feet. It glowed silver, bright as a full moon. Calling Dobbins Air Force Base half an hour later, she was told their phones were "burning up."

THE 1960s

SEE ME, SMELL ME—ALIEN TOXIC WASTE

One of Georgia's most reliable sightings occurred in Turnerville, a Habersham County community near Tallulah Falls, on June 29, 1964. Jimmy Ivester was visiting his mother, father, and siblings that night when the television they were watching developed so much interference that they turned it off. Then they walked outside to sit on the porch and chat. There they spotted a UFO at treetop level. It moved to within three hundred feet of the house and hovered across the highway, just a few feet over a neighbor's garden. The bottom of the bowl-shaped craft was clearly visible, but the top of it was dark, broken only by three blinking lights in a row—red, clear, and red. When the lights disappeared, the UFO rose, shining from its bottom a bright green beam so bright it illuminated the woods.

The sight was unnerving enough, but worst of all was the smell the ship left behind, described as "something like embalming or brake fluid."

Habersham County sheriff A. J. Chapman was called after the sighting. He arrived from Clarkston just in time to see the UFO return. He viewed the object flying high overhead as it disappeared and also experienced the terrible odor. Chapman vouched for the honesty of the witnesses.

The UFO had hovered above the property of Mrs. Russell Hickman, who watched the object with her sixteen-year-old daughter Diane. After the UFO departed, Mrs. Hickman complained of a stinging, burning pain on her arm and face. In the morning Diane's face was red and drawn, her eyelids swollen nearly shut. Mrs. Hickman told *Atlanta Constitution* reporter Tom Winfield that she hesitated to take Diane to the doctor because she feared he would think they were crazy.

Another family in the same neighborhood had also watched the UFO, making a total of nine witnesses.

Confirmation of this sighting arrived with Beauford E. Parham, a businessman who was driving home late that evening near Lavonia when he noticed a very bright light in the sky that rapidly flew straight toward his car. Suddenly, it was directly in front of his headlights, giving him a clear view of the UFO. It was a spinning, top-shaped object, amber colored, six feet in height and eight feet in width, with what he described as a mastlike object protruding from the top. Through small portholes that ringed the bottom of the craft "flames" could be seen. The "top" was tilted toward him, and the object issued a hissing sound "like a million snakes."

The craft vanished, then immediately reappeared again five feet in front of him, where it remained for about a mile at sixty-five miles per hour. Parham followed it in what he called a "near trancelike state." The UFO then flew over the car, emitting a powerful smell described as embalming fluid and a gaseous vapor. The object reappeared for a third and final time in front of him and again approached the car. His motor began misfiring while the UFO spun "like crazy," then the craft flew off to disappear in a "split second."

Finally free of the harassing UFO, Parham realized that he had a burning sensation on his arms. He drove to the nearest airport and reported the encounter to the Federal Aviation Administration. Although this detail is not recorded in the official records, traces of radioactivity were detected on the car. Parham repeatedly washed his hands thoroughly, but the pain continued. Despite repeated washings, a mysterious oily film remained on the car's exterior, and the hood had been warped by the incident. Rubber hoses in the engine compartment also deteriorated rapidly.

This was Georgia's first "physical trace" UFO. It had affected three humans and various components of a car, and was witnessed by at least ten individuals, one of them a respected law officer, in three separate locations.

CENTRAL GEORGIA REPORTS

Things were different in 1966. The air force still investigated UFO sightings, and we were more likely to believe their findings. The days of

"Trust No One" and "The Truth Is out There" were a quarter-century away.

Such was the state of affairs on Saturday night, April 23, 1966, between 11:00 P.M. and midnight, when several people spotted UFOs in the sky over Barnesville. A number of folks were rousted the following morning at 6:00 A.M. by a loud noise that had no apparent origin. In between these two incidents, a private citizen and four policemen watched a round, bright UFO hover over downtown Thomaston, a central Georgia city northwest of Macon. James C. Burke saw it first, an object four to five feet in diameter that glowed white like a fluorescent light and occasionally displayed a red tint and a green light. Burke spotted the UFO hovering above his house when he left at 4:30 A.M., a Sunday morning, to go fishing.

Burke immediately alerted Thomaston police, who dispatched patrolmen Bill Mewbourn, Earl Campbell, and Tony Webb, and Lt. Kennie Salton. From 4:57 until 6:15 the object hovered and circled, moving against the wind. Danny Ballard, manning the radio at the Georgia State Patrol post in Manchester, saw it, too. It was reported that both the local police radio and the state patrol band had experienced considerable static while the UFO was in sight, but the interference disappeared when the UFO did.

Barnesville police officer E. O. Pitts spotted a red object that "turned light orange and then almost white and back to red," and which was "about the size of a softball."

Thomaston police notified nearby Robins Air Force Base, where duty officer Sgt. Robert McCommon dispatched a U3A plane from the base to overfly the area. Nothing unusual was spotted, nor did the UFO register on the Robins radar.

Because the air force had standing orders to investigate all UFO reports, a team from Robins interviewed the Thomaston witnesses hours after the sighting occurred and again on the following day.

Emboldened by these reports, two Barnesville residents, Alpha Wilson and Lois Hooks, reported that a week earlier, on April 16, a fireball "the size of a basketball" had hit the pavement directly in front of their car.

"I first noticed the ball of fire above the trees," Wilson told a newspaper reporter, and pointed it out to Mrs. Hooks, who was driving, and she started slowing the car. "When the object fell right in front of us," Wilson continued, "we stopped and watched.

"It lay on the pavement about thirty seconds before burning out. We were scared to death. I first thought it was a bomb and expected it to explode any minute. But it didn't. It just burned out.

"We got out of the car and inspected the pavement. There were no ashes or anything."

27

WE NOW RETURN CONTROL OF YOUR TELEVISION

A curious event in Barnesville occurred to Mrs. W. A. Beavers, a former resident of Boston, Massachusetts. She was listening to her television in April 1966 during this wave of UFO reports, when a familiar voice caught her attention. She looked at the screen to find Jack Chase, an announcer for WBZ, a Boston TV station, describe an aerial mystery thought to be a meteorite. Such a long and selective atmospheric skip is extremely unusual. Remember, this was long before the days of satellite technology that made cross-country and international TV feeds an everyday thing.

Several days later, on April 30, a group of ten people at Lake Sinclair reported a UFO that hovered above the water.

"It looked like a red and green light," said Walter Bush of Macon, "and it stayed right over the lake for a while and then started moving toward Macon at a pretty slow rate of speed."

The soundless, basketball-sized object was flashing its lights when spotted at 9:20 P.M., and departed to the west after ten minutes.

Later that night Macon police investigating a reported UFO landing on I-75 found a cardboard box with holes cut out and a flare burning inside. Despite the inference, it had never been airborne.

DON'T TRY THIS AT HOME

Imitation UFOs often appear after legitimate sightings are reported in the press. What usually happens is a group of boys or college students fashion frameworks of balsa wood, secure candles to the contraption, and place them in the bottom of laundry bags. When the bags hit air currents they scoot across the sky in mystifying fashion. Of late, these hoaxes have evolved into helium-filled balloons dangling flares or glow sticks. In 1973 an editorial on the topic wrote, "Boys will be boys, and what's wrong with that?" Nothing, one hopes, for in the late 1960s I built several such devices myself.

POLICE CHASE, OR DON'T CHASE, UFOS, OR VENUS

A year and a half passed before UFOs struck Georgia again in an episode apparently embellished. The first spate of reports surfaced at 1:00 A.M. on Friday, October 20, 1967, at the lonely ridge-top Manchester state patrol post. Trooper Jerry Goldin spotted two objects—one was an ice blue ball about a mile in altitude, and the other a yellow triangle shape with one red side that hovered about one hundred yards above the tree line.

Police in eleven communities, including Milledgeville, Fayetteville, Greenville, Dublin, Sandersville, Greensboro, Thomson, Warrenton, Bowman, Talbottom, and Butler, also spotted UFOs, but it was in Newnan where a UFO made national news.

Patrolmen Dale Spradlin and his partner Gerald Masdon heard the earlier reports, but they had almost forgotten about them as they cruised the quiet city. Then they "saw this light off to the east," Spradlin said. "I don't know what it was and have never said it was a flying saucer. I saw a light that moved all around, and I've got no idea what it was."

They pulled into a car dealer's lot to observe the object, which was "to the east beyond a railroad bank" and seemed about as high as the tracks, but its distance could not be determined.

"We left the lot and went to where we could get a line of bearing on the light by marking it with a building," Spradlin continued, "and then we started toward it. We followed it about eight miles out of town east on Poplar Road."

After encountering a state trooper observing the same thing, they turned around to resume their rounds.

"I was driving," Masdon said, "and Spradlin was watching the light through the back window. It seemed to get higher like it was gaining on us. It was a bright light and looked a lot like one of those mercury vapor lamps—with a sort of bluish glow. It moved around."

The North Star was clearly visible in the dark sky, and the UFO seemed to be equidistant between it and the ground.

Returning to the station, Masdon told others about the phenomenon they had seen. Some left to look for themselves. When Masdon went off duty at 7:10 A.M., the stars had disappeared but the UFO and moon were still visible.

Officers across the region watched the object as it slowly flew higher into the sky, moving erratically, and faded away at dawn.

The Suwannee River, located in extreme southeastern Georgia, has been the scene of UFO and bigfoot sightings, and ghost slave ships are heard at night. Petroleum prospectors believe Georgia's first petroleum deposits may lie below the surface.

PARADISE BY THE DASHBOARD LIGHT

When the object caught up with the patrol car, this account continued, it rose into the sky and emitted a beam of bluish light which illuminated the road. Spradlin did not know how close the UFO approached, but reportedly said, "A boy and girl parked at a lake who witnessed the chase said it seemed to be right above us."

Later accounts did not include the word "chase," nor was the blue beam mentioned.

Spradlin later stated that he and Masdon had seen the light, so to speak, but emphasized that "we were not chased by the object, nor were we almost blinded by flashes of light from it. Reports of the incident have been blown up out of proportion, and some of the statements attributed to us are absolutely untrue."

In Milledgeville, two experienced policemen, an Officer Niblett and Charles Mixon, were on routine patrol east of Milledgeville on GA 22 at 4:36 A.M. on October 20 when Niblett spotted what he interpreted as a new streetlight, but as they approached a UFO flew away from them. They pursued the object, which was football-shaped and changed from a clear light to red. It accelerated and disappeared eight miles from the city. Niblett and Mixon returned to Milledgeville, and at the city limits they discovered that the UFO had rejoined them.

Mixon, admittedly shaken, spotted it through the rear window of the patrol car and drew Niblett's attention to it, saying the UFO had "caught up with us. The light from it lit up the police car enough to make the hands on our wristwatches visible."

The officers radioed their situation to headquarters, then stopped and left the car to view the UFO more carefully. As they did, the UFO, described as the size of a large water tank and at treetop level, veered off and flew out of sight into the darkness.

Returning to the police station, Niblett and Mixon picked up another patrolman, J. M. Poole. They drove to a hill to scan the skies, and were joined by a fourth officer, Alan Council. Eventually, all the policemen saw a UFO that changed shape from a football to a four-leaf clover and shifted color from bright red-orange to brilliant blue. After twenty minutes, near dawn, the object flew off and disappeared.

The Milledgeville UFO returned on the night of October 22, when a resident phoned police to report a UFO had followed him down a highway. Niblett responded, radioing headquarters that he saw UFOs—one several thousand feet above the first, high in the sky. They "were still hanging" in the sky, having floated together across the sky as the hours passed, when he clocked out in the morning. Niblett described the lower object as like a piece of drifting tinfoil. When other policemen submitted additional reports on October 23, Niblett and another officer drove to the scene and reported a "bright, starlike" UFO. Soon a companion UFO was above the horizon.

It had been arranged for a local pilot to take off and maneuver for a closer look at the UFOs. Soon after 5:00 A.M. the pilot and a friend, in radio contact with the police, took off. Unfortunately, the aerial crew had difficulty distinguishing UFOs from other celestial light sources. The police official pointed the spotlight from his car at the UFO to guide the pilot, but the cops soon informed the pilot that he "flew under it."

The frustrated pilot reported that the UFO was elusive, backing off and "moving higher and away from us." He contacted Robins Air Force Base to inquire if the object registered on their radar. The air force controller reported one target, which he assumed was the chase plane, but for one minute he tracked an unidentified object that then disappeared. After landing at 6:00 A.M., the pilot said the brilliant white shape he chased was still visible.

During this period a thirteen-year-old boy took his Polaroid into the woods to photograph a UFO and emerged with two shots, taken in daylight, of an object shaped like a Mexican sombrero. Few believed the photographs were genuine.

VENUS ATTACKS!

A speedy investigation of these widespread UFO reports was initiated on two fronts. Two research scientists, Dr. Ray Craig, a physical chemist, and John Ahrens, of the University of Colorado, contracted with the air force to evaluate UFO phenomenon in the government's last official investigation, known as the Condom Committee, arrived to investigate the Milledgeville reports while the sightings continued, on October 25. They joined an air force team from Robins that was on a similar but independent mission.

When Milledgeville policemen pointed out the recurring UFO to them, the scientists identified it as Venus, unusually bright due to its close approach to earth. It rose above the eastern horizon at 3:50 A.M., an hour before the first UFO sighting on October 20. The second UFO, according to the researchers, was Jupiter.

As to the radar return noted on October 22, Philip Klass, a noted UFO debunker, suggested an overflying airplane, a swarm of birds, insects, or freak atmospheric conditions.

Dr. J. Allen Hynek, a highly respected UFO researcher, agreed that the UFO "was most definitely Venus!" He believed the "case should be read by all UFO investigators. It is a fantastic example of how persuasive the planet Venus can be as a non-screened UFO. Police in eleven counties were 'taken in' by this planet."

Klass explained that once someone misidentifies Venus as "a UFO, he will find that no matter how far or fast he drives, when he looks back, the UFO seems just as close and just as bright. The logical conclusion is that the UFO must be following him."

Milledgeville was surprised by the reaction to the phenomenon observed there. The *Milledgeville Record* received inquires from news agencies as far away as New York and Los Angeles.

UFOs had been sighted over the Atlanta area earlier in October, on the sixth, seventh, and eighth. In Mableton, C. C. Curry and a number of friends observed several luminous aerial objects for over four hours on the eighth. Other reports originated from policemen.

MY NAME'S RAGSDALE: I CARRY A BADGE

In late October the state of Georgia stepped in to debunk some of the UFO sightings as the work of mischievous teenagers. Maj Barney Ragsdale, head of the Georgia Bureau of Investigation, released a report written by Lt. H. M. Spurling of McRae, supervisor of the GBI's District Three. Several weeks earlier Spurling had found a group of male teenagers cutting out cardboard platforms for candles that were then fixed inside blue plastic laundry bags. The lighted candles filled the bags with warm air, which lofted the contraptions to considerable altitudes. Some colored balloons were inflated with propane or other gases and released.

"When they hit the wind currents they really go," Spurling marveled. "It's almost frightening to see them."

The stern Bureau agent warned that substantial penalties awaited any pranksters whose manmade UFO started a forest or property fire.

It was no surprise that Spradlin and Masdon emphasized that their encounter did not involve a chase. A year and a half earlier, on April 17, 1966, exactly ten days before the four policemen in Thomaston saw their UFO, a police chase in Ohio of a UFO garnered national attention and notoriety for the two pursuers, one of whom lost his job and the other was reassigned after their stories were debunked by Project Blue Book. This was even after they had been told via radio during the incident that radar was tracking the UFO and that two jets had been dispatched to check out the UFO—two jets that they then saw with their own eyes being chased by the UFO. Obviously, they weren't alone in knowledge of the UFO's presence, but they were the fall guys.

PERSONAL STORY

In the fall of 1967 I was a fourteen-year-old Boy Scout in central Georgia. We camped regularly at Camp Benjamin Hawkins, located in the wilds of Crawford County. Traditionally, on the first night of a campout, we waited for the adults to sack out and then we chased each other through the woods until dawn. On the second night we slept like the dead.

On a weekend in mid-October there must have been six or eight of us sitting around a campfire sometime in the dead of night, swapping lies and talking about girls we wished we knew. I doubt I spotted it first, but someone noticed something in the sky which should not have been there. It was a bright orange light, much larger than any object in the sky except the moon—and that was accounted for—and hung far above the pine trees. While we speculated about what it might be, this definitely unidentified aerial object began swinging from side to side like a pendulum, with each swing bringing it closer to the ground in what I later discovered was a classic "falling leaf" maneuver. At length it disappeared behind the tree line.

I can recreate the dialogue in my mind to this day. "Let's go check it out." "You go check it out!" "You're scared." "Am not!" "Mr. Smith told us not to leave camp." (Like we had ever listened to him before.)

After nearly thirty-five years I honestly can't remember if the UFO remained behind the trees and we retreated to our tents or whether we jawboned until it ascended in the same manner that it had "landed" and disappeared into the cosmos. I don't know what it was, but it was certainly unidentified. It was my first and, so far, last UFO.

GEORGIA'S LAST BLUE BOOK UNKNOWN, NO. 12567

In *The Hynek UFO Report*, Dr. J. Allen Hynek related a case he investigated called "The Willful Car," the last unsolved Blue Book case from Georgia. At 8:05 P.M. on Saturday, November 23, 1968, Conway Jones, identified as an Albany bank accountant, was driving his 1967 Ford through a sparsely inhabited area ten miles west of Newton. When he topped a rise and rounded a curve he saw a brilliant light hovering seventy feet directly over the road only two hundred feet ahead.

The "self-luminous, oval-shaped object between forty and fifty yards in diameter which glowed with a yellowish white light" was nontransparent, Hynek wrote, and had a "fuzzy outline."

Jones stated that as he approached the UFO "a beam of light came down to my car, causing the engine to stop and all electrical components to malfunction." First the radio faded to static, then went dead as the engine stopped running. The light beam, which was six feet wide, well defined, and illuminated the woods, was then retracted "like a ladder" into the UFO, a common feature of CE-II (Close encounters of the second kind) cases, Hynek wrote.

After four minutes the UFO changed colors "to a brighter reddish orange and moved straight up at a very high rate of speed" and "was completely out of sight in less than fifteen seconds."

After the departure of the UFO, the car, left in drive, started again by itself—an impossibility—but Hynek accepted the fact. The scientist noted that he investigated the incident at "the same time as the Condom Committee was to make public its report dismissing the entire UFO phenomenon as having no substance," which occurred early in 1969. The Condom Report (officially designated *Scientific Study of Unidentified Flying Objects*) was highly flawed but largely mollified the media and public opinion until the great UFO sightings of 1973. (The greatest tragedy of the Condom Report—it led to the cancellation of my favorite TV show, *The Invaders*.)

According to Lt. Col. John E. Cadon, assistant chief of operations at Moody Air Force Base in Albany, Jones was one of several who reported UFOs that weekend near Newton.

LUSTING AFTER JIMMY CARTER AND HIS UFO

Georgia governor and U.S. president Jimmy Carter had his UFO coming-out on September 12, 1973, in the midst of a record number of sightings being reported across the state. Governor Carter was visiting Statesboro as part of an effort to understand the issues concerning Georgia's people and

Although the locals have no memory of the incident, Jimmy Carter reported that he sighted a large UFO in Leary in 1969.

communities, a program dubbed Operation Feedback. During a press conference at City Hall, Carter was asked to comment on the continuing UFO reports. The future president surprised everyone when he described a personal UFO encounter.

Just after dark, about 7:15 P.M. on the night of October 6, 1969, before speaking to the Leary Lion's Club in southwest Georgia, the attention of Carter and ten to twelve others was drawn by a large, oval, glowing light in the sky. It varied in brightness, changed color, and appeared to approach

34

them and then move away several times, varying in distance between three hundred and one thousand yards. "It was about thirty degrees above the horizon and looked about as large as the moon," he said. "It got smaller and changed to a reddish color and then got larger again." After a ten-minute observation, it vanished. He was unsure about the source of the phenomenon—"probably an electronic occurrence of some sort" or a gaseous reaction (he was an engineer, you know). One account has Carter claiming he had immediately dictated a description of the event to a tape recorder.

"I am convinced that UFOs exist because I've seen one," Carter said, calling it "a very peculiar aberration." He remembered it as "a very remarkable sight . . . obviously there, and obviously unidentified." Despite the speculation of those gathered at Leary, "none of us could figure out what it was."

"I saw it before I became governor," Carter said in a lame attempt at humor. "I haven't seen any UFOs since I have become governor."

Four years after the sighting, on September 18, 1973, Carter completed a thorough sighting report form for NICAP, the National Investigation Committee on Aerial Phenomena (although the International UFO Bureau claims Carter wrote his account longhand on a form they sent him; they then forwarded a copy to NICAP, where the information was typed on their form, which is now available on the Internet). He listed his occupation as "Governor" and his address "State Capitol Atlanta." Under education was "Graduate in Nuclear Physics." According to the report, the single UFO was self-luminous, brighter than the background sky and sharply outlined against it. It appeared to stand still for a time, flew erratically, and changed brightness, shape, and color. "Came close, moved away, came close and then moved away," he said, describing its motion.

In 1975 Carter described the UFO to a *Washington Post* reporter as a light which "appeared and disappeared in the sky. It goes brighter and brighter . . . I have no idea what it was . . . I think it was a light beckoning me to run in the California primary," he joked.

While running for president in May 1976, Carter described his UFO experience. "It was the darndest thing I've ever seen. It was big, it was very bright, it changed colors and it was about the size of the moon. We watched it for ten minutes, but none of us could figure out what it was. One thing's for sure, I'll never make fun of people who say they've seen unidentified objects in the sky." He then unveiled a UFO plank for his platform, saying, "If I become president, I'll make every piece of information this country has about UFO sightings available to the public and the scientists."

Although President Jimmy remembers the event with great clarity, reporters had difficulty identifying any of the dozen or more Lions alleged to have seen the phenomenon with Carter.

35

"Not one resident recalls anything unusual about that particular January evening," Tom Tiede wrote for the Newspaper Enterprise Association on February 2, 1978. "The townsfolk are mildly amused," he continued, and "have in fact been chuckling" since the media focused on Carter's sighting. "Some think that Carter actually viewed the town's silver water tower," the article revealed.

Leary mayor Stanley Shepard told Tiede that he had spoken with everyone who was at the meeting, "and nobody remembers anything about flying saucers," Tiede related. But they did remember that his speech was dull.

A check with the headquarters of Lion's Club International in Illinois revealed that Carter had made a mistake in dating the UFO encounter. He remembered it as occurring in October 1969, but records prove the meeting was held in January 1969.

Allan Hendry, chief investigator of the Center for UFO Studies, and UFO skeptic Robert Sheaffer calculated the time and place of Jimmy Carter's sighting and compared it to the position of Venus. Carter's object was thirty degrees above the western horizon, while Venus was twenty-five degrees to the west-southwest. "This almost perfectly matches," Sheaffer wrote, and most scientists concluded that Carter had seen the planet, which through earth's atmosphere appears to expand and contract in size. It is "not at all uncommon for atmospheric conditions to create the illusion the president saw. Many people misinterpret Venus," Sheaffer wrote in *The Humanist* magazine in 1977.

"No other object generates as many UFO reports as the planet Venus," he continued. Although the planet is obviously not as bright as the moon and cannot approach or withdraw from a viewer, "descriptions like these are typical of misidentifications of a bright planet. Every time Venus reaches its maximum brilliance in the evening sky, hundreds of 'UFO sightings' of this type are made." During Carter's sighting, Venus was one hundred times brighter than a first-magnitude star.

"Mr. Carter is in good company in misidentifying Venus as a UFO," Sheaffer stated. "Many highly trained and responsible persons, including airplane pilots, scientists, policemen, and military personnel, have made the same mistake." A number of U.S. pilots attempted to shoot Venus down during World War II.

Many UFO researchers have accepted this explanation, and Carter has no complaints either.

Considering the lack of witnesses to Carter's sighting in Leary, perhaps he spoke somewhere else in October and saw his UFO there. However, Sheaffer, a member of the UFO Subcommittee of the Committee for the Scientific Investigation of Claims of the Paranormal (whew), did locate one Leary witness who somewhat substantiated Carter's account. In 1969 the Leary Lions Club president was Fred Hart, who had vague memories of watching an aerial light with Carter, although he thought it could have been a "weather balloon." The event left little impression on Hart, who believed the object was nothing unusual and also readily accepted the idea that it might have been Venus.

One final note on the Carter files. In late September 1995, according to Reuters, in response to questions from college students, Carter denied knowledge of government evidence proving the existence of extraterrestrials.

"I never knew of any instance where it was proven that any sort of vehicle had come from outer space to our country and either lived here or left," the former president said.

If you think this story is out of character for a president, bear in mind that Carter once admitted to the press that a rabid "killer rabbit" had jumped into a pond, swam to a fishing boat occupied by himself and secret service agents, and attempted to climb into the vessel. Carter also had a faith healer sister, and his wife, Rosalyn, reported ghosts in a home they lived in as newlyweds.

WALK THIS WAY

At 6:30 P.M. on February 1, 1971, a married couple was driving near Waverly Hall when they spotted a "bright circular object," the husband stated, nearly directly overhead. It descended to hover one hundred feet over the ground two hundred yards from the highway. The phenomenon paralleled their route, slowing, speeding up, and stopping with the car while remaining at the same height and distance from the car. After five miles the couple pulled over and the man walked toward the UFO. After an observation of fifteen minutes, he felt the object had disappeared, but it "simply faded slowly as it left behind a mist." The UFO changed from a bright, full moon to a football shape, and had huge red and green blinking lights.

OUR FIRST TRIANGLE

Near midnight of August 1, 1973, a young man was saying good-bye to his girlfriend in Morrow, when he spotted a triangle with rounded corners hovering at treetop level 150 feet away. The UFO was fifteen feet to a side and had rows of white lights as bright as car headlights. After five minutes it began to rotate slowly onto its side, then disappeared.

Georgia had experienced a number of classic sightings by the start of the 1970s, but what happened next was unprecedented in UFO history.

2

Creature Features

Reports of animals such as the Loch Ness monster and the Abominable Snowman date back hundreds of years. Surprisingly, as humanity has spread out into the world, such reports have not diminished, but have substantially increased. Aquatic critters are reported not only in large lakes, but in many rivers and all the oceans. Big, hairy humanoids have been found in virtually every locale—mountain wilderness, impenetrable swamps, the piney woods, and quite close to densely populated areas.

Nor are sea monsters and bigfoot our only curious fauna. There are big phantom cats where they shouldn't be, and bizarre unions of tigers and lions prowling the countryside. As a bonus, giant dinosaur-era birds have been seen flapping their great wings on several occasions.

THE WOG

The Cherokee called them *Nun Yunu Wi*, "the stone man," and *Kecleh-Kudleh*, which means "hairy savage." Besides Native American myth, Georgia has few stories of mystery animals in its early history. The most impressive account was Jefferson County's Wog, which occasionally appeared in a radius of several miles around Jug Tavern (modern Winder), from its settlement until about 1809. The Wog was the size of a horse, only shorter, and was covered with jet-black hair. The rear legs were twelve inches shorter than the front pair, which rendered the appearance of a large dog sitting on its tail. It seemed to walk almost sideways, sliding first on one side and then the other. The head was bearlike, with menacing red eyes, and the mouth contained "a set of great white teeth over which his ugly lips never closed," noted an early county history. This feature enabled its forked, eight-inch-long tongue to play "in and out his mouth like (that) of a snake."

A truly unique aspect of the Wog was a large tail, which did not taper to a point like other animals, but was uniformly thick. It ended in a dense bunch of white hair eight inches in length. This great tail was in constant motion, no matter if the creature was walking, standing, or sitting. The appendage moved "with a quick upward curve which brought it down with a whizzing sound which could be heard thirty feet away," the history stated.

Local Indians advised settlers that the creature would occasionally visit their houses at night, if it saw light. The Wog would announce its presence by the whirling tail and poke its wicked tongue through any chink or openings in their cabins, but would leave if left unmolested. The pioneers apparently abided by this wise counsel. There are no stories of attacks against the Wog, nor of it molesting people or their animals, although an appearance frightened barnyard denizens. Chickens fled for the trees, horses snorted, cattle moaned, and dogs and cats raced away. Occasionally, some animals reportedly died of fear. Finished with its inspections, the Wog would emit a loud snort and depart. As more settlers entered the area, the Wog shambled into folklore.

SWAMP THING

The Okefenokee Swamp was truly a land of mystery in June 1829, when a bizarre story about it was published by the *Milledgeville Statesman*. The tale was related by a John Ostean, "residing on the borders of this swamp in Ware County," and others who lived on the opposite side in Florida. Locals had long heard from Creek Indians of an enchanted island inhabited by "mortals of super-human dimensions and incomparable beauty." The story goes that two men and a boy had taken advantage of a long dry spell and pushed deep into the swamp for two weeks to seek this island. However, "their progress suddenly arrested at the appearance of the print of a footstep so unearthly in its dimensions, so ominous of power, and terrible in form," that they paused. The print was eighteen inches long and nine inches across, the stride of this giant over six feet. The party hastily returned and spread the tale of the "Man Mountain."

Hearing the story, nine Florida hunters ventured into the swamp. After several days' journey, they found a similar print and others. The men followed the tracks for several days and had camped on a ridge when two of their members "simultaneously discharged at an advancing and ferocious wild beast" whose screams made the swamp "reverberate with a deafening roar." The creature came "full in their view advancing upon them with a terrible look . . . Our little band instinctively gathered close in a body, and presented their rifles. The huge being, nothing daunted, bounded upon his victims, and in the same instant received the contents of seven rifles. But he did not die alone; nor until he had glutted his wrath with the death of five of them, which he effected by wringing off the head from the body." The four surviving men examined the prostrate giant as it died, "wallowing and roaring. His length was thirteen feet, and his breadth and volume of just proportions." Fearing that the struggle might have alerted similar beings, the men gathered their comrades' guns and fled for home.

Another mystery creature appeared in late November or early December of 1926. A young son of Elmer Smith was walking to school near Sand Hill Ford on Mill Creek in Bulloch County when a "large strange animal" stepped out of the bushes and blocked his path. The lad pitched his lunch pail at the creature and ran home. Local residents put their dogs on the path of the monster, but a "number of hounds showed great fear and refused to follow the trail." One month earlier, it turns out, something had killed and eaten a large bulldog two miles west of Statesboro.

KILL THE MONSTER!
The earliest bigfoot report from Georgia was gathered by California researcher Rich Grumley. He spoke with a man who had been a boy somewhere in Georgia in 1943. An unknown animal had been killing sheep and calves by ripping off their limbs. Tracked down on a ridge by a number of men, sixty shotgun slugs were required to put it down. One round finally penetrated an eye and entered the brain. The thing was then stuffed into the bed of a pickup truck and taken to town. Although its head was propped up against the cab, the feet dragged on the ground. There was little hair on the head, and none on the palms and soles of the feet, but the remainder of the creature was thick with reddish brown hair. All agreed it stank terribly. The being was buried beneath a rock cairn and reputedly remains there today.

One other American bigfoot, this one in Missouri, has been reported killed, but both are lost to history—or mystery—assuming either event is true.

THE ABOMINABLE SANDMAN
One night around 1951 in the Boston, Georgia, area, near Valdosta, a woman heard her dogs raising a ruckus and walked outside to investigate. "Treed" on the front porch by the canines was a giant, manlike creature covered with hair. After her husband fired at the animal, it ran into the night.

This poor bigfoot also dodged a pistol shot fired by the woman's stepfather, who spotted what he thought was a seven-foot-tall man peering through a window of his cabin late one evening. He ran outside and fired, inducing the dark-colored creature to make for the woods. On the following morning the man found twenty-inch-long tracks outside his home.

THE GRAY GHOST
Some researchers connect the fantastic alien entity encounter experienced by Mrs. Symmonds (see chapter 1) to a series of creatures that had the

Bigfoot, up close and personal on Fort Gordon property near Augusta. The witness estimated its height at ten feet and its weight at eleven hundred pounds. The creature was all big-boned muscle, with thick arms and legs. (© 1999 by Bill Asmussen,www.door.net/hominid artwork)

good citizens of the Peach State snickering for a month. A short, hairy wildman was running amok one hundred miles to the southwest, around Edison and Bronwood.

This strange series of summer sightings started on the afternoon of July 20, 1955, when Tant King, a farm worker, was mowing alfalfa in a field adjoining dense woods on the Three Springs Ranch. He spotted "a hairy little gray man without clothes," which he estimated to be three and a half to four feet tall, emerge from the trees and walk along a fence which enclosed the field. Although frightened, King continued working, keeping an eye on the creature for twenty-five minutes, when it reentered the woods.

At the end of the workday Wayne Dozier, owner of the farm and a vocational-agricultural teacher at Edison High School, picked King up. The hired hand immediately told Dozier of his experience. Dozier suggested that King had been seeing things, and inquired why he did not get closer to identify the apparition.

"He said that he thought he was a ghost," Dozier explained fifteen years later, "and did not want to crowd him." That sounds reasonable enough.

Dozier took the account seriously enough to examine the fence line, where he discovered fresh tracks "the size of a hand with four claws turned out sideways."

After Dozier related the story to friends in town the next day, they wanted to inspect the site. This time Dozier found new tracks and a tuft of "white, curly hair about three inches long" stuck in the fence at the place where King said the creature had emerged from the forest. Dozier immediately sent it to the Georgia Bureau of Investigation crime laboratory in Atlanta for analysis.

Additional fresh tracks were discovered on July 21. By that time the rural area was buzzing with speculation about Dawson County's "hairy ghost."

On the afternoon of July 24, just a few miles from the Three Springs Ranch, Mrs. Elberta Donnell, a mother of five, and her son, Toby, noticed "all the cattle runnin' up this way and I wondered what was after 'em. Directly, we seen this thing walkin' up this way."

She described the thing as "shaggy, about four feet high," and "mole-colored," presumably brown. She and Toby watched the creature "waddling across the pasture." It ambled toward the house, then walked behind a tree and never reappeared. Afterward, she explained, the cows refused to approach the spot where the thing had left the woods. Apparently, she was staying put as well, stating, "I got a heap o' cotton down yonder by the woods that needs pickin' bad, and it's gonna rot if they don't hurry up and find that thing."

Mrs. Donnell's daughter, Martha, spotted the creature on the following day in the same place. She confirmed that it walked upright, was brown, and "shoulder high."

Dozier discovered more tracks on his land on July 27, along with partially eaten citrons, which bore animal tooth marks. On Julian Lane's neighboring farm the animal had eaten parts of cantaloupes.

Dozier and others lay in wait for the little hairy man, but he never reappeared, much to the farmer's annoyance. Dozier expressed hope that the thing would be caught or killed so people would stop teasing him about it. Calhoun County sheriff Ivan Jones seemed to give the incident credence, announcing that his department was cooperating in the search.

It was apparently a slow summer in Georgia law enforcement. By August 2 the director of the Georgia Bureau of Investigation crime lab, Dr. Herman Jones (see chapter 1, "Monkey Men from Mars"), declared the hair sample to be human, but pointed out that "there was no proof" that it had come from the mysterious being. The hair "could have been deposited there by a human being climbing over the fence." His wife, a toxicologist at the lab, proposed that a worker mending the fence could be the source of the hair.

Sheriff Jones announced that the creature was "more of a mystery than ever. It's spooky. Those who say they have seen it declared it walks on two legs like humans." The sheriff never personally saw the thing or located any tracks.

On August 3 the *Atlanta Constitution* published an anonymous report that the creature was an escaped coyote from Early County. Unfortunately, this source did not explain the creature's size, humanlike appearance, or how it came to walk erect on two legs.

BIGFOOT ATTACKS!

The controversy was not yet ended. Shift northeast to Terrell County. The state had recently erected new highway signs along GA 118 near Kinchafoonee Creek, three miles northeast of Bronwood and eleven miles from the county seat of Dawson. Joseph Whaley, a twenty-year-old employee of the Georgia State Forestry Commission and resident of Dawson, was using a scythe to cut bushes and tall grass that obscured the signs.

Hearing a "strange noise" in a thicket near the creek, "I walked to the edge of the woods and heard the bushes rattle," Whaley said. He ventured into the forest to investigate and spotted a threatening figure approaching. It "reminded me of a gorilla," the worker recalled, exceeding six feet in height and "built something on the order of a man." The animal was covered with "shaggy gray hair" which he described as "like a wire-haired terrier dog." But this was no terrier. Prominent features on the head included "tusklike teeth and pointed ears," and it was "grunting like a wild pig." The creature's arms looked "heavy but its hands not very large."

Fearing attack, Whaley launched a preventive assault. "The creature . . . walked toward me," he related. "I still had my scythe. I took a couple of swings at him and struck him on the arms and the chest. But he kept coming at me." Whaley missed on his first swing, then landed two blows on the right paw and another on the chest.

Causing no apparent harm to the beast, Whaley fled for his Jeep, which was parked beside the road. He grabbed the microphone and tried to reach the nearest ranger tower, but was unsuccessful. He was unable to crank the vehicle before the creature was upon him. The entity rained blows upon the young man, ripping off his shirt and leaving three lines of scratches on his left arm and shoulder. Whaley hastily exited from the other side of the Jeep and ran back into the woods, thinking he could distance his attacker, which pursued in "a lumbering and slow-moving" gait. Whaley circled back to his Jeep and had gained enough space to start the engine and escape.

Whaley drove immediately to his superior, forest ranger Jim Bowen, to report the incident, and later repeated the tale under oath. Bowen went straight to the site, where he found "very definitely a trail." He stated that "something was there that looked like a large object."

It was officially a slow summer in Georgia crime, for on August 4 GBI director Maj. Delmar Jones dispatched Agent T. E. Faircloth to investigate the unusual hominid activity in southwest Georgia, saying he had read the reports "with interest."

Terrell County sheriff Zeke Matthew initiated his own investigation, which lasted one day. Matthew bowed out, stating, "If I believed there was anything to it, I would be out looking for it." He said there were no signs of a struggle or unusual footprints near Whaley's alleged encounter.

Major Jones concluded his investigation on the following day in an even more unsatisfactory manner. His agents had purportedly found an unidentified farmer who had attempted to scare off trespassers who were fishing out of his private pond. This inventive (or invented) agriculturist draped himself in a sheet, donned a Halloween mask, and wandered across his land.

"He scared the pants off the trespassers," Jones reported with amusement, "but he also fired the imagination of others until they began seeing 'monsters' everywhere."

The GBI director believed that the prank sparked the series of sightings around Edison and inspired a panic. In conclusion, Jones stated there was "nothing to the reports." As to Whaley's attacker, the GBI decided he had been assaulted by "a hog-bear—a little black bear."

In *The Complete Guide to Mysterious Beings*, John Keel wrote that O. K. Fletcher, identified as a zoologist, "speculated it could have been a kangaroo!" which would have been as bizarre as a bigfoot.

However, the creature near Bronwood was gray-colored and looked like a gorilla, not a man, and nobody there or at Edison reported a white creature with a grotesque face.

AFTER THE CAT!

Before the creature sightings in southwest Georgia concluded on this desultory note, a different mystery animal appeared near Lincolnton, in Lincoln County along the Savannah River bordering South Carolina. News accounts stated that "a long, slender, puma-like creature" was seen chasing a dog at Soap Creek Fishing Camp. Witness Pete Hall got a shot off at the phantom puma. "It scampered away into the woods faster than any four-legged animal I've ever seen," he stated.

The "puma," this time snarling like a wolf, made a second appearance in Columbia County near Martinez, at the confluence of the Savannah and Little rivers.

A fragmentary report from John Green's *Sasquatch, the Apes Among Us*, dated a year later, has a number of people sighting a seven-foot-tall creature walking upright along a road near Columbus, northwest of Edison and Bronwood.

BIGFOOT AND MISS PIGGY

Just south of the Heard County line shared with Troup County, a young boy who lived along Ridge Road in 1955 or 1956 was feeding a hog when he saw an odd creature. It was eight feet tall and covered with "long, light-brownish hair." The boy's brother noted large, four-toed footprints near the hog pen. A neighbor chased off the four- to five-hundred-pound bigfoot with shots from his 30-30 rifle on several occasions. The animal was locally called "Bung-a-Dingo."

SHAKE OFF THE DEMON OR, IT WAS A ONE-EYED, ONE-HORNED, FLYING PURPLE PEOPLE EATER

About 9:30 one night in 1960, an eleven-year-old boy near Liberty Hill was gathering firewood for his grandmother when he felt something grab him around the waist. "Cut it out," he yelled, assuming his twin brother was playing a trick on him. But then he saw the brother cutting wood thirty yards away. Something still had ahold of his waist, so the boy started screaming and running toward home, one hundred yards away, with the entity securely latched on to his waist. As the two rounded a corner of the house, centrifugal force threw the thing off. More curious than afraid, the boy continued around the house and crept up to the last corner. Peering out carefully, he shined his flashlight at the spot where the creature had been detached. Seventy-five feet away stood a figure "half the size of a monkey," two to three feet tall, with red-brown skin, one large dark eye, and a horn in the forehead extending down to the eye. Long, slender, antenna-like ears on the creature were several inches long.

On sighting his demon, the boy lit out for his grandmother's house (no one was home in his house) literally running out of his shoes. The entire encounter took three to four minutes.

MANGLED BIGFOOT

A sighting phoned in to researcher Gordon Strasenburgh reported an eight-foot-tall creature that was spotted near Tarrytown in 1965. It appeared "mangled," which leads one to wonder what could mutilate an eight-foot-tall monster.

DON'T CROSS THE RIVER

According to an account filed with the Georgia Swamp Ape Research Center (to be explained), in the spring of 1972 a young man identified as P. Phelps returned from a tour of duty in Vietnam and went to work for the Corps of Engineers surveying the Flint River. One morning as he and his partner rounded a bend in the river in Talbot County, the partner nudged Phelps and said, "Bear." A creature was in the river at the shoals, one hundred yards upriver.

GSARC member pointing out bark harvested from a tree in the Flint River area. The creature that did it is very, very tall. (Courtesy of James P. Akin)

When the men started their engine to maneuver around the shoals, the "bear" stood up and turned to face them. His "mind could not comprehend" what he saw, Phelps testified. It was "a creature of a tall stature, seven, eight feet tall, completely covered in thick black hair." Detecting the men, it "galloped to the opposite bank with incredible speed" that resembled "a sprint runner in track." The creature rapidly disappeared into the woods.

A BOY AND HIS BIGFOOT

Another report forwarded to the GSARC detailed an encounter in the Okefenokee Swamp. While a fourteen-year-old boy and his family were camping at Stephen Foster State Park in 1972, the boy was walking along a waterway when he heard footsteps behind him, drawing closer. He assumed it was his siblings. "I figured they were going to scare me, and I decided to let them sneak up and I would jump out and scare them." Moments later "a thing that looked like a cross between a chimpanzee and a little man" approached along the path. "It saw me and let out a sound like a hill," then crouched down and nimbly sprung on the boy. "It knocked me down and tried to get its teeth in(to) my neck. I screamed. I thought I was dead."

Fortunately, the youngster's parents heard the scream and shouted back. "It raised up real slow and sniffed the air for a few seconds," he continued. "Then it just got up and walked into the canal and swam across to the other side," disappearing into the woods.

TWO FOR THE SWAMP

Our final swamp stories have sites but no dates. Two farmers deer hunting near Waycross saw a seven-and-a-half-foot-tall creature covered with grayish brown hair crossing the Southern Railroad. It stopped and stared at them for a while, and they looked back. The bigfoot finally disappeared into a swamp.

Years ago a family visiting their grandmother's house in the Okefenokee Swamp was passing the time fishing. Suddenly, the mother "began screaming and pointing at this thing that was carrying away our stringer," said a man who was twelve at the time and related the story recently to the GSARC. The creature was thirty yards distant, loping along a creek. The father shouted angrily at the animal and pursued until he got close "and it turned around and screamed at us."

The father turned and ran, quickly gathering the family into the car and leaving. That night Granny informed the family that "she heard stuff around all the time but stayed in the house at night."

The Okefenokee X-Files Web site describes a bigfoot creature that inhabited the swamp until recently. Known as the South Georgia Pig Man by old swampers, it was "a large apelike being that walks upright, has abundant hair and a nose similar to a pig." A skunklike odor accompanied the animal, which never displayed hostility or aggression and "was referred to as timid and shy with sad expressive eyes." Most reports originated from deep within the swamp. This animal might be related to the skunk apes frequently reported in the Everglades. It was suggested that they could easily migrate along a path consisting of the Kissimmee River Valley, Lake Wales Ridge, and Saint John's River Basin, where bigfoot has been seen lately.

JELLYSTONE BIGFOOT, OR SMARTER THAN YOUR AVERAGE "GAQUATCH"

According to the *Yeti Newsletter*, a bigfoot appeared at Blackburn State Park near Dahlonega at 4:30 A.M. on September 2 in the early 1970s. Three Saint Petersburg, Florida, residents, Loes Alexander, Bob Martin, and Chris Stevens, were camping when they saw an eight-foot bigfoot eating out of trash cans (imagine the futility of *safeing* foodstuffs by suspending them above a campsite with a Sasquatch in the area). It emitted a high-pitched howl (perhaps lamenting its being reduced to plundering with common possums, raccoons, and bears). Local residents informed park rangers that they had seen a similar creature, dubbed Billy Holler Bugger, in the area. Tracking dogs refused to follow the animal, perhaps indignant at being asked to follow a creature with such a dreadful name. Or perhaps they knew it did not exist.

One month earlier, on July 29, seven Georgians had spotted an eight-foot bigfoot, this one clad in brownish black fur, exit a swamp near a cotton mill. This one gave and took—taking "shiny" objects from a pickup truck and leaving footprints in our legendary red clay.

MALLED

A variety of bigfoot creatures were spotted by a group of fourteen-year-old boys from March until June 1974, in Gwinnett County, several miles from Norcross and seven miles from the Chattahoochee River.

The first incident occurred while the boys were building a fort of bamboo stalks in a swampy creek bottom not far from their neighborhood. After a while it dawned on them that the woods had gone completely quiet. Then they heard a large branch break no more than seventy feet away. "We heard the animal scream and run toward us by the sound of the stomps in the leaves," one of the boys later said. They escaped without sighting their pursuer.

Over the following week they discovered tracks with three and five toes, heard "far-off animal sounds," and located an area of depressed grass. Soon after they spotted three-toed tracks and "a series of tracks that looked like the bare feet of children." The teenagers agreed that the screaming bigfoot they heard was "a female with babies." Farther back in the woods they located a single large print on one side of a stream and a similar print on the other side, indicating a massive stride. "A *big* step!" remembered one.

Early one morning, Mike, a friend of the man who related the story, ran to his house from two doors down in an excited state. While getting dressed for school he had heard a neighbor's dog bark wildly "and could hear the creature running through the woods" behind their houses. He had also spotted the shadow of the being.

The sun was rising as the boys walked to their bus stop. They looked down a cul-de-sac toward the woods and swamps and saw, beneath a street lamp, a "large cone-shaped dark" mound that should not have been there. Suddenly, the mound stood up, walked several yards, leaned over to pick up something off the ground, then darted into the woods.

They all agreed it was about seven feet tall but skinny, with wide hips, arms dangling nearly to its knees, and with "what appeared to be a sagittal crest" atop its head.

The next fall the narrator and Mike were headed toward the bus stop when they heard a distant call originating from the swamp. It was described as "a two-toned call—a high-pitched note that turned into a low-pitched note." The boy imitated the call, and several seconds later he was answered—this time it was closer. The boy again called back, "and immediately we heard a return call, again much closer, as if the creature were moving through the swamp toward us." A third imitation brought a response that sounded as though it came from the edge of the swamp. At this point the boy's stepfather shouted at him to stop shouting. The creature sounded one last note, "coming from far, far away." It was apparently a good-bye call.

MOUNTAIN MAN
In mid-June 1978 a twelve-year-old girl was visiting friends, thirteen-year-old twins who lived ten miles northwest of Toccoa. The mountainous area was remote and densely wooded, populated only by six related families. As the three children walked into the woods at midday, they spotted a "bulky, lumbering figure coming toward us" about thirty-five feet away. The seven-foot-tall being, described as "a cross between a man and a bear," had a hairy face and "a strong, musty animal smell." The children ran for the nearest house and the creature pursued. At one point it was only fifteen feet behind, but stopped at the edge of a clearing. It made no sound.

HARRY, THE HAIRY APE
About 2:00 P.M. one day in late fall 1979, a man walking on the U.S. Signal School-Fort Gordon Small Arms Impact Area in Richmond County, near the headwaters of South Prong Creek, spotted a creature. "A large man/ape creature, ten feet to ten feet, six inches tall (estimated weight eleven hundred pounds)" approached him "with an unhurried pace," he recorded. From a distance of twenty feet the man saw that the body, except for face and palms, was "covered with neat short (one-inch) dark-brown-to-black hair flecked with gray." It was "not especially threatening," and assumed a defensive stance. The face was "like a gorilla, dark skin and dark, deep-set eyes, the head sloped back and was Neanderthal-shaped, had no eyebrows, prominent lips but not protruding, jutting square chin, prominent nostrils, slight nose, not flat like a gorilla, and an aged look to the face. The body was all big-boned muscle, no body fat and had thick arms and legs." He saw no ears or teeth, and the creature issued neither sound nor odor. The man backed away and walked quickly to his truck.

ICKY POOH
In the area the witness had noticed a footprint twenty-two inches in length, six inches wide at the heel and nine inches at the ball. The toes

were angled, but straight. He also found a pile of vomit which "contained deer skin with hair attached, acorns not well chewed." A stool deposit consisted of "deerskin, acorns, and tree bark." A tree had bark stripped from it at a height eight to ten feet above the ground.

HAVE YOU SEEN YOUR BIGFOOT, BABY, STANDING IN THE SHADOWS?

About midnight in 1982 three young men decided to seek out a ghost reportedly haunting Beards Creek Church cemetery near Glennville in Tattnall County. They admitted to having a beer or two on the way, but were nowhere near drunk as they approached the site down a dirt road through farmland and swamp. Passing the church, they noted someone standing in the shadows. When they turned for a better look, the figure ran into the graveyard. About the time the boys thought it had eluded them, the creature suddenly stood up from behind a large headstone. "We froze as it stared at us," one wrote. "It was very tall, about seven or eight feet, and had long brown hair that covered its entire body, including the face." The eyes appeared red. After a few seconds it ran into the woods.

SWAMPFOOT, AKA THE SKUNK APE

A creature rarely seen but often heard and smelled haunted a rural section of Paulding County during the early 1980s. The story became public after Emazell Elliott crossed GA 101 from her house to check her mailbox on September 17, 1984. Glancing down, she spotted twenty-four-inch-long footprints stretching fifty feet to a dirt lane, which led into a wooded, swampy area beside her home, where she had lived all of her fifty-seven years. There were a few prints on the rough lane, but apparently the creature that had made them elected to detour into the wilderness. The giant prints were deeply impressed into the earth and spaced nine to eleven feet apart. Emazell's husband, Heslip, a retired mail carrier, noted, "You know that thing has to be heavy and tall." The prints were so deep that a street cleaner swept over the tracks without disturbing them.

This was the first physical manifestation of a thing they had long suspected existed in Hannah's Swamp, a fifteen-square-mile area near the Union community, located in southwestern Paulding County. At one time the Elliotts fished regularly in the swamp, but an incident three years earlier ended that recreational pursuit.

"We were midway into the swamp," Mrs. Elliott related, "and were fishing when we heard a sound which I can't describe, except to say it sorta sounded like a hyena. The sound came nearer and then it was blood-curdling. It was in the evening, and after we heard that noise we got our poles and came out from there faster than we went in," she concluded. They never returned.

After being happily confined to the swamp for some time, what would have motivated this swampfoot to leave its secure, isolated home for a more hostile environment? One theory points to the land's owner, who supposedly was attempting to drain the swamp in an effort to transform it into pastureland. That activity apparently disrupted the creature's native habitat.

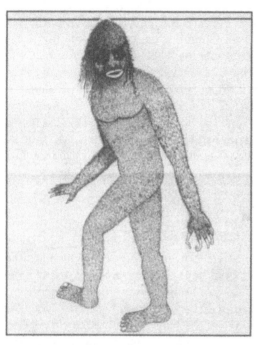

One of several different bigfoot creatures sighted by numerous witnesses in the mountains around Summerville in September 1986. (Courtesy of the Summerville News)

BIGFOOT FAMILY VALUES

Five years earlier, Nan McQuillen, a staff writer for the Dallas New Era, had been told of two bigfoot creatures inhabiting a swamp in neighboring Douglas County, in the vicinity of the Southern Empire Egg Farm along Sweetwater Creek. The creatures had apparently homesteaded there for years and were spotted on several occasions. One was dark colored and large; the second was lighter in color and smaller. On every occasion the creatures were smelled before being sighted. Speculation was that they lived off chickens and eggs and fish from the creek. An area family admitted to several encounters with the swampfoot.

"We call it a 'Skunk Ape,'" said Lucie Luallen, "because it smells so badly. I have never seen it, but my son George has. I have heard it from time to time. The only way I can describe the sound is something similar to a child yelling and a bull bellowing."

For the previous five years of their eight-year residence in the swamp, the Luallens had encountered the creature. At one point Chester Luallen and his son took a high-powered hunting rifle and struck out into the bottomland to kill the animal.

"My boy got ahead of me, and after we got well into the swamp, we heard it," Chester recalled. "Then my son came running as fast as he could and said, 'Daddy, get the hell out of here!' He said it stands like a man and is a little over eight feet tall."

That son described the creature as walking upright. A second son later saw the same being in a pasture, after first detecting it by smell. Mrs. Luallen heard a racket late one evening as the creature made off with a calf.

The last member of the Luallen family, their German shepherd Princess, also confirmed the existence of the monster. She was fearless in the face of any danger, except for this mystery animal. "She can tell when it is nearby for she always gets underneath the house," Mr. Luallen said. "She was with us when we ran out of the swamp. And she wouldn't leave me for anything, but she got to the house faster than I did."

WOOF, WOOF

In 1986 a fifteen-year-old boy and his two older brothers were deer hunting in Sumter County, between Plains and Richland, in a pine forest owned by a paper company. One had wounded a deer, and the two older siblings followed the blood trail, leaving the youngster at the bottom of a gully to watch their equipment. It was twilight, just after sunset. The younger boy had waited about half an hour when "something woofed at me" from the tree line ten yards away. Frightened, the boy climbed to the top of the gully to wait for his brothers. They soon appeared, having failed to locate their prey, and the three gathered their gear and started for their truck.

As they walked, heavy footsteps in the woods on the side of the trail could be heard. The brothers would stop, and seconds later the footsteps in the woods would stop. The oldest brother yelled into the woods, thinking a hunter might be lost, but there was no response. The trio continued, and so did the sounds. The boys stopped and the brother shouted again. Getting no response, he then fired ten rounds into the air as a warning. They continued along the trail, concerned that if their shadow continued on its present course it might cut them off from their truck. When the sounds continued to pace them the alpha brother warned the stalker that he would fire if they were followed anymore. They started walking again "and so did the 'animal' in the woods." One brother then fired into the woods where the sounds emanated. The hunting party was able to continue unmolested to their truck.

BIGFOOT CALL

About 8:00 P.M. in March 1988, a boy and his father were driving on dirt roads through wooded hills in rural Polk County, their purpose to ferret out turkey roosts. They planned to return in the morning for a hunt. The pair would drive a short distance, then blow an owl whistle and wait for a

53

response. They soon "heard something walking through the woods on two legs." At first it "was walking the ridge parallel to the one we were parked on," but then "began coming toward us," stalking down the opposite ridge and climbing up the one they were on. They found it strange that the creature did not stumble once while breaking through the tangled landscape in the dark, and its approach "meant it wasn't scared of us." They had no gun with them, so when the intruder got close they executed the smarter part of valor and left.

WOLF, WOLF?

In late 1991 pets started disappearing along Douglas County's Dog River. Mary Mitchell lost three cats. Then something climbed a six-foot-high fence and ate one of Donald Glover's four beagles, leaving only a paw and the head. At that point residents became alarmed.

Jason Mauldin, alarmed that a small child might be the next victim, circulated a flier which read, "Wolf at Large?"

"We've lost all sorts of animals out here," Mauldin said. "Everyone has an idea—a bear, packs of wild dogs, coyotes, bobcats, mountain lions. Everyone, of course, thinks they've seen something."

But no one had seen anything definite. Mary Mitchell heard something one night in July as she checked on an animal pen.

"Something bellowed," she said, "a deep guttural sound, not a growl. I know animals, but I don't know what that was. We had a shotgun, but we ran for it."

She also found unusual tracks, which resembled a raccoon's, "except it'd have to be two hundred pounds. God help us if a raccoon got that big. It's some big, bad mother that's getting old and wants the easy pickings. I wouldn't go by that river at night. Hell, no."

Asked his opinion of the affair, Bill Fletcher, a Department of Natural Resources wildlife biologist, acknowledged the incidents "sound strange." He thought a bobcat, weighing no more than thirty-five pounds, would not have engaged four dogs, and a bear would have inflicted more damage.

One man told Perry Poe, executive director of the Douglas County Animal Control Office, that the culprit was a bigfoot. "He wasn't joking," Poe said.

"HAVE GUN, WILL TRAVEL" READS THE CARD OF A BIGFOOT HUNTER

The Douglas County creature seemed to be related to the skunk ape, "a prehistoric creature" seen in Florida and southern Alabama, said Mike Clark, of Dothan, Alabama, a skunk ape hunter by avocation. "They're notorious for the same thing—killing animals—horses, goats, hogs. It's not a bigfoot, technically," he said, adding that the government covered up its

54

investigation. The skunk ape obviously has an atrocious odor, and has clawed feet and seal skin. Douglas County's edition seems foul tempered and emits a guttural growl. The initial Douglas County reports mentioned sightings across a wide area.

"It was about 11:30 P.M., and my baby started crying," said Henry County's Connie Mulvaney. "We went in and heard a growling noise and a challenge at the window. It was more than a growl; it was a deep, rough sound. It frightened us so much that we called the police."

The only physical evidence police found of the mysterious creature, which attempted to enter the bedroom, was a tear in the screen.

Meanwhile, in Fayette County, Mike Redman, principal of an elementary school, was cleaning a deer in the woods when he heard "a deep, awful, ferocious, guttural sound," attributed to a creature he felt was after the game. Redman immediately grabbed his rifle. "It was big, but not a bear," he said. "It was an overgrown varmint, and it's blood-and-flesh-seeking." Redman had previously lost two cats in the area, and he later saw a wolverine-like creature playing in a field.

Near Lithia Springs, Jim Pirkle had repeatedly spotted a black panther in a swamp not far from his house. "He comes through this way at spring and fall. It's like clockwork."

Official state and federal biologists hate hearing black panther reports. After an extensive study, they "never did come up with any evidence that we could attribute to a large cat," said Steve Johnson, a wildlife biologist with the Department of Natural Resources.

"People see something at night and it gets three times bigger," he continued, and attributed the recent attacks to bears, bobcats, or wild dogs. No documented report of a cougar/mountain lion had been recorded in decades, he claimed. There are naturalists who fight the legend of black panthers as hard as they fight reports of bigfoot. However, bigfoot and phantom panthers often share the same elusive realm.

Bigfoot Syndrome

"People want something to be out there," stated anthropologist Grey Keyes of the University of Georgia. "The real beasts, the wolves and panthers, are gone; we've killed them. People miss that element of danger in the environment—something that isn't human." So we apparently invent bigfoot, phantom panthers, and other elusive creatures.

Maybe it was the television crews, print correspondents, Bigfoot Research and Investigation Team, or "nut cases with guns," as one local put it, but the elusive creature soon departed.

Poe said the act that sparked the entire controversy, the killing and eating of the beagle, was a hoax, although he offered no evidence. He concluded that a homeowner killed two dogs, a car hit one, and the other dogs cannibalized the beagle.

The man who filed the original report, Jason Mauldin, said Poe did not know what had happened. "He just didn't want all this happening around here," he stated.

SLEWFOOT

David Brown, forty-four, had been hunting ginseng, a medicinal herb that grows wild in the north Georgia mountains, for years without incident. But at 9:30 A.M. on August 24, 1986, he was in a hollow at Jenkins Gap, just below the crest of Taylor's Ridge in Chattooga County, when he saw someone walking toward him from the far side of the hollow. He thought a friend had spotted his parked pickup truck and was coming in search of him. He shouted for the man to join him, but then "it got deathly quiet."

Brown continued his search. He had entered a second hollow when he sensed movement behind him.

"It came up behind me some sixty or seventy feet without me ever hearing it," Brown reported. When he turned, he saw a strange creature only twenty feet away. Brown described it as seven and a half feet tall and weighing 350 to 400 pounds, with large eyes, a pointed head, flat nose, and arms which hung down to its knees. It stood upright, but was definitely not a bear.

A sketch of the bigfoot creature seen harvesting honey from a tree along the Flint River near Butler. (Courtesy of James P. Akin)

"I stood and stared at him three or four or five minutes, and it was nothing like any bear I've ever seen," Brown swore. The creature was content to stare back, panting heavily as if winded.

"I was frozen to the ground," Brown continued. "I couldn't move. I was afraid it would attack me." He thought remaining motionless might prevent aggression from the bigfoot, but he was ready to "go up that mountain like a rocket" if it moved closer to him.

SENIORS DAY AT THE BERRY PATCH

Brown took this singular opportunity to study his newfound companion. The face was "monkey-like," he thought, with a flat mouth and thick lips but no teeth. That convinced him that it was old, but "I think it could still eat me," he added. Its left arm, which ended at a paw containing long fingernails which curved "like corkscrews in a knot," appeared useless, and "something seemed wrong" with its left leg. This bigfoot had seen better days. The right paw had short nails and appeared functional. The animal was covered with locks of thick, long black hair, and Brown was unable to determine its sex.

Apparently finished with its own scrutiny of Brown, the bigfoot grunted, turned, and started down the ridge. Brown likewise turned, but he sprinted uphill.

"I've got bruises as big as half-dollars all over my legs where I slid on the rocks," Brown admitted. "I went up that mountain in three or four minutes, and when the deputy and I went back down there it took us fifteen minutes. I guess I did go back up the mountain 'like a rocket.' I thought I was going to have a heart attack. When I got to the truck, I'll bet I tried every key I had before I got it cranked."

Brown said that he vomited after the ordeal, not from the creature's smell, which was revolting, but "because that's how scared I was."

He immediately reported the incident to the Chattooga County Sheriff's Office, but there was no evidence of the creature.

"I'd give anything if there'd been somebody with me or if there'd be any way to get a picture of it," Brown lamented. He acknowledged that his account was "unbelievable. If somebody had come up to me and said they'd seen that, I'd have said, 'You're crazy!' but I know what I saw!"

BIGFOOT CAM

An amusing incident occurred after an Atlanta television station sent a crew to interview Brown at the site of his encounter. When the clip started on the evening news, Brown was seen walking with reporter Neal Craig, but the clip blacked out abruptly. "I don't believe it," Chuck Moore said on camera to his coanchor John Pruitt. "I don't believe it." The two then lightly bantered that perhaps the bigfoot had taken control of the station's equipment, because an attempt to air the story the previous night had also failed.

The official explanation from station management was that the crew had edited the story on unfamiliar equipment at the station's Rome Bureau when its manager was absent. What viewers saw broadcast was a "false start," which was on the same tape as the finished take. Deciding the story was "jinxed," it was dropped.

A report that the Chattooga County Sheriff's Office had arrested a man for impersonating a bigfoot turned out to be false.

A Clothed Bigfoot

Around the same time Walker County residents Robin Avans, Kevin Petti-grew, Todd Rope, and Tommy Brooks were coon hunting near Centre, in northeastern Alabama. There they spotted a huge creature in the middle of an extensive soybean field.

"He was real tall," Avans said, describing it as about ten feet in height, slender, and wearing what appeared to be yellow-brown "overalls." This animal was only covered with fur from its feet to its knees. It was upright and walking in long, stiff-legged strides. "It could walk in fifteen minutes what it would take a man to walk in an hour." When it entered the woods, the four hunters declined to pursue it.

Avans reported that earlier in the summer a friend of his had "got a real good look" at a similar creature, clad in what he described as a "kind of monkey suit," near Pigeon Mountain, west of Lafayette in Walker County.

Homeless Bigfoot

"It looked like something you'd see in a horror movie," stated Selma Lamb of the being she encountered at 10:15 P.M. on GA 100 between Kincaid and Simms Mountain, near the Floyd-Chattooga county line at the south-ern end of Taylor's Ridge. It was September 18, 1986, less than a month after David Brown's sighting. She initially thought her thing was a large dog, because it was on all fours. When Lamb hit her brakes to avoid hitting it, the "dog" stood up on two legs and "snarled" as she passed within four feet at ten miles per hour. She accelerated to her home twelve hundred feet away and immediately returned with her mother and brother, but the crea-ture had disappeared.

Her up-close-and-personal sighting revealed a being with long hair and an apparent injury. The right side of the face was swollen "like it had a knot on it" which extended down the back. It wore no shoes, but it seemed to be clad in "ripped-up and nasty" clothing, a green shirt and brown pants cut off at the knee, although the latter could merely have been dirty rather than brown.

In recent years at least one bigfoot creature has been prowling the bottomlands of the Flint River in Taylor County.

Lamb described the creature as "just real ugly, scary looking," and thought it might have been a deformed human, although it was described as being over six feet in height. Lamb's mother thought it might be an afflicted man who lived in the mountains on scraps of food. These north Georgia bigfeet seem to be a motley bunch.

The Chattooga County Sheriff's Office again investigated, but found no prints or other evidence to support the incident.

WHO LOOKS FOR DEER AT NIGHT IN A CAR?

About two o'clock one morning in November 1993, Delton Lord, suffering insomnia, was driving around looking for deer when he observed a dark gray figure cross the road in front of him. "It's stride was long," he related, quickly crossing an eighteen-foot-wide road in three steps. It disappeared in the rolling hills west of Waleska in Cherokee County.

BIGFOOT BAMBI HUNTER

On July 3, 1998, two boys were fishing from a boat on the Flint River near Manchester, just below Red Oak Creek. During a lunch break they heard a

59

creature crashing through the forest. "We were startled to see a small doe burst from the woods and jump into the river," one related. The thrashing sound from the woods continued and the fishermen watched intently, expecting to see another deer. They "were shocked when a black hairy creature on two legs emerged from the trees." It stood still until the other boy shouted, *"What the hell is that?"* At that point "the thing slowly turned and walked back into the woods."

TRAPPED IN THE MIDDLE OF A BIGFOOT MATING RITUAL
Late on the evening of August 4, 1998, a man and his girlfriend climbed in his pickup to seek solitude in the densely wooded ridge and valley country of Pigeon Mountain, near Lafayette in Walker County. They drove eight miles down an isolated rocky lane and stopped at a clearing to build a fire. At 1:00 A.M. on August 5 "we heard a loud, high-pitched scream that reverberated through the dense forest," the man reported

The frightened woman asked her boyfriend, a self-professed "outdoorsman my whole life, hunting, fishing, camping, and studying animals like a religion," what it could be. Despite his extensive experience, he admitted he had "never heard anything like that scream." The macho guy looked up and down the trail, lit by a bright moon, and in "the middle of the trail a large, bulky figure stood" only thirty yards away and facing him. The man quietly glanced away to collect the woman and when he looked back the creature was gone, but not very far. It screamed again, behind them, but worse was "a similar, more distant call . . . from the forest in front of us." They jumped into the car and lit out "a lot faster than we drove in."

THE BIGFOOT BUREAU OF INVESTIGATION
"Somewhere in the dense forests and swamps of the United States, an enigma is alive and well." So began the Web site of the Georgia Swamp Ape Research Center, one of a number of organizations that have sprung up in recent years to investigate the existence of big, hairy hominids, a semi-recognized science called *cryptozoology*. The GSARC was established specifically to concentrate study on Georgia's bigfoot creatures.

One of the first cases the GSARC investigated occurred on September 14, 1998, involving a woman walking near her home in Butler. She entered a swampy area of hardwoods and underbrush near the Flint River and "heard this noise like a big buzzing and a loud cracking noise," she said, and then "smelled something like a cross between a dead animal and a muskrat. I began to feel really nervous—then I saw it." It was a creature over eight feet in height, covered with light brown fur and "looking into a hollow tree. It turned to look at me, grunted, and began slowly walking into the woods" in a casual fashion.

The woman "ran away and screamed. It scared me to death. I just couldn't believe that something like that was around." Asked if it could have been a bear, the woman was adamant. "No way. What I saw walked away on two legs. It had a face like a cross between a human and an ape. It couldn't have been a bear—I've been to a zoo—it wasn't a bear."

Swamp Ape agents found a colony of bees inside the tree and decided that the bigfoot was attempting to satisfy its sweet fang. Chewed honeycomb was found, and the outside of the tree bore deep scratch marks.

Similar creatures had recently been seen in the area. A large bigfoot was spotted harvesting garbage and eating cow feed stored on a farm near the river.

THE MEN FROM GSARC

On May 15, 1999, a "Pursuit Team" from the GSARC entered the bottomlands of the river and stopped atop a hill surrounded on three sides by impenetrable swamp. Most of the team set up camp and went about normal activities, while one member sat in a blind away from the camp with night-vision equipment.

First a bobcat alarmed the camp before fleeing. At 12:30 A.M. a large creature was detected by sound. The "noise was intense" and enabled the team to track it as the animal scouted the camp, "always staying just out of the range of firelight." It circled north to south, making no attempt at stealth. The team "heard large limbs and sticks break under the weight of the animal," which then began vocalizing a "hootlike sound." Every few minutes the team sounded a commercial turkey call, which drew a response from the creature, sometimes sounding near the camp, sometimes far away.

"The big surprise came as we were startled by the deepest growl I've ever heard," one team member wrote. Although it sounded only 150 feet away, nothing could be seen through the night-vision gear. A "long lonely howl" just before sunrise concluded "a thrilling, satisfying night." Before leaving the area, the task force also located prints that measured sixteen inches in length, nine inches in width, and had a stride of seventy-two inches. The tracks disappeared into the swamp.

The GSARC believed the scream they heard was aggressive. Analysis of the footprint showed dermal ridges and other physiological structures proving the foot could support a massive creature and was not a fake.

Researchers in the area have found trees stripped of bark to a height of twelve feet and pine trees broken and twisted by a creature obviously much stronger than any human. Cattle and deer are occasionally killed by the brute force of some animal, which has an appetite for certain internal organs.

The GSARC thought the Flint River bottomlands definitely support a bigfoot. Sightings of it have occurred regularly for several years. Investigators

A GSARC research team believed a large, unidentified creature was shadowing it in the woods. Computer enhancement indicates something was here, centered in the hand-drawn circle seen here, but it can't be positively identified. (Courtesy of James P. Akin)

propose that it migrated into the area because "the creature used a local food supply until exhausted, and then moved on." It would travel along rivers and creeks because of their isolation and abundant food supply. The streams also tend to run north and south, a primary migratory pattern. Bigfoot hunters warn that bigfoot is "aggressive and territorial," because it is "often reported as menacing and belligerent." It is also willing to eat whatever comes its way. Although the big hairy primate exploits the overpopulation of white tail deer, "aggression toward children and canines" is not out of the question. Bigfoot is a "caloric opportunist" that eats "what it can get." Dogs often disappear in areas that report hominid activity.

Researchers in the southeast have located three-, four-, and five-toed tracks, a puzzling characteristic. Despite fairly large differences among humans, a set number of toes are the standard. How did bigfoot's diversity originate? Another divergent feature is hair color, which varies between our bigfoot and those found further north. Those in Georgia tend to darker hair.

Bigfoot is generally considered to be a resident of the rugged, deep woods of the American Northwest, so why would it exist in the Southeast? The Appalachian Mountains that extend through the region are still largely wilderness, and the area also sports large tracts of woods, extensive systems of rivers and creeks generally inaccessible to humans, and vast swamps.

The GSARC believed that Southern bigfoots are seven to nine feet in height, with attendant long strides. They average eight hundred pounds, are covered in hair, and give off horrid odors. The organization proposes that the creatures have always lived in the region and point to Indian legends of spirits who abducted children and the monster stories told by early settlers.

Another incident investigated by the GSARC occurred at 11:30 P.M. on January 12, 1999, in south Georgia, when a man was frightened by a gorilla-like figure outside his home. The hairy creature fled at great speed, leaped fences, and ran into the woods while the man's pit bulls cowered in fear. He believed it might have been after the dogs. When investigators arrived they found the area "strangely quiet" and a "strong 'sour' odor" hung in the air.

The GSARC had an outstanding Web site, which offered a number of interesting features. Included was a reproducible Sighting Report, which asked for the where and when of your encounter and the creature's estimated height, weight, color, fur coverage, eye color, sound, and smell. It also requested physical evidence such as footprints, and personal information (yours, not the bigfoot's; they wanted to make sure you're not a flake—well, not too much of a flake).

An Evidence Submission Form would accompany your physical evidence, forwarded to several institutions with which the GSARC had made arrangements. One was Idaho State University. Blood samples had to be packed in a paper bag, because plastic ruins it. Hair, for DNA testing, had to include at least one follicle. Original videotapes and audiotapes had to be submitted; copies are only suitable for voice stress and/or deception analysis, and plaster casts of tracks had to be the original. You were required to notarize the forms.

IF YOU GO INTO THE WOODS TODAY

The Web site included fascinating articles and essays. Advice was given for establishing your own Pursuit Team, which should be small and mobile. Certain equipment was recommended, including cameras, films, audio and video recorders, and guns (*big mothers*). Tips on collecting and photographing evidence was offered. A recommended tactic involves sending a noisy

Sightings of bigfoot in Georgia are often associated with arrangements of trees and limbs into territorial markers. (Courtesy of Jon Butler III and the Gulf Coast Bigfoot Research Center)

lead expedition into the target area, which would be shadowed by any local bigfoot. A second, stealthy team follows to shadow the bigfoot. The GSARC explained that we must use our hopefully superior intelligence because bigfoot is adapted for an elusive life in the wilds, has superior senses, and may even see in the infrared and ultraviolet ranges. Camouflage is advised, including chlorophyll tablets that (honest) make you smell like a tree.

Bigfoot hunters were warned that bigfoot might be hunting them. The "creature is more than capable of out-running, out-stalking, and possibly out-thinking you in the woods." Casual hunters "run the risk of being literally 'torn to pieces'" and devoured. "We do not endorse hunting the animal," the GSARC emphasized. The debate over whether bigfoot should be studied from afar or bagged, autopsied, and stuffed still rages.

The GSARC had an irregular on-line newsletter called the *Swamp Times*, plus a chat room, sighting reports, research articles, and links to other creature features.

UPDATE ON THE GEORGIA SWAMP APE RESEARCH CENTER
Shortly after posting a $250,000 reward for "the capture and/or collection of a specimen and/or body part of the creature commonly known as 'Sasquatch,' 'Bigfoot,' 'Skunk Ape,' etc.," their Internet operations succumbed to cyberterrorism. The site had been "hacked, cracked, and attacked," they stated, but they hoped to return in the future with better security.

THE LATEST FROM THE BIGFOOT FRONT
Late on the evening of May 8, 1999, a married couple was leaving the husband's parents' house after dinner. The four were saying good-bye in the yard, located on the edge of Lake Allatoona near Acworth, when they "heard an extremely long and loud howl," the husband reported. It lasted five minutes and set "dogs in the area to barking and howling in response to the strange howl." They knew it wasn't a dog "due to the length of the howl and tone." They listened to bigfoot recordings on the Bigfoot Field Researchers' home page and found it "almost a perfect match" with what they had heard.

The man's father was working on his back deck on May 19 when he heard a "squall" from the direction of the earlier howl, which also set off the canines. A third incident occurred at 2:00 P.M. on June 16 during a heavy rainstorm. It came from the same area and again alarmed dogs, but was only half as long as the earlier vocalizations.

At 6:30 P.M. on August 1, 1999, two boys were riding four-wheelers near Buckhead, in rural Morgan County, when they "heard growling and looked and saw a big black figure running" toward them. They said the creature, which had intelligent-looking eyes, was seven feet tall, ran hunched over like a chimpanzee, and smelled like a wet dog. Area residents had also noted cracked trees, unusual footprints, and strange sounds.

ANIMAL FARM

BIG BIRD—THIS AIN'T SESAME STREET, KID

At 6:45 P.M. on June 10, 1994, a married couple driving along Mountville Road, between Mountville and LaGrange, noticed a great bird, standing three and a half feet tall, beside the road. At their intrusion the big avian jumped into the air and started flapping great, wide, but slender wings and flew low across the pavement in front of the car at an altitude so low that the wife screamed, fearing they would hit the winged monstrosity. The big black bird continued flying low and disappeared into thick woods. The wife thought it "flew like an airplane would fly over you."

After reflecting on the apparition, they decided this caped avenger had a ten- to sixteen-foot wingspan. At closest approach it was one hundred feet distant, and in sight for several seconds.

The husband, while trapping as a boy, inadvertently caught several buzzards and was consequently familiar with the creature. Both agreed it was not an eagle or turkey.

The local and long-serving game warden denied knowledge of such a creature and classed it with the "black panthers" reported so frequently to him—there was no proof that they existed. Local UFO researcher John Thompson reported that he believed the story about black panthers because he had received "more reports than I can count."

FREE BIRD, ALBUM VERSION

A second close encounter with "Big Bird" involved a hunter sitting in his tree-mounted deer stand at 5:30 P.M. on November 18, 1995, near New River, west of Corinth in Heard County. Seeing a large object with straight wings overhead, he assumed it was a glider or silent airplane. Raising his binoculars, he was startled to see a giant black-brown bird with odd feathers—curly rather than straight. He estimated its size as at least "twice the size of a buzzard," the wingspan twelve feet or wider. The bird glided directly overhead, a hundred feet away, then started flapping its great wings. After being observed for two minutes, it disappeared. The hunter could not see the head or estimate the size of the body, but he glimpsed two feet, colored like the wings. He was certain it was not a buzzard.

John Thompson has received reports of other "Big Birds" in southern Heard and northern Troup Counties. One occurred a mile away from the first hunter on Charles B. Johnston Road in February 1996. Although the bird was nearby, he could not hear any sound when the massive wings were flapping. UFOs have often been seen nearby.

HERE BE MONSTERS

"Quagmire" is one of my favorite X-Files episodes. Scully's dog Quee-queg gets eaten, a freaked-out kid kisses a toad seeking enlightenment, and Mulder and Scully wax philosophic after the guest monster sinks their cabin cruiser and strands them on a rock. The writer chose to locate this great aquatic creature in a huge natural lake in Georgia, presumably extremely north Georgia, because the mountains of British Columbia are prominent in the background. Unfortunately, there are no sizable natural lakes in Georgia, although I suppose the creatures could spontaneously generate in the wake of the Corps of Engineers, and precious few water monsters have been reported from our region. Anyway, our aquatic creatures are far more elusive than the land monsters with one exception: Altamaha-ha.

THE LOCH NESS MONSTER OF GEORGIA

What's dark, twenty to thirty feet in length, thick as a man's body, has two or more humps, and inhabits an eastern Georgia river? It's Altamaha-ha (note: I am not responsible for the name), Georgia's water monster, seen on at least 350 different occasions.

The Altamaha River ends in a tidal estuary. This vast network of meandering rivers and creeks, interspersed with extensive tracts of marsh and old rice fields and drainage systems from the plantation era, ebbs and flows with the tide from the Atlantic Ocean. The last town along its route is Darien, a historic community dating back to the days of Oglethorpe.

The first reports originated far upstream, where the sightings date to prehistoric times. The Tama Indians had a legend about an enormous water creature seen frequently in the Altamaha. They described a giant snake that bellowed and hissed when frightened.

The first historic sightings were made in the 1920s when a major industry in the region was logging. Trees were felled and trimmed, then formed into giant rafts that were maneuvered downstream to sawmills in Darien. Timbermen reported a "snake monster" sighted in Wayne County near Doctortown. In 1935 three hunters in Appling County, near Carter's Bite, spotted a "big snake." In the late 1940s a troop of Boy Scouts sighted a "long, snakelike thing" swimming across the river.

Roger Carter and a friend, both officials at Reidsville State Prison, were crossing Mills B. Lane Bridge near Glennville in Tattnall County during the summer of 1959 when they spied something in the river. "At first we

Witness Kathy Howard Strickland made this painting of Altamaha-ha. (Courtesy of Kathy Howard Strickland)

thought it was a big old gator," Carter said. "But it looked too much like a snake. It was long and dark-colored and stretched maybe more than thirty feet from what we could see." It was in sight for several seconds and may have broken the surface a little bit later. It was suggested to them that they had seen driftwood or a diamondback rattlesnake, but Carter responded, "What we saw wasn't no log. And it sure wasn't no rattlesnake."

Sightings were sparse until about 1970, but consistent reports have continued until the present.

It was high tide during the summer of either 1969 or 1970—Donny Manning is not certain of the year—and he and his brother were on their father's houseboat in the Altamaha River at Clark's Bluff. They were cat-fishing when something grabbed a hook and ran. When the creature broke the surface the boys could see that it was ten to twelve feet long, had a snout like an alligator or duck-billed platypus, a horizontal tail, a spiny, bony, triangular ridge running along the top of the body, and a dorsal fin on the back. It was the color of gray gunmetal on top and oyster white or yellow at the bottom. Sharp, pointed teeth gleamed in the sunlight. As it left the area, the animal moved up and down vertically like a porpoise, not a fish, and snapped a forty-pound test line as easily as if it were kite string. Manning believed it weighed seventy-five pounds or more.

In the early 1970s Benny Coursey and a friend ditched church one Sunday to spend the day fishing on the Altamaha near Baxley. They were making their way back to shore when "All of a sudden," Coursey told writer Randall Floyd, "we saw this thing heading straight for our boat. It looked like a big snake, a real whopper, with its head reared out of the water and looking straight at us like it meant business."

Just before contact, the serpent submerged, surfacing again twenty yards on the other side of the boat, and disappeared around a bend. "The good

Lord was with us, I reckon," Coursey concluded. "That was the last time we went fishing on Sunday."

HA-HA IN THE EIGHTIES

Fast-forward to the summer of 1980, when Barry Prescott and Andy Greene were driving north on U.S. 95 between 3:00 and 4:00 P.M. Glancing toward the river, which was at half tide, they saw a creature stranded

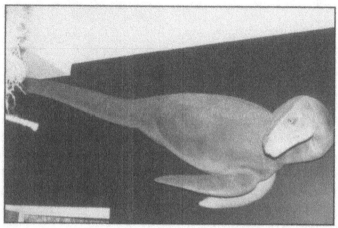

This model of a ten-foot-long adolescent Altamaha-ha is displayed in a natural history museum at the Rock Eagle 4-H Center near Eatonton, where the prehistoric effigy is preserved. It was crafted by Rick Spears.

on a mud bank a hundred yards from them. The monster, estimated to be thirty to forty feet in length and three to four feet thick, was thrashing violently in its efforts to get free. Much of the body was out of the water, and the men could clearly see about twenty feet of it. The object was brown or black, the skin pebbled in texture, although perhaps from mud splashes, and gills or some appendages could be glimpsed beneath the surface. Its back looked triangular, and its powerful movements were again undulating, unlike the movement of fish. After ten minutes the creature freed itself and sank quietly into the water.

Ha-Ha has often been seen in tributaries of the Altamaha. Six months later, in December, Larry Gwin and Steve Wilson were fishing for eel at Smith Lake, farther up the Altamaha, when they spotted a huge creature. It was fifteen to twenty feet in length and "as big around as a man's body with two brownish humps about five feet apart," one stated. "It dove in a big swirl of water" and disappeared, but a swell "like a wake of a racing boat" boiled up above its route.

Next came the account of two anonymous men hunting wild hogs, common game in this area, from a boat in Minnow or Hammersmith Creek, three miles from Two-Way Fish Camp, a noted local institution on the Altamaha. They were quietly waiting for their hunting dogs to return when two hundred yards away a creature they described as being twenty feet long and as thick as a man's body surfaced two or three times as it crossed submerged logs. The head resembled a snake, but the body was described as a helicopter without wings, a smooth, tapered shape without gills, fins, or any other appendages. It looked greenish-brown to them. At a later date the two men again saw the creature near the same place.

Harvey Blackman described an encounter with the monster at Two-Way Fish Camp to Hugh Mulligan, a local newspaper columnist. Blackman was standing on a floating fish dock when a large wave rocked the platform. Swimming by in the river was a grayish brown aquatic animal, fifteen to twenty feet in length and thick as a human body. When it raised up out of the water, Blackman saw a snakelike head.

On a cold, windy day in 1981, two men entered a creek from the Altamaha near Two-Way and spotted "that thing" which had been reported in the newspaper. Lying on a mud bank, it was gray-brown, ten to thirty feet long (hard to judge), and twenty inches in diameter. Apparently sensing the boat, Ha-Ha slid into the water and swam toward them, looking them over as it passed. The men feared for a moment that it would attack them. The great serpent had two to three humps and undulated as it swam. It had no projections or fins and did not lift its head out of the water.

BABY HA-HA

Several years later one of the men and his wife were fishing in the rice field dikes at Champney River when they spotted a "baby" monster beside the bank. It was twenty-six inches long and had two humps on its back. The infant had a flat, nonfish-like tail that was vertical instead of horizontal, reddish fins behind the head, and undulated through the water. The couple spent ten minutes attempting unsuccessfully to get the creature to take hooks baited with shrimp and worms.

Numeorus other Ha-Ha sightings have been made and reported over the years. Each provides details different from the others, but descriptions commonly make mention of the creature's excessive length and thickness, as well as its unique coloring, head shape, and the presence of two humps on its back. One such observor, crab fisherman Ralph DeWitt, described the creature as "the largest eel known to mankind."

THIS ONE TOPS JIMMY CARTER AND THE KILLER RABBIT

In May 1988 Frank Culpepper, owner of Two-Way Fish Camp, related a story told to him years earlier. When three men saw the creature in the Altamaha, one ran inside and asked Culpepper for a rifle. The owner complied, but all he saw was the wake. On another occasion he was fishing on the river when a long, brownish serpent, so large he could not have reached around it, attempted to climb into his boat. Admitting the encounter frightened him, he immediately returned to the camp. "It looked like a big snake," he said.

In 1989 an L. Lowe entered the Altamaha from the Intercoastal Waterway when he "saw an odd sight that caught my full attention" about one hundred yards away. He shifted the boat into neutral to give it his full attention. According to Lowe, "a hump had risen out of the water and slowly went back down. In a few seconds, it rose again at the same spot about one-half the height . . . The hump was about two feet above the water line and maybe the same across. It came slowly straight up with no forward motion. The rise up was slow and then slow back down. It was a near-perfect one-half circle. The hump was solid and not the donut look. The color was a dark shade, maybe dark green or dark brown." It remained in view for about ten minutes.

LANDSHARK

Chip Croft, then owner of Two-Way with his brother Bill, related another story from the Champney. Two fishermen, one a minister, had tied their boat to an old power pole when they spotted a large, snakelike apparition approaching them. The frightened men watched it swim past close to the boat. They described the usual shape, but this one did something different—it crawled up the riverbank and disappeared into the undergrowth.

In August 1995, Barry Prescott was transporting a man from Hird Island in the Carneghan River when he saw three humps undulating through the water. He observed about one and a half humps at any one time, and they were two to four feet above the surface of the river. This creature looked black or brown and was about thirty feet long and thicker than a snake. It apparently ran aground—its first movements were gentle, then grew violent—which produced a boil of water and mud from beneath the body.

A local fisherman identified as T. O. has spotted four different-sized creatures in his four sightings. He believes they were the same species, just different members of it. Two were seen in the Altamaha at Broughton Island, one at the mouth of South River, and the last near Hird's Island. During the first encounter, his father grabbed his rifle to shoot, but T. O. stopped him. On one occasion, the animal looked directly at the man, then smoothly submerged without a ripple, resurfaced, and fixed its gaze on him again. On each occasion, the monster submerged and reemerged or undulated through the water. The mouth was always closed, and the eyes were noticeable.

Former Wayne County sheriff Red Carter investigated a number of sightings. He said some residents believe an unidentified creature, perhaps a survivor of earth's ancient past, lives in the Altamaha. "Since the river runs into the Atlantic Ocean, God knows where its home is. It can swim in and out of here at will, whenever it wants to."

That might be the case, for the monster has been seen near the ocean and far upriver. One Wayne County resident, Buster Hagen, of Madray Springs, believes it travels upstream to spawn, like an eel. He has witnessed the creature several times, calling it a "prehistoric monster, just like one of those things you see in the movies—long and snakelike, with a long neck and a long tail and flippers."

Darien resident Ann R. Davis is Altamaha-ha's chronicler. She also runs a gallery and bookstore in Darien and has crafted miniatures of the creature. Check out Ms. Davis on the Altamaha-ha page on the Internet.

OTHER SNEAKY SNAKES
Fortean journals provide a short list of other water monsters in Georgia. A lake monster occupies No Man's Friend Pond, which that invaluable reference book Georgia Place Names locates southwest of Adel in Cook County, but it is "actually a dense woody swamp or (Carolina) bay, which is so thick that a person can easily get lost in it." Something has been seen in the Chattahoochee River at Roswell. A ship's captain reported a sea monster in the Atlantic Ocean off Cumberland Island. Please send me any details you may have about these or other bizarre aquatic creatures.

Douglas County had a big snake problem back in 1915, according to the annals of the Douglas County Sentinel. Early in May it reported that Mr. and Mrs. H. G. Lowe were planting a field when they heard an eight-year-old girl struggling with a six-foot-long "coachwhip" that had knocked her down. The child was rescued. Later a snake, "sixteen or eighteen feet long, and as big around as a stovepipe," was seen around McWhorter. Many hunters tracked the massive reptile, and one, T. W. Friddell, "said he found a snake track six or seven inches wide." Another man, a carpenter named J. G. Chapman, reported seeing the serpent in his pasture.

AFTER THE CAT! PHANTOM PANTHERS AND OTHER CURIOUS PUSSIES
A prime Georgia mystery cat was spotted by farmer J. H. Holyoak down south in Berrien County between Enigma (!) and Alapaha. Holyoak was driving his pickup to check on his cattle when he spotted what he thought

at first to be a big dog chasing a calf. When the creature was one hundred feet away, the farmer realized that he was seeing what he described as a combination panther and lion. It was basically a panther model but sported a long-flowing mane like an African lion.

Holyoak snatched up his shotgun and fired a round of birdshot at the animal. According to his son Ken, Holyoak "saw blood running out of it, but it didn't do much damage." The hybrid fauna leaped the fence and disappeared into a wooded swamp that bordered the pasture.

Ken stated that the incident had occurred in broad daylight and "there was no mistake about it." The elder Holyoak had killed mountain lions in his native Arizona, and could distinguish between them and a lion.

In late April and early May 1972, Cobb County was in an uproar over the appearance of an apparent "mountain lion," although one man insisted he saw two large cats together. The cougar had reportedly attacked cattle, killing a calf, and killed several hunting dogs and ate several ducks. A sighting of the cat by Ray Rozelle, who worked in the stables at the North Georgia fairgrounds, brought out hordes of hunters—official and otherwise. Attacked while tracking the big cat, Rozelle suffered scratches on his arm. "I was tracking it and suddenly it was jumping through the air on me," Rozelle told reporters.

Police officers and self-proclaimed big-game hunters were soon in the wooded area around the fairgrounds with hunting dogs and high-powered rifles and shotguns. Several days later workers from the state Game and Fish Commission and the Atlanta Humane Society, armed with tranquilizer darts and lures of fresh horse meat, took over responsibility for the search.

A spokesman for the Atlanta Humane Society believed the lion might be dangerous. "We're shutting this place down and not allowing anyone in. (The lion) has been shot a couple of times, I think. If these people had called us first time they saw it, we would probably have caught it with a piece of meat in our hands." Game and Fish workers also believed their chances of seizing the elusive cat had been spoiled by the yahoos. If they captured it, they planned to tend any wounds and release it in the Okefenokee Swamp because the Humane Society's "main concern is that this is an endangered species."

Game and Fish employee Hubert Handy never publicly ridiculed reports of the cat, but he found it highly unlikely that a cougar would remain in an area where people and dogs were stomping through the woods. Handy said a real mountain lion, which he called a very shy creature, would be "forty miles away" at the first sign of trouble. He did allow that a tame animal turned loose might remain in the area where it was released.

After a week's fruitless effort, Handy noted that no searchers had spotted the cat and said, "We haven't found him and we don't believe there's one there." When the search was terminated, Handy stated, "If he were here, he's sure gone now. He snuck out on us." Col. R. K. Fansler of the Commission noted, "We've had no evidence of the animal, other than the word of the people involved." However, one Humane Society worker stated that tracks had been seen, which proves something had been present, however elusive.

A perfect example of a phantom panther occurred three years later near Stockbridge, in Henry County. In the spring of 1975 James Rutledge spotted one while plowing his garden. He picked up his rifle and killed the animal, then quietly buried it in the woods and kept the encounter to himself because he feared upsetting his neighbors. By September other residents had spotted a second panther in the same area, apparently the mate of the first one, and Game and Fish officials set out humane traps baited with fresh meat. Unfortunately, no one could locate the second animal or the grave of the first one.

Five witnesses to the second cat described it as having a long black tail, a black coat, and eyes "as big as a silver dollar." The coat was described as "jet" or "soot" black. The observers were certain that it was a black panther, a mystery the experts were unwilling to accept.

Dr. Ernest Provost of the University of Georgia's Forest Resources Department said that Georgia's native panthers had been brown. "There may be panthers here, but they are not black," he said. "This black business has never been proven. No one has ever gotten a black panther." Furthermore, he stated, "No one has positively gotten (a brown panther) for many, many years." There may be brown panthers in isolated parts of south Georgia, other experts said, but they would be Florida panthers, also brown, with black fur being found only on the muzzle, tip of the tail, sides of the nose, and back of the ears. Atlanta Zoo curator of mammals Ron Jackson said, "I don't know of any (black panther) in any zoo in the country." Jackson continued to say that people confuse terms. What people think are black panthers are actually black leopards, which are found in Asia and Africa.

"As far as I know there would be nothing like that unless someone released it," Jackson allowed. "It's possible that some circus had it and it escaped," although no black leopards had been reported missing in Georgia.

Confusion arose after Mrs. Gloria Seymour found a gray hair in the wire that surrounded a pen where a goat had been mauled one night. Jackson determined that the hair did not match a big cat, but looked "awful similar to a German shepherd's hair," he stated. However, Mrs. Seymour had later seen the black animal.

"It was gray hair and the animal we saw was black," she stated. "I gave them that hair even before I heard about the black animal." Local residents never believed the hair belonged to the mysterious creature they had spotted.

A mystery creature, which was probably more a mystery cat than a bigfoot, prowled DeKalb County and attacked and killed sixteen dogs and cats during the summer of 1983. It returned the week after Christmas and killed two hogs penned along Whites Mill Road. The hogs, weighing 250 and 150 pounds, were so badly mutilated that owner Alvin Bowman was forced to destroy them. Bowman thought the attacker was a bear or bobcats, not dogs. Whatever was responsible, he said, local residents "are a little afraid to get out of their houses at night."

KILLER PEACOCKS

In early July 1985, residents in western Hahira, a town of two thousand located fifteen miles north of Valdosta, began reporting bloodcurdling screams between 10:00 and 11:00 P.M., as well as early in the morning. The mysterious, frightening cries were attributed to a panther prowling the woods, but game warden L. C. Taylor believed they were fugitive peacocks: "I can't even halfway believe it's a black cat," he said.

Penny West disagreed, stating, "One of our neighbors saw a black panther the other morning. It is scaring my children to death." Another described the cry as "like a blend of a goat and a cat."

BLACK PANTHERS (ANIMAL DIVISION)

In the early 1990s a number of western cougars, genetic relatives of the endangered Florida panther, were released in northern Florida to see if they could survive. They failed the test, particularly the six known to have wandered into southern Georgia. Three joined the NRA Club (one survivor, but when guns are outlawed, only panthers will . . . live?), one joined the Possum Club (bump, bump), and two survivors were trapped and repatriated at the end of the study.

The "experts" are grimly determined not to acknowledge the presence of black panthers in Georgia. Since 1978, state and federal wildlife experts have undertaken a massive study of the possibility. The state effort, "Cougar Investigation Project," has scrutinized more than three hundred panther sightings. Bob Downing, a biologist retired from the U.S. Fish and Wildlife Service, tracked the phantom beasts for five years and examined more than five hundred sightings in the southern Appalachians. His finding was "that people are going to keep seeing cougars whether they are really there or not." Such cynicism from a scientist. He concluded that none of the studies have produced any physical trace of the animals—no

74

tracks, feces, hair, photographs, or bodies. Chris Belden, the Florida Game and Fresh Water Fish Commission specialist, claimed, "Where we know we have panthers, we have no trouble locating them. They get hit by cars or we see tracks, and they are easily treed by the dogs. They aren't ghosts." But they could very well be phantoms.

Panthers, often called cougars or pumas, can be found from Canada to Argentina. A solitary species, their home territory can consist of three hundred square miles. The eastern panther suffered when the forests were destroyed in the eighteenth and nineteenth centuries. Fearful settlers and later farmers hunted them to extinction. The last Georgia panthers were killed in the Okefenokee Swamp during the 1920s.

The panther was thought to be extinct in Florida until 1978, when forty were located in wilderness swamps. Texas is the nearest documented habitat for modern panthers.

Georgia does have bobcats, a cousin to the panther that has been misidentified. These cougars average twenty pounds in weight; panthers 120 to 130 pounds.

Bob Downing finds that 5 percent of the panther reports are difficult to reject, especially those made by "experienced wildlife biologists, naturalists or hunters—people who should know."

In late December 1905, a "lion" measuring seven feet in length and weighing 132 pounds was killed by D. T. Beasley in Bulloch County. Another report claims that a black panther leapt against a car in Rome in 1958, leaving muddy paw prints on the vehicle. In February 1987, a policeman in Valdosta shot a Bengal tiger, its origin unknown.

In 1932 the *Statesboro News* printed a story about seventy-seven-year-old Henry Dugger of Briar Patch. Back in the 1820s Dugger lived in southern Bulloch, where he "came into contact with a tiger that was roaming" the woods. While feeding his hogs, he heard a panther scream. He went to investigate on horseback. The creature leaped at him, but his swift horse removed him from danger. Several days later, he heard his hogs squealing and thought an alligator was after them. Venturing into the swamp with his musket, he again encountered the big cat. His weapon merely pestered the creature, so Dugger climbed a tree and continued potting away at it. A neighbor, Sam Davis, arrived with a rifle and killed the "tiger" with a bullet to the brain. It measured eleven feet, and weighed four hundred pounds.

Northern Hart County used to be home to the now-drained Panther Lake, which a local history book, *The Hart of Georgia*, assures us, does not refer to "the cougar, but the jaguar." That fact is established by the Cherokee name for the lake, *Awehsa Untari*, which means "the cat that lives in water." This jaguar, a prominent feature in Cherokee mythology, was known as the "underwater panther." A number of places along the upper Savannah River are associated with the figure.

Between 1835 and 1845, a number of full-fledged tigers prowled the wilderness of Ware, McIntosh, Pierce, Atkinson, and Wayne Counties. No wildcats, bobcats, or even our elusive black panthers, but real tigers of the Indian-African variety. These stories were collected in the book *This Magic Wilderness*. "It is recorded that the Asiatic-oriental beasts did roam this area," it was claimed. "Eyewitnesses testified to their appearances near this Okefenokee Swamp."

Around 1840 the wife of James I. Inman was walking home from a building, where members of the community weaved cloth, when she saw a very large "yellow dog." Her husband felt it was somewhat considerably more ominous and found "slash" and "rip" marks from a large animal around the weaving house. Believing the animal would return, a neighbor whose last name was James armed himself with a rifle and hid in a mulberry tree. Mr. James killed the ten-foot-long animal, which had yellow and black stripes. He displayed it locally.

JUST CALL ME LEFTY, OR CALCULATOR (PUTS DOWN THREE, CARRIES ONE)

A woman neighbor of the Inmans' was going about her chores, her young baby placed on a pallet near the stick (covered with clay) chimney. Hearing a scuffling sound, the mother turned and saw a great claw probing through a gap in the chimney. She quickly hefted a hoe and whacked the great clawed appendage off. A search party soon killed a tiger missing one paw.

Judge E. May, in *Gaters, Skeeters, and Malary,* recounted a third and far more dramatic epic in this kitty drama.

Jimmie Stewart, fourteen, led a group of children into the forest to fell hardwood trees and reduce them to ashes for making soap. Their dog raced ahead into a swamp, then it barked, yelped, and raced back to the children with a huge tiger bounding right behind it.

Bravely, Stewart yelled for the younger children to run while he braced himself with ax held at the ready. The enormous animal knocked Stewart down and he lost the ax. The boy played dead, lying on his chest, as the tiger stripped flesh from his back. Temporarily satiated, the creature raked leaves and pine straw over its "kill" and loped to a creek to drink.

Stewart lurched to his feet and half crawled, half walked two miles to the nearest house, where armed adults were organizing an expedition to hunt down the tiger. The pioneers were horrified by Stewart's appearance, back gnawed and slashed ribs exposed. It was thought he would die but Stewart rallied and lived a long life, showing many people his scars to prove his remarkable story.

A hunting party of mounted men and their dogs left at once. The monster tiger whipped the dogs and the horses shied away from the swamp. Tip Padget and Hamp Guthrie ventured in, Padget with a shotgun and Guthrie carrying an old flintlock. Guthrie wounded the tiger, which only infuriated it. The animal leaped upon Guthrie and fixed his jaws around the man's head. Padget, fearing he would hit Guthrie with a shot, picked up Guthrie's flintlock and beat the tiger to death with it. Padget was forced to pry the tiger's jaws open to release his friend.

Guthrie, grateful for his salvation but angry that Padget had ruined his antique firearm, sued his buddy for ten dollars, arguing that Padget should have shot the animal. Judge May found for Guthrie.

Where did the tigers come from? One runaway circus animal, okay, but three in the middle of nowhere? Judge May "offers no explanation for the presence of jungle cats" in southeastern Georgia.

We have been spared one element of the queer animal kingdom. Occasionally across America, phantom kangaroos and other exotic creatures will haunt an area, leaving behind footprints and puzzled witnesses, and then they leave as abruptly as they arrived. Some researchers believe they appear when an alien teleporter misses his mark, while others think the animals are wanderers through the space-time continuum.

3

UFOs: The Clash of '73

It started when hundreds of observers, largely law-enforcement personnel, were treated to strange lights maneuvering across the sky. Two unidentified objects then crashed into the ground, and that was followed by a diving craft that drove two military policemen off the road. Then the really weird stuff started to happen. It was August 1973, and the most intense wave of UFO sightings in American history had begun in Georgia.

CLOSE ENCOUNTERS OF THE FIRST KIND— LIGHTS IN THE SKY

The flood began just before midnight on August 30 when four government workers driving on GA 118 from Bronwood to Dawson in southwest Georgia sighted two unusual, oval-shaped lights in the sky. They stopped a Dawson police car at 12:10 A.M. on August 31 and reported "something quite weird in the sky."

Dawson patrolman Gary Ellington, who had a background in military intelligence, soon spotted the UFOs. He said he saw two objects "sort of shaped like a football about the size of a car. They would come in several hundred yards, then back off and fade out."

Ellington described the UFOs as "real bright, and the lights were changing colors from white to a reddish orange color to a sort of greenish yellow color."

Other Dawson city and county officers observed the UFOs through a telescope. With magnification the objects appeared to be very bright in the center and were surrounded by a gray haze. One witness said his "knees started shaking" when he saw them.

A normally quiet Thursday night in rural Georgia came alive as law-enforcement radio transmissions squawked out hundreds of messages describing UFO encounters. Across the region several state patrol stations reported disruptions in radio transmission.

A significant portion of the Camilla Enterprise *staff observed UFOs on the morning of August 31, 1973, as the great wave started. Photographer Bill Burson caught this UFO hovering above southwest Georgia at 5:30 A.M. (Courtesy of the* Camilla Enteprise*)*

"Suzanne, you won't believe this, but we have three unidentified flying objects spotted over Dougherty County," State Trooper William Revel told *Albany Herald* reporter Suzanne Shingler via telephone at 1:00 A.M. "I have a Dougherty County police unit out on the Dawson Road at the Lee County line watching them now. If you want a story, go on out."

Shingler joined four Dougherty County sheriff's deputies watching "as three and then five UFOs played games in the sky, flashing like neon signs gone mad."

After half an hour, "their activity began to increase. The object to the right of the biggest one suddenly moved straight up, stopped, and resumed changing colors. A few minutes later, two more objects, which appeared to come from nowhere, shot across the sky under the three we had sighted."

By that time law officers from Lee County, an Albany city commissioner, and several curious citizens had joined the UFO-watching party. Reports from across southwest Georgia continued to pour in. As the morning hours passed, the UFOs spread throughout Sowega (regional shorthand for southwest Georgia). According to Officer Ellington, police "all over southwest Georgia . . . reported seeing the objects."

A patrolman in Doerun rousted Mayor B. C. Crowell, who, along with employees of Crowell Auto Parts, watched one UFO described as an "oversized morning star" hover directly overhead.

At Pelham, Lt. Melvin Perkins thought the light he watched was perhaps "some secret military experiment by the air force."

When Robert Welch, Camilla's police dispatcher, heard about the eruption of UFO sightings, he stepped outside at 1:45 A.M. and saw a strange light in the sky, then he went back inside and monitored messages—on the Georgia Crime Information Computer terminal—regarding sightings from across the region. He broadcast local sightings to state patrol units and city and county law-enforcement agencies throughout southwest Georgia. Periodically, he ventured outside to keep an eye on his UFO, also seen by at least six others.

PHOTOGRAPHS AND MEMORIES

Frank Veale Jr., owner of the *Camilla Enterprise*, and his son, Frank Veale III, a reporter, raced out of the city on U.S. 19 and spotted a UFO about 3:20 that same morning.

They left the car, Veale Jr. wrote, and "suddenly from near the UFO a stream of light, in some ways resembling a shooting star, but in other ways resembling what might be a laser beam of incandescence . . . went in a fraction of a second from near the UFO toward the earth." Later, north of Camilla, the Veales saw a similar phenomenon.

Another father-and-son team from the newspaper also became involved in the excitement. Bill Burson had just returned from a trip to New Orleans and was asleep at 2:00 A.M. when his father, Thomas, got him out of bed to watch the intensely bright objects in the sky. Bill set up his camera near Cotton and attempted several time exposures of the UFO he had under observation. Only one, exposed for an hour around 5:00 A.M., produced anything useful. In that shot the tracks of stars and other celestial bodies are evident, but in the center of the picture is an object many times brighter than the others. The photo shows that the UFO moved to the left at the beginning of the exposure, then returned to its original position.

Thomas Burson wrote that the photo made it "obvious that the light is not a part of the earth's gravitational system." The UFO remained still in the air as the earth (and camera) "rotated away from it."

Although observers of the phenomenon heard no sound, some area residents reported a noise like the whine of high-voltage wires for some time after the UFOs disappeared. There was a power outage in Mitchell County while the UFOs were present.

WAR OF THE WORLDS

Things were a little livelier in Cordele.

"Women tourists were coming in off I-75 screaming the world was coming to an end," Cordele patrolman Vernon Pridgen said of the early morning events of August 31, "and reports from officers all over this area were filling the airways on the statewide police network."

Around 1:00 A.M. Cordele desk sergeant Ronnie Culpepper received a telephone call from a motorist who had been traveling between Hawkinsville and Cordele, "when all of a sudden the inside of his car lit up. He said it got so bright he could look at his watch and tell the time."

In Adel, Sgt. Henry B. Morgan and three other police officers watched a UFO hover above the town for a minute before it raced away toward Waycross. "All we could see were flashing white, red, blue, and orange lights," Morgan said. "It would sit in one position, then move around in a circle at a rapid rate of speed, then come back to its original position."

Georgia news services were flooded with UFO sighting reports and sent them out over the wires to the Associated Press and United Press International. Television stations in Albany, Tallahassee, and Atlanta also gave full coverage with prompt updates to the strange events in southwest Georgia. Before the day was over, Georgia's UFOs had received national coverage. In the following days media from coast to coast swamped tiny local newspaper offices, TV and radio stations, and police agencies for updates on the sensational UFO activity. Three regional air force bases and the National Weather Service were frequently queried but could never explain nor confirm the phenomenon.

The great UFO wave (known at the time as a "flap" in early UFO-speak) occurred while I was at home between summer and fall quarters at Georgia Southwestern College in Americus, Georgia, about fifty miles north of the epicenter of initial UFO reports. I stumbled out of bed on the morning (or afternoon?) of August 31, 1973, to find the sightings splashed across page 1 of the *Macon Telegraph* and the *Atlanta Constitution*.

If school had been in session, I would have gathered my buddies and we would have bedeviled rural farmers for a week while scouting locations for a close encounter of our own. But I was sixty miles northeast of Americus and my friends were scattered from Waycross to Baltimore. I ventured to a local radio station to ask about initial reports that had come in over the wires. They directed me to the trash bin in the back lot, and I waded in. Half an hour of dumpster-diving netted me a dozen coffee-stained items torn off the wire services the previous night. It was interesting to note how the sightings developed and spread through that first night.

The second night of the saucers saw silent, flashing, multicolored lights reported in Albany, Dawson, Camilla, Cordele, Leary, Pelham, Ashburn, Vienna, Moultrie, Leesburg, Tifton, and Waycross. They also spread north to Macon, Gwinnett County, Walton County, and Marietta. A dispatcher at the Albany State Patrol headquarters reported that a trooper trained a portable radar unit, normally used for catching speeders in cars, at a UFO but received no reading.

The UFOs apparently followed I-75 north, because the hot spot on August 31 was Macon, where police officers, firefighters, and private citizens spotted objects that winked, blinked, and sped across city skies at treetop level.

A fire vehicle took off in hot pursuit of one UFO, but lost the object on I-75.

At 2:25 A.M. that night Cordele police called their Macon counterparts and alerted them to a UFO that seemed to be flying in their direction. The craft made damn good time, for only three minutes and seventy-five miles later in Clisby Place, police officers R. M. Barreth and H. E. Hathaway saw it. It was traveling east and "has about six green and red lights around it and it's shaped like a diamond with a tail," they said.

Macon police recorded twenty UFO reports from every part of the city between 7:00 and 10:00 P.M. on September 1, according to Sgt. Gene Collins. "They came from everywhere. We even had one call saying one of them had landed."

The latter report had a UFO hovering at treetop level and landing on Zebulon Road near I-475, but responding police found nothing.

"I'll go against any man who says these things are a planet or scrap metal falling from space," said Macon officer Dennis Brown, referring to early "explanations" for the phenomenon, after observing four UFOs through a ten-power rifle scope. "I believe the yellow or white lights are from the propulsion system," he speculated. "There is something inside. I believe the American government is experimenting with something and don't want us to know about it."

One young man in Marietta reported that he (and presumably many others) had seen a UFO hovering over the Wheeler High School football game. Mrs. Bob Griffin of Cordele was a bit "shaken" by her experience Saturday night. She had gone outside around 11:00 P.M. to check the sky for rain clouds, when she spotted a "big round object" to the southeast. It gave off radiant orange colors from its center while the outer edges contained multicolored blinking lights. It "appeared to be at great height and moving at great speed from southeast to northwest," she stated, and remained in view for five minutes.

Back in southwest Georgia, in Camilla late Saturday night, Chester A. Tatum, publisher of the *Sowega Free Press*, used a Polaroid camera to photograph a bright object with blinking, multicolored lights. It appeared to have a "ribbed-type design with some sort of center down the middle," and left a luminous exhaust or trail.

That night many residents of southwest Georgia were out on the streets and in their yards scanning the sky. Two UFOs appeared to be shuttling back and forth over Camilla, according to reports received by the police station. Another, seen by hundreds of people, hung motionless in the sky to the southwest of the city.

The early days of this phenomenal wave of sightings produced similar descriptions of a veritable fleet of UFOs that whirled and danced each night, primarily for an audience of state troopers, sheriff's deputies, and city policemen. Communications radios crackled continuously, causing high-ranking officers to roll out of bed and rush to the scene in various stages of undress. Despite popular opinion, few of these witnesses were under the influence of any intoxicating substance nor were they unfamiliar with the night sky. From midnight to dawn, glowing, round or football-shaped objects, blinking red, orange, green, blue, and white lights, raced at fantastic speeds and made immediate halts, meandered slowly, hovered, and drifted up and down from high in the sky to barely above the ground, remaining in view for seconds or hours. They emitted neither sound nor smell and did not register on radar.

Southwest Georgia would have only a few additional sightings, but those were substantial. One occurred about 6:45 A.M. on September 5, when twenty-two-year-old Kenneth Parker, a resident of Hahira (soon to be made famous by Ray Stevens's "streaking" song), was driving west on U.S. 41 to his job at Elcona Mobile Homes. The student-pilot first spotted an unusual light hovering near I-75 in northern Valdosta.

"It was glowing and looking like a big ball of flaming red gas," Parker stated.

Thinking it was a reflection from the windshield, he stopped and got out of the car, but the object was still visible. Two minutes after his observation began, a second UFO joined the first.

"They were identical in shape and size," the young man continued, "but they were not football-shaped, nor were they completely round."

After another minute, they vanished, one at a time.

Later that day, twenty-one-year-old Dave McDaniels, owner and operator of Quitman Flying Service, was returning to the airport near dusk after crop-dusting soybean fields when he spotted his UFO.

"It was late—about 7:30 or 8:00 P.M.—and I was coming back in to land," he told a reporter. "I happened to glance out my left window and saw a bright, shiny object shaped like a football about ten to fifteen miles away" and "flashing like some kind of lit-up Christmas ornament."

It was hovering over a field, but when McDaniels turned his plane for a better look, the UFO "just dashed away into the clouds and disappeared." He described the object as "real white and bright . . . it was shiny, sparkling," and seemed large.

On the following afternoon two state troopers observed a UFO floating lazily over the courthouse in Lakeland for five minutes before it disappeared

Dozens of residents of west-central Georgia, centered on Pine Mountain, saw UFOs cruising through the air in 1973. Police in Woodland found that one UFO was a hoax, accomplished with a common highway flare. (Courtesy of the Griffin Daily News*)*

in a cloud of smoke. A farmer in Dougherty County "nearly had a heart attack" as a round, shiny, motor-home-sized craft buzzed his tractor.

The sighting of UFOs in southwest Georgia declined sharply as the phenomenon's interest shifted elsewhere. On Saturday night, September 10, citizens in the western part of Albany observed glowing objects in the sky that alternately displayed red, yellow, and green colors. Some flew rapidly across the sky, others slowly. After that date the UFOs apparently had more pressing appointments, but would return in late October.

RUBE POLITICS

Georgia state senator Franklin Sutton of Norman Park, who had previously established his claim to be class clown of the General Assembly, provided an amusing sideshow early in the sightings. On September 6 he petitioned Senator Culver Kidd, chairman of the Senate Committee on Economy, Reorganization, and Efficiency in Government, to investigate reports of UFOs in his district.

Sutton believed Kidd's "committee can get to the bottom of this," adding, "This is the most reckless bunch of saucers that we've had to contend with. Due to their total disregard of safe operating procedures, they have flown into silos on the farms of Jim Mack Odom and C. O. Smith Jr. and completely demolished them. It is also rumored that they are rustling cows and carrying them back to Mars to relieve the beef shortage there. Your immediate attention to this matter would be appreciated."

Sutton maintained that two concrete silos had been demolished from some unknown cause. "They were up one night and down the next," he said, noting that, indeed, a crop-duster pilot had sighted a UFO.

Senator Kidd had recently completed a controversial investigation of the Georgia Board of Pardons and Paroles and had been accused by Gov. Jimmy Carter of attempting to whitewash the situation.

"I don't want to whitewash," Sutton said, referring to the UFOs. "I think those saucers are much prettier in psychedelic colors."

A week later Sutton talked about the response to his statement. He obviously relished the notoriety that resulted from his tongue-in-cheek declaration.

"I have been interviewed by a Los Angeles TV station, been invited to speak to the London Society of Occult Phenomena, and propositioned by thirty-two advance-fee publishers and moviemakers."

On the negative aspects, "My electricity has gone off, gas given out, tires gone flat, and the fish quit biting Friday.

"I have been subpoenaed to appear before a congressional committee to swear that UFOs don't exist . . . and sixteen psychiatrists from the U.S. Air Force have convinced me that we're experiencing mass hysteria because of the low intelligence of the natives, compounded by the heavy use of corn-buck liquor."

Regarding strange phenomena in general, he concluded, "I intend to deny it on the basis that if you hadn't seen it, you wouldn't believe it, and I didn't see it."

Seemingly with pride, Sutton said that his credibility had cratered "to a new low."

PINE MOUNTAIN—A UFO BEACON?
UFO activity had moved north to the pleasant countryside around Pine Mountain in west-central Georgia, where sightings were reported on August 31. On Saturday night, September 1, several calls were received from citizens who observed unidentified lights moving around the sky for several minutes near Woodbury.

At 12:30 Sunday morning, September 2, Sgt. Gene Bartlett, of Georgia State Patrol Post 34, and Woodland police officer Jim Davis were on the north side of Woodland when an oval-shaped light was spotted at about three thousand feet flying from Manchester toward Columbus. When the object passed over, no noise was detected, and it was determined that each side of the object was lighted.

At 11:30 Sunday night, Georgia state troopers Bill Tatum and Tony Caldwell, along with two troopers from the LaGrange Post and several civilians, one armed with a telescope, were at the intersection of Highways 18 and 190 near Durand when a "perfectly oval white light" appeared to the east, Tatum said. "It moved steadily but in circular and swaying motions." According to state patrol radio operator A. W. Pole, Caldwell and Tatum said the bright white light had blue lights on either side and remained in view for two hours. The UFO occasionally emitted flashes of light that illuminated the entire sky.

For a week hundreds of curious people crowded the hilltop occupied by the Manchester state patrol post, where substantial sightings had been reported in 1966 and 1967. They brought folding chairs or just laid out on the lawn, scanning the skies with high-power binoculars and telescopes. Many were rewarded by fleeting glimpses of the UFOs.

The objects persisted in the area for another week. On Saturday, September 8, Leonard Walker, a Columbus resident, saw "five or six UFOs darting back and forth. They looked to be yellow," Walker said, and each would sprint in one direction, stop, then dart back in the opposite direction.

At 10:00 P.M. on September 8, Trooper R. E. Traylor was in his patrol car in Palmerton when he received a radio message that a UFO had been seen over Manchester, fourteen miles away, and it was heading his way. Two minutes later "a large glowing object came into my line of sight traveling due south at a high rate of speed," Traylor said.

That same night a television crew from an Atlanta station captured on tape one UFO that was described as a stationary white dot. Unfortunately, it was so distant that it appeared only as a bright star on television screens. On September 9 the same news team observed but failed to capture on tape a second UFO that moved across the sky, a sighting witnessed by over a dozen people.

Near Manchester, State Patrolman Sammy Taylor, his wife Shirley, and Joanne and Gary Corwell searched the skies for UFOs at 10:30 P.M.

"We followed the first UFO across the sky until it disappeared over the tree line on Pine Mountain," Shirley said. "We watched it for at least a minute as it glided slowly through the sky."

The four continued the vigil until four the following morning and were rewarded with a second sighting that lasted two and a half minutes.

That same night Talbot County deputy sheriff Charles Pope and Patrolman Traylor were two miles east of Talbottom at 11:15 P.M. when they spotted a UFO. The two men pulled off the road and extinguished their headlights.

"When we turned off the lights, it reversed and went in the opposite direction," Pope said. "It was about three hundred feet in the air and a quarter of a mile away."

"It was floating like a balloon," Traylor said, "only much faster."

Barely across the Georgia state line is Lanett, Alabama (My brother Ray lives there. Hi, Ray!), where, in the early morning hours of September 9, a policeman observed an object he estimated as the size of a car descend within 150 feet of the ground. What officer Keith Broach of Auburn saw was as large as an airplane and changed colors from red and white to green and then white again before disappearing. The craft also visited Tuskegee, Carrville, and Notasulga, Alabama.

The UFOs also moved north and east for Sunday night's show. On September 9 Alton Hutcherson was adjusting his television antenna in Carrollton at 9:10 P.M. when he saw a white, silent object "like a falling star going sideways."

At 4:40 A.M. Sunday, Virginia Smith noticed her cat acting strangely. Opening the door to put the "growling" cat outside, she spied a large UFO with "something shiny sticking up from the top like a fin. It stayed at the treetops for about fifteen minutes and then moved quickly and silently to the northwest." She described it as orange in color and the size of a large airliner with "pipes" protruding from the top, bottom, and side of the craft.

At 7:30 P.M. James R. Wyatt II spotted three glowing UFOs that moved in an erratic, zigzag pattern. At that moment all the lights on his side of the street went out. The objects "continued flying zigzag" as they flew off to the north, Wyatt said. Alma Ethridge, who lived due south of Wyatt, saw three similar objects at the same time.

UFOs favored Columbus with another visit late on the evening of September 10. Mrs. L. H. Webb of Midland told her husband, "Sugar, I'm going to go out and look for flying objects." Her husband laughed and accompanied her. Suddenly, Mr. Webb "started yelling to me," Mrs. Webb said. One after another, three UFOs appeared from the northwest and disappeared at high speed behind a cloud "just like they were going somewhere." Although the UFOs were spotted at high altitude, Mrs. Webb could see that they were circular and had three prongs and a tail.

During the first week of sightings, a few reports of UFOs were received in Houston and Peach Counties in central Georgia. A spinning object with red and white blinking lights was seen near Warner Robins Junior High by three residents at 8:35 P.M. on September 1. It hovered about 150 feet off the ground and resembled "two saucers put together," said witness Hank Bates. After five minutes the craft left, still spinning.

STARS IN THEIR EYES?

On Thursday night, August 30, residents saw UFOs over Sandersville and called radio station WSNT to describe their experience. Disc jockey Ray Smith invited one witness out to the station, located several miles from town, at 11:15. She pointed out several UFOs to Smith, including a cluster of eight to the south.

The UFOs resembled stars, but, Smith said, they were "much smaller. They are basically blue, but the colors red and green and occasionally gold revolve around them." Smith viewed the objects for half an hour, then called UPI.

Returning to the station later in the day, Smith was inundated with calls from radio and TV stations and newspapers across the country requesting interviews with him. Because of Smith, Sandersville briefly became the center of the UFO universe.

Because of the recurring nature of the Sandersville UFOs, I decided to pop over there one day and pretend to be a legitimate UFO investigator (weren't we all pretending in college?). I met Ray Smith, who was gracious and still glowing from his personal fifteen minutes of fame. I was given a grand tour of the radio facilities and Ray pointed out where all the UFOs appeared. I took notes and photographs, gravely shook his hand, and departed, convinced that he and his listeners had been caught up in the UFO mania sweeping the state and had honestly misidentified stars and planets that glittered brightly in the rural sky. Undoubtedly, many other UFO reports resulted from similar circumstances.

HIT AND RUN

Meanwhile, UFO mania had reached high gear in Savannah. On the night of September 5, William and Mary Fisher saw three brightly lit UFOs from Chatham Street. The first was spotted around 11:00 P.M., then the second arrived and "rendezvoused" with the first. The original object shot straight up like a shooting star in reverse. The Fishers' third UFO appeared and consorted with the second object before those two moved off together. The silent objects were in sight for an hour.

Around 10:00 P.M. on September 6, a UFO witnessed by many, including city officials, crashed into the ocean off Tybee Island. Three observers in a parking lot on Sixteenth Street saw the object splash a quarter-mile off the beach. The UFO "was bigger than a bread box," one said, made a "whooshing noise" as it flew overhead, and was bright enough to cast shadows. Michael K. Deal, acting chief of the Thunderbolt Police Department, was sitting in his patrol car in a parking lot on Tybee Road at 9:40 when he and a passerby saw a UFO with a light that was "greenish with a slight orange tint." It remained in sight for at least six seconds. "It made an arc toward Savannah Beach," Deal said. "I've seen shooting stars and this didn't drop. It made a definite pattern toward the beach."

At the same time, Savannah Beach patrolman Mike Kelly and recruit Jim Brown were on U.S. 80 on Tybee Island "when all of a sudden we saw this big light in the sky." Startled, Kelly brought his prowl car to "a screeching halt" to observe the object that initially had "a reddish tint, but it changed almost immediately to a bright green." As they watched, they heard Deal report the same object on the police radio. Kelly and Brown believed the object crashed into the Atlantic Ocean a mile off Sixteenth Street. "Just before it hit, it turned a bright white," Kelly said.

Not only did the Coast Guard station on Tybee Island receive a half-dozen UFO reports that night, a spokesperson revealed: "We saw some lights up here ourselves." However, they took no action.

Late on the night of September 7 sightings were reported by a dozen residents of southern Savannah who saw "bright yellow" UFOs hover over the city for three hours.

The fourth night of UFO action over Savannah escalated spectacularly. In the early morning darkness of September 8, two military policemen patrolled Hunter Army Airfield, adjacent to the Forest River-Armstrong State College area in Savannah. Spec. 4 Bart J. Burns and Spec. 4 Randy Shade were driving along the perimeter road near Cobra Hall at 2:30 A.M. when they spotted an unidentified object in the sky. It was "traveling at a high rate of speed from east to west about two thousand feet above ground level," according to a report they filed immediately after the experience.

The mystified MPs continued their rounds. Ten minutes later they were adjacent to Montgomery Crossroads, near the 702nd Radar Squadron building, an ammunition dump, and the base golf course, when the same UFO "came in at treetop level and made a dive," Burns's official report stated. It passed just above the blue lights on top of their car. This aggressive move caused the soldiers to duck and forced the patrol car to leave the road and enter a ditch.

It took the MPs fifteen minutes to get their vehicle out of the ditch, a harrowing time while the UFO hovered only two hundred yards in front of them, blue, white, and amber lights "flashing brilliantly." After they regained the pavement and headed for headquarters, the object paced them, remaining fifty to one hundred feet away until they neared their office, when it flew away.

Because the Pentagon has "no normal channels for a communication of this type," stated Lt. David Anderson, a Hunter-Fort Stewart public information officer, he directed the MPs to report the incident on forms used for reporting accidents.

Half an hour before the sighting, at 1:40 A.M., Marcus Holland, executive sports editor of the *Savannah News-Press*, was exiting I-16 onto Lynes Parkway when he observed a UFO with red, green, and white lights racing across the sky. It resembled a baseball.

"I was traveling at seventy miles per hour and it outran my car like it was tied to a post," Holland reported. The lights blinked off and on, and the UFO seemed to circle the city. The newsman turned off the highway to follow the light and saw it fly across Hunter Air Field.

"I called the county police when I got home and they said they had five cars watching it," he stated.

Mrs. Dick Halliard was one of a dozen residents of Mayfair who observed a UFO, twice the size of the North Star and colored a bright yellow, maneuver over Lake Mayer for two hours. When she first sighted it at 10:30 P.M., she thought she heard a motor. The object had a "tail" that appeared whenever the UFO moved.

In Meldrim, a loud "thud" startled Miriam Tolver and her daughter Davey and shook their house for a full minute. They ran outside to investigate and spotted a large UFO hovering two hundred feet away from their house. It had a large orange searchlight mounted on top, with smaller blue lights, and even smaller orange lights circling the searchlight.

A bureaucratic haze soon engulfed the MP sighting. One MP amended his report and denied that their car had entered a ditch. Then a duty officer deleted the part about the vehicle leaving the pavement at all. Burns, who had been quite cooperative with the press, had promised early Sunday to tell the "whole story" to a reporter. However, he failed to keep a scheduled appointment Sunday afternoon. Contacted early Monday, September 10, Burns revealed that he had been instructed not to discuss the encounter. "I'm afraid we aren't allowed to say anything," he said, referring all questions to the duty officer. A spokesman acknowledged that the "situation has changed," but was "not at liberty to say" what the change was or why the MPs had been forbidden to speak with the press about the incident. Later that day the MPs were given permission to talk openly with the press, but they could not be reached. Burns and Shade had been given three days' leave, and there the matter ended.

The UFOs ignored the controversy and continued to descend on Savannah for the fifth straight night, Sunday, September 9. This night hundreds observed UFOs, even entire neighborhoods. By 10:00 P.M. the Savannah Police Department had logged over fifty telephoned UFO sightings. Police responded to nineteen, and half a dozen officers radioed in personal observations.

Things turned quite strange when four callers informed authorities that a craft had landed in Laurel Grove Cemetery, doused its lights, and disembarked "ten big, black, hairy dogs" that then raced through the grounds. This might be dismissed as a hoax, except "big, black, hairy dogs" have a long and storied history in paranormal literature.

In Emanuel County farmer Raymond Williamson of Oak Park watched four UFOs fly over his house at 10:00 P.M., apparently bound for Savannah, but he took it in stride. "They've been landing in the pasture near my house for the past six years," he stated. The ships were "about the size of a camper shell attached to the back of a pickup truck," Williamson said. They seemed to land whenever cattle were in the pasture, although no bovines turned up mutilated or impregnated with alien embryos.

On September 10 two patrolmen and a county police lieutenant first spotted an aerial curiosity over Largo Drive and tracked it down Abercorn Extension and Middleground Road. Many others also observed it.

This was the third consecutive night that Mrs. Dick Halliard and her neighbors had watched a colorful UFO in the sky over Queensbury Street. Chatham County patrolman Paul C. Lupica was dispatched to the area and spotted two UFOs through binoculars. The bright objects changed colors from blue to red, green, and white.

In Meldrim Lake Acres, Carolyn Nobles reported a "bright red, round, very large object about 250 feet above her house." Blinking red lights were on top and a tail trailed behind. Ms. Nobles watched the phenomenon for twenty minutes before it raced away. In the same neighborhood, Mrs. Romie Myers had seen a saucer-shaped object with a tail change color from red to white for the past three weeks.

At 8:50 P.M. Nancy Love of Kingsway Street saw "a red flashing light" over the Lake Mayer-Mayfair area, north of her house. It blinked, but not constantly, for five minutes before it disappeared. It returned at 9:35 and climbed into view beyond the tree line and hovered before again disappearing a few minutes later.

Near Waters Avenue, Penny Black and neighbors witnessed a red, football-sized object hovering in the sky over her house. Their attention had been drawn by a noise "like something brushing across the trees."

In Williamsburg, Eddie Chapman saw an object "about the size of a very large star" as it moved slowly from east to west near Memorial Stadium at 9:20. Before it disappeared he saw an orange glow and three separate orange spotlights.

On September 24 half a dozen reports of UFOs came in from southern Chatham County. William H. Whitten, a News-Press reporter, saw an object with blinking red, green, and white lights near Thunderbolt at 10:35 P.M. It hovered above a radio transmitter on Oatland Island and alternately grew brighter, then dimmed. Several people spotted a UFO over Thunderbolt Bluff that was stationary for a time, then ascended and flew off.

UFOs reached Griffin on Sunday night, September 9, when Mrs. Hugh D. Beall called the Spalding County Sheriff's Office to report an "upside-down-cup-and-saucer-shaped object" hovering at treetop level above her house. It had gold, red, and green lights on the bottom that changed colors, and made a "funny" noise, pitched too low for a conventional aircraft.

GREAT BALLS OF FIRE!, OR CHICKEN LITTLE WAS RIGHT!

At 4:00 P.M. on September 10, Ress Clanton, a retired textile worker known by his friends as Shorty, was sitting in a yard chair beneath the shade of a large magnolia tree beside his house in Orchard Hill, five miles south of Griffin. Clanton was contemplating supper while scanning a beautiful, sunny afternoon sky. He was focused on a small thunderhead crossing the face of the sun "when the thing dropped."

The "thing," variously described as having the size and shape of an egg or baseball, was bright gold in color, but its most curious aspect was that it did not plummet rapidly to earth, but appeared to be descending at a controlled rate of speed, floating, apparently under intelligent control. The object did not spin, it "just come down plumb straight—didn't come down too fast, just take its time," Clanton recalled.

When tree branches blocked his view, Clanton jumped out of his chair and ran to a yard swing, which he climbed onto for a better look.

"I stood on the swing till it come down," Clanton said. "It didn't make no racket, now, when it hit the ground. When it hit the ground it stay there for a second, and, directly, white smoke raise up. It never did spread, it just stay together about as big as a nail keg, it just keep going up till it was a little wisp of a thing, and then one line of smoke come out toward the evening star, another toward the morning star."

Ress "Shorty" Clanton of Orchard Hill, near Griffin, watched a glowing UFO fall at a controlled rate of speed and disappear on contact with the ground, leaving extremely high concentrations of certain compounds. (Courtesy of the Griffin Daily News)

CLOSE ENCOUNTERS OF THE SECOND KIND—
PHYSICAL EFFECTS

The projectile vanished when it encountered the ground, apparently destroyed during the curious impact. Once the white smoke dissipated, all that remained was a smoldering, scorched patch of lawn the size of a basketball, about a foot long and five inches deep. Strangely, there was no crater.

Clanton started to go look at the point of impact, then he wisely changed his mind and detoured to a neighbor's house. He then enlisted a second neighbor, a former deputy sheriff, and the three ventured toward the scorched site, twenty-five yards from his house and on the property of an adjacent warehouse, sandwiched between grain elevators and the municipal water tower.

When the men knelt beside the smoking spot, Clanton passed a hand three feet over it. The heat was so intense that it nearly burned his palm. Clanton unfolded his pocketknife and ran the blade through the soil for several seconds. When he extracted the blade, the metal was too hot for him to touch.

Clanton reported the curious incident to the Spalding County Sheriff's Office. Before a deputy arrived, a crowd of patrons from the convenience store across the road had gathered, attracted by the commotion. None of the assembled multitude had any notion what the mysterious object could have been, but one of the radiomen had the presence of mind to call Dr. O. E. Anderson, head of the agronomy department at the Georgia Experiment Station in Griffin.

Anderson waded through a crowd four to five people deep. Although he arrived at the scene two and a half hours after the incident, Anderson could still feel the intense heat emanating from the grounded object when he placed his hands near ground zero. It was still smoldering, and he estimated the temperature at that time to be two hundred degrees. Presumably, it would have been far hotter immediately after impact—Anderson later ventured an estimate of three hundred degrees. He said a normal afternoon soil temperature for the area in summer would be 115 to 120 degrees.

The soil scientist took three samples—from the impact site, a spot two feet away, and a third site thirty feet distant. Anderson also collected the soil excavated by WKEU and departed to run a soil analysis, a reluctant scientific participant in a bizarre event. He estimated it would require three days to determine if anything unusual had been found.

Shorty Clanton had no need to await test results. "I tell you, I believe it to be a piece of brimstone from heaven come down here to show people how He can burn the earth with it," he proclaimed.

By nightfall WKEU had received at least three reports of area UFOs.

"Something definitely elevated the temperature of the soil," Anderson soon informed the press. "The soil was unusually hot for just grass to be burning. It was hot down to a depth of at least a half an inch and as much as an inch of the soil was very, very hot." He also said a "glob about the size of your little finger of molten metal or slag had remained on the ground. They are seeing some form of energy, but what?"

Anderson was also convinced of Clanton's sincerity, saying he "had the feeling he was telling us what he thought he had seen." After a second interview with Clanton, Anderson said, "He stuck to the same story. It is a credible story. I don't think he dreamed something up and went out and set a fire."

Anderson's initial analysis revealed nothing out of the ordinary—no signs of radiation were present—but he planned chemical tests "in hopes there may be something in the analysis that will give us a clue to what heated the organic matter in the soil." Tests of the soil samples would reveal the presence of certain inorganic and organic material.

"If it was a magnesium flare, we would expect to find a high amount of magnesium compared to the soil around the burned site," he added.

Anderson declined to speculate on the cause of the charred spot, emphasizing that he was not conducting a flying saucer investigation. However, he did term the incident *puzzling*.

Results of the chemical analysis raised as many questions as it answered. The absence of hydrocarbons eliminated the possibility that the use of gasoline or other petroleum products initiated the ignition of natural organic material in the soil at the impact site. The use of flares was ruled out when the content of magnesium and strontium, commonly used in flares, was not found to be higher than normal.

What was found in unusual amounts were copper and chromium, metals commonly found in alloys. The concentration of copper at the impact site was two thousand times greater than in control samples taken a distance from the site, 43,050 parts per million, while thirty feet away it was 7.4 parts. Chromium was two hundred times higher at the impact site.

The evidence did "lend support to the observation of an individual who observed the area immediately after the alleged occurrence," Anderson's report stated. "He observed what was described as a small metal-like object at very high temperature slightly embedded in the soil."

At least Clanton had been vindicated.

"I'll tell you what I think it was," Clanton maintained five years later. "And nobody can convince me different. A piece of brimstone. It's the only thing could burn pure dirt. Before this happen you couldn't get nobody out to Sunday School or into church. Now it's full all the time."

The soil required time to regenerate. Years later the spot was still bare of grass, the soil grayer and finer than the earth surrounding it.

HIT AND DISSOLVE

The hits just kept coming. Roy Lawhorn was a tenant farmer living in Brook, a rural community eight miles from Griffin and twenty miles southeast of Orchard Hill, with his five-year-old daughter Donna. He was awakened about 2:00 A.M. on Friday, September 14, by "a sound like locusts and a bright light outside the house.

"I grabbed my rifle, because it looked like it was coming towards the house. I shot at it about three or four times and it just disappeared into the ground."

The object, "as big as your head," demonstrated the same characteristics as the earlier one in Orchard Hill. "It came down like an umbrella," he continued, "it gradually came down. I thought the devil had come to get me." For fear that he would be thought a fool, he waited until September 17 to report the incident.

The object left a charred spot on a dirt road located ten yards from the house. Dr. Anderson was again called upon to exercise his expertise. This impact also left no crater, but there were markings on an area one foot long by six or eight inches wide, nearly the exact dimensions of the earlier incident. Beneath the top layer of soil, Anderson excavated a wide area composed of charred soil and organic matter.

Test results revealed nothing unusual in the soil. A high organic content indicated that the site might have been a dump site for plant remains, charcoal, and other common farm residues that were later covered by clay when the road was constructed.

This analysis was released on September 20, accompanied by reports of UFOs seen over Griffin the night before. Police received a number of UFO calls, three from members of local government agencies. Police captain Larry Howard and neighbors observed a disc-shaped UFO festooned with lights and which darted around the sky. It was white or silver, noiseless, and would stop in the air, then race off at high speeds.

The wife of probation officer Eddie Freeman was returning home from church when she saw lights being shined on the ground by an aerial object. The lights separated, then came back together. Excited, she rushed home and described the experience to her husband. The couple drove to a high point on Teamon Road to search for the object. Before long two disc-shaped UFOs appeared in the sky, hovering 150 yards above the pavement. One object had three lights pulsing from bright to dim. Described as the size of a Volkswagen, it had a light on each side and in the middle, and alternately moved rapidly and slowly.

Griffin resident Harry Lambert saw a golden colored, football-shaped vehicle that was sixty feet long. "Everybody thinks I'm crazy," he stated, the Georgia mantra of the month, "but I know what I saw."

On September 9 eleven people saw a UFO in Evans, but sightings from the Augusta area remained curiously light.

The UFOs finally made it past Atlanta in some strength on the night of September 5. *Marietta Journal* reporter Penny McHan was driving on I-75 near Marietta when a companion exclaimed, "Hey, what are those strange lights in the sky?"

McHan looked and "spotted a small, eerie light almost due north, directly in front of us, hovering, gently bobbing in the black, 10:30 P.M. sky.

"Not as fixed as a star and beaming more steadily than a planet, the light seemed to mother two smaller lights underneath and to the lower left of where it hovered, moving only slightly now and then." The larger light moved "ever so slowly, followed by the two smaller, pinpoint twinkling lights.

"Suddenly, to the left of the horizon, a helicopter swiftly approached the lights, but they immediately dimmed themselves to darkness," and never reappeared.

On September 10 a Forsyth County sheriff's deputy reported seeing a UFO. That night in Marietta officers were called to investigate a UFO report at the residence of Mark Headrick on Lanier Road. There they found a group of people staring at a UFO that moved slowly to the southeast at three to five miles an hour. Through a telescope, the policemen saw a light-colored football shape with a red tinge around the edge. It would hover, then accelerate rapidly, only to slow again.

NORTH GEORGIA REPORTS

Charles Meeks, his wife Cornelia, and their daughter Susan were making a run to the Floyd County dump at nine that evening when they saw a bright round object the size of a dime moving to the northwest. It changed color from white to a dull red or pink, then back to white. The fast mover traveled from horizon to horizon in fifteen to twenty seconds, abruptly changing directions and zigzagging all the way.

"That's what was so amazing," Meeks stated, "as fast as it was moving and changing direction and turning so fast. If it had been an airplane, it would have torn the wings off."

At 11:00 P.M. on September 11, a Forsyth County woman observed a UFO for fifteen minutes near Coal Mountain, just north of Cumming. The silent, stationary object hovering at treetop level had flashing red, green, and white lights.

Apparently, Cathy Puckett, her husband, and their son saw the same object. Their UFO was not as bright as the North Star, but clearly distinct from the stars. It seemed to hang twenty feet above the tree line a third of a mile away. The object had a circular movement, like a lighted, turning cylinder, but no shape could be distinguished. It moved very slowly between the trees before rapidly disappearing over the horizon.

UFOs returned to Forsyth County on September 10. H. B. Tallant, who lived in Friendship Circle west of Cumming, was driving when he spotted an object "brighter and a little larger than a star." It started flashing red lights, then white. Over the next two nights he observed two other UFOs.

West of Cumming is Heardsville, where Junior Roper spotted one UFO the previous Saturday, two on Monday, two on Tuesday, and two on Wednesday, September 12. During the course of the evening they "drifted down behind the trees, but they were too still for too long a time to be a plane."

Also on September 12 three teenagers watched a UFO near Sawnee Mountain, which several of my associates believe is the center of all manner of paranormal phenomena. Another man saw two. He had observed a bright UFO a week earlier that "could be seen through the trees as it passed by."

As in Sandersville, a number of people in north Georgia were undoubtedly observing ordinary celestial phenomena, which is inevitable when people unfamiliar with the sky start searching the night for UFOs. If you focus on Venus or a star long enough, you can easily imagine it "dancing" around the sky and shifting colors.

Rome's first visitation by UFOs occurred on Sunday, September 16, and continued for three straight nights, according to reports from the state patrol. In response to a call at 10:30 P.M., a *News-Tribune* reporter went to Simpson Drive, where the Russell Kessler family had watched UFOs for the previous three evenings. These objects seemed to be several white lights of angular shape, set close together, and rotating around a common center. Red lights were followed by white lights, and at times a red spark or light separated from the object and shot quickly across the sky. The formation would hover stationary for a while, then move around the sky, only to return to their original spots. Many area residents reported similar sights to the Georgia State Patrol.

Extreme-north Georgia finally got a UFO sighting on September 24 when Carlton Shaw and his two children stepped outside their home in Young Harris at 8:45 P.M. and spotted a red UFO west of Venus. It seemed to swing like a pendulum, first clockwise, then counterclockwise. Through a rifle scope the thing appeared to hop up and down. Earlier, on September 19, four north Georgia residents, Carl and Debbie Collins, Clyde Collins, and Preston Turner, saw an unusually bright object in the western skies. It was reported as being "brighter than a full moon and comparable in size."

In October 1973 two adults and a child were pursued by a giant, cigar-shaped UFO in Warner Robins. Minutes later an identical craft was seen at close range by a sheriff's deputy at the Houston County Fairgrounds, which has a commanding view of the surrounding countryside.

At 10:15 P.M. on September 26 Tim Richardson, a newsman for radio station WKRW in Cartersville, spotted two UFOs, one in the sky and another that apparently landed near the Etowah Indian Mounds (visiting relatives? Sorry, an ancient astronaut fantasy). The aerial object was a flashing light that zigzagged across the sky at high speed, while the grounded one was circular, about forty feet in diameter, and featured flashing lights that changed from green to white to red to yellow.

On October 1 at Stillwell, in Effingham County, a number of residents were watching the sky at 9:00 P.M. when they saw a bright white UFO flying fast at treetop level, apparently in pursuit of a small plane flying to the west. Half an hour later it returned, chasing a similar plane to the east.

On the night of October 4 in Bulloch County eight people observed UFOs, some for up to four hours. In Clito, Myra Waters and six friends spotted a UFO with red, green, and blue lights, some of them rotating. It hovered to the southeast at 8:30 P.M., then moved from right to left just above the horizon. On U.S. 301 North, Linda Bazemore saw an object with a "red, pulsating light in the middle of it" which was "smaller than the moon" and disappeared behind trees after half an hour.

99

This UFO was photographed by Spalding County juvenile probation officer Ed Crawford on October 10 over his house in Highland Hills, near Griffin. (Courtesy of the Griffin Daily News)

HONEST OFFICER, PART ONE

On the morning of October 11, three men observed a car-sized UFO fly slowly and silently through Albany's skies. As the aircraft passed, one began bobbing up and down vertically. Hours later, at 8:42 A.M., a man was driving south on GA 333 in Albany when a bright flashing light from the sky penetrated his windshield. "I blacked out," the witness claimed, and awakened in Phoebe Putney Hospital. Police had found him passed out in his car, which had run into a ditch. The experience "has really left him uptight," his wife said. "Something has got him shook up. And he won't talk about it." An early abduction, perhaps?

UFOs continued to be observed by newspersons in Floyd County. On Tuesday night, October 16, a *News-Tribune* photographer and three reporters had sightings. Reporter John Ronner and photographer David Bailey were driving down rural Reeceburg Road at 10:15 searching for UFOs reported by residents when Bailey shouted, "There it is! I think we've found it!" Ronner hit the brakes and the pair bailed out of the car for a closer look at what Ronner called "an eerie sight."

"What is that?" Ronner exclaimed, while scribbling notes in the dark as Bailey snapped away in futility. What fascinated them was "a reddish flying object looking like an oval pea, moving slowly and silent westward over treetops . . ." It was composed of six to twelve clustered, twinkling red lights, and slowly changed course, flying south before disappearing behind a hill.

In southern Rome, Thomas C. Byars was driving home about three miles northeast of the previous sighting when he spotted a UFO, whose brightness fluctuated as he watched. It would grow very bright, then dim, and brighten again in the sky. He called the Floyd County Sheriff's Department to report the sighting and was soon joined by two deputies. They and Byars's wife Anne, his sister Virginia, and her husband Rayford all watched the reddish "oblong pea" that hovered soundlessly, "alternately approaching us and backing away," Byars said. They also saw a second red UFO tracing the tree line along Reeceburg Road.

In Coosa, Linda Swanson glanced out the window while preparing a bottle for her baby and saw a "big bright white object" hovering "very far away." While she was phoning her neighbors to alert them to the sight, it vanished. Later, while speaking on the phone to her sister, Anne Byars, she peered through a curtain and saw the UFO rematerialize "out of nowhere." Frightened, she broke into tears.

Two other reporters, Steve and Laurie Craw, were returning to their home in Polk County on Booger Hollow Road (no joke) when they sighted a bluish white object at 8:15 and observed it for fifteen minutes. It was distant, seemed to alternately hover, then continue flying southwest "in jerky motions." It glowed brightly even when passing through clouds, which ruled out "the possibility it was a plane or a star," Steve said.

On Wednesday evening, October 17, David Bailey finally captured a UFO on film. It was east of Cave Springs and changed from red to blue to yellow. Bailey hit paydirt again at 1:00 A.M. on Sunday, October 21, from the hilltop East View Cemetery in Rome. His first photograph had been taken with a three-hundred-millimeter lens; this time he was armed with an eight-hundred-millimeter telescopic lens and took timed exposures of ten to twenty-five seconds. The UFO primarily hovered, but also approached and moved away from him and slowly moved to the north. The object appeared to be flexible, leading to speculation that it was a large balloon.

On the night of October 17, deputies Charles Fowler and Ray Hanson responded to a UFO report made by a Pinkerton security officer in Athens. The object had vanished when they arrived, but as they talked to the guard "we saw an object rise from the ground," Fowler related. "The object appeared to be about twelve feet in diameter with rotating red, white, and blue lights."

Also on October 17 two substantial UFO reports came from Warner Robins, in central Georgia. The two incidents were separate, but they occurred within thirty minutes and one mile of each other.

At 9:00 P.M. Lawrence Smith, Peggy Stepp, and her daughter Kathy spotted a large, cigar-shaped object about one hundred feet above the ground. They followed it down Dunbar and Bateman roads. "I was petrified," Smith said. Suddenly, "there were two of them. And then they started getting close, and we started getting scared."

Kathy began to scream and Smith raced toward a more inhabited area. "The UFOs began to close in," Peggy said, and then, "my God, there was one right behind us. My daughter screamed hysterically, and the thing stopped right above us and put this bright light on the car."

Smith called the Houston County Sheriff's Department to report the incident at 9:30. Meanwhile, Cpl. Bobby Fisher was dispatched to investigate a UFO sighting near Elberta and Dunbar roads. He reached the Houston County Fairgrounds, an elevated area with a commanding view of the surrounding countryside, at 9:57, and apparently saw the same object hovering above the trees.

"It approached a clear field," he reported, "and then took off in a westerly direction. It was huge with red, blue, and green lights. I chased it when it zoomed over me. It made a humming noise, sort of like electricity going through a wire."

Fisher, who described his UFO as being "big as a building," bravely pursued the craft and overtook it on Dunbar Road a mile east of Houston Lake Road.

"It stopped there right over me, and I got out of the car," he continued. "I took my flashlight and pointed it at the thing. Hell, it was only about one hundred feet above me. I couldn't see anything for the bright light. I think I got some type of reflection off of it when I pointed my flashlight at it. That's how close it was. I thought that damn thing was going to land right there in that field.

"I stayed on the radio trying to get someone else out there. I didn't want anyone to think I was crazy."

Jim Cosey, executive editor of the *Warner Robins Daily Sun*, believed that Smith, Stepp, and Fisher "saw something. They sounded sincere and nearly hysterical on the phone."

Cosey rousted three reporters (which would have included several of the paperboys) out of bed and joined them on a nocturnal tour around the city that produced no aerial anomalies.

Griffin's spectacular UFO sightings ended with a bang on Wednesday, October 17, when Harry Lambert, superintendent of the LBI Quarry, spotted a large, gold-colored UFO at 8:30 P.M. on County Line Road. The sixty-foot-long, football-shaped craft was near ground level when he first saw it. "I tried to follow it, but it went straight up into the air," Lambert said.

UFOs returned to Ashburn in southwest Georgia on October 17 when Elbert Lee Sims, a trustee at the Turner County Public Works Camp, was changing oil in a state patrol car just before dawn. After "a real bright light caught my attention," Sims said, he "saw a saucer-like thing moving slowly across the sky" until it disappeared from sight.

AND NOW FOR SOMETHING COMPLETELY DIFFERENT . . .
ALIEN CREATURE FEATURES
Paul Brown, a minister and car dealer, tooled for home in his brand-new yellow Volkswagen Beetle on the night of October 18. He was traveling on U.S. 29, a mile and a half north of Danielsville, on his way home from Hartwell.

"I was listening to the World Series," he related four years later. "Then my radio went out. As anybody would do, I reached over to get the channel tuner. So I started turning and everything was the same way, it was just dead, a scattering sensation, static, no voices. So I thought, 'That's crazy.' My radio had never just gone out like this before."

"Everything lighted up" suddenly, Brown said. "I could see the road and the fields lighted up all around me. My first impression was that it was a small airplane trying to land."

The "descending airplane" turned out to be a craft that had chosen his car to pace at sixty miles an hour, about two hundred feet overhead. After Brown got a good look at the object, he decided it was not configured like an airplane and made no engine sounds. However, it was descending so rapidly, "I realized if I don't stop I'm going to hit it. So I came to a screeching halt," which was fortunate because the ship had landed in the road one hundred yards in front of him. "I don't know why I did it," he said after slamming on his brakes and pulling the emergency brake as well, "but I opened the car door and managed, frightened as I was, to get one foot on the ground." The minister had started to pray when a light abruptly shone in his face.

"I don't think I've ever seen, could ever describe, how bright the light was," Brown said. "Like a round beam, much bigger than a basketball in size. It's in my face . . . and it's blinding me. And then I realized I didn't see any wings. I heard no propellers. It was a deathless quiet except for my engine running."

He estimated the craft to be about fifteen feet in diameter and six feet high.

CLOSE ENCOUNTERS OF THE THIRD KIND
—ENTITIES SIGHTED

"Two subjects came out," Brown continued. "Where they came from I don't know. I couldn't see a flap, a drop door, or anything. When I finally got my vision clear I could see a clearance underneath, so it was not belly-landed; it had some kind of landing gear. And they came out, and they had on the most beautiful outfits I've ever seen—silver, blousey, come down to where your wrists are, then they had what appeared to be white gloves. Very tight around the neck, like something a priest would wear. Down to the feet, like a jumpsuit. It looked like if you pulled a gun and shot it, it would glance off, yet it moved. They could move, yet it looked like it was heavy, because of the way they walked, very slow. I estimated them to be four to five feet tall.

"They just started walking down the road toward me, very slow. I could see a face, you know, place where eyes would be, ears. The faces were reddish. Hair was almost like cotton, no discoloration, which leads me to believe maybe it was a mask of some kind. I never got close enough to really say—closest I ever got was 150, 200 feet away, which is not too far away when you're there by yourself."

This robotlike being reportedly caused several cars on I-75 to stop in October 1973, and then "inspected" the vehicles. (Courtesy of the Center for UFO Studies)

The creatures "had two arms and two legs like a man," he noted. And they were getting closer. At that point Brown reached into his car for a .22-caliber target pistol he carried for protection when depositing money from his business. The creatures had taken half a dozen steps toward him, but at the sight of a weapon "they turn around, walk very slow back behind the shadow to the bright light. All of a sudden they disappear behind the light, and I try to see where they go, if they go in a hatch or what, but I couldn't."

When the aliens disappeared, "the lights went out almost instantly and stung my eyes again. It took off at an angle and made a sound I would describe as like a million fans," or "a whizzing sound, like golf balls coming by my ear." The spectacular exit "almost stood my hair on end."

After the craft vanished among the stars, the car radio resumed playing. Shaken, "my legs about buckling," Brown drove to the nearest telephone and called the Madison County Sheriff's Department in Danielsville. After hearing the story, Deputy Jimmy Mattox returned to the site with Brown and found twenty-five-foot-long skid marks. He described Brown as "real nervous. He was shaking all over." On the following day, investigators discovered that the grass beside the road was "fan swept."

On October 20 Brown revealed that air force experts had made arrangements to speak with him. He contacted Falkville, Alabama, police chief Jeff Greenhow, who had seen red-skinned aliens clad in silver suits similar to Brown's. Greenhow had snapped four photographs of his creatures and promised to send copies to Brown.

The same night that Brown had his encounter (October 18), UFO activity resumed in the Savannah area. An unidentified woman reported that at 9:15 P.M. she and several other ladies were returning home on U.S. 17 in Effingham County after a church function when she spotted a tiny silver figure standing beside the highway. A "whole line of traffic slowed down to about ten miles an hour," she stated, to stare at the creature, but "I guess everyone was just too scared of what they might find" to stop and investigate.

Nearly an hour earlier in nearby Pembroke, Rev. Hanie Burnsed, pastor of Northside Baptist Church, said he and a number of families stood beside GA 67 and observed a large, bluish, circular craft with a long tail that hovered for half an hour around 8:30 P.M. When the tail neared the ground, Burnsed said, several "ladies thought they might be sucked up."

AAA SERVICE

At 3:30 P.M. on October 19 an unidentified woman was traveling south on I-75 near Ashburn in Turner County when every system in her car suddenly stopped functioning—engine, power brakes, and steering. According to one report a UFO had passed by close overhead. After coasting to the side of the road she had a "strange feeling" and reluctantly turned to her left. Standing beside the car was a "four-foot-tall metal man who appeared to be wearing a metallic pewterlike outfit capped with a bubble or dome made of the same material—there were two openings for the eyes. The slits were rectangular."

The creature was so close that had her window been down "I could have touched it." This odd experience continued for six minutes as the entity circled her car. "He didn't bother me," she stated. "He just walked away, just disappeared."

When a Georgia state trooper stopped to help the stranded woman, she described the encounter. The patrolman replied that he had heard identical stories from several other motorists that day. The car was towed to a garage, where the engine remained too hot to touch three hours after the incident.

At 7:55 P.M. that night a woman was returning home to Rutledge in Morgan County when she sighted twin narrow beams of fluorescent-like lights in the sky. They blinked, and after passing behind a tree "formed into a larger mass that looked sort of like the moon" and turned blue-green. Closer, the UFO became a turquoise-colored oval and followed her car even as she accelerated. Frightened, she pulled into a driveway and got out to find the UFO hovering fifty feet over the house. She ran inside with her child and blurted out her story. The residents stepped outside and watched the object for five minutes, until it rose, blinked, and faded to nothing. The woman's face was burned during the encounter and remained inflamed for a week.

BEAM ME DOWN, MARS

Mars Walker was a twenty-year-old University of Georgia art student who lived in an apartment near Airport Road in Athens. At 2:00 A.M. on October 20, his reading was disturbed by "a high-pitched, sirenlike sound." Glancing toward the window, he noticed a "glow like a watch dial" shimmering outside. When he opened the door, outside lights illuminated a craft that slowly descended from the sky about fifty yards away. The object was round, varying in diameter from ten to seventeen feet, and smooth-surfaced. It "had no definite color, just a vague shade of purple, like a midnight sky," he said.

After five minutes the pitch of the sound became sharper "and a thing took shape within the doughnut shape of the middle." It required another minute before the form became clearly visible. According to Walker, "It was a humanlike being standing erect," and colored "a sea green opaque, like a hologram." The most prominent aspect of the creature was its "medusa-head," composed of objects resembling tentacles that surrounded the head. Each hand had three or four fingers, but otherwise seemed human.

"The odd thing to me" Walker continued, "is how little attention it paid me, no interest in communicating with me or threatening me or any other activity, besides observing."

The scene was surreal, the creature bathed in the pale green light like "an electrical field," the student thought. Perhaps it was a hologram.

Apparently finished with its duties, the entity went back inside the craft. After a half hour, the UFO departed.

THROW THIS ONE BACK

Another physical effect on a car occurred at 11:30 P.M. on October 20 in Terrell County. A man driving to his girlfriend's house spotted flashing

106

Drawing of a Medusa-headed alien observed in October 1973 by Mars Walker, a University of Georgia art student. Appearing like a hologram, it seemed to be taking readings of our alien enviornment. (Courtesy of the Center for UFO Studies)

lights ahead, which he assumed was a police car until a beam shone on his vehicle. "Everything stopped on my car," he said. "Everything went out. It blew every fuse in the car."

A UFO hovering one hundred feet above the ground pulled the car off the pavement, then returned it to the highway. The car cranked immediately and the motorist raced for safety. "It followed me for a ways, and I could see the cornstalks blowing around underneath it, but I don't think there was anything burned," he concluded.

CLOSE ENCOUNTERS OF THE FOURTH KIND— ABDUCTION, OR HONEST OFFICER, PART TWO

During this period, Clarence Patterson was driving near Loxley when his pickup truck was "sucked" into an enormous, cigar-shaped craft. He was removed from the cab by several creatures that appeared to be robots. They conducted a physical examination, Georgia's first recorded such incident, and Patterson claimed they were able to read his mind. He blacked out and returned to consciousness to find he was careening down the highway at ninety miles an hour.

After a radio station reported a sighting south of Fitzgerald on October 24, Ralph Smith and Johnny Brown drove out to a firing range near

107

the airport, where they observed an unusual light, larger than a star, which moved around the sky. Through a telescope they saw it make a circle before disappearing. Numerous other area residents described the same event.

SEVEN FOR THE ROAD

At 9:00 P.M. the same night a number of Upson County residents, including a reporter from the *Thomaston Times*, spotted a light that flew "an erratic run southward sometimes fast, sometimes slow." It dropped below the horizon, only to reappear several minutes later. The UFO abruptly disappeared, but six more arrived over the following thirty minutes.

Georgia's last reported UFO from the dramatic 1973 campaign originated from Colquitt County on October 24. An employee of the County Extension Service was driving on GA 133 at 11:00 P.M. and was starting across the Ochlochnee River Bridge when he saw an oval UFO occupying the center of the road. He managed to stop fifty feet away, and he studied the craft in awe. The man described it as shaped like the top of a grain silo, six to seven feet high. As he watched, "lights started coming on—red, yellow, blue, and green—in that order in a clockwise motion. There was no sound at all. I couldn't see any type of door, windows, or anything other than just dull-gray metal."

When the witness grabbed for a gun under his seat, the UFO ascended and flew over his car and the tree line and disappeared.

The UFO next decided to play chicken. Half an hour later a carload of people on Sylvester Road watched the craft drop close to the pavement and head straight for them. The driver wheeled the car into a yard and doused the lights. The UFO hovered for a moment, then rose and vanished into the night.

The incredible wave of UFO sightings that inundated Georgia and spread across the country in the late summer and autumn of 1973 ranks as the greatest long-term series of UFO events in American history. Since that time there have been impressive UFO displays over various parts of the world, but never in such a wholesale manner, particularly within the United States. UFOs appear but in restricted locales. Since 1973 U.S. ufology has focused on cattle mutilations and silent, black helicopters, Roswell, Area 51, government cover-ups, and abductions. Unfortunately, the joyous days of good-humored UFO sightings have been replaced by rumors of dark secrets and sinister plots. The truth may indeed be out there, but if it is we still don't have a clue to what it is. The Wave of 1973 had absolutely no useful function, at least so far as human minds can divine.

OFFICIAL RESPONSES, EXPLANATIONS, AND MASKIROVKA

Whenever UFOs are sighted, there always seems to be someone around to attempt to debunk them. The massive sightings of 1973 provoked intense efforts to explain them, including some patently ridiculous offerings.

The initial official response to the sightings occurred when the Albany State Patrol Post alerted the Albany naval air station of the first UFO sightings at 12:40 A.M. on August 31, according to Capt. Dean Webster of the navy.

"We were unable to sight anything on radar or visually," Webster stated, beginning a familiar litany. "The naval air station had no aircraft or helicopters in the air at the time of the reported UFO sightings. Our last conventional aircraft was on deck at 10:17 P.M. Our last helicopter landed at 10:45 P.M. We had no aircraft in the air between then and 8:30 A.M. today."

A spokesman said the navy "is concerned about this and will look into it."

A spokesperson for Moody Air Force Base in Valdosta reported no aircraft in the area between 12:20 A.M. and 5:30 A.M., and nothing appeared on their radar.

Albany assistant police chief J. J. Lairsey said on September 1: "The Albany Police Department has received no direction from the U.S. Department of Defense or any other government agencies about what to do about these sightings of unidentified flying objects."

Also alerted were Eglin Air Force Base in Fort Walton Beach, Florida; Maxwell Air Force Base in Montgomery, Alabama; and Robins Air Force Base in Warner Robins, Georgia. All denied radar contacts. No planes had been sent up to investigate, there had been no aircraft in the sky to account for the sightings, and there would be no investigation. At one point a spokesman at Robins responded that they would be sending investigators to southwest Georgia, an apparently erroneous report, for it never happened and they had no teams to dispatch.

On another occasion a Robins spokesman acknowledged receiving UFO reports, but all calls were referred to the military police, "which makes all investigations of UFO reports."

"Most of the calls we've received have been from the press," stated Lt. Col. Richard Davies, information officer at Robins. "There have been two reports from police and one from a military policeman here but none from any private citizens."

A later statement from Robins explained that the air force no longer investigated UFO sightings because a twenty-one-year project never revealed any sightings that could not be explained and yielded no evidence of "extraterrestrial vehicles."

"No UFO report investigated and evaluated by the air force has ever given any indication of threat to our national security," the release stated.

The latter statement was correct, the former untrue. Project Blue Book officially declared several hundred sightings "unknown."

Colonel Douglas Embry, public information director for Georgia civil defense, said the UFO reports had been logged, but admitted, "We don't do anything with them." He knew of no "logical explanation" for the sightings and said if there was a "danger of life and property" his office would ask the governor to take steps to investigate.

Georgia's adjutant general "would oversee any joint military-civilian operations," Embry continued. "But even after all these reports, I don't know of any concerted investigation underway." He suggested that the National Weather Service might explain the events.

"One thing is, this type of situation just hasn't come up in Georgia before," Embry concluded. "We have never had any UFO sightings of this frequency before" in the fifty years he had lived in the state.

WHO'S ON FIRST?

On September 1 *Albany Herald* reporter James Sheppard bravely stepped through the looking glass and into the U.S. Government's version of Oz. His trip down the yellow brick road led him to a number of unusual encounters with denizens of the military netherworld.

Starting in the Pentagon, Sheppard contacted Maj. James A. Durham, speaking for the assistant secretary of defense for public affairs. Asked about the military's interest in the recent UFOs and involvement in an investigation, Durham responded: "The Department of Defense does not have a statement to make." He would acknowledge that the military had been informed of the sightings in southwest Georgia, and stated that they were concerned and desired for citizens to continue reporting their experiences to local police departments.

Asked why the Department of Defense had no statement, Durham replied: "I can't answer that question."

Asked if any military organization, the Defense Department, air force, army, navy, marines, or others would be investigating, Durham said: "I'm not going to be able to answer that for you."

Sheppard was nothing if not persistent. "What is the Department of Defense policy of unidentified flying objects?" he asked.

"I'll have to skip that question, too, but I will say that we are concerned about all this, and civilians should continue to report any UFO sightings to their local civilian law-enforcement agencies. Beyond that, I can't tell you anything."

Asked how long the Pentagon had been aware of the sightings, Durham said: "We have been aware of this for three days, but I can't tell you anything else." Then he added, "Maybe I should point out that the air force was involved in studies of these phenomena, but these studies were terminated about 1969, I think."

Asked to explain further about the studies, Durham concluded, "I'll try to call you back on that," but did not know when he would.

Sheppard next called the office of Adm. Thomas H. Moorer, chairman of the Joint Chiefs of Staff, who was attending a wedding. The reporter talked instead to Col. Jack Powell, described as the emergency actions officer. Powell had nothing to say on the subject and referred Sheppard to "someone else here who may be able to help you," a Lieutenant Colonel Williams, public affairs officer at the national military command center in the Pentagon. Williams came on the line.

Asked about recent UFO sightings, Williams said, "I can't talk to you about that. Our public affairs people who handle that will have to talk to you." He suggested a "Mr. Willibee," also in the Pentagon. Asked for his first name, Williams refused. Asked how to spell Willibee, the officer said he did not know. "Maybe it's spelled W-I-L-L-I-B-E-E," he suggested. Asked again for his full name, Williams stated, "I don't see why you need that." At that point, Colonel Powell jumped in and said, "If Lieutenant Colonel Williams doesn't want to give out his first name, that's his business. I don't know his first name myself. Why don't you follow Colonel Williams's suggestion and call Mr. Willibee?"

Sheppard finally reached O. G. Wiloughby, "chief of the defense news branch in the Pentagon," the gentleman said. He added that he had just spoken with Powell and Williams about the reporter's call, then concluded: "It's time for me to go off duty, and I cannot talk to you."

Pressed for an official Pentagon statement about the UFOs, he said, "Major Durham is in charge of that."

The Federal Aviation Administration in Atlanta did not receive any UFO reports from pilots, and the National Weather Service announced that weather balloons were normally launched between 8:00 P.M. and 7:00 A.M., but the lights they carried would have been too small to account for the sightings.

In contrast to the chaos of federal agencies, the Georgia State Patrol was instructed on the morning of August 31 to investigate UFO sightings.

WINKING, BLINKING, AND NOD, OR THE XYZ AFFAIR
On September 4 the astronomy department at Fernbank Science Center in DeKalb County put together a tag team to knock the wind out of the UFO sightings.

Dr. Ralph Buice led the attack. An astronomer specializing in satellite tracking, he believed many of the recent reports were simply based on satellites breaking up during reentry into the earth's atmosphere. He noted that the orbits of two satellites had decayed and plunged them back to earth in spectacular deaths. One was estimated to fall on August 28, the other on August 30.

Not only does the satellite itself reenter, but also, we were informed, debris accompanies it. NORAD, the North American Air Defense Command, tracks every manmade object ever shot into space, starting with NORAD 1 in 1957. They had tracked seven thousand individual objects, each with its own designation, and three thousand were still circling the globe in 1973.

"Only one thousand of those are satellites," Buice stated. "The other two thousand are discarded rocket stages, shroud panels, and other assorted bits of debris associated with the launch. There can be several pieces of junk for each satellite. Skylab, for example, has about thirty bits of debris associated with it." Skylab would have an uncontrolled reentry of its own several years later.

All of that "space junk" reenters over a period of several days, producing bright flashes of light, puffs of smoke, and other spectacular atmospheric events.

"Conceivably, a satellite that breaks up could deposit a cloud of ionized gas in the upper atmosphere, perhaps seventy miles above the surface of the earth, that would glow and take several hours to dissipate."

Such phenomena could produce the bright lights reported in southwest Georgia, as happened several years earlier during a test launch of a booster rocket.

"The top stage was loaded with sand to simulate the weight of a fully fueled vehicle, and when it reentered, all the sand burned up in the atmosphere and created quite a spectacular sight."

Buice did add that if "you get reports of UFOs chasing cars, landing and doing other things like that, it's obviously something else." However, "In all the years I have been looking, I have never seen anything suspicious. I would like to see something like that so I could try to determine what it is."

Enter astronomer Robert Hayward, who attempted to explain sightings of flashing red, green, and blue lights. They were planets, he proposed, specifically Venus, Mars, and Jupiter, which were brightly visible at different times during the night.

"When Venus sets in the evening, you have to look at it through several miles of the atmosphere," Hayward stated. "The atmosphere diffracts, or scatters, the light, causing you to see different colors. I talked to one woman who said she had seen an object with flashing lights on it and didn't believe it could be Venus because it wasn't round. People don't realize that Venus goes through phases just like the moon and does not always appear round viewed from earth."

Hayward also noted that UFO sightings come in spurts, because "when one person reports seeing something, a lot of other people go out and look and see things, too, which they then report. The second person to report something might not have even seen the same thing that the first person saw."

The third team member was James Buckley, a meteorologist who blamed some sightings on cirrus clouds that are at such a high altitude and so thin that at night they are invisible to ground observers, but they still scatter light. A bright satellite seen through cirrus clouds would appear to be flashing multicolored lights.

Buckley added that electrical phenomena, including ball lightning, could explain some sightings.

"These phenomena are usually associated with thunderstorms, and there was a line of thunderstorms across southern Georgia Thursday night," Buckley said. "This line was moving slowly northward and the UFO sighting reports followed the same pattern."

Hayward did not categorically deny the existence of UFOs as alien spaceships, quipping that he needed "a Martian for a class on Mars I have to teach this fall."

In September 1973 hundreds of Savannah residents observed UFOs executing a variety of maneuvers over the city. One UFO, watched by several police officers, crashed into the Atlantic Ocean off Tybee Island. Coast Guard employees at this station on Tybee also saw strange objects in the sky.

These speculations, which received widespread publicity, were accepted by many authorities and newspapers as the gospel. The *Atlanta Constitution* used the story to make an environmental and anti-UFOs editorial.

On September 7 a spokesman for NORAD, which tracks all orbital material, announced from headquarters in Colorado Springs, Colorado, that no manmade space debris had reentered the atmosphere over Georgia during the UFO sightings. This authoritative refutation received far less attention than the original, erroneous statements did, which reflects a typical pattern.

By September 8 APRO, the Aerial Phenomenon Research Organization, one of the country's most respectable UFO groups (I was a teenage member), operating out of Tucson, Arizona, had four field agents investigating the Georgia flap. Their team had interviewed witnesses from Moultrie to Augusta and many places in between.

Commenting on the space debris theory, one unidentified agent remarked: "Man (astronomer) has plenty of credentials, but in this case he seems to know less than a high school science student."

Stanton T. Friedman, a nuclear physicist from Redondo Beach, California, who left his profession in 1959 to study UFOs from a scientific standpoint, defended the good people of Georgia on September 12.

"I've talked to enough policemen in Georgia in the last two weeks to convince myself that the UFOs seen are not due to astronomical observations," Friedman said. "I also find that most astronomers know little about UFOs."

Bruce Henne, a psychology teacher at Gordon College in Barnesville and a twenty-year member of NICAP (the National Investigations Committee on Aerial Phenomenon), another highly regarded UFO investigation organization, was critical of the report labeling the Orchard Hill event the result of fallen space debris.

"A meteorite would leave a crater," he said. "So would a piece of space junk." Also, "The conclusion that the object was a meteorite might be just barely supportable if you ignore the eyewitness account. But if you take the eyewitness account into consideration as well, there is no way that object could have been a meteorite."

Sam V. Jones thought sightings around Griffin were the result of airliners approaching Hartsfield International Airport in Atlanta, circling in holding patterns and descending for landings. Their multicolored flashing lights seemed to form an image that was fixed on layers of atmospheric pollution. However, the planes had circled for many years earlier, and three decades since, without provoking UFO sightings.

After the UFO crashed into the ocean off Savannah, skeptical experts and a lack of research funds were attributed to the lack of an investigation.

The Coast Guard post on Tybee Island sent no search craft to look for the object. Their effort was confined to calling the local coast guard air station, which asked the air force base in Charleston, which blabbed about the abandoned study years earlier. In Charleston, Capt. David Duggan said the reports were logged, but he knew the air force no longer investigated these things. He suggested space debris as a cause.

At the Savannah Science Museum, director Charles Milmine had received reports, but noted there was no budget to examine the sightings closely. He said recent UFOs over Brunswick had been determined to be marsh gas, but added that the phenomenon was not likely to occur off Savannah.

Dr. E. J. McCranie, a psychiatrist on the faculty of the Medical College of Georgia in Augusta, suggested on September 10 that "misperception of reality" (a term he preferred over "mass hysteria") could account for many sightings.

"This is not an uncommon type of occurrence," Dr. McCranie said. "People get activated, alerted, and see something—a stimulus—and misinterpret it. They are looking for something and are apt to be overly apt to see it.

"There are two possibilities. One, there may be something out there and they are misperceiving a stimulus, or, two, they might actually see something when there is nothing at all. Man's brain is an interesting phenomenon, and it plays all kinds of tricks on us."

Obviously, McCranie did not believe in UFOs.

Debunking this debunker was Dr. Berthold E. Schwarz, a psychiatrist who had examined hundreds of UFO witnesses. He concluded that they were not suffering from hallucinations, seeking publicity, or psychotic. These reports are neither "conscious or unconscious fabrication," he said. He submitted that a substantial body of UFO reports had been reported by competent witnesses and investigated by competent researchers.

Several aviators suggested that weather conditions that time of year could explain some sightings, as well as swamp gas and the northern lights.

Other authorities suggested Skylab, orbiting 293 miles overhead, as the source of UFO sightings. However, NASA officials at the Marshall Space Flight Center in Huntsville, Alabama, regularly notified the public weeks in advance when the orbiting space laboratory would pass overhead. During this period Savannah newspapers published full information of an appearance by Skylab, which included exactly when and where it would be visible and the length of time it would be in sight.

Gas Bags
UFO reports from Gwinnett County on September 6 had an acceptable explanation. At 3:00 P.M. a purple and white hot-air balloon ascended from the Gwinnett County Airport near Lawrenceville with two human

passengers. Citizens across the county soon reported UFOs. People crowded around the courthouse in downtown Lawrenceville, looking and pointing into the sky. Gwinnett *Daily News* reporter Ralph Heussner took off in pursuit and stopped two miles north of town on Collins Hill Road, where the balloon was only a few hundred feet in the air. There was also a line of twelve cars that had pulled over to observe the phenomenon. Few viewers were fooled, and the tendency was to discount all sightings. As a man said: "I bet that's what all the fuss is about with these UFOs. They're probably just these balloons running at night with lights on."

In mid-October the National Weather Service launched several enormous meteorological balloons and a series of rockets that released brilliantly colored chemicals into the sky. These events were heavily publicized in advance, and only completely ignorant dolts reported them as UFOs. Of course Homer Simpsons are with us always, and these scientific tests generated plenty of sighting reports. Unfortunately, authorities and media alike used this situation to discount all UFO sightings made during the period, but by this time many reliable witnesses were reporting close encounters of the third kind, which could not be explained by weather experiments.

On October 16 the National Weather Service released two balloons, one from Montgomery, Alabama, the other from Palestine, Texas. Both were 150 feet in diameter and floated from west to east with substratospheric currents at altitudes of fifty thousand to sixty thousand feet above the earth to collect data for weather predicting. At that height, because of the earth's curvature, the devices reflected light long after the sun had fallen below the horizon as seen from the ground. The balloons were observed across much of central, north, and east Georgia.

The *Macon Telegraph* took an excellent photo of the balloon that showed instruments hanging beneath it. Thousands of middle Georgia residents spotted it about dusk. One typical report to the newspaper was of "a great big light bulb, burning brightly." Some said it changed colors from white to red and blue. Many witnesses refused to believe the "pat" balloon answer and stubbornly insisted it was a UFO. Crowds gathered in parking lots and pointed toward the sky as they speculated and argued, then swamped switchboards at police stations, newspaper offices, and radio and TV stations. The Macon Weather Service seemed remarkably incompetent, feinting ignorance of its origin but suggesting it was from a forecasting station in Texas. A spokesman did know that it was a "very large" balloon involved in a research project to take atmospheric samples.

A Warner Robins resident said the light hovered over Robins Air Force Base for a "good while" then quickly flew away. He thought it was too big for a star.

On the night of October 17, a Dublin newspaper photographer caught on film an object which was probably one of the weather balloons. The image was of a bright device floating high in the late afternoon sky that was reported by many residents. Some used telescopes to view the phenomenon closely.

The shiny object appeared just before sunset in Griffin, where it was photographed, and was clearly visible in Thomaston and Atlanta, resulting in a flood of UFO reports to police departments and the media. By this point in the massive wave of UFO sightings, citizens were easily set off by any stimuli.

As in Macon, local bureaus of the Federal Aviation Administration and National Weather Service often did not know who had launched the balloons, and the government agency responsible had failed to file a flight advisory, even though the balloons traversed heavy air traffic areas. It also seemed to be traveling at a much lower altitude than the FAA and NWS estimated.

"It was extremely bright," astronomer Hayward said. "It was reflecting quite a bit of sunlight. I could see what appeared to be an instrument package hanging under it. I also noticed that it wasn't completely filled out yet, which means it had probably not reached its maximum altitude."

At Emory University, religion professor John Fenton watched the big gas bag through a thirty-power telescope from 6:50 to 7:15 P.M. and could also see an instrument package, or a gondola, hanging beneath it.

Most of the residents of Warner Robins are either military personnel or civilian workers at Robins Air Force Base, which is central Georgia's largest employer, and they habitually watch the skies. Thousands crowded the streets on October 17, staring skyward at the spectacle, and the Warner Robins police department logged over four hundred calls reporting UFOs. All but perhaps two sightings were explained by the weather balloons, but those were substantial reports from four persons—including a law enforcement officer—who chased and were chased by mammoth aircraft. Also, for the record, those sightings occurred an hour after the weather balloons had cleared the area.

GASEOUS CLOUDS

At 7:40 and 7:50 P.M. on October 19, Eglin Air Force Base in Florida sent two sounding rockets sixty miles into the atmosphere to release glowing clouds of red, green, and yellow gases. They were used to test wind currents at an altitude too low for orbital satellites to register and too high for weather balloons. The gases, sodium and barium, were high enough to reflect sunlight after complete darkness had covered the ground. The poisonous gases were too diffused to harm anyone and moved at forty to fifty miles per hour. The glowing, multicolored clouds were visible as far north as Memphis, south to Miami, west to Corpus Christi, and east to Charleston. Authorities in hundreds of communities prepared for the inevitable UFO reports.

Because of the scheduled rocket tests, Hayward expected a significant rise in UFO sightings. In Macon, the *Telegraph*, weather service, and civil defense department received reports of blue streams high in the sky that turned green. Tens of thousands saw glowing, bright silver shapes in the sky that changed to a bluish color, then a dazzling green. I was twenty years old and stood in my front yard in Warner Robins to watch the evolution until it disappeared. The sight was spectacular.

In Athens on October 19, a homemade balloon, composed of a large laundry bag powered by candles stuck to a balsa frame, created UFO sightings. It was captured after landing at Westchester Manor Apartments. Similar contraptions had previously been discovered in the latter stages of UFO sightings in Savannah and Griffin, where Dr. Anderson, the soil scientist, observed boys launching such devices.

Columbus Ledger employees photographed a third high-altitude balloon, launched from Montgomery, at dawn of October 20, one day after residents were deluded by the atmospheric rocket tests. Most of the 150 reported UFO sightings that flooded the local police and sheriff's departments could be readily explained by the weather balloon.

The same night that Brown had his alien encounter (October 18), UFO activity resumed in the Savannah area for the first time since September. Between 8:00 and 10:00 P.M. at least twenty-five people reported UFOs around the city.

There are two points to this exercise: 1. Not all objects reported as UFOs are "unidentified." 2. Easily explained aerial phenomena cannot be used to explain all sightings.

4

Ancient Mysteries

Despite tremendous advances in archaeological techniques, the past doesn't speak—it mumbles. Even literate societies did not record all of its affairs, particularly those of lesser classes and mundane events. Prehistory leaves us with even less to work with. Controversy in archaeological circles is rampant among professionals, and when the ignorant rantings of amateurs are stirred in, some truly bizarre claims emerge. There are legitimate archaeological mysteries, and there are patently false, if not fraudulent, theories advanced. Both archaeologists and crackpots often dismiss incontrovertible evidence, and both diminish an important field of study.

I have tackled a number of archaeological mysteries in this chapter. Some survive close scrutiny, others don't, and some await additional evidence. Just don't yell at me for my conclusions, as college professors and the lunatic fringe occasionally have and no doubt will in the future.

ACROSS THE UNIVERSE

In 1963 astronomer Gerald Hawkins astounded the scientific world when he suggested that the famous English archaeological site Stonehenge had been used as an astronomical computer that could mark the spots where the sun rises at the summer and winter solstices and even predict eclipses. During the last several decades archaeologists have discovered many similar prehistoric sites in America, including three in Georgia. Fort Mountain is detailed elsewhere, but here follow the other sites.

June 21–22 marks the summer solstice, which not only signifies the official start of summer but also the longest day of the year. As the earth makes its yearly journey, the sun appears to travel very slowly across the sky, rising at a different spot on the horizon each day. In late June the sun reaches its northernmost rising point, then it will reverse its path and travel back the way it came until about December 21, the winter solstice, which is the start of winter and the shortest day of the year. This is the farthest point south that the sun reaches, and it will again reverse its path and start a return journey back toward summer.

Many prehistoric cultures recognized the astronomical significance of these events, particularly the summer solstice, and they developed a system that alerted them when these days were approaching. From one fixed land-

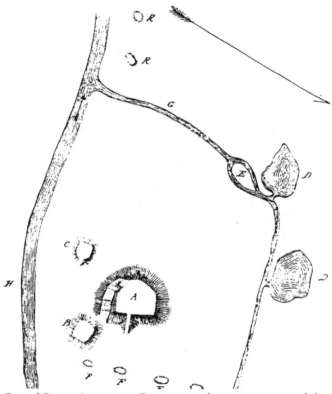

One of Georgia's great pre-European civilizations constructed the village of Etowah, dominated by Mound A and flanked by twin burial mounds from which the skeleton of a giant and exquisite artifacts have been excavated. A wet moat and palisade surrounded the community. (Charles C. Jones, Antiquities of the Southern Indians)

mark, the fore sight, the Indians located or constructed a second fixed point, called a back sight, over which the sun would rise on the solstice morning. As the solstice approached, the sun would rise closer to the back sight point.

Most Georgians are familiar with the Etowah Indian Mounds, a state park located on the outskirts of Cartersville. It dates to the Mississippian

Mound A and a burial mound at Etowah, as seen from the riverbank.

culture, which flourished between A.D. 900 and 1550. The site occupied an area of fifty-two acres along the Etowah River. At its peak, five thousand people lived at Etowah, which was a heavily fortified village. An outer moat twenty-five feet wide and fifteen feet deep surrounded the city. Inside that obstacle was a twelve-foot-tall stockade made of wooden posts. The inhabitants lived in small houses within the enclosure and grew corn, pumpkins, and beans in the rich valley soil. They fished and hunted deer and other animals to supplement their diet.

Using dirt taken from the moat and gaping borrow pits located nearby, Native Americans constructed seven mounds. The large central structure,

Ancient Americans constructed this ramp to the tallest mound in Georgia at Etowah to align with a gap in a distant mountain. On the summer solstice, people standing at the top of the ramp can watch the sun rise.

121

designated simply Mound A, is sixty-three feet tall, contains 4.3 million cubic yards of earth, and covers three acres. On the eastern edge was a clay ramp stepped with logs that led to the top of the mound.

On the summit of this mound was a large, thatch-roofed temple where religious and political leaders lived and conducted ceremonies for the dead and to ensure crop fertility. From here the chiefs exercised social and economic influence over much of what is now northern Georgia and Alabama. According to a publication from the Georgia Department of Natural Resources, the ramp is oriented to an important solar event: "On the horizon to the east lies a sharp notch in the Allatoona range of mountains," it reads. "The sun rises in that notch on the summer solstice." Someone standing at the top of the ramp and sighting along it sees the sun rise through a gap in distant Hogback Mountain.

Henry Tumlin, whose family owned and preserved the mounds for a century, was once curator of the museum located at the mounds. He acknowledged that the Department of Natural Resources has established this orientation, but he was not so certain that it was intentional.

Twenty years ago my wife Earline and I attended the solstice sunrise ceremony at Etowah. As we ate omelets in the predawn darkness at a Cartersville Waffle House, a lonely waitress asked what we were doing out at that ungodly hour.

When we described how the sun rose over Hogback Mountain on the summer solstice, the only other customer there, an elderly farmer, scoffed, "Hell," he said, "the sun rises over that mountain half the year."

Undaunted, we drove out to the mounds and found that Mr. Tumlin had opened the gate to the parking lot and gone back to bed. When we had labored to the summit of Mound A (eighty-eight steps, exactly), we were surprised to find seven other people and a very large, affectionate dog awaiting the dawn.

The dog, named Tucker, accompanied two young, bearded graduate students from the University of Tennessee. The denim-clad men had packed a tripod camera and tracking device up the mound and both instruments were trained on the gap in the distant heights.

Tucker, a beautiful but vain golden retriever, trotted among the observers demanding attention. If you stopped petting him for a moment, he would place a big paw on your leg and nuzzle your shoulder until you resumed.

Perched on the edge of the mound were three students from Berry College in Rome. They passed the time until sunrise quietly discussing how American Indians have always been portrayed as savages by movies and television shows. They considered this mound and its solar orientation as proof of the intelligence of Native Americans.

Sitting apart from the rest of us were two hippie types left over from the sixties. The man and woman both had long, flowing hair and were clad in army surplus fatigues. They sat cross-legged on the grass and burned incense. The wind kept blowing the incense out, and they struggled to keep it lit. Both chain-smoked cigarettes, which seemed inharmonious with the universe. I dubbed them Latter Day Druids.

The only things awake besides the seven of us and Tucker were cows in neighboring pastures, but they were not impressed with the sun's eternal journey across the sky.

There was a mist on the mountains, and the horizon we stared at was a dark blue. Heavy, dark clouds floated across the tree line of Hogback Mountain as rays of sunlight sparkled above through white, fluffy clouds.

The weather forecast had not been good for observing the sunrise. An hour after official daybreak the sun was still hiding, so we could not tell if it actually rose over the notch in the mountain. The disgusted graduate students packed up and left, with Tucker bounding behind, followed by the girls. As we descended the steps, the Druids were still smoking and fumbling with a lighter in yet another attempt to light their incense.

I decided that being a Druid isn't what it used to be. Undoubtedly, our ancestors on England's Salisbury Plain had even worse weather conditions to contend with three thousand years ago.

I returned ten years later and was treated to a spectacular dawn. The sun rose directly through the notch in an awe-inspiring event. Among the spectators that morning were John Burgess, an astronomer at Agnes Scott College in Decatur and the Fernbank Science Center in Atlanta. We discussed his research, and he told me that he planned to spend the next morning at Fort Mountain. He took note of an ancient stone structure atop Horseleg Mountain near Rome that I knew about and promised to check it out for astronomical alignments in the future.

A MYSTERY ALIGNMENT

Ocmulgee National Monument in Macon marks a site that has been inhabited for ten thousand years. Archaeologists estimate that around A.D. 1200 one thousand people lived in a city constructed around a number of mounds. Like Etowah, this community was also protected against hostile neighbors by a log palisade and ditch. The public area of the city, which included a large ceremonial square, was painstakingly leveled. Dirt taken from the project was used to build the mounds.

Of the seven mounds remaining today, the largest is the Great Temple Mound, which is forty feet high and was the center of the prehistoric community. The mound was covered with red clay, making it a beacon to the surrounding countryside. A large wooden temple was constructed on its summit.

When the late Dr. A. R. Kelly, professor emeritus of archaeology at the University of Georgia, began excavation of the site in 1933, he found a low heap of earth half a mile from the Great Temple Mound. Archaeologists across the country were excited to find that this had been a circular, subterranean council chamber. It was made of heavy logs covered with earth, and a long, low tunnel led inside. The floor was a raised clay platform with a large fire pit in the center. Along the wall were arrayed forty-seven seats that

Ocmulgee National Monument's council chamber is the only structure of its kind found in North America.

increased in size as they neared the center. In the middle of the chamber was a clay eagle effigy with three large seats, where important citizens sat.

Twice a year the sun rose exactly in front of the tunnel entrance. Its light spilled onto the eagle head and illuminated the esteemed person who occupied the center seat. Eight hundred years later, we can only speculate about the rituals that accompanied these sacred mornings.

Although the ceremonial lodge had been purposefully burned when the inhabitants abandoned Ocmulgee, archaeologists have reconstructed this remarkable building and were able to preserve the original floor. Today visitors crawl through the tunnel to examine the chamber exactly as it appeared long before Columbus set sail.

A second ceremonial chamber discovered seven miles south of Macon at Browns Mount (see "Mystery of the Stone Mounds") has apparently not been examined for astronomical alignments.

A nonastronomical mystery is found between Ocmulgee and Browns Mount at the Lamar Mounds, a successor to Ocmulgee and preserved as part of the national park. Unfortunately, the site is so isolated in the river swamps that it has never been developed. Featured at Lamar are two temple mounds two hundred yards from each other. Each is twenty feet high and one hundred feet wide. Access to one of the mounds, designated "B," is not via the traditional ramp of clay or log stairs but a spiral path running counterclockwise from the ground to its summit.

THE STONE MOUND BUILDERS

As every visitor to Rock Eagle knows, there were once prehistoric inhabitants in Georgia who built massive structures with stone. These people are the oldest known mound builders in North America. Dr. Kelly believed the culture existed five thousand years ago.

ROCK EAGLE

The most famous stone mound in America is located on the grounds of a 4-H camp near Eatonton. To construct the Rock Eagle, Indians ingeniously piled tons of loose quartz rock, carried from a considerable distance, to form the shape of a giant eagle with wings spread. The bird has a wingspan of 120 feet, and the body, built to a height of ten feet above the ground, is thirty-five feet wide and sixty feet long. The eagle is so massive that it can only be appreciated from above. A three-story tower has been built overlooking the effigy for just that purpose.

The Rock Eagle is always open to the public. A beautiful walkway leads from a parking area to the effigy, which is protected by a high fence. Stroll around the grand mound to view it from every angle, then climb the stone tower and pause at each level to view the eagle as its builders intended for the gods.

Georgia Power owns the land at Lawrence Shoals Recreation Area on which a second, similar mound is located along the Oconee River, about ten miles from the first eagle. The land was purchased for the development of Lake Oconee, but ten acres around the effigy was donated to the Georgia Board of Regents. In 1990 Georgia Power, the University of Georgia, the Putnam County Commission, the Oconee Regional Planning and Development Office, and the Georgia Department of Natural Resources joined forces to preserve the artifact. For the moment archaeologists have decided not to restore the mound, which remains in a dilapidated state due to the ravages of treasure hunters over the past 150 years, plus road construction and vandals. A stout chain-link fence surrounds it. Believed to be a hawk, the only way to appreciate this mound is to study sketches made in 1877 by Dr. Charles Colcock Jones, an early Georgia historian-archaeologist who studied the mound when it was still relatively intact.

Like Rock Eagle, the Rock Hawk lies on its back, head turned to the east and wings spread wide. It is located on the highest elevation in the vicinity and was constructed entirely with white quartzite stones also transported to the site from a distance. A single person could have handled most of the stones, but the larger ones would have required the concerted effort of two to three individuals. Cracks between the large stones were filled with small fragments of quartz. Rock Hawk has two unique features missing at Rock Eagle. First is a low stone wall, which was twelve to eighteen inches in height, surrounding the effigy. Also, the hawk has a narrow bifurcated tail, which marks it as a hawk. Rock Eagle has a long, wide, unsplit tail. Rock Hawk is 132 feet wide, while the eagle measures 120 feet. Both are 102 feet from head to tail, but the body width of the hawk is seventy-six feet, the eagle only thirty-three feet. The hawk has a thicker body but shorter wings.

Excavations by University of Georgia archaeologists at both sites in 1935 and 1954 revealed no artifacts. Those experts located no village site or quartz rock within a twenty-mile radius of the mounds. Dr. Kelly believed Native Americans traveled from a wide area to observe cultural ceremonies at the sites. Birds were often totems for Indians, and the eagle was often considered a creature of prophecy. Several pottery and stone effigy pipes shaped like eagles have been found in the area.

Scientists also found other stone mound sites in the area. Two miles northwest of Rock Hawk they discovered a large mound on top of a ridge and many smaller mounds. Eight miles from Eatonton was a stone mound several feet high which measured sixty by twenty feet, and thirteen adjacent mounds were eight feet in diameter at the base and four to seven feet in height.

The largest prehistoric stone mound in Georgia and possibly a third immense bird effigy were found on a hilltop near Juliette in Monroe County, not far from Rock Eagle. This heap was originally forty feet high, composed of quartz stones ranging in size from pebbles to boulders. Whoever constructed it used a huge, natural outcropping of stone as a base on which to build. A number of small stone rings surrounded the primary body.

Story time, boys and girls. In 1974 Georgia Power moved to purchase the land through condemnation. Being in college and bored, I drove up one day and introduced myself to the Williams family, who were naturally upset at the legal seizure of their land.

Mrs. Williams took me on a comprehensive tour of the wooded property. Atop one hilltop was a set of defensive fortifications dating back to

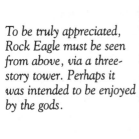

To be truly appreciated, Rock Eagle must be seen from above, via a three-story tower. Perhaps it was intended to be enjoyed by the gods.

the Civil War. A hill opposite contained probably the largest stone mound in America. I returned later in the day when a news crew from WMAZ-TV in Macon taped a story on the controversy.

I managed to make myself part of the story. Apparently, I spoke much too confidently, because on the subsequent televised report I was identified as an archaeology professor at Georgia Southwestern College in Americus—the institution and I both appreciated the compliment—Southwestern had yet to initiate its archaeology program and I was a semiprofessional undergraduate. Perhaps it was my distinguished gray hair (dating back to age fifteen) which fooled station personnel.

Note to my parents: You always wondered what the hell I did with my time in college. Now you know. At least part of it.

On this twelve-thousand-acre property near Juliette (of *Fried Green Tomatoes* fame), Georgia Power established massive Plant Scherer, a coal-fired, electricity-generating facility. In 1977–1978 the University of Georgia conducted extensive archaeological surveys there, identifying 377 prehistoric and historic sites, including twenty-two sites containing stone mounds. Each of those sites contained from one to more than eighty individual mounds measuring from one to fifteen meters in diameter.

The largest prehistoric site was the Williams Mound. Constructed of large quartz stones on Berry Creek, it was ten meters in diameter and two meters high, surrounded by eighty-one smaller stone mounds. Its construction was dated to between 2000 B.C. and A.D. 500. When I visited the site an intramural war was being fought by several archaeologists from the state and the University of Georgia. Unfortunately, the mound was declared nonprehistoric. The popular theory was that early American farmers had piled the stones to clear fields—a clearly preposterous position—and the land was seized. I met Dr. Kelly at Macon College not long before he died and the professor strenuously disagreed with his colleagues. He was firmly convinced that the site was prehistoric. On a color aerial photograph of the site the white stone mound stood out like a beacon. Unfortunately, this stunning artifact did not survive the development of the power plant.

FORT MOUNTAIN

One of our most popular archaeological mysteries are crumbling stone enclosures found scattered across the state, from middle Georgia through the mountains. The best-known example is Fort Mountain, located atop a windswept peak in the rugged Cohutta Mountains of Murray County. This enigma is also the only preserved example of a stone fort in Georgia, and the sole one which can be reached with any degree of ease.

The fort from which this elevation takes its name is an 885-foot-long wall that meanders across the ragged, 2,800-foot-high summit. The wall is twelve feet thick at the base but only two to three feet in height. Some experts believe the wall was once seven feet high, or perhaps topped by a wooden palisade. At each end of the wall is a large, square pit. Twenty-nine inexplicable holes, often called foxholes, appear at irregular, but usually thirty-foot intervals. The pits average three feet in depth.

The thousands of rocks that compose the wall range in size from small stones to rocks that would require several strong men to transport. Enormous natural boulders peaking above the surface of the slopes were incorporated into the work. The wall is composed entirely of granite rocks gathered from the mountain and piled loosely, similar to the Rock Eagle. The enclosure commands the practical route to the northern summit, which is 250 feet higher than the remainder of the peak and encloses eight acres of reasonable level land. The wall zigzags irregularly across the mountain's northern face, the angles and length of each varying considerably.

CHARIOTS OF THE INDIANS

The mysterious wall at Fort Mountain has been the object of much speculation. Various theories claim Hernando de Soto built it for protection against the Indians during his fifteenth-century wanderings across the southeast in search of gold, but he was only in the region for several days. Other ideas: Phoenician explorers two thousand years ago; Vikings, who reached our northern shores in the twelfth and thirteenth centuries; Madoc, a Welsh prince who supposedly visited in 1170; and from Cherokee legend, a "moon-eye" group of albinos, perhaps descendants of ancient European seafarers. The latter, quite popular theory, comes from *Myths of the Cherokee*, a 1900 publication written by ethnologist James A. Mooney, who compiled Indian tales. One Cherokee legend held that when they arrived in Georgia they discovered a race of blond-haired, blue-eyed, white-skinned people who lived by night and shunned the daylight, perhaps because they were albinos. Many years were required for the Cherokee to wipe out and seize the territory of this fierce, savage race. According to these carefully preserved legends, Fort Mountain was one of their primary defensive positions.

Perhaps the Cherokee constructed it to defend against the Creek Indians to the south, and the pits provided protection for sentries. The silliest proposal has the site a honeymoon haven for newly married aboriginal lovers.

BLINDED BY THE LIGHT

The anti-Indian theories reflect racist views that existed through the middle of the twentieth century that Native Americans did not have the ability or motivation to handle such projects. A superintendent at Fort Mountain acknowledged that "it was fashionable—to doubt the Indians had enough engineering ability. But the Indians were no dummies."

Archaeological evidence can neither prove nor disprove any of the fanciful ideas regarding the identity or purpose of the builders. The purpose of the wall has generally been assumed to be defensive, an idea disregarded by modern archaeologists. The defenders would have their backs against a cliff and lacked a water and food supply. Fort builders are not supposed to be stupid. Archaeologists also cite a complete lack of artifacts and human remains. No implements have ever been excavated from the fort or surrounding area—no arrowheads, flint chips, refuse, or a single shard of pottery. The area is absolutely barren of artifacts, except of course the wall. This fact has led professionals to hypothesize that the wall enclosed a sacred, religious area. After each ceremony the grounds would be cleansed of all evidence of human intrusion. Native Americans may have conducted religious rites here, or perhaps priests received divine revelations from their deities. Males might have been initiated into manhood.

The recent discipline of archaeoastronomy has lent another twist to the mystery. Built on a northeastern axis, the wall could have been used to mark the rising of the sun at one end of the wall, and its setting at the other end. This artifact could have been used to mark solar solstices, worship the sun or moon, and function as a calendar to guide the planting and harvesting of crops. Another proposal is that the wall was a map of the region controlled by an ancient Native American nation.

"Religion, ceremony, the sun, and seasons were all tied together in Indian culture," says astronomer John Burgess. His extensive research at Fort Mountain revealed that "the northeast end of the wall lines up precisely with sunrise at the summer solstice, June 21–22."

Burgess points out that the "wall was built by an unidentified society for an undetermined reason at an unknown date." His theory "is that these agriculturally oriented Indians built the wall so they could determine when to plant and harvest their crops. Other sections of the wall could have been used as sight lines to the rising sun and moon—a calendar device similar to those found in many ancient societies. A shaman with knowledge of the seasons would have had considerable standing in the tribe."

However, the Cherokee arrived too late to have knowledge of the wall's original purpose. "They have a tribal legend that their ancestors displaced a race of moon-eyed people," Burgess explained. "In the Cherokee language, *moon-eyed* could also be translated as moon watching. If those early Indians were interested in astronomy, they may well have built the wall."

The term *moon-eyed* might also relate to their practice of keeping track of the movements of the moon and sun through their stone calendar.

In 1985 Burgess was present at Fort Mountain on the summer solstice in an attempt to observe the sunrise, but thick forest obstructed the sight line. Another problem is that after two thousand years the stones of the wall have shifted and fallen, widening the structure to such an extent that accurate measurements of the wall's alignments are now difficult. In 1990 Burgess convinced the U.S. Forestry Service to survey the site with a hand-held satellite receiver connected to a computer that triangulated signals from three different satellites to establish the exact position of the wall. Unfortunately, the system was only accurate to within ten feet, which is not precise enough to prove astronomical alignments.

"All I've been able to do so far is get a rough survey of the wall and look at the rough alignment of certain features," Burgess stated. "It does appear that there's a heavy clustering of features toward the northeast, toward the point of sunrise at summer solstice."

A major element in one Cherokee myth about a giant serpent named Uktena featured a bright, magical gem embedded in its head—perhaps the sun rising each year at the end of this calendric Sun Serpent. The serpent slayer also received an ability to locate game, perhaps a corruption of a major purpose of the device. Knowledge of the seasons could guide planting, harvesting, and the migration of animals.

Moon Struck

A number of Native American cultures observed and could correctly predict the phases and cycles of the moon, which inspired festivals and other ceremonies. The angle of the earth's orbit around the sun and the moon's circuit around the earth shifts moonrise over a nineteen-year period by up to twelve degrees. Because of this complicated cycle, ancient astronomers had to mark those alignments in some manner. Burgess suggests several pits near the center of the wall might have marked moonrise at different points during the year.

There may be truth in the legend that the mythical Uktena serpent fell from the sky, broke into pieces atop the mountain, and fossilized. Billy Townsend, a historian with the Georgia Department of Natural Resources, noted that the snake is "a recurring motif in Cherokee religion." Further, "when you see an aerial view of the wall, it could be a feathered serpent stretched across the mountain."

Tied into that theme are two documented "sun serpents" in the Midwest, one in Ohio, the other in Kentucky. Both are connected with a prehistoric culture known as Hopewell, and both are aligned with the sunrise at the summer solstice.

Another startling hypothesis is that the contours of the wall were a model of the surrounding mountains. "If you walk along the wall and look away from the crest of the mountain," Townsend said, "the dips and turns in the wall seem to correspond with the skyline, almost as if the wall were some kind of shadow projection." However, he quickly adds a disclaimer, noting that he had "no idea how accurate that correspondence is or what its significance may be."

Charles Faulkner, a professor at the University of Tennessee who has studied many of the South's mysterious prehistoric stone structures, suggested that historic treasure hunters or the growth of large trees created the pits. However, their near regularity and similarity tends to discount the idea. Until the site is excavated, Faulkner concluded, it "is a site we professionals can only scratch our heads about." A singular aspect of Fort Mountain that distinguishes it from similar artifacts is "the size of the rocks used in its construction."

Atlanta office supply magnate Evan Allen grew up in nearby Dalton, where as a schoolboy his teacher, Confederate general Byron Thomas, spun fanciful tales of the mysterious wall. In 1926 Allen fulfilled a lifelong dream when he purchased Fort Mountain from a bankrupt family. At that time much damage had been caused to the wall by treasure hunters, who threw rocks from the construction in search of a mythical treasure. He donated 119 acres of the property to the state of Georgia in 1934 with the stipulation that it be used as a state park. One of the most popular state parks, Fort Mountain is known for its tranquillity and beautiful surroundings. Trails lead visitors to the stone wall and scenic overlooks with panoramic views of the surrounding countryside.

In *The Haunted South*, Nancy Roberts tells the story of the Willard family, husband and wife Frank and Meg, and their precocious seven-year-old daughter Sarah. While they slept in a friend's cabin on Fort Mountain one night, Sarah heard music that escaped detection by her parents. She upset her father the following morning by asking if people can die and "come back and play the music they used to play?"

THEY WENT TO THE LIGHT

The family spent the following night in sleeping bags near the stone wall. As the witching hour approached, Sarah awoke to the sound of distant, muffled drumming. She started in the direction of the music and was delighted to see fireflies, but then the girl realized the lights were a line of torches being carried through the forest toward the wall.

Then a huge, round, incandescent yellow-white light appeared at the eastern end of the wall. It was the brightest moon she had ever seen and it illuminated the figures carrying the torches. They wore clothes made from animal skins and had white skin and blue eyes, presumably Madoc's mad band.

They trod in step up the wall toward the light, their arms raised in supplication. Sarah ran forward to speak to them, but she fell on the rocks. Looking up, the last figures, drawn irresistibly to the moon, vanished, the drums ending their beat at the same instant.

The experience might have been a dream, except for the bruises, scratches, and dried blood she found on her hands and knees the following morning.

A number of similar "forts" were once found all across Georgia. East of Atlanta is the famed Stone Mountain. Its two thousand feet of abrupt prominence has become a well-known tourist attraction and monument to the Confederacy, but few visitors realize that in antiquity a five-foot wall of loose granite boulders completely encircled its summit. There was only one opening in the barrier, just large enough for one person at a time to squeeze through. Most of the wall was removed for safety when construction began on the Confederate memorial in 1923, but segments can still be seen on the mountain. One writer, Elizabeth Austin Ford, claimed that a second stone wall once surrounded the base of the mountain, apparently thought sacred to some ancient society.

Other stone forts are not readily accessible to the public. On the crest of the tallest peak in the Pine Mountain range, appropriately called Indian Mountain, are two concentric circles constructed of stone. The outer ring is fifty feet in diameter. The figures were formed by carefully piling stones, each six to ten inches in diameter, until the walls were an average of three feet in height.

In neighboring Talbot County is a wall of sizable stones, tumbled apart in places, located halfway up a ridge above the Tigner-Morris-Callier House, located off Po Biddy Road near Collinsworth Church.

Habersham County has two of these curious artifacts. On Alex Mountain is a stone "fort" that has the same type "foxholes" as Fort Mountain. A broad oval in shape, it has a diameter of 107 feet and stretches for ninety-two feet from east to west. My wife, Earline, and I have climbed the steep slope to visit it. We have also seen another circular stone wall in Habersham that has a wonderful Cherokee legend attached to it.

Along an old trading path that led from South Carolina to the old Cherokee Nation, near the head of the Tugalo River, is a "noted circular depression," reported James Mooney in *Myths of the Cherokee*. The stone wall forms a circle roughly one hundred feet in diameter, which Mooney thought was roughly the size of a Cherokee council house, and waist high.

"Inside it was always clear as though swept by unknown hands," Mooney wrote. "Passing traders would throw logs and rocks into it, but would always on their return find them thrown far out from the hole. The Indians said it was a *Nunnehi* (a supernatural race) townhouse, and never to go near the place or even to talk about it."

Eventually, the Nunnehi tired of cleaning up after the white man. After traders threw logs into the hole on one occasion, the trash was allowed to remain. The Cherokee believed "that the Nunnehi, annoyed by the presence of the white men—abandoned their townhouse forever."

Twenty years ago the property, near Soquee on the river of the same name, not far from Batesville, was owned by a gracious retired elementary school teacher who had learned every secret the good people of Habersham County thought was safely hidden away (children tell tales to teachers). The elderly woman energetically led us up the ridge to see the well-preserved work.

In 1881 the Smithsonian Institution published the first scientific examination of the Etowah Mounds, conducted by Charles Whittlesey. He also surveyed Ladd Mountain, which he called "a rock hill" two and a half miles to the northwest. There he found an irregular oval, with diameters of 220 and 200 feet, composed of "loose unhewn stones." Six openings, ranging from ten to sixty feet in length, pierced the wall at irregular intervals. He described the appearance of the artifact as "a heavy stone fence which has fallen down." He found "nothing in this structure suggestive of a fort," particularly the gates, which were too many and too wide to be defended. He imagined "imposing public processions and displays" attended by throngs of people. The mound was dismantled for road-building material.

Near the railroad crossing of Petit's Creek, half a mile from the fort, Whittlesey studied a great cone-shaped stone mound eighteen feet in height and 160 feet in circumference. Like the Williams Mound in central Georgia, it was surrounded by smaller piles of stone. By 1880 the mound had been considerably damaged by treasure and relic seekers, who had cratered the center of the cairn almost to ground level. Known as the Shaw

Mound, excavations revealed one burial accompanied by several large sheets of mica, a trapezoidal copper breastplate, and two greenstone celts, establishing a cultural relationship with Copena, the Southern cousin of the Midwest's Hopewell Culture, centered in Ohio.

A different type of wall was discovered recently in Bartow County between U.S. 411 and the Etowah River. This wall, five feet high and thirty inches wide, was built of closely laid stones without mortar. A few hundred yards away are thirty stone mounds, knee high and five feet in diameter, made of the same type stones as the wall. Unlike the other stone walls in the region, which conform to the contour of a slope, this one extends vertically up and down the ridge.

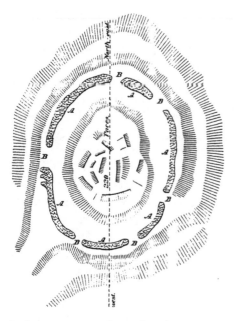

Prehistoric stone enclosure found in Bartow County near a giant stone mound. Both have been destroyed. (Charles C. Jones, Antiquities of the Southern Indians)

On Rich Mountain in southwestern Pickens County are more than ninety unexplained stone mounds—some intact, others gutted by looters. The mounds could be described as altars, stacks of carefully chosen stones arranged on a north-south axis. On top of nearby Oakey Mountain and an unnamed ridge are huge stone walls similar to those at Fort Mountain. Around Padgett Falls are a number of L-shaped rock piles, usually found in groups of three.

Another "fort" is found at the summit of Horseleg Mountain near Rome. A shorter stone wall atop Sand Mountain in Catoosa County has six accompanying stone cairns. It is not an enclosure and was built between two cliffs.

One "fort" is unique for its location, not in north or west Georgia, but in the central portion of the state. Browns Mount, near the Ocmulgee Indian Mounds, is located seven miles south of Macon on a unique elevated point that contains unusual forms of plant life. Early settlers found an enclosure, encompassing about sixty acres, around the summit. It followed the contour of the hill, at times only twenty yards from the edge. The wall, built of boulders, stones, and earth, was four feet high and five feet wide, bordered by an interior and exterior ditch, the former ten feet wide and four feet deep, the latter three feet wide and three feet deep. The excavated earth was incorporated into the wall. Within the enclosure were two small earthen mounds and a circular depression forty feet in diameter. Excavation determined it to be a second council chamber, a near twin of the restored one at Ocmulgee. The builders were Mississippian and recent compared to the stone enclosures further north, which probably are a thousand years older and related to Hopewell. Browns Mount, once a popular place for dances and other social gatherings, has been protected as a natural area. The prehistoric features are gone, but the unique fauna and flora remain.

In the late 1970s I was researching Hopewell and Adena culture mound sites in the Midwest when I came across a collection of archaeological essays published as *Hopewell Archaeology, the Chillicothe Conference,* a collection of articles by experts in the field. I was astounded when I read a short piece by Dr. A. R. Kelly. He described a vast set of stone mounds that formed a huge serpent effigy winding along a ridge in Gwinnett County, at that time a relatively sleepy area east of Atlanta. Checking a Gwinnett County history book, it mentioned an "Indian cemetery," a circular wall of white flint rock enclosing graves near Luxomni.

I wrote Larry Meier, for seventeen years the Cobb County archaeologist, who was handling the investigation. He seemed positively shocked that a layperson had stumbled upon this closely guarded secret. To his credit, Meier gave me substantial information that I could not have developed elsewhere, and he asked that I not publicize the site until it was protected. It's been twenty years and the stone mounds of Gwinnett County have been a hotly debated topic for ten years, so I now relate the story.

ROCKING IN GWINNETT

Plans for a sprawling community near Dacula were announced in December 1989. The complex, projected to occupy 1,158 acres, would have consisted of nineteen hundred houses, office buildings, an eighteen-hole golf course, a sewage treatment plant, and commercial buildings. The announcement led Native American activists to hold a fifty-day "camp-in" through the winter. They and local residents filed suit to halt development of the site. Why were they so upset?

Noted archaeologist Patrick Garrow, hired a year earlier by the Gwinnett Convention and Visitors Bureau to conduct an archaeological survey of the land, had located two hundred ancient stone mounds. He described the site as "highly significant," although somewhat disturbed by looters and loggers, and thought the mounds dated back two thousand years. The president of the Gwinnett County Historical Society called it a "phenomenal site" and "a major find."

135

The mounds are located on a narrow strip of steep, rocky ledge along the banks of the Apalachee River, from Gwinnett to Barrow County. Each flat-topped mound was four to five feet in height, a round structure composed of carefully stacked, three-cornered, flat rocks wedged in tightly to a diameter of four feet. The river is an important drainage, with the water on one side of the divide draining into the Atlantic Ocean and the other side flowing into the Gulf of Mexico. Garrow, while admitting it was a guess, stated, "I think it was a complex for burying the dead and a ceremonial complex." An absence of ordinary artifacts indicated that those responsible for the mounds lived in villages located elsewhere, probably downstream.

During the camp-in, one Native American activist, Michael Haney, a Seminole from Oklahoma, reported feeling the presence of his ancestors. "I feel like I'm home," Haney said. "I can hear the wind and imagine my ancestors. I close my eyes and hear village life and see the dances."

Over the next decade developers would retreat for a while, only to rally with revised developments, which always seemed to lead to the discovery of hundreds of additional mounds. "There may be thousands of them," Garrow said at one point.

Each entrepreneurial foray drew protests and court battles by groups of local citizens and an array of Native American groups such as Guardians of the Planet, Inc. and Preservation of Native American Indian Sites (ProNas). A sticking point was whether burials lay in or beneath the mounds. If burials were present, state law required special permits to allow development. Without burials, contractors were allowed carte blanche to bulldoze precious two-thousand-year-old archaeological sites.

Problem number one: After two thousand years in Georgia's moist, humid climate, survival of remains becomes doubtful. Problem number two: The absence of burials does not prove that a site was not considered sacred. The careful removal of all human traces besides the mounds indicates a reverential devotion to a holy place. Problem number three: Native American groups opposed *all* excavation, even by professional archaeologists, as sacrilege (would we allow JFK's remains to be removed from Arlington for study?). Problem number four: Developers and their tame archaeologists usually argued that American farmers formed the stone piles to clear fields or gather stones for dams, chimneys, and other projects.

Locals wanted the area protected as a county, state, or national park, while developers saw prime land for development. The county seemed to favor growth, but followed state regulations concerning grave sites. The problem for the state was complex rules regulating disturbing or moving human remains. In this case Georgia determined that the decision would be left to local governments.

A Gwinnett County superior court judge ruled that the county had to decide if graves were on the properties to be developed. The county defaulted on their responsibility, claiming that state law did not tell them how to determine the existence of graves. "Everyone is passing the buck," a Native American correctly observed.

The suggestion was raised that after two thousand years, the Native Americans who turned up to protest and litigate had little if any cultural connections to the builders of the stone mounds. Can the modern English claim a spiritual connection with the Celts? That did not bother the activists. Regardless of whether the "graves are five or one thousand years old," one announced, "spiritual life is there—do not disturb the monument or—you disrupt the spiritual world."

After an archaeologist hired by developers declared the mounds to have been formed by farmers over the past 150 years, Garrow retorted that his logic was "faulty" and the report "an excuse to allow the destruction of the mounds." He doubted farmers would litter their land with hundreds of small mounds. A professor emeritus in geology at the University of Georgia also stated that the rock, amphibolite, broke easily and made poor building material.

The resultant anarchy allowed developers to destroy a number of mounds in 1995, an incident that sent Garrow "ballistic."

By 1998 a private group, the Trust for Public Land, acquired more than one hundred acres for preservation, and there was hope for hundreds of other acres. Plans are to preserve the mounds, with proper interpretation, and develop other areas as ball fields and playgrounds. But the controversy rages on in a county that was the nation's fastest growing county for nearly a decade.

In Cobb County, John Cissell, superintendent of Kennesaw Mountain Battlefield Park, announced in April 1993 that hundreds of mysterious rock cairns had been found in remote areas of the park, aligned perfectly up the sides of ridges. They were dated A.D. 900 to 1000.

A striking feature of most of the stone mounds found in Georgia is the great care taken in their construction. Two to three thousand years of age, few have toppled without outside force. They were built without mortar on flat stone bases with stones specially selected. The dry stone constructions are found by the thousands, but all were painstakingly pieced together with flat, triangular stones.

Stone mounds, singular and in large groups, are distributed across the state above the fall line. There were once many stone cairns located at passes between high peaks along well-traveled trails in the mountains. There is a worldwide tradition that travelers must contribute a stone to such mounds to ensure safe passage over treacherous heights. Many cairns were six feet in height and diameter, and all were composed of loosely piled stones.

The most famous Georgia stone mound is Trahlyta's Grave. The single stone mound at a highway junction north of Dahlonega marks the traditional grave of Trahlyta, an ancient Cherokee princess who remained young by bathing in the water of a secret spring. When kidnapped from her home by a suitor, Trahlyta quickly withered and died of old age. She was buried there under a stone cairn, and pass-

This stone mound covers the grave of Trahlyta, a Cherokee princess who remained young by drinking the water of a magical spring. She rapidly aged and died when kidnapped by a suitor and taken away from the spring.

ing Indians added more rocks. There is an alleged curse on anyone who would desecrate her grave. According to legend, when the highway was built, her cairn was targeted for demolition because it obstructed the intersection. After several tractors wrecked and workmen were injured near the stone mound, the highway department decided to build around it. True or not, the mound stands in the center of the intersection of U.S. 19–GA 9 and GA 60.

Another easily visited stone mound site is at the State Botanical Gardens, operated by the University of Georgia on 313 acres along the Oconee River two miles south of Athens, where nature trails explore local flora and fauna. A short loop off the Orange Trail leads to a two-acre site, where at least thirty conical stone cairns, each three feet high and ten feet in diameter, are located.

Skilled hikers may ascend Chimney Mountain, northwest of Anna Ruby Falls just northeast of the intersection of GA 356 and GA 197, where three hollow rock cairns, each four feet high, can be seen.

A significant archaeological site is located on the western slope of Lookout Mountain near Lookout Creek in Dade County, the extreme northwestern corner of the state a few miles from Trenton. The Tunacunhee Mounds consist of three limestone mounds covered with earth and four small mounds of limestone that covered thirty burials interred with beautiful, elaborate works of art. Artifacts included panpipes, which were elaborate musical instruments made of copper plated with silver, copper earspools, rectangular copper plates and gorgets, and drilled bear teeth. Dated 1000 B.C.–A.D. 1000, the remains were part of the Copena Culture.

Also located in Dade County is Bone Cave, where more than one hundred burials were discovered, a rare find in Georgia.

Near U.S. 278–GA 12 at Robinson in Taliaferro County, near the headwaters of the Ogeechee River, is a high hilltop crowned by three enormous mounds comprised of white stones and surrounded by numerous smaller rock cairns. Archaeologists assume they are burial or ceremonial in nature. A historical marker that once stood along the highway suggested they were the works of the Yuchi, known as "Children of the Sun," who were unlike the historic Creek and Cherokee Indians. More about the Yuchi later. My wife and I traveled to Robinson a number of years ago and spoke with local residents who had visited the mounds many times. Our attempt to see the mounds personally was thwarted by the crackle of firearms. It was opening day of deer season and sounded like the soundtrack to *Platoon*.

Atop Big Mountain, six miles east of Lexington in Oglethorpe County, is a large circular pile of stones carefully fitted together, with an opening in the center. Local lore maintains that it is the grave of an Indian chief.

In the center of a plateau along Little Tennessee Valley in Rabun County are piles of stones thought by locals to mark the graves of warriors killed in a conflict with Americans during the Revolutionary War.

Near the mouth of Reed Creek, at what was Hatton's Ford in Hart County, a ridge that runs southwest across the county accommodates numerous groups of stone mounds similar to others found in the state. Known in the area as Indian cemeteries, some have been destroyed, while others remain intact.

In southeastern Paulding County is an earthen mound twelve feet high, 120 feet long, and fifty-five feet wide. Rocks are plotted along the site, including some that appear to be in a row.

WRIT ON ROCKS: GEORGIA B.C.

Columbus Day is a time to celebrate all the explorers who chanced upon the New World. It is also an occasion to argue about who was the first to discover America. Columbus certainly was not, and evidence has been presented that he was preceded by the Vikings, Welsh, Chinese, Jews, Celts, Phoenicians, and many other cultures from ancient world history. This was a topic of great interest in the 1970s, and since that time considerable new evidence has come to light regarding ancient explorations in Georgia.

PAX ROMA

I teach economics, and the definition of money is whatever people will generally accept in exchange for goods and services. Georgia's ancient visitors doubtless brought the coins of their realms, and we have found them.

Minna Arenowitch found this Roman coin in a Columbus garden in 1945. Portrayed is Antoninus Pius, who governed the Roman Empire in the second century A.D. (Courtesy of the Mahan Collection, Simon Schwob Memorial Library, Columbus State University)

The first evidence of pre-Columbian contact with America came from a number of Roman coins found in widely scattered parts of the country. In the 1930s two boys exploring a cave on the Coosa River near Gadsden, Alabama, found a cache of Roman pottery and ceramic lamps. While digging in her garden in 1945, a coin was found by Minna Arenowitch in Columbus. Dated to A.D. 138–161, it featured the figure of Antoninus Pius.

The next coin appeared directly across the Chattahoochee River from Columbus in Phoenix City, Alabama, where in 1955 a small boy noticed a coin in a field while searching for arrowheads at Coweta Falls, along the Chattahoochee River. He took the coin to a store and was given fifteen cents' worth of candy for it. The grocer was intrigued by the unfamiliar artifact and gave it to Preston E. Blackwell, a professor of history at the Columbus Center of the University of Georgia, presumably the predecessor of Columbus College (yeah, I know we made every post high school in the state a "university" a few years back, but that doesn't make them real universities). Blackwell sent enlarged photos of the artifact to the Fogg Art Museum in Boston.

The obverse side identified the coin as dating to 490 B.C., its origin Syracuse, located on Sicily. Unfortunately, Blackwell kept the coin in his wallet, and when he was hospitalized for a stroke it disappeared.

After Columbus city workers scraped five inches of earth off Third Avenue, three hundred yards from the Chattahoochee between Fifth and Sixth streets, John Carroll took his metal detector on a search for artifacts. A metallic object was signaled, and Carroll found a coin at a depth of eight inches. He sold it to Michael Smith, although neither could identify the coin. Carroll had known the late Dr. Joseph Mahan, of the Columbus Museum, since childhood, so the coin was brought to his attention. Mahan's distinguished career included being a teacher at the University of Georgia; director of research and education at the Columbus Museum (where he also served as curator); director of restoration at Westville, a recreated early-nineteenth-century village in southwestern Georgia; and a famed archaeologist and ethnologist.

The coin has a hole drilled through the top, with four dolphins swimming around the profile of a nymph wearing a pearl necklace on the obverse. The reverse has a horse head, a fallen date palm with five roots, and four marks that represent three Punic letters. The horse head was a symbol for Carthage and the palm stands for the word "Phoenicia." Phoenicians established the city of Carthage in North Africa.

That coin and seven other identical coins found in Alabama, Arkansas, Oklahoma, Nebraska, Kansas, Pennsylvania, and Connecticut were made in 146 B.C., during the Third Punic War. The seven coins came from the same die, which proves that a large number of Old Worlders were doing considerable business in ancient America, including Georgia. There are doubtless many other coins undiscovered or unidentified.

This Georgia connection is not isolated. There are thousands of pieces of evidence that ancient America was in regular communication with Europe, Asia, and Africa, and additional coins, engravings, sculptures, and other artifacts are uncovered every year.

THE METCALF STONE

Manfred Metcalf, a civilian worker at Fort Benning, was an artist, amateur archaeologist, and collector of Indian artifacts. His father was an army sergeant who retired in Columbus, and Manfred and his brother John grew up roaming the vast expanse of the military reservation, one of the largest in the country. They hunted and collected artifacts, turning over important pieces to the Columbus Museum. Much of Fort Benning consists of overgrown and forgotten farmland and buildings purchased in the 1930s when the facility was expanded to accommodate modern, large-scale military training. Huge segments of the training base are live firing zones, obviously dangerous to enter, and the occasional unexploded dud round makes them still more forbidding.

Over a three-year period Manfred searched the area for flat rocks for use in a barbecue he was constructing in his backyard. He built a portion of the barbecue, then dismantled it. Returning to the project again in September 1966, he flipped a stone over and noticed a sunburst symbol inscribed on it. A thorough washing revealed an inscription that filled one side of the five-pound, twelve-inch-square stone. Metcalf quickly examined the other slabs, but found nothing. He immediately took the stone to Mahan.

The Metcalf Stone was the evidence Mahan had been seeking to prove what at the time was a controversial idea. Mahan, the leading authority on the Yuchi Indians, the most conservative of Southern tribes, had been involved in "a running argument with Southern archaeologists for years," he stated. The Yuchi had lived in the Chattahoochee River Valley for a thousand years before Christopher Columbus arrived, and remained until forced to Oklahoma in 1836. Even there they preserved their language, which is not related to any other Native American linguistic group. Hundreds of the one thousand surviving Yuchi still speak their pre-Columbian language.

"We've long suspected that the religious ceremonies of the Yuchis were influenced by early Mediterranean religions," Mahan said. He had recorded their history-legends-myths from Chief Samuel W. Brown Jr., who died in 1957 at age eighty-four. Brown could recite the lineage of twenty-eight hereditary chiefs from memory.

"In their religious ceremonials these Indians have a tradition that their ancestors originally came in boats from the east, following a great natural catastrophe," Mahan said. He thought this sounded "like a volcanic eruption."

Those familiar with the ancient world know that the great Minoan civilization in the Mediterranean Sea was destroyed by the explosion of a volcano on the island of Theta, which may have inspired the Atlantis myth. In 1967 American and Greek archaeologists unearthed an entire thirty-five-hundred-year-old city covered by tons of ash and pumice located on the small island north of Crete. The titanic explosion caused part of the island to sink into the ocean. This was the scene of the catastrophe that ended the Minoan civilization.

"They (the Yuchi) came to a new homeland and stayed a long time," Mahan continued. "We take that to be northern South America. After more disturbances a group of them came north—to a cape, which may have been Florida—and from there they spread north and west.

"Yuchis claimed to have come from the east," Mahan continued, "and if you reach Georgia from the east, you can only come from across the ocean. Aztecs and their predecessors have a tradition about the arrival of Quetzalcoatl, a white being who came from the east and brought the arts of civilization with him." The Mayans in Yucatan and the Incas in Peru told similar tales.

This supposition may not be as exciting as the idea that Minoans came to Georgia directly from the eastern Mediterranean, but it is more plausible. Before the Metcalf Stone surfaced, what supported Mahan's startling idea? Anthropological proof, Mahan explained.

"The Yuchis celebrated a festival, which began on the full moon of the harvest month. They made a pilgrimage, lived in booths with lattice roofs that they covered with branches. They built a fire in the middle of the enclosure and spent eight days in circumambulations. A couple of people held branches of leaves and shook them.

"Where do we read about a ceremony like this? In the Bible, in Leviticus 23. This feast of the tabernacles is the same religious ceremony. It began on the full moon of the harvest month, lasted for eight days, and during this time the people lived in booths. The festival is still observed by the orthodox Jews. The similarity of one of these details could have been coincidental. But not this cluster of details. The festival was not a Hebrew invention. Both Leviticus 23 and the American Yuchi festival perpetuate an ancient agricultural cult from the Mediterranean."

The Metcalf Stone, found on the vast expanse of Fort Benning, proves that America was discovered two thousand years before Columbus. The people who produced this stone apparently settled here and became the Yuchi Indians. (Courtesy of the Mahan Collection, Simon Schwob Memorial Library, Columbus State University)

The Yuchi continue to observe two of five aspects of the harvest festival that modern Jews have abandoned—gathering at their cultic center, where they maintain a sacred fire. These are no longer practiced by Jews because of the destruction of the Temple in Jerusalem in A.D. 66 and their subsequent dispersal.

Mahan and other experts have found striking similarities between the written Mayan glyph language, nearly destroyed by Spanish priests in the fifteenth and sixteenth centuries, and Minoan glyphs. There are also many similarities between Minoan symbols and those found on ancient Yuchi pottery.

"We see certain artistic designs in the pottery and architecture—particularly the mounds—that are identical to religious symbols and art forms from the Bronze Age, prior to 1500 B.C., in the eastern Mediterranean area," Mahan said. "Similar things are found in Palestine, Syria, Turkey, and particularly on Crete in the Aegean Islands. Enough was retained in the art forms and religious philosophy of the Yuchis to show a cultural descent from Mediterranean religions . . . Characteristics of the Yuchi culture and religion show they would have had to break off the parent stem about the time the writing on the stone was in vogue."

From their center on Crete, the Minoans proved themselves excellent navigators and skilled seamen. Their influence was extensive throughout Europe in the mid and late Bronze Age. For example, their imprint has been found at Stonehenge in Great Britain, where a double ax was discovered on a standing stone.

Mahan's theory is that the Yuchi "are possibly descendants of ancient Minoan people, from a Mediterranean civilization, which flourished in the Bronze Age. A small caste or group or somebody could have retained a knowledge of writing for a long time."

Hundreds of years, perhaps more than a millennia, after the Minoans came to America, "somebody in this area—retained this writing system and carved this on a Georgia rock," Mahan believed.

These valiant seafarers deliberately navigated across the Atlantic Ocean to explore, trade, and apparently settle in the Americas. In their new home the symbols continued to evolve, as any language does. The language has become peculiarly American and is not now fully decipherable, but it is obviously related to the ancient Minoan script.

When the Metcalf Stone was presented to Mahan he immediately noted that the characters resembled the Minoan that he had been comparing to pottery designs on prehistoric Georgia pottery. Comparing Minoan script with the Metcalf Stone, he found nine of the thirteen symbols had "a close relationship."

One of Mahan's first actions was locating the site where the stone had originated. It was obviously a broken fragment and the remainder might

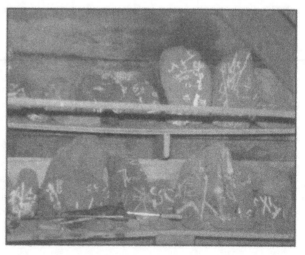

A north Georgia resident believed ancient navigators who discovered America thousands of years before Columbus left these inscribed stones. Historians have discounted their authenticity.

still exist, along with additional inscribed stones. Mahan also needed to know if the inscription had been carved locally, or brought from another place. Metcalf had gathered the stones across a wide area, so a geologist was consulted and each potential site explored. By comparing the mineral and sand content of stones from different places, the geologist matched the inscribed rock with a particular locale. It was a site where Metcalf remembered taking a stone from an old foundation, numerous large square pillars, or chimneys of the Underwood Mill, a gristmill constructed around 1820 on Pine Knot Creek, or associated houses. There were many red sandstone slabs of the size and shape of the Metcalf Stone, all of them heavily covered by vegetation. Despite repeated searches, no additional inscribed stones were uncovered.

An examination of the symbols under a microscope convinced Mahan that "they were not made in recent times," for the grooves displayed distinct weathering. Dr. Cyrus Gordon, chairman of Mediterranean studies at prestigious Brandeis University in Waltham, Massachusetts, and an expert on the ancient history of the Near East, agreed. He estimated that the marks were at least one hundred years old in 1968.

The next step in proving the authenticity of the inscription was locating an expert in ancient languages who could determine if the stone was a hoax.

"I'm convinced it is not," Mahan stated. However, because of his "running argument with Southern archaeologists," he "wanted to bring in an outside authority." Mahan selected and contacted Gordon, "the man in this country who is most knowledgeable about eastern Mediterranean symbols."

Gordon wrote Mahan that the "glyphs have a certain second millennium B.C. look." He considered it an important link between the old world and the new. Gordon was intrigued by the reddish slab of sandstone, whose flat surface undoubtedly attracted the attention of an ancient scribe. On that surface someone engraved dots and lines which were the predecessors of Greek letters, and a classic double ax, a box-tie-shaped figure familiar in the ancient world. The script was believed to date from 1500 B.C. and originated from the famed Phoenician culture of the Mediterranean.

Several symbols can be deciphered. Two vertical lines with dots beneath them probably represent numbers, perhaps twenty-two. That is what they meant in ancient Minoan in Crete. Three symbols resemble ancestors of the Greek characters for *delta*, *pi*, and *theta*. The double ax had both a phonetic and symbolic value. The sunlike character, composed of a dot and seven rays, probably indicates a very large number. A curious parallel line, in an ancient Phoenician script, meant value. Several characters represent a large number—one thousand or ten thousand, or perhaps seven hundred or seven thousand.

"There's no chance of an accidental duplication by a primitive people of these ancient symbols," Gordon stated. However, he cautioned, "I haven't implied that we can read this stone. The text is not Minoan—we're not sure what the language is. Minoan characters were used for two different languages on Crete—Semitic Minoan and Greek—just as Latin characters are used to write many languages. But if we compare the symbols on the rock with the known scripts of the world, the symbols most closely resemble Minoan."

Although searches have not revealed additional finds, there are almost certainly other rocks with engraved inscriptions. There is no reason why there would be only this one extraordinary exception.

In his book *Before Columbus*, Gordon found "affinities" between the characters on the Metcalf Stone and an Aegean script from "the latter half of the second millennium B.C." Minoan Linear A and Mycenaean Linear B were written syllabaries from the Aegean Sea area. They also resemble letters of the Phoenician language, and seem to be an intermediate stage between that syllabary and an alphabet.

Gordon consulted with Stanislav Segert, professor of Semitic languages at the University of Prague, Czechoslovakia, who thought the symbols were four thousand years old.

Another argument against the inscription being a modern hoax were traces of red clay and mortar, which had cemented the stones together, found embedded in the symbols. The latest dates for the mill and other structures where the stone originated were 1889. Sir Arthur Evans did not locate the first clay tablets containing Linear A until 1899. Those records were estimated to be thirty-five hundred years old.

What purpose might the inscribed stone have had? Probably commerce, Gordon thought, suggesting an inventory of goods including a problematical reading of the last line as "one double-ax weighing one mina, made of copper." Gordon also believes the language was limited to inventories and commercial transactions.

THE HEARN TABLET

Gardening was the passion of Mrs. Joe Hearn of LaGrange. As she dug and planted through the years, she unearthed a number of arrowheads and other Amerindian artifacts that she placed in a cardboard box for her grandchildren's amusement. In 1963 she excavated a lead tablet the size of a matchbox, about an inch square. The symbols on its surface meant nothing to her, so she added it to her collection.

Eight years passed. In June 1971 Mrs. Hearn's daughter, Mrs. James R. Wilbanks, read a newspaper article about Dr. Mahan's work on the Metcalf Stone. It reminded her of a photograph of an ancient tablet she had noticed in a Sunday school magazine. Recalling her mother's artifact, she was astounded to discover that the two appeared to be identical.

Mrs. Wilbanks brought this curiosity to the attention of Mahan, who kept the discovery confidential while he investigated its importance. He conferred first with Dr. Lynn Holmes, history professor at West Georgia College. They interviewed Mrs. Hearn in LaGrange and decided the script was Sumerian Cuneiform, used about 1800 B.C. Mahan thought it was a receipt for silver, the exchange evidently occurring in Georgia.

"I got out the *Who's Who* and several scholarly journals to find the name of a competent scholar who might help me out," Mahan said.

Dr. Cyrus Gordon was selected. Among Gordon's numerous books were the first grammar and dictionary textbook for the Ugaritic language, extensively used in fourteenth-century B.C. literature on the north coast of Syria. It had significant impact on the Old Testament and influenced interpretations of early Greek literature, including Homer. Gordon heard the story but remained skeptical until he received a plaster cast of the tiny Hearn Tablet. Mahan said that "as soon as he saw it he got in touch with me immediately," and flew to Columbus to examine the artifact. Gordon was so impressed that he consulted with Dr. Benjamin Mazas, a professor at Hebrew University in Jerusalem.

The cuneiform that covered the surface of the small metal tablet was first discovered in 1850 at the legendary city of Ur in Mesopotamia.

Gordon and Mahan agreed that the tablet found in Mrs. Hearn's flower garden was a receipt for sheep, written in a Minoan script used in the Middle East four thousand years ago. Mahan revealed that Mazas thought the object originated in the eastern Mediterranean and was "amazed when he learned it came from Georgia."

The surface of the tablet had developed a whitish gray patina, but "precise inscribed characters were visible and were unmistakably cuneiform," Mahan wrote in his book *The Secret*. "The tablet was in the bun shape characteristic of cuneiform tablets from Mesopotamian sites. It measured almost exactly one and one quarter inches in length and width. Closely spaced lines of the carefully impressed letters extended around the surface covering the two faces and one of the sides of the tablet. One was smooth and somewhat flattened."

After the patina, which forms as lead ages, was chemically removed, "the entire inscription became clearly legible except for a few characters on the face that had been damaged by the spade with which Mrs. Hearn discovered it."

Even more curious was the discovery that this was not the "original" artifact. That had undoubtedly been a clay tablet, so prevalent in the Mideast while the Sumerian culture flourished. The Hearn object was a cast of such a tablet.

The Hearn Tablet is apparently a copy of a clay tablet made with the lost wax process. A wax original is impressed into a moist clay tablet. When dry, the wax was heated and drained off and molten lead was poured into the clay impression. When it cooled, the clay mold was broken off. Microscopic examination of the lead tablet disclosed tiny particles of clay embedded within the symbols that make up the inscription. This technique was common among the Sumerians and other ancient cultures that also used copper, gold, and silver to make casts.

Mahan and other professionals sifted through Mrs. Hearn's garden, but found that her energetic work had previously unearthed every artifact in the area. She had earlier discovered a smaller piece of the same material, which appeared as if it had been cut from a similar tablet. Unfortunately, she had lost it before 1971. During her gardening Mrs. Hearn had found evidence of ancient fires, indicated by deposits of charcoal, and near them had been located several thin, irregularly shaped pieces of lead that must have splattered onto the ground while molten. These droppings were also covered with a heavy green patina.

Mrs. Hearn retained several dozen stone projectile points and a half gallon of quartzite chips and broken points and knives that dated from the Archaic Period, which ended before 1000 B.C. The area had never been cultivated. Mrs. Hearn's house had been constructed in the 1850s or earlier, and was surrounded by ancient oak trees.

The evidence indicated that the site had not been disturbed between at least 1000 B.C. and the 1950s. The implication is that four thousand years ago an immigrant, refugee, or commercial trader had crossed the Atlantic Ocean and lived and traveled in the Americas. At first experts thought that perhaps an original clay tablet had become a treasured family or tribal heirloom and at some late date a lead cast was made of it, but that idea has since been rejected. It should be noted that this is one of a handful of cast-lead objects discovered in pre-Columbian America. None seems to have been made by Native Americans.

The tablet itself was impossible to date—carbon dating is not applicable, and there is no technique for dating lead. Archaeologists compared the patina to that on lead "Minie" bullets from our Civil War. No date could be established for the casting of the Hearn Tablet, but the examination indicated it was far older than the bullets. Another indication of age are the Indian artifacts associated with the tablet.

What does the Hearn Tablet say? Because of damage caused by Mrs. Hearn's digging, several signs were "problematical," but the text was obviously Sumerian cuneiform. The reminder plainly was a receipt for a transaction involving eight assorted sheep and five goats. From the text we know that a scribe named Enlila, apparently recently arrived from the city of Ur in Sumer in the thirty-seventh or thirty-eighth year of King Sulgi's rule (about 2040 B.C., during the Third Dynasty), gave a receipt to two men, one named Zabardab, the other name obliterated, for animals meant to be sacrificed to the sun god Utut and the goddess Lanma-lugal.

Mahan wrote that Ur did not possess the important metals for the tools and weapons necessary for the survival of a civilization and sent out expeditions to secure supplies. He believes that one party reached the southern coast of North America and wandered through what is now Georgia. Such an expedition would include metallurgists to mine and reduce ore to pure ingots, saving transportation space and making each trip more profitable. They could easily have produced the Hearn Tablet, and Georgia's rainy climate may not have preserved clay tablets. As to the pre-Columbian presence of goats and sheep—expeditions until recent times often brought live animals with them to provide fresh meat on the hoof, as did the Spanish conquistadors.

Adventurer Thor Hyerdahl proved decades ago that ancient Egyptians could cross the Atlantic Ocean in a reed boat. If so, "the Phoenicians and Minoans could have done it with ease in their far more sophisticated crafts," Mahan wrote.

THE BAT CREEK STONE

Mahan was responsible for another piece of the pre-Columbian puzzle in August 1970, when he examined a book published by the Smithsonian Institution's Bureau of Ethnology in 1894. It described a Smithsonian-sponsored excavation conducted by Cyrus Thomas in 1885 of a burial mound at Bat Creek, Tennessee. Nine graves were revealed, but only one had been interred with artifacts. Beneath a male skull was a polished stone with inscriptions, two copper bracelets, a drilled fossil, a copper bead, a bone tool, and several small pieces of polished wood. Thomas concluded that the Bat Creek Stone bore an excellent example of the Cherokee language developed by Sequoyah in the early 1830s.

Mahan, who was fluent in Cherokee, knew that assertion was incorrect. He turned the page upside down and recognized it as an ancient script from the Middle East. He sent a copy of the photograph to Dr. Gordon, who initially thought it was Canaanite, then decided that it was actually made by Bronze Age Hebrews from Palestine. The Bat Creek Stone was at least two thousand years old, dating between 1000 B.C. and A.D. 136. After checking with experts, Mahan "positively and unproblematically" identified the stone as Canaanite, a developmental stage of Hebrew.

It was first translated as reading "for (the land of) Judah," although a later interpretation is "For Jehu" or "belonging to Jehu," presumably the man buried with it. Jehu was a common name in ancient Palestine. Five Jehus are listed in the Bible, including a prophet and king.

Mahan felt the Bat Creek Stone vindicated his work. Archaeologists could call the Metcalf Stone and Hearn Tablets hoaxes, but this artifact could not be dismissed or discounted. It had been excavated by reputable Smithsonian scientists in an indisputable archaeological context—an ancient, undisturbed burial mound.

"Awfully hard for the Smithsonian to question its authenticity," Mahan said. "They found the thing and have had it in their possession ever since." The possibility of a hoax, he concluded, "is totally implausible."

"There are literally hundreds of pieces of evidence which prove to me beyond a shadow of a doubt that there was a migration to the Americas from peoples living in the eastern Mediterranean," Mahan concluded.

For those wishing more information, Mahan's papers reside in the library of Columbus University.

GEORGIA GIANTS IN THE EARTH

In 1524 Lucas Vasquez de Ayllon landed on the coast of either Georgia or South Carolina. It is impossible to determine exactly where, since his expedition was not destined to be remembered as one of the great adventures of humanity. Ayllon remained on the coast with the ships and half his force while two hundred men ventured inland to explore and conquer what they found. Indians fell upon this party and slaughtered them all, then turned on the ships and forced the Spanish to abandon the coast. Ayllon limped back to Santo Domingo in disgrace.

Back at the Imperial Council, Ayllon and a friendly native he brought back, Francisco Chicora, befriended historian Peter Martyr, who later chronicled Ayllon's ill-fated expedition. Martyr included a number of fascinating stories told him by Chicora. One story described a gigantic king called Datha, and his queen, of like stature, who ruled many tribes in a land called Duhare, located somewhere in the interior of Georgia or South Carolina.

"The secret of their huge stature was not known," Martyr wrote, "but was said that while the children of this royal house were babes, their bones were softened with an ointment of strange herbs, then kneaded and stretched like wax by masters of the art, leaving the poor objects of their magic as if dead. The infants were then wrapped in warm covers and revived with milk from the breast of a nurse who had been fed on food of a special virtue. This treatment was repeated many times."

Historians of the time questioned this process of stretching, but believed it was likely the children were fed a secret formula of herbs "given them principally at the age of puberty, when it is nature's tendency to develop."

In *Martyr's Decade, Volume IV*, he urged the Spanish government to send an expedition to discover the formula, "lest some enemy find it first and then have the Spaniards at their mercy."

The idea of Martyr lying awake nights awaiting an invasion by giants is precious.

When the Cherokee Indians were removed to Oklahoma, a portion hid and remained in North Carolina. There, in the last bastion of Cherokee tradition, James Mooney, the Smithsonian ethnologist, lived among them at the turn of the twentieth century. His 1900 classic, *Myths of the Cherokee*, included several legends describing giants.

According to one account, at a very remote date a young maiden married a man who only visited her at night and always insisted on leaving before dawn. The girl's shrewish mother grew suspicious of this behavior and demanded to meet the husband of her only daughter. The giant, named *Tsulkalu*, refused, but he was a powerful hunter and consequently a good provider. When he departed in the morning he always left plenty of fresh meat for his wife and her mother. One day the mother grew tired of chopping wood and wished aloud that the husband would leave some firewood the next morning instead of meat. At dawn on the following morning she found "several great trees lying in front of the door, roots and branches and all."

Tsulkalu finally gave in to the harping of his mother-in-law and agreed to stay one morning.

"The old woman came and looked in," Mooney related, "and there she saw a great giant, with long slanting eyes, lying doubled up on the floor, with his head against the rafters in the left-hand corner at the back, and his toes scraping the roof in the right-hand corner by the door."

Mother ran off screaming.

Another legend, localized in Georgia, tells of a visit by a hunting party of giants to the early Cherokee. These large men were twice as tall as the Indians and had slanting eyes, so naturally they were collectively called *Tsunilkalu* in honor of the ancient legend. Of these giants, Mooney said they "lived far away in the direction in which the sun goes down," or west. The Cherokee treated the Tsunilkalu kindly, prompting them to stay a while before returning home. The Cherokee did not consider them to be Indians. Perhaps they were the remnants of a lost race.

An early history of Georgia described the contrast between Cherokee women, "the smallest race of women yet known," and Cherokee men, "of gigantic stature, a full size larger than Europeans, many of them above six feet, and few under that." They were also "by far the largest race of men I have seen," the writer continued.

During the 1870s an expedition from the Smithsonian was excavating a burial mound at Etowah when it made a startling discovery. An Athens newspaper of the period, preserved in the scrapbooks of Judge Richard H. Clarke, reported that after the top layer of dirt had been removed, excavators came to a vault made of hand-dressed stones.

"These stones were removed," the article continued, "and in a vault beneath them was found the skeleton of a giant, measuring seven feet and two inches. His hair was coarse, and jet black, and hung to his waist, the brow being ornamented with a copper crown. The skeleton was remarkably well preserved and was taken from the vault intact."

On the dressed stones were found "carved inscriptions, and if deciphered will probably lift the veil which has shrouded the history of the race of giants which undoubtedly at one time inhabited the continent."

Several skeletons of children were found with the giant, each covered by a layer of bone beads. Discoveries such as these were common in past centuries, but unfortunately the skeletons and artifacts were scattered to the winds and lost to history.

In 1968 excavations by modern, professional archaeologists at Etowah revealed the skeleton of a man who was six feet, ten inches in height. Perhaps this is evidence of a royal family of giants.

A letter written in August 1870 by George W. Williams, whose father was one of the first settlers in northeast Georgia, described a significant find on Captain J. H. Nichol's farm in the beautiful Nacoochee Valley near Dukes Creek. Not far from an Indian mound (note: there are more than just the prominent one with the cupola on top beside the highway near Helen) a plow struck a stone that was part of a tomb, lined top, bottom, and sides with polished stones. Among the many skeletons was "a giant, or a man much larger than the present race" of Indians. With those remains were "immense conch shells, pipes, tomahawks," and a "most remarkable relic—a piece of in-wrought copper." Walker considered "the huge men skilled in art. The tomb itself showed that the builder understood the use of tools."

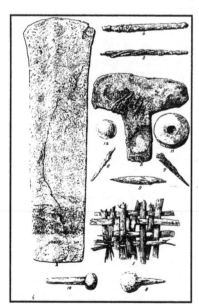

Artifacts found with the Nacoochee Valley giant included textiles and stone and bone instruments. (Charles C. Jones, Antiquities of the Southern Indians)

Accounts of this discovery appeared in a number of publications more than a century ago. "When did this race of men live?" asked Lucian Lamar Knight in *Georgia's Landmarks and Memorials.* This was the same area where a sub-terranean village, described later in this chapter, was uncovered.

Trackrock Gap Archaeological Area is located thirty or so miles north of the Nacoochee Valley, where a group of 136 petroglyphs were carved into soft soapstone boulders. There are concentric circles (bisected vertically and horizontally), crosses, and human, animal, and bird prints. The human footprints vary in size from four inches to "great warriors which measured seventeen inches in length and seven inches in breadth across the toes," wrote an early chronicler of Georgia history. "What is a little curious, all the human feet are natural except this, which has six toes." The remains of six-toed giants have been excavated in Crittenden, Arizona.

Across the state on the Atlantic Coast are the scenic Sea Islands, where in 1936 workers constructing a new airport uncovered numerous Indian artifacts. Smithsonian archaeologists were called in and excavated 150 burials and recovered twenty-one thousand artifacts. These ancient people had been hunters who occupied the area seasonally over a long span of time.

There was only one burial mound on the island, composed of sand, which stood six feet high and fifty feet in diameter. Burials in the mound were covered with a heavy layer of hematite, a red substance favored by the ancient Adena culture in Ohio, and one skeleton was clothed in an apron of 225 shell beads. In a place of honor at the bottom of the mound was the most important burial. This was the skeleton of a male, judged to be over six and a half feet tall, although his skull was missing, a peculiar cultural trait common among some Southern Indians.

Preston Holder, director of the excavation, deduced from the bones that the individual had been a teenager, even though his position in the tribe was thought to be great, judged by his grave goods. With him were six bone awls, four mussel shell pendants worn over his left shoulder, a chipped stone flint spear point, and a string of eight sea snail shell beads on his left knee. These were very rich grave offerings for the area and period. Evidence indicates he was a young king, like Tut, or a "Mico," son of a king.

Skeletons found in mounds near Savannah were cremated and the remains stuffed into urns, making it impossible to determine height. However, many charred bones became petrified and were well preserved. The *Savannah Republican* commented, "It may also be remarked that their processes and spines for the insertion of muscles are bolder and more prominent than those we find at present; their muscular force must have been proportionately greater."

Perhaps they had been enormously strong giants.

A number of large mounds have been found in Hancock County, primarily along Shoulderbone Creek. Unfortunately, the land was so productive that early settlers leveled the works for agriculture. Many ordinary artifacts were found in a mound surviving on the plantation of M. W. Harris. Also discovered was a male skeleton "of great stature," found in perfect condition and now reportedly residing in one of those dark forgotten storerooms at the Smithsonian.

An account written by "Bro. Gautt" that appeared in the March 28, 1884, *Greensboro Herald* described his exploration of two mounds in northern Greene County at Scull Shoals, mounds preserved today along a hiking

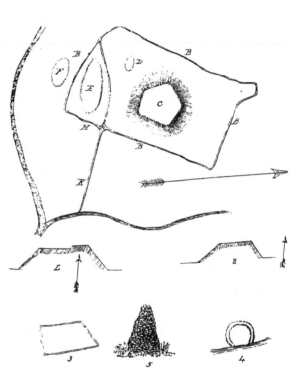

Ancient structures found by settlers in Hancock County included a large mound of piled stones. Hundreds, if not thousands, of similar mounds have been found across Georgia, particularly in Gwinnett County. (Charles C. Jones, Antiquities of the Southern Indians)

trail in the Oconee National Forest. One mound was large, "looking like a huge sugar loaf rising in the valley," and the other, thirty yards away, was about fifteen feet in height. Floodwaters had exposed the base of the larger mound, where Gautt discovered "a great many relics and a part of the skeleton of a giant." He claimed that acres of the valley were "one vast cemetery," which he believed resulted from a great aboriginal battle.

Down in the extreme southeastern corner of Georgia is the legendary Okefenokee Swamp. The freshwater swamp covers seven hundred square miles in four Georgia counties and two in Florida. Local legend holds that Spanish explorers who ventured into the vast area swore the forests turned into giant warriors who launched showers of arrows at them. Today phantom deer, bears, and panthers that can only be killed by special bullets roam the islands at night, and on stormy nights ghost slave ships slip up the Saint Mary's River amid sounds of clanking chains that can be clearly heard by observers. Skeleton crews sail the boats up the channel and unload their forbidden cargo on isolated islands.

During the 1920s a railroad was built to transport lumber out of the swamp. While crossing Floyd's Island, the largest in the swamp, it became necessary to cut through an extensive half-moon-shaped Indian mound. Within it workers found the skeletons of several huge men accompanied by pottery and beads.

Tom Chesser, who owned Chesser Island in Charlton County, had a sizable mound in his backyard. In 1969 he told the *Atlanta Journal and Constitution Magazine* that a professor from a northern university hired him to excavate the mound in the 1920s. They discovered thirteen skeletons in all.

"Some of the skeletons were crossed," Chesser said, "one on top of the other. Some were facedown. All of them were perfect when they were first discovered. Teeth even still had some glaze on them, but when air struck, it crumbled them. They were giants. Those jawbones would go over my whole face."

The formation of the burials, crisscrossed and in tiers, was also noted in a burial of giants in North Carolina. Further, many people who discover the remains of giants believe the skulls could fit over their own heads. Unfortunately, far too many of the skeletons crumble into dust.

I researched giants while in high school and early college. I wrote many museums and universities in search of information. When a professional archaeologist deigned to answer, it was usually to roast me for following such a silly, far-fetched, and unfounded line of study. It was an attitude I understand to an extent: Professors and curators can easily lose face in the academic community for lending credibility to such trivial pursuits.

I received only one note of encouragement. Instead of instantly dismissing my childish interest in giants and chiding me, one associate professor of anthropology at the University of Georgia thought the proposition through and wrote the following: "It is possible that in some populations a relationship may have existed between tall males and high-ranking status positions in the tribe. This could mean that men of high status (and possibly tall stature) were buried with special ritual, with an abundance of grave goods, in a select spot . . . This is not merely speculation, as there have been some reports issued of Southeastern archaeology recently indicating such a relationship with stature and status."

This archaeologist has become a leader in Southern archaeology, and I withhold his name in case he would regret having encouraged me (others have).

In *The Mound Builders*, Robert Silverberg's research into the human remains found in Midwestern Adena mounds led him to propose that "a small elite of round-headed giants" dominated the Ohio Valley two thousand years ago. Charles Snow, author of the definitive *The Adena People*, theorized that social selection might have developed a distinctive chin of leaders in the culture. Don Dragoo, in *Mounds for the Dead*, noted the massive protruding chin and added another prominent characteristic of the Adena: "The second trait is the large size of many of the males and some of the females," he wrote. "A male of six feet was common and some individuals approaching seven feet in height have been found."

Dragoo excavated a male skeleton over seven feet tall in West Virginia's Cresap Mound. "All the long bones were heavy and possessed marked eminences for the attachment of muscles," which was noted in the Savannah area skeletons. Dragoo commented that the man "would have been a splendid figure in any society and the darling of a primitive basketball team."

Several female skeletons from the Dover Mound in Kentucky "were more than six feet in height. Not only were these Adena people tall but—the massiveness of the bones indicates powerfully built individuals. The head was generally big with a large cranial capacity."

If these high-ranking persons had bred only with those who possessed the same chin and stature, the two genetic characteristics would have been enhanced in future generations, which would also have been held in awe and given status burials for us to excavate. So there, those who smirked at my youthful interest. The idea of prehistoric American giants has at least some basis in fact.

A FEW ODD ARTIFACTS

OWL ROCK

At historic Owl Rock Methodist Church, located five miles west of I-285 on GA 166, is the Owl Rock. It was named several centuries ago by Cherokee Indians and early settlers who believed that it resembled an owl. To modern eyes it looks amazingly like the neck and head of a prehistoric dinosaur, and has been labeled "Cecil" by those who remember the seasick sea serpent of cartoon fame.

The first six feet of the eight-foot-high monolith resembles the curved neck of a sea monster. The top has a well-defined head with an astonishingly lifelike eye peering out. A snout divides the long face, which seems to jut out from the neck, giving the stone an animated quality. Anthropologists have suggested that the Indians revered this unusual rock as a sacred object and carved the stone to bring out its natural features. The word *owl* was chiseled on it at a later date.

Early settlers noticed a large, intricately engraved stone near Silver City in Forsyth County. It was featured by Georgia's earliest archaeologist, Charles C. Jones, in *Antiquities of the Southern Indians*, and had been mentioned in 1855 by George White in *Historical Collections of Georgia*. In the 1940s it was rediscovered by Margaret Perryman, who described it as a "fat gray granite whale." Later, Professor T. M. N. Lewis at the University of Tennessee recognized it as an "owl totem" lying horizontally with clearly distinguishable beak, eyes, and taloned feet. It was moved to the University of Georgia campus for safekeeping.

Owl Rock is a tall stone artificially shaped by ancient Americans to resemble an owl, or Cecil the Seasick Sea Serpent.

It is nearly impossible to date petroglyphs and sculpted rocks, but the owl and concentric symbols are frequent designs on Mississippian pottery of the Etowah period.

OH, GIVE ME A HOME WHERE THE BUFFALO ROCKS ROAM

In northern Fulton County near Birmingham, along the Little River, is a fourteen-foot-high boulder that resembles the head of a buffalo. The huge eyes, mouth, and nostrils are readily apparent, and from one side the stone appears to be charging. It is questionable whether this huge stone is entirely natural or if the Native Americans noticed a general likeness to the buffalo and did a little sculpturing. A local legend says the Indians sacrificed young people to their gods in an effort to bring the buffalo back to the Southeast, where the animal had once roamed in abundance.

At the top of the rock is, according to some, a sacrificial basin drained by twin grooves where victims were allegedly slain. Their blood flowed down the sides of the great buffalo head. Carved footholds are on either side of the basin, where the chief priest and executioner may have stood, perhaps to deliver the coup de grâce. Stains, some say blood, can still be seen on the rock, and smoke from many ceremonial fires tended at the base of the stone in ancient times has blackened the buffalo.

BEAR WITH ME

While certainly not a sculptured stone, Mount Yonah, framed so prominently to the southwest of the beautiful gazebo-capped burial mound in the

157

Nacoochee Valley, was held sacred by the Cherokee because its shape reminded them of a sleeping bear. The Cherokee word *Yonah* means *bear*, or so I've been told.

GRAY EAGLE'S CHAIR

Gray Eagle was the last Cherokee chief until either his death or deportation to the reservation in either North Carolina or Oklahoma (local legends are a cafeteria—choose what you want, leave the rest for others). His home had been in the gap between Tallulah Mountain and Hickory Nut Mountain, where he presided from a throne carved from a one-ton piece of stone. After the Cherokee Removal in 1835, the great chair was

The Nacoochee Valley in North Georgia has a number of mysteries, such as an ancient giant skeleton and a mysterious subterranean village. Behind the prehistoric mound is Mount Yonah, which Native Americans thought resembled a bear.

transported to a field belonging to the Vandever family; one member had been part of the Cherokee council, a white man and friend of the Indians. In 1924 Adam Vandever loaned the large artifact to Tallulah Falls School for ninety-nine years with the stipulation that it would never be sold or given away, but would always belong to Gray Eagle.

The chair sits beside a walkway between buildings. Over the years students have formed the belief that sitting on the stone furniture while studying ensures good grades. Note that Tallulah Falls is a private school, and visitors should immediately check in with school authorities before seeking out Gray Eagle's Chair (this warning is based on personal experience).

HEAP BIG ARROWHEADS

The people of Sumter County's DeSoto have a tradition that Hernando de Soto's expedition struggled out of the Florida swamps and recuperated at the site of their little community. After they wore out their welcome by abusing the locals, the natives poisoned their water supply. The conquistadors then dug an oblong, six-by-eight-foot artesian well, surrounding it with ground-level rocks. The Spanish departed on March 31, 1540, but the well still runs.

Gray Eagle's Chair was the throne of a Cherokee chief. Left behind when the Cherokee were removed, it is now preserved at a school in Tallulah Falls.

Spring Head, which the natives poisoned, still exists in Leslie, where several carved rocks, one in the shape of a giant arrowhead, are located. J. C. Gazaway showed me a great arrowhead-shaped stone near his museum several years before I heard of the one at Leslie. Although I never saw it, he said another stone throne was hidden in the surrounding hills of Forsyth County.

From left to right: Judge Gary Hamilton, Larry Itson, Steve Redden, Jeffery Raymond, and Gene Richardson, with the Spanish sword from Hernando de Soto's expedition. The three men in the center found the fabulous artifact. (Courtesy of Eunice J. Autry and William S. Autry)

A UNIQUE PETROGLYPH

A strange stone bearing a petroglyph was found in 1909 by W. H. Roberts near Sweetwater Creek in Douglas County. Perched upon a bluff, the artifact was apparently revered because carved stone steps led up to it. The granite boulder, four feet high, one and a half feet wide and one foot thick, weighs six hundred pounds and bears the carved image of a pie-faced man wearing a skirt.

The state of Georgia came into possession of the stone and displayed it on the porch of the old state archives building. When the current structure was built, the stone was sent to the Columbus Museum, where it was displayed for years. Renovations sent the stone into storage, where it remains.

The image is so odd that it led Frank Schnell, archaeologist for the Columbus Museum, to doubt it was an Indian artifact.

"There are Indian petroglyphs that have designs on them," he said, "but they're all purely abstract in Georgia. So there's nothing really to compare it to in my own mind, except for early, nineteenth-century homemade gravestones.

"This might be a descendant of what's called the 'death's head' gravestone. In the colonial period, it was fairly common to have a stone with just a death's head carved on it. That's what this reminds me of, except that it's a lot more elaborate."

Douglas County would like to display the artifact locally, but the Georgia Council on American Indian Concerns stepped into the picture. If the stone is determined to be of Native American origin, it belongs to descendants of the Indians who produced it. If the stone is determined to be historic, the state and family of W. H. Roberts may wrangle over possession.

For the present, the stone remains in storage at the Columbus Museum, a baffling enigma.

IT'S NOT THE SIZE—

Dr. Warren K. Moorehead was apparently dismayed when he discovered several stones shaped like the human penis at Etowah. He cast them aside, but a farmer rescued one. Others had previously been found there and more would later be excavated from the site. Charles C. Jones noted that one twelve-inch phallus, "perfectly resembling the natural object," and a sixteen-inch model were found. Also, three clay phalli were found at Etowah, one at Ocmulgee. Similar representations have been found at aboriginal sites in Tennessee, Ohio, and Oklahoma. Archaeologists suggest they were ceremonial objects similar to ones used in ancient Egypt and Greece.

ECCENTRIC FLINTS

There are three types of eccentric flints. The first are chipped or flaked-stone objects with unusual form and no obvious practical application. The second are giant flints, often called leaf-shaped implements. These are unusually large, show no signs of use, and would generally be useless for any normal chore. Third are caches, where a large number of unique stone products, again never utilized, were buried in one place. Georgia has one of each, all rolled into one.

I encountered Georgia's cache of giant eccentric flints at an Indian artifact show held either at Kolomoki Mounds or Bowens Mill about twenty years ago. Displayed on a velvet fabric, the artifacts made a stunning sight. The owner told me he had dug them from an earthen Indian mound in southern Georgia. He was asking professional archaeologists about their origin, he continued, but had received no concrete answers to his ancient riddle.

I snapped several photos of the artifacts, which I later showed to the late J. C. Gazaway, my dowser friend, who also directed me to Owl Rock and the stone mounds in Gwinnett County. He informed me that the artifacts' owner had approached him for information. Gazaway told him that the relics were ancient and very sacred to their owner (OK, I could have made the same prediction, but it was all in his delivery).

I would appreciate hearing from the current owners of these artifacts or anyone who has recent information about them or similar objects.

The most famous giant eccentric flints originated in Mayan sites in Honduras and Guatemala. Large flints, less exotic than Georgia's and generally shaped like batons, maces, axes, and blades, have been excavated in large numbers from Mississippian sites, including those in Etowah in Georgia and in Tennessee, Alabama, and Oklahoma. They were certainly used as ceremonial objects and accompanied high-ranking officials to the grave.

Not as exotic, but still intriguing, is an article from the *Smithsonian's Report of the National Museum of 1897*, which mentions the Steiner

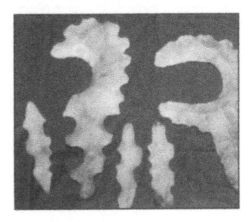

Giant, eccentric flints are rare outside of Central America, but these were extracted from an ancient mound somewhere in Georgia.

Collection of Indian artifacts gathered in Burke County. This collection contained "a number of asymmetric arrowpoints or spearheads" made of gray flint with a yellow patina, common to the area. The Smithsonian noted that they could not have been used as projectiles but were utilized as scrapers or knives and attached to short handles. Described as "lopsided," they were sharpened only on one side.

Curious implements such as these have been found around the world. They resemble "arrowpoints and spearheads in material, method and style of manufacture, and general appearance, though by reason of the peculiarity of their form are totally unfitted for any projectile purpose and, indeed, it is impossible that they should have served as such," stated the Smithsonian. Objects of this sort are "entirely without utility and solely to gratify an artistic desire." They were obviously religious-ceremonial in nature or manufactured by bored prehistoric art students. One is obviously a serpent, another tree-shaped, and a third resembles a normal arrowhead but with a misplaced notch. However, none of them are large.

Another report documents a number of flint and jasper outcrops found in Burke and neighboring Jefferson counties and numerous ancient workshops where implements were manufactured. In an area of forty acres, one Smithsonian team discovered sixteen thousand shaped objects.

PREHISTORIC BAKING?
An interesting archaeological mystery is found at Rhodes Ferry on the eastern side of Spring Creek in Decatur County. Called Jackson's Oven by locals, it is an artificial construction made with limestone slabs. The walls of the oval-shaped building measure fifteen feet long and nine feet wide. The walls are five feet high and three inches thick, and the floor is sunken two and a half feet below the surrounding land. An arched roof of stone slabs remained until about fifty years ago, when they were removed and used for chimneys in area houses. The stones are of all sizes, and a single opening, eighteen inches in diameter, pierces the southern end.

Local tradition has Andrew Jackson's troops constructing and using the structure for baking bread. Some consider this an Indian temple, granary, stone house, sweat lodge, guard house, fortification, tomb, oven, or pottery kiln. A few have suggested it was the refuge of deserters or evaders of the Confederate draft during the Civil War. However, there are no signs of fires being tended in the building, nor pottery shards, which suggests a ceremonial purpose.

STAIRWAY TO?
An 1886 article in the *Athens Weekly Banner* described an ancient stone mystery from Scull Shoals along the Oconee River: "At a famous washing

162

hole near Old Scull Shoals is a set of stone steps about the length and dimensions of stairs and perfectly smooth and regular beginning on the bank and leading down to the bottom of the river. They are evidently the work of some extinct race of man, but for what purpose they were fashioned no one can surmise."

An early Greene County diary refers to "the old Indian fish ladder," suggesting it was a device used to catch fish. However, those were usually a narrowing V of stones or logs which allowed fish to be caught in wicker baskets at the end, but the stairway does not seem to fit that bill.

SOLVING AN ARCHAEOLOGICAL RIDDLE: GEORGIA'S MYSTERIOUS SILVER CROSSES

In 1832 Robert Gilbert of Macon excavated a pair of unusual silver crosses at Coosa Old Town in Murray County. The crosses, made of pure silver, had four arms of equal length, each six inches long, and one a thirteenth of an inch thick. Col. William B. Johnston, also of Macon, bought them in December 1832, and in 1881 they passed into the possession of Charles C. Jones. Jones, a historian and antiquarian, was intrigued enough to write a report about the objects, and it was published by the Smithsonian Institution.

Jones theorized that the crosses had been left by Hernando de Soto's expedition. The Spanish undoubtedly visited that area of northern Georgia, although their exact route is still disputed. Jones believed the Conquistadors stopped at that exact spot before moving down the Oostanaula Valley to Chiaha, thought to be the present city of Rome, where they spent June 1540.

The site where the crosses were found was probably de Soto's Conasagua, which is now the name of a river that flows not far from Coosa Old Town. Jones noted that the settlement was inhabited by the Cherokee Indians until their removal in 1838.

Jones's research revealed that de Soto's expedition had included twelve priests, eight clergymen, and four monks. Certainly one of the purposes in exploring this newly discovered continent was to convert the natives to Christianity. The Spanish brought crucifixes, crosses, and rosaries to distribute to their converts. Presumably, the excavated crosses were given to professing Indians. When they died, these prized possessions accompanied their bodies to the grave.

"These silver ornaments were doubtless held in high esteem," Jones wrote, "because, in beauty of material, symmetry of form, and excellency of manufacture, they far excelled all the products of aboriginal fabrication."

So far so good, but a controversy soon to erupt involved decorations engraved on the crosses. Both sides of each artifact were inscribed, apparently by the manufacturer, with circular engravings and geometric and floral patterns. Crudely added later to one cross is a complete image of an owl within an ornamental circle. On the opposite side, the head and neck of a horse had been scratched between the circles, and within the circle below an enigmatic inscription read "IYNKICIDU," or from right to left, "UDICIKNYI." This "word" intrigued Jones and has continued to excite pseudoarchaeologists for over a century.

Jones thought it obvious that an unskilled person had executed these rude engravings, probably an Indian, using a clumsy tool.

Jones went on to "suggest that the native, into whose ownership one of these crosses passed, endeavored with a flint flake to perpetuate his recollection of this animal (the horse) which, in his esteem, was not less remarkable than the pale-faced stranger or his shining gift?"

The myth-making process began with Charles Fort, the original collector of UFO reports and encounters with strange creatures and phenomena, who also sought out intriguing archaeological anomalies. In the early twentieth century he wrote about the crosses in *Book of the Damned*, casting doubt on Jones's suppositions.

"In the Rept. Smithson. Inst., 1881–619, there is an account, by Charles C. Jones, of two silver crosses that were found in Georgia. They are skillfully made, highly ornamented crosses, but are not conventional crucifixes; all arms of equal length. Mr. Jones is a good positivist—that de Soto had halted at the 'precise' spot where these crosses were found. But the spirit of negativeness that lurks in all things said to be 'precise' shows itself in that upon one of these crosses is an inscription that has no meaning in Spanish or any other known, terrestrial language: 'IYNKICIDU,' according to Mr. Jones. He thinks that this is a name, and that there is an aboriginal ring to it, though I should say, myself, that he was thinking of the far-distant Incas; that the Spanish donor cut on the cross the name of an Indian to whom it was presented. But we look at the inscription ourselves and see that the letters said to be C and D are turned the wrong way, and that the letter said to be K is not only turned the wrong way, but is upside down."

Worse was yet to come. In a 1950s book about UFOs, the crosses were theorized to have been left by ancient extraterrestrial visitors. Other writers wondered if they were artifacts originating from the lost continents of Mu, Lumeria, or the more familiar Atlantis.

Brag Steiger's 1974 *Mysteries of Time and Space* is a good example. While noting that the engraving of the horse suggests post-European influences, he proposed, "According to copious fossil evidence—the horse was not unknown to this continent in *prehistoric* times."

Steiger next criticizes the hypothesis that "IYNKICIDU" was carved by "some semi-literate Amerindian" and incorrectly claims that Jones suggested it was the name of his tribe.

"But I never heard of any tribe of Amerindians named the Iynkicidus," Steiger continued, "nor any tribe even phonetically similar." Spelling it backward "offers even fewer possibilities. Is Iynkicidu a Latin or a Spanish word?" That would be unlikely, Steiger wrote, "unless a semi-literate silversmith or priest engraved a corruption of the name of a person, place, or thing on the cross," which is undoubtedly what actually occurred.

Steiger then trotted out his theory, asking, "Should we at least entertain the possibility that they may be artifacts from an unknown civilization that once flourished on the North American continent? A civilization that we might christen 'The United States of Iynkicidu.'" A culture that might have moved south and formed the Aztec and Maya cultures, he continued. "The empire builders of our forgotten nation may even have established outposts in North Africa and the Middle East, for whoever these forgotten people were, they were technologically more sophisticated than even the walls of these buried mystery cities would indicate."

All this from the evidence of two crude crosses.

Now for reality.

In 1966 Dr. George Irving Quimby of Washington State University in Seattle devoted several pages of his book, *Indian Culture and European Trade Goods*, to silver crosses.

"Silver crosses of several kinds were common ornaments used in the Indian trade," he wrote. "They were worn by the men as chest ornaments or sometimes as ear ornaments."

Quimby estimated that thousands of crosses were manufactured for use as goods in the fur trade. Because the fur trade demanded only the best quality silver, the craftsmen who made the crosses were well known and handsomely paid American, British, and Canadian silversmiths. For example, in May 1759, Phili Syng of Philadelphia was paid 115 pounds for 720 silver ornaments, including eleven dozen crosses. Over a four-year period one fur-trading company, McGill, spent more than four thousand pounds on silver ornaments.

Dr. David J. Hally at the University of Georgia kindly located for me an unpublished paper from the Laboratory of Archaeology that examined the cross controversy in detail. Titled "Explorations in Sixtoe Field, Carter's Dam, Murray County, Georgia," its primary author was the late Dr. A. R. Kelly, former professor emeritus at the university. The report detailed three years of excavations at Coosa Old Town between 1962 and 1964. Three mound sites—Sixtoe, Bell Fields, and Little Egypt—were explored. The crosses were taken from one of those.

Kelly's work proved that the site had been part of the historic Cherokee Nation. The Cherokee secretary of the nation had lived there, and a Methodist mission was established in the early 1800s. The community was on the primary Indian path that crossed the region and on the Federal Road, a heavily traveled thoroughfare in the early United States.

Within a burial mound, which is where the crosses had been found, Kelly's group discovered an intrusive eighteenth-century burial in a pine box, fastened with iron screws and containing glass beads.

In the *Etowah Papers*, noted archaeologist Dr. Warren K. Moorehead mentioned several iron objects, including a sword or knife, which he recovered from Little Egypt in the late 1920s. The UGA manuscript indicated this portion of the site exhibited more evidence of historic contact than the other two mounds. The crosses probably came from there.

When asked his opinion of the crosses, Clemens de Baillou, former director of the August Museum, suggested to Dr. Kelly that the famed Sequoyah was responsible for the added decorations on the crosses.

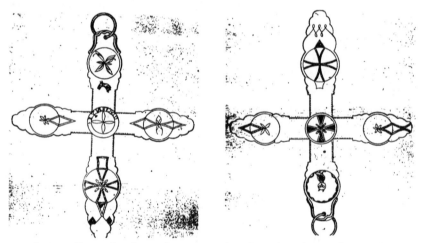

A view of one side of two silver crosses found in a burial mound in northern Georgia. Hypothesized to have been left by ancient astronauts, Atlanteans, or various prehistoric seafarers, they are actually European trade goods about two hundred years old. The inscribed owl may have a supernatural meaning. (Smithsonian Annual Report, 1881)

"It seemed a very primitive work," Baillou stated. "This alone speaks for Indian work influenced by white man's gadgets and ideas, especially to mention the Indian ornamentation with sun circles and zigzag-rayed motif underneath and the owl, which was in this area a ghostly symbol—It seemed to me rather a dabbling with Roman script as the illiterate Sequoyah did for many years until he developed his famous syllabary. As we know he was silently, but deeply, opposed to Christianity and that could be the reason that there are no Christian symbols on the cross, while the cross itself was also an Indian symbol."

Albert Manvey, a National Park Service Historian at Castillo de San Marcos in Saint Augustine, Florida, dismissed the idea that the Spanish had left the crosses.

"The basic designs are not in the Spanish classical tradition, and the engraving impresses me as the product of a relatively unschooled mind."

Dr. Quimby believed our mysterious artifacts were imitations of European trade goods, a "poor copy or job by apprentice of trade silver crosses of the period 1750–1820. Engraved design done for most part by compass. Also no touch (identification) mark. In my opinion crosses are made about 1770–1790 or later and may be work of an English trader or possibly work of an Indian silversmith."

Quimby also suggested that Sequoyah was responsible for the crosses.

Arthur Woodward, another researcher of silver trade goods, wrote: "My personal belief is that these crosses were made by Indian silversmiths somewhere in the south, eighteenth or early nineteenth centuries." Woodward also found that other silver ornaments of historic origin have been excavated at Indian sites. He found a "general distribution of trade and gift silver ornaments" by French, English, American, and Spanish governments. This was not a large-scale operation until after 1750, and the period 1750–1765 saw a "flood of silver" as Europeans vied for Indian allies during the French and Indian War.

The consensus of opinion from knowledgeable historians is that the crosses were made by Indian or American craftsmen between 1790 and 1850. The artifacts were not crafted by Atlantans, ancient astronauts, or even Spanish conquistadors. Many legitimate mysteries remain in archaeology, but the origin of Georgia's silver crosses has been identified.

At last report, the crosses were owned by a Belmont, Massachusetts, family that purchased a collection of Indian relics from Jones's heirs in 1922.

THE SUBTERRANEAN VILLAGE OF DUKES CREEK

In 1829 gold deposits were discovered along Dukes Creek, which flows into the Chattahoochee River a few miles south of Helen in Habersham County. The precious material was found both as placer gold in the creek bed and in alluvial deposits in the banks and surrounding floodplain. Miners dug a number of canals to divert the stream, which allowed them to exploit gold-bearing gravel and sand from ledges and potholes in the creek bed, provided water to operate sluice boxes, and washed out material excavated from the valley floor.

In 1834 Colonels Merriwether and Lumsden were excavating a canal at the "Eaton Diggings," fifty to one hundred yards from the creek, when they discovered a wooden construction made of logs, hewn at the ends and stacked and notched at the corners. Further digging revealed a roofless "cabin" attached to a second. Intrigued, workers followed the logs and eventually discovered a string of thirty-four connected cabins or "rooms" which extended in a straight line for three hundred feet. They were buried at a depth of three to nine feet, some embedded in alluvial gravel. Every early-nineteenth-century account of this find emphasized that the cabins were built in a style contemporary with common Southern cabins. These structures were either constructed subterranean (doubtful) or rapidly inundated by spring floods in the narrow valley (evidence that this was not the product of Indians—they were too wise to build on the floodplain.) Cut marks on the wood proved they had been prepared with sharp iron axes, which indicated it was not the work of prehistoric Indians.

Twelve years before the excavations, the forest had been cleared from the land for cultivation of the rich bottomland. Ages of the hardwood trees, two to three feet in diameter, ranged from 150 to 200 years, or dating back to around 1630, more or less.

According to an account from 1850, one cabin contained "three baskets made of cane splits and a number of fragments of Indian ware." Other artifacts were excavated in the vicinity, including a one-gallon-capacity crucible located ten feet below the surface and beneath an oak tree five feet in diameter. A double mortar, also called a stone trough or sand crucible, was discovered in Dukes Creek. It was five inches in diameter and had an inch-thick depression on each side.

Charles Lanman, an explorer/writer who traveled through the area in 1848, wrote a year later in *Letters from the Allegheny Mountains* that in the vicinity "something resembling a furnace, together with iron spoons, pieces of earthenware, and leaden plates, were disinterred."

Early credit for the construction went to Prince Madoc, who did a little mining before fortifying Fort Mountain. The Vikings and de Soto were long thought to have passed through the Nacoochee Valley. One writer suggested they were pigpens that restrained de Soto's meat on the hoof. The cabins were much too elaborate for hogs or even for fast-moving conquistadors. However, the time frame seems consistent with the Spanish era in southern North America.

The probable solution to this mystery was proposed by George William Featherstonaugh (whew!), an Englishman of long-term U.S. residency who worked for the Bureau of Topographical Engineers surveying gold fields in the southeast. His exploits were later chronicled in his book, *A Cane Trip up the Minnay Sotor* (beats me).

In 1837 Featherstonaugh visited the area of Dukes Creek, where he heard about the strange wooden cabins and examined a "micaceous stone trough" associated with them. He did not visit the site but continued to Murphy, North Carolina, where he heard about the remains of an ancient mining endeavor near the Valley River. There he found a familiar stone trough, an incomplete iron smelting furnace, and eleven old mining shafts, each about one hundred feet deep. Beneath a pile of rocks at the bottom of one was found a number of human skeletons. In 1854 miners working in the area located five additional shafts with two-hundred-year-old trees growing among the ruins. They also found several well-preserved wooden windlasses banded with iron, and a shaft hacked through twenty-five feet of hard rock with sharp metal tools.

An elderly Cherokee woman related a legend to Featherstonaugh concerning a group of yellowish-skinned people who arrived long before and started mining operations. More of the strangers arrived until they annoyed the Indians enough to kill them all.

Featherstonaugh returned to Dukes Creek in 1840, when he examined the site and a piece of remaining wood, which soon crumbled to dust. He believed the cabins were not habitations but containers for a cache of some material.

Dr. Thomas Lumsden, a Clarkesville doctor and descendant of one of the subterranean village's discoverers, believes that Spanish colonists in Florida or the Caribbean heard reports of gold in the Appalachian Mountains from de Soto's survivors and mounted an undocumented mining expedition that operated in Dukes Creek and Murphy.

Antiquarian Charles C. Jones developed a possible scenario. He suggested that Spanish leader Luis de Velasco, acting on information gathered by de Soto's expedition, dispatched General Tristan de Luna to open an avenue of advance into the area. A force of three hundred Spanish soldiers were dispatched to northern Georgia and spent the summer of 1560 near Rome. Juan Pardo was directed by Florida governor Aviles to build a fort at the foot of the mountains. From these historic accounts we know the Spanish were active in the region.

Johannes Lederer, who traveled through Virginia and the Carolinas in 1669, wrote that the Spanish were mining gold and silver in the Appalachians. He produced samples of their ore as proof. In 1690 Indians informed James Moore, on a tour of the mountains, that the Spanish were operating mines just twenty miles away.

Mystery solved and case closed. The Spanish did it.

ANCIENT IRON ARTIFACTS

In March 1928, Dr. Warren K. Moorehead, director of the department of archaeology at Phillips Academy in Andover, Massachusetts, began excavating the largest of three mounds near Coosawattee Old Town. Two weeks into the dig, amidst a number of aboriginal skeletons, he discovered the remains of heavily oxidized iron swords and pikes.

"The longest of these objects is six and one-half inches," his report, published by Yale University Press, related, "while the lengths of the others are, one sword fragment three and three-quarter inches, the other four and one-half inches. The slender pointed objects are four and three-quarter and five and three-quarter inches. These fragments of swords and pike points, or whatever they are, were found with skeleton H, fairly well preserved, and buried some six feet below the surface. The ground was disturbed and we considered H as an intrusive interment."

The iron artifacts were shipped to the Metropolitan Museum of Art in New York City for scrutiny by an expert in the area of weapons and armor. His report was less conclusive, stating that the objects were old and "not of American Colonial period." He could not determine if they were of Spanish origin because the artifacts had "no hilts or maker's marks, and the dates could not be distinguished."

According to William Conner, a reporter for the *Columbus Dispatch*, Moorehead found "the remains of what must have been a pit iron smelter inside a mound at Etowah." Moorehead himself accepted a local story that a nearby plantation owner's slaves had constructed and operated the furnace. Such devices had been used in Africa for centuries, but no other furnaces, or even stories of additional such devices, have been located in Georgia.

Conner believes that prehistoric Native Americans were responsible for the pit furnace. North Georgia certainly had iron ore. A well-known ironworks, Cooper's, operated ten miles from Etowah until after the Civil War.

While the romantic is tempted to accept the theory of a prehistoric American "iron age," the iron in Georgia mounds can probably be attributed to the Spanish. Witness the following story.

THE SWORD IN THE RED CLAY

In 1539 six hundred Spanish conquistadors under the command of Hernando de Soto landed in Tampa Bay. Over the next four years they wandered seventeen hundred miles across ten Southern states, including a trek through modern-day Georgia, before ending in Texas with half the expedition, including de Soto, dead. Since that time historians and archaeologists have vigorously attempted to trace de Soto's path. At long last, we know one spot in Georgia where they definitely stopped.

During the summer of 1982 David Hally, an anthropologist with the University of Georgia, and a team of archaeologists excavated three acres of land at the King Site near Rome. Located on Foster Bend along the Coosa River, King Site was a significant village inhabited when de Soto passed through Georgia. The team ate lunch each day in an adjacent wooded grove. At summer's end the artifacts and skeletons they excavated were crated and stored for study at Georgia State University. The landowner then sold the property and the wooded lot was leveled.

Several years later three local men, Larry Itson, Steve Redden, and Jeffery Raymond, were searching the fields for Indian relics when one of them spotted bones. Excavation revealed a pitted steel sword form the sixteenth century, making it one of the most important historical finds in the history of Georgia.

The weapon was loaned to the Etowah Indian Mounds for five years, until 1988, when the men received an offer for the historic treasure. At that point the property owner claimed it belonged to him. The state retained custody while the lawsuit wended its way through the courts. In July 1989 the discoverers were awarded the sword.

The sword is not the only proof of a Spanish presence at the King Site. A large number of skeletons unearthed there reveal both unusual slash marks and gnawing marks from rodents. Deaths from American Indian combat resulted primarily from puncture wounds inflicted by sharpened sticks, which were thrust. Edged Indian weapons were not designed for slashing.

Spanish soldiers were trained to kill with the long-bladed iron swords they carried. Against armored foes in Europe, most wounds were inflicted on exposed limbs and the head. The wounds on skeletons from the King Site were compared to wounds inflicted at a Danish battle in 1361. In both cases 78 percent of the wounds were slash marks to the skull and extremities.

An analysis by the New York Metropolitan Museum of Art proved that the sword had been manufactured between 1530 and 1568 in Europe. Pottery and other artifacts found with the burials also date to the same time.

DEM BONES

Was there a great battle near Rome? No, but a study of expedition records revealed that at this site Europeans enslaved a number of men and women and forced them to accompany the Spanish on their journey west.

"Many of the wounds—were clearly inflicted by metal weapons," one archaeologist involved in the study of the Georgia skeletons said. "Because there was only one battle of this magnitude that fits the place and time, we have to conclude that these people were killed by de Soto's men at the battle of Mabila on October, 18, 1540."

171

Somewhere in southern Alabama, Native Americans sprung a trap on the Spanish. When the desperate battle of Mabila (the name of my childhood Boy Scout camp in the same area, which might explain those voices at night) concluded, twenty-five hundred to five thousand Indians had been killed, making this one of the largest battles in American history. The Spanish prevailed, but eighteen were killed and 150 wounded. After a month of recovery, the Spanish continued west.

At this point the second unique feature of the skeletons is explained. Historians believe that the inhabitants of King were required to wait a month before recovering their dead and taking them home for burial. By that time mice, rats, opossums, and other scavengers had fed on the decaying bodies.

Archaeologists are confident that the site of Mabila has been discovered a few miles below Selma, Alabama, on the west bank of the Cahaba River where it joins the Alabama River. This is also a significant place in American history—it was the site of Alabama's first capital and a Confederate prison for captured Union soldiers. Excavations have revealed traces of a shallow moat and a defensive wooden palisade that had been burned—all elements of the place where Indians attempted to annihilate the Spanish 460 years ago.

Other evidence related to the Conquistadors in the state have surfaced for years. Pieces of iron described as "Spanish armor" have been reported from the Okefenokee Swamp to DeSoto Falls in north Georgia. A documented discovery in the possession of the Georgia Department of Natural Resources is the lid of a Spanish burial urn found near Dahlonega.

THE DARE STONES
Perhaps John White was thinking "Third time's the charm" when he landed on the island of Roanoke, now in North Carolina, in July 1587, with 119 other English citizens. Two earlier settlement attempts had failed, but White worked hard to help this one succeed by smoothing relations with local Indians. He left a month later, leaving his daughter, Eleanor Dare, her husband, Ananias, and a granddaughter, Virginia, the first English child born in America and named for the virgin queen, to attend to urgent business in England. He expected to return within a few months. It was agreed that if the settlers had to abandon Roanoke in distress, the colonists would carve crosses on trees; if they left with friendly Indians, they would carve a message.

RESISTANCE IS FUTILE
War with Spain intervened, delaying White's return until 1590. He found the settlement abandoned, no crosses, and the single word "CROATOAN"

carved on a tree, apparently referring to a neighboring tribe of Indians. Speculation ran rampant for 350 years—the English had been wiped out by hostile Indians or willingly absorbed when their food ran out. Reports of fair-skinned and fair-haired "Indians" speaking a curious dialect were legion, but the leads never produced anything of substance.

Fast-forward to November 1937, when L. E. Hammond of Georgia entered the hallowed halls of Emory University. He carried a twenty-pound rock found in a North Carolina swamp that had indecipherable carvings on both sides.

The curiosity circulated through the faculty until it reached history professor Dr. Haywood Pearce Jr., who was also vice president of Brenau College in Gainesville, where Pearce Sr. was president and owner.

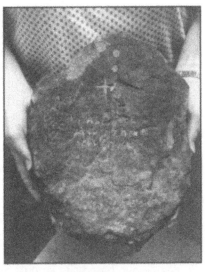

Dozens of the infamous Dare Stones are stored on the campus of Brenau University in Gainesville. This is the original stone, kept in the library, and it is the only one of the stones believed by historians to be genuine.

Pearce's interpretation of the stone shocked America. "Ananias Dare & Virginia went hence unto heaven 1591." It was apparently the gravestone of John White's son-in-law and granddaughter. A longer but fainter message on the opposite side took longer to decipher, a task made no easier by the Elizabethan English in which it was written.

At length Pearce announced that the message, initiated by Eleanor White Dare, described their peaceful refuge but later decimation by a different Indian tribe. Only seven of the English survived; seventeen were buried on a hill near the gravestone. Linguists agreed that it was authentic Elizabethan English, and geologists determined that it had been produced about four hundred years earlier.

L. E. Hammond led Pearce and other scholars to a swamp on the Chowan River near Edenton, North Carolina, eighty miles east of Roanoke. Nothing was found then or during five subsequent searches mounted by Pearce Jr., who was sometimes accompanied by Pearce Sr. Frustrated, he made a controversial move, offering locals a reward for locating the cemetery.

The historical mystery quieted for a while. Pearce remained intrigued, but others began to question Hammond's motives—and his identity. The stone's finder was interested in exploiting his discovery for cash, and no one knew who he was—his California address was a post office box. The Pearces moved the stone to Brenau, the family business, and sent Hammond the pricey Great Depression sum of one thousand dollars for full ownership of the stone. Hammond was never heard from again.

Early in 1939 William Eberhart, an Atlanta carpenter and stonemason, produced two pieces of soapstone he found on a hill near Greenville, South Carolina, hundreds of miles from Roanoke. Pearce paid Eberhart a small sum, which apparently encouraged him to find more in the same place. Dated 1591, they listed the names of the seventeen colonists allegedly buried in North Carolina. "God hab mercye," it pled, and was signed "Eleanor Dare."

Why the stones were found so far from North Carolina was a mystery, but the carpenter, who had only a third-grade education, could not have manufactured them.

Pearce purchased the land in South Carolina for fifteen hundred dollars. He personally discovered nothing, but others found thirteen additional stones there. Perhaps this was the cemetery, and the gravestone had been displaced, Pearce theorized, in an attempt to take it to John White.

One stone contained a message from Eleanor: "Father wee goe SW," and by thunder that is where the next stones were found, on the banks of the Chattahoochee River near Atlanta. Produced in late 1939 by I. A. Turner, a local handyman, the inscriptions on these were intended to inform John White that his colonists had gone to live with friendly Indians in the "primeval splendor" of Southern forests. "Father, God brynge you hither," one note pleaded.

The year 1940 turned into a banner one for Dare stones. Two additional Georgians, T. R. Jetty and William Bruce, found several inscribed stones. Eberhart, a source of engraved rocks from South Carolina, discovered more, also from Georgia.

YES, SPELLCHECK HAD A FIT WITH THIS

The now extensive series of hard-copy letters home revealed that Dare had remarried, this time to an Indian king, and birthed a second daughter. In 1598 she wrote (or carved), "Father, I beseeche you had mye dowter goe to englande." A final stone, from Griffen Jones, a fellow Englishman, announced, "Eleanor dye February" 1599.

By this time scholars and the press were flocking to tiny Brenau College in Gainesville to study the stones and interview Pearce Jr. Replica stones were proudly displayed at the Georgia exhibition during the 1940 New York World's Fair. Pearce lectured and wrote scholarly treaties on the stones and was frequently interviewed on radio. However, he did not unequivocally pronounce the message rocks genuine, but stated that a hoax of this magnitude would be "more fantastic than the story itself."

FOOL ME ONCE

To stamp *settled* on the controversy, in October 1940 a team of nationally esteemed historians, led by Harvard University's finest, Samuel Eliot Morrison, the world's leading expert on early American exploration, descended upon Georgia.

These learned men scrutinized the stones, interviewed the finders (minus the elusive Hammond), and examined a cave on the banks of the Chattahoochee River a short distance north of Atlanta, where several Dare stones had been discovered. "Eleanor Dare heyr sithence 1593," an inscription on the cave wall declared.

"The preponderance of evidence," the academic dream team declared, "points to the authenticity of the stones commonly known as the Dare stones."

With this endorsement, Pearce penned a popular article about the famous stones for the *Saturday Evening Post*. With Morrison's blessing, the editors purchased the piece, but dispatched Boyden Sparkes, a hard-boiled investigative reporter, to check the facts. Sparkes began his investigation at Roanoke and the Dare stone sites in North and South Carolina, then fell upon Atlanta. In Georgia he interviewed Pearce, inspected the stones, which now totaled forty-eight, questioned the men (again minus Hammond) who had discovered them, and examined the places where the rocks were found.

Sparkes's conclusion, published in the *Post* in April 1941, stunned the world. The four men who had produced stones from Georgia and the Carolinas had criminal records. Worse yet, they knew each other.

Sparkes also questioned the coincidence of nearly fifty stones, hidden for 350 years, all suddenly coming to light within three years. He wondered how one simple man found Dare stones in South Carolina and Georgia, the last ones only four miles from his house. And don't forget the shadowy Hammond, a Californian who found the original stone in North Carolina and brought it to Georgia.

Experts decided that some stones seemed to have been engraved recently, and linguists questioned whether certain words used in the messages had been in use around 1600.

Pearce was quoted as saying that a hoaxer in this case would be "deranged, but brilliant with great imagination and tremendous creative ability." Sparkes suggested Pearce had described himself.

STONED

The fame enjoyed by Pearce Jr. turned into infamy overnight. He considered legal action against the *Post*, but soon accused one of his stone sources of fraud. The accused called Pearce and his family fakes. The stones were no longer displayed at Brenau, and Pearce admitted that they were "discredited."

This last sad saga started, according to Pearce, on April 18, when Eberhart called to report a new stone found near where Long Island Creek entered the Chattahoochee.

"There was a face of rock about as big as the side of a room," Pearce stated. "It was very rough and covered with moss and lichen, all except one smooth place, which had carving on it." The artifact "looked phony," he said, "the first stone that looked wrong. It looked fresh." When Pearce admonished Eberhart, the mason "got very sulky and angry."

Suspicious, Pearce returned with Professor Count Gibson, a Georgia Tech chemist, who discovered a bottle containing purple fluid in a burned-out tree trunk. The carving was tinged a distinct purplish hue. After a minute's examination, Gibson declared, "This is a fake." A state chemist, Reynolds Clark, found the liquid to be a vegetable dye.

Stung by the incident on the Chattahoochee, Eberhart refused to deal with Pearce or his father. On May 4 Eberhart called Pearce's wife and "said he had a stone, fully covered with moss and undisturbed, which would prove it all," Pearce Jr. stated. It was a week before Mrs. Pearce could meet with Eberhart. She was driven to Buckhead by her father-in-law, who remained nearby. Eberhart showed Mrs. Pearce an engraved stone that read, "Pearce and Dare Historical Hoax. Our motto is—We Dare Anything." He "said the *Saturday Evening Post* would be interested in buying the stone and his story."

Mrs. Pearce contacted her husband, who met Eberhart at his shack in the woods that evening and scribbled out two statements. The first statement, unsigned, was written in pencil. It read: "In consideration of $200 paid to the undersigned, I agree not to divulge anything regarding the fraudulent character of stone delivered to H. J. Pearce in the past and not to deliver any other carved stones to other parties than said H. J. Pearce and not to discuss with or communicate with other parties any matter pertaining to the so-called Dare stones."

Because Eberhart wanted his money first, he declined to sign the paper. Pearce wanted some proof of Eberhart's duplicity before he left, so he wrote a second statement on the back of an envelope, which Eberhart signed. It read: "I agree to accept from H. J. Pearce Jr. $200 on Thursday night, May 13, in connection with the matter between us. W. A. Eberhart." Pearce claimed that Eberhart held a rifle across his knees during the proceedings and would not allow Pearce to approach him.

Pearce conferred with Judge Jule W. Felton, who sat on the court of appeals, and Bone Almand, solicitor of the county criminal court, before returning to Eberhart's shack Wednesday night with Professor Gibson. Eberhart said in front of Gibson that the statements written Monday and his signature were genuine.

Pearce accused the mason of trying to "foist off a fake carving" on him. He said Eberhart told his wife that if she did not pay him two hundred dollars, he would tell the *Post* that the stones were fakes. Pearce immediately called his lawyers. However, Pearce had to admit that he had given Eberhart twelve hundred dollars and Hammond one thousand dollars to keep their stones.

Between the two meetings with Eberhart, Pearce located and obtained statements of authenticity from every other person who had found stones, with Hammond the exception.

In mid-May 1941, Eberhart, who had discovered most of the Dare stones, signed a statement that said all save one of his stones had been found where officials at Brenau College directed him to search. He strenuously denied carving any of the stones or having any knowledge of such a scheme.

Eberhart explained that his first stone had been found accidentally in 1937 when he walked into a field for a rock to use as a jack when his truck had a flat tire. He noticed carving on it and took it home, where it stayed in his shack near Atlanta for two years, until "I read in the paper about these old stones" being sought by the Pearces. He took it to them and they purchased it for fifty dollars, saying, "it was just some sort of Spanish trail marker." They sent him off for more, and he soon located eight others within an area of fifty square feet near Piedmont, South Carolina. He also noted "signs of digging around there," implying that someone had recently deposited the stones.

Eberhart turned over the stones and did not hear from the Pearces for a time. "Then they told me to go up above Gainesville and look along the banks of the Chattahoochee," where he found thirteen additional engraved rocks, he claimed. "They were, some of them, buried in the dirt, with the writing on them facedown, and some were sticking up out of the ground, and some were on top of the ground. They were all in a place about fifty to one hundred feet square.

"I was getting my expenses paid on these trips and they cost a right smart (amount) of money," Eberhart continued. "With expenses, and what I got out of the stones, which averaged nearly fifty dollars a piece," or $2,000. When the Pearces purchased the land in South Carolina, they gave Eberhart a half interest but later bought it back.

The final stones were found "along the Chattahoochee near Atlanta." The site was close to an old Indian village where artifacts were frequently found, "in a stretch about a mile long" where "the Pearces told me to look.

"The last one I found, the one which said, 'Pearce and Dare Historical Hoax. We Dare Anything,' was found along the Chattahoochee, too. It looked just like the rest of them, the writing did, I mean.

"I called the Pearces about this stone, and they came down and I showed it to them. Then I put it under my bed and the first thing I knew it was gone."

Eberhart denied admitting to manufacturing fakes and the blackmail attempt. He maintained that several weeks earlier he had stumbled across the hoax stone and showed it to Mrs. Pearce. Eberhart disappeared shortly thereafter.

Pearce immediately and vigorously counterattacked, intensifying the controversy by releasing the two documents, which he believed proved that Eberhart admitted faking the stones in an effort to extort two hundred dollars from him.

"We are interested in but two things," Pearce said. "One is to establish the truth. The other is to keep Brenau College, as always, in the clear."

Pearce acknowledged that "The whole proposition is badly discredited," but stated that five stones, unconnected to Eberhart, might be genuine, and that three of Eberhart's early discoveries could be also.

A *New York Times* editorial stated that the stones "just reeked with the kind of information about the lost colonists which people have been thirsting for. Genuine archaeological finds are never so explicit. They leave the scholars to piece out the information from fragments and shadows." An adept description of archaeology, a field I nearly entered. But that was before I realized that it involved squatting in the heat for lengthy periods of time.

Morrison had declared the stones either genuine or a "fantastic hoax." He had scrutinized many high-caliber fakes, but they "were not in the same class" as the Dare stones, he concluded. In 1971, the year Pearce died, Morrison insisted that he had "politely—declared the stones to be fake" back in 1940.

The Dare Stones are stored out of public view at Brenau, where history professor Jim Southerland is the reigning expert and has dealt with inquiries concerning the stones for years. Pearce, "a good, respected historian," he believed, was not guilty of fraud, just losing "his objectivity" in the excitement of achieving fame in his field. He believes there is a chance that the original stone submitted by the enigmatic Hammond might be authentic.

WRIT ON ROCK

In central Georgia, five miles south of Dublin in Laurens County, is Blackshear's Ferry, an early crossing point of the Oconee River. It was established, local tradition states, by members of the Lost Colony from Roanoke. We know that it existed prior to 1790, operated by Creek Indians, before David Blackshear took control of the ferry and removed the Creeks from this part of the state.

A mile north of the ferry site is Indian Spring Rock, a stone seven feet long and four feet high. One side of the rock, artificially smoothed, has characters reminiscent of Egyptian hieroglyphics carved into it. No one has ever been able to decipher these markings. From beneath the rock flows a stream of clear water.

Decades past I was attempting to get information about another prehistoric site from a certain archaeologist at the University of Georgia. I thought a trade of information was in order, and offered to guide him to this site. He refused my request, but demanded to know where the petroglyph was. I told him to go to hell.

It is amusing to think about future archaeologists examining our long-vanished culture and asking, "What gods were they worshipping at Stone Mountain?" (Actually, considering the fierce devotion many Southerners have to figures associated with the Civil War, they might be correct.)

5

UFOs: The '70s, '80s, and '90s

It would have been difficult for the UFO phenomenon to trump the massive incursion of 1973, so it didn't try. It mutated. Enter contactees, long-vanished labor leader Jimmy Hoffa, perhaps a crashed UFO, and spectacular but isolated bursts of sightings. The UFO community also went political in an unintentionally humorous manner.

LATE HARVEST MOONS

A brief but concentrated flurry of UFO activity descended upon southwest Georgia on the morning of November 20, 1975, witnessed primarily by law-enforcement personnel.

The sightings started in Leary, twenty miles southwest of Albany, where Police Chief James Spivey spotted strange lights outside the station at 2:00 A.M.

"When I first saw it, it was only two hundred to three hundred feet high," Spivey said the next day. "The middle of the thing was white, a glowing kind of white. There was a revolving red light on top and a blue revolving light on the bottom."

The large, round object was directly overhead. Spivey noted that the central, pulsating white light was dull, but when it lit up "It was so bright you couldn't tell what it looked like. It was so bright, it lit up the whole front of the building."

The UFO slowly climbed to about ten thousand feet and moved to the southeast.

A number of neighbors witnessed the phenomenon and supported Spivey's testimony. "Everybody from city councilmen to deputy sheriffs saw it, too," he pointed out.

At 3:15 A.M. Camilla police lieutenant David Chapman and patrolman Freddie Martin spotted an unusual light in western Mitchell County. At the police station, dispatcher Edna Stock fielded several reports from

181

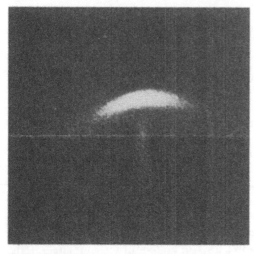

Michael Williford was a high school student when he photographed this UFO at 11:45 P.M. on October 26, 1974, in his backyard three blocks from the center of Camilla. (Courtesy of Michael Williford)

local residents. After hearing numerous UFO sightings over his police radio, Mitchell County sheriff lieutenant Jimmy Ray Sanders drove to a field just east of Camilla and joined six men observing one of the lights.

"There were three of them," Sanders stated, "but one dropped down below the trees." One was a bright light, and another, estimated to be twenty-five miles distant, had a slowly flashing red light. The latter slowly ascended into the sky.

About 3:00 A.M. an unidentified woman who had been traveling on U.S. 84 between Bainbridge and Donaldsonville called the sheriff's office to report a "huge round ball with blinking lights on it," according to Decatur County deputy sheriff Mike Phillips. The object was "about as high as a radio tower," Phillips continued, around two hundred feet high, and resembled a "flashlight when the batteries are about to go dead."

State patrol communications officer James Oldham in Albany received additional UFO sighting reports from Valdosta, Moultrie, Blakely, Adel,

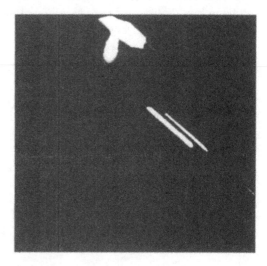

A second photo snapped by Michael Williford appears to show objects leaving the UFO. (Courtesy of Michael Williford)

182

and Arlington. C. W. Duffy, a state patrol dispatcher, said most sightings were of objects with red lights on top and green ones on the bottom.

John Everett, an Albany flight specialist, found only one plane aloft at the time, and that near Dothan, Alabama, too distant to account for the local sightings. Everett thought the active lights were a result of watching through cheap binoculars. Chief Spivey retorted that he "was looking at the thing with my naked eye."

At Fernbank Science Center in DeKalb County, astronomer Robert Haywood believed the sightings described the rising or setting of planets, which were clearly visible in the cold, clear morning sky. Venus, rising at 4:00 A.M., was a bright white light to the southeast, and Mars, colored red, and Jupiter both set in the northwest.

On a personal note, my college roommate, now a Waycross physician who shall remain anonymous (but you know who you are, so pay up or I'll use your name in the second edition), was driving from Columbus to Americus that night and observed the same phenomenon. He described it to me before the other sightings were publicized, unfortunately waking me from a sound sleep.

Bo & Peep, the San Diego UFO-Suicide Cult, and Contactees in Georgia

America was stunned in late March 1997 with word that thirty-nine members of a UFO cult had killed themselves in a $10,000-a-month mansion in San Diego. The number was shocking, the method bizarre. The dead dressed in identical black "uniforms" with new black Nikes. They placed a passport, driver's license, five-dollar bill, and roll of quarters in their pockets (for cosmic snack machines?), took a combination of alcohol and Phenobarbital, a sedative, and lay down quietly on their dormitory bunks to die. They had shed their earthly "containers" and hoped to hitch a ride with a giant UFO purportedly trailing the comet Hale-Bopp.

Their leader was Marshall H. Applewhite, seminarian, professional singer, music teacher at the University of Alabama, son of a minister, and father of two children. In the early 1970s his life disintegrated. Applewhite was fired from Saint Thomas University for a homosexual relationship with a student, and spent time in a mental hospital. He divorced his wife and had himself castrated to eliminate sexual urges.

Applewhite then met a nurse named Bonnie Lu Trusdale Nettles, who believed Applewhite had been chosen by extraterrestrials for a special mission. He and she believed aliens occupied their bodies and minds. The pair, now known as Bo and Peep, and later Do and Ti or simply the Two, went looking for "sheep," recruiting across the country and streaking to brief national prominence in 1975 when they and twenty disciples were stood up one night by a UFO in rural Colorado.

One city they hit was Atlanta, where their appearance provoked concern over cults and "brainwashing" techniques. In early fall 1975 the first reports in Atlanta surfaced that a bizarre couple had been in the area recruiting people to join their UFO cult. Inductees were instructed to quit their jobs, sell all their worldly goods and donate the proceeds to the group, and abandon their children on the promise that aliens would take them away in a flying saucer to nirvana (no such place, right Kurt?).

Various officials stepped forward to discredit this effort, including Rev. Tim Smith, head of the Alexandrian Temple of Light, who should know the truth—he had long been in contact with the aliens. He had learned of this group's effort months earlier from the aliens, who were really ticked off about the sham.

"This is not the way the extraterrestrials operate," Smith explained. "They aren't taking people from earth to another planet. The space beings aren't interested in money. Money won't buy you a trip on a spaceship."

THE CITY TOO BUSY TO BE INCREDULOUS

Smith maintained that Atlanta had developed into the spiritual capital of the world. "The extraterrestrials have selected Atlanta and a four-hundred-mile radius as its main area of concentration," he claimed.

The aliens supposedly first contacted Smith in 1973. Before that time he "knew they existed," but "had never contemplated or been fascinated by UFOs. I wasn't interested at all," until one night after a service. "I was asleep and I heard a voice. I thought it was clairvoyant at first, but then the voice identified itself and told me to take down what he said."

The voice, which belonged to an entity known as Zandark, ordered Smith "to get in the center of the room and as far away as possible from all electrical appliances and outlets." Smith learned that the aliens "would be contacting in various places all over the world," particularly in the United States and Asia. Although in the Americas their primary point of interest had been Vancouver, British Columbia, "it is now moved to Atlanta." Better weather, one supposes.

According to a transcript of Smith's encounter, Zandark said they "have been here from time to time over a period of thousands of years, and at certain times have stepped in to advance the science, technology, and medicine of your cultures—these cultures only forget who helped and aided them."

A Short Diatribe (contactees and their channelers are typically verbose and condescending)

Zandark continued: "We built the Sphinx, the pyramids, and other structural phenomena as proof of what we can do in a constructive way. These were built for you and with you in a time when your civilization could not possibly, on their own, have constructed and engineered these feats.

"Despite their benevolence toward humanity, the aliens would not allow us to destroy ourselves, and they did occasionally abduct humans.

"They will take earth beings when the time comes so they can resow the earth. They don't want to manifest fear and hysteria, but it has happened."

"We can see them when they allow us to," Smith said, and the aliens gave messages to selected humans, like him. "They haven't released it before because they haven't felt confident. First people would not believe it, and, second, people didn't need it. It was something people could not handle.

"They are watching us particularly carefully because of the atomic bomb and our pollution. Our pollution, not just garbage, but mental pollution, is hurting the other planets.

"They have said if we don't take them more seriously they can withdraw and leave us with the knowledge we have and we will destroy ourselves eventually. The knowledge is nuclear power.

"The people in Atlantis destroyed themselves with their machinery. The people there destroyed themselves with their thoughts. In fear they used their machinery wrong and it destroyed them."

Cue Donovan

Bill O'Hara, another Atlanta psychic, also believes that Atlantis has been reborn in Atlanta. "Many people have migrated to Atlanta in the past few years from all over the world without even knowing why . . . I believe those coming here are reincarnated from Atlantis."

O'Hara dared to make a prediction several months ahead, saying that between October 15 and October 25, 1975, "There will be quite a display of UFOs in the area of Dougherty County, Georgia." He was wrong, but only by a month.

Bruce Henne, then Georgia director of MUFON, used the recruiting effort to address UFOs and organized religion. He believed that churches had to acknowledge the existence of UFOs to prevent people from being deceived by UFO cults. "We have to get the church to talk about UFOs," Henne said. "People need to get the straight information," and he offered to speak in churches on the matter.

"It is obvious something is going on up there," Henne continued. "The longer the churches keep quiet about it, the longer the nuts are going to run around saying God is an astronaut."

After the Colorado debacle, Bo and Peep assumed a lower profile but continued their work, even surviving the death of Nettles in 1985. The organization regained prominence in the 1990s through the Internet and promotional videos. Georgia's last contact with the UFO cult came in March 1994, when a recruitment team, traveling in two new vans, gave lectures in Atlanta. Apparently, Applewhite was not among them.

"They were a very strange group," remembered Robyn Quail, a UFO researcher who attended a session. "They gave you a chance to join them. You had to give up everything: sex, money, possessions." All the men "had the same haircuts," Quail said, and the "men and women all look kind of the same."

Those who met the recruiters called them "warm, wonderful people" and "very sweet and mild-mannered," although "a bit androgynous." And completely deluded. An interest in UFOs is a harmless pursuit until the passion leads to cultism.

BUT SIRIUSLY, FOLKS! WELCOME TO OZ

Jenny Randles, a veteran and reputable researcher of UFOs, developed what is known as the "Oz" factor. There was a time when outlandish tales were dismissed by all but the most fanatical devotees of flying saucer-Fortean lore, even though witnesses to said phenomenon were competent, sober, sane, educated, community-leader types who had nothing to gain and everything to lose by revealing their experiences. Also troubling were perfectly believable accounts marred by one ludicrous detail.

Hence the Oz factor. We must occasionally expect and accept the ridiculous as having been sincerely experienced by an honest person.

CAN JIMMY COME OUT TO PLAY?

Tom Dawson made his living selling cars in Florida, then retired to the peaceful, rural community of Pelham. He was sixty-three years old on August 6, 1977, living in a mobile home park on Vada Road with his wife and seven-year-old daughter. He arose early that Saturday morning, then took his girl to visit Linda and Jimmy Kolbie, owners of a house adjacent to the mobile home neighborhood. Dawson was a frequent visitor to the Kolbie home, where he enjoyed playing with their infant son.

After chatting with Linda for a few minutes, Dawson declared that he was going to walk to a nearby pond with his two dogs and see if conditions looked right for fishing.

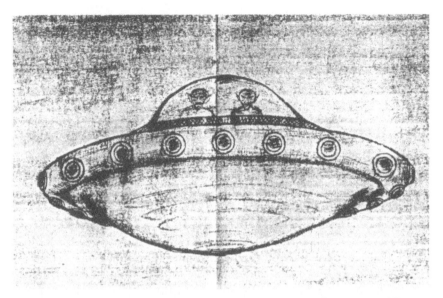

The occupants of this UFO immobilized Tom Dawson near Pelham, stripped him, and subjected the man to a physical examination. (Courtesy of Billy J. Rachel)

It was a beautiful day, the countryside quiet as Dawson neared the pond. When he was about a hundred feet from the water, a circular spaceship instantly appeared and hovered four feet above the ground in front of him. It produced barely a whisper of sound, and was forty to fifty feet in diameter and twelve to fourteen feet high.

Dawson found himself frozen in place—he could not move a muscle. All of the cattle in his field of vision were also frozen, as were his dogs—one had a leg suspended in the air, apparently stilled as it took a step.

A hatch immediately opened on the ship and an occupant emerged. Dawson dubbed him the "leader," and he was apparently hesitant to disembark. His first step onto terra firma was tentative. Finding it solid, he motioned four more aliens to join him. At the same moment, two "sentries" appeared on top of the craft.

Of the five humanoids that approached Dawson, three were men and two were women. He described the women as beautiful and shapely. Their skin was a bloodless, powder-puff white. Their ears were sharp and their small noses upturned. They had no neck—their heads sat directly on their shoulders. The aliens' heads were bare of hair, as was every portion and crevice of their bodies. Dawson knew this because two of the "crew" were nude, a male and a female. To satisfy your prurient interest, the woman's vagina was located where a human's navel would be, and her breasts were positioned higher on her chest and widely separated—almost under the hairless armpits.

If anyone cares, the man's penis was small, the size of a six-year-old boy's. The other three wore identical clothing.

After hesitantly approaching Dawson, the aliens proceeded to conduct a medical examination of this new species. A device similar to a skullcap was placed on his head. It was connected by several cords to a large ring the size of a hula hoop, which contained an extensive series of dials.

While the electronic survey continued, the creatures stepped to within two feet of Dawson and dropped his pants, apparently to check his sex, and lifted his shirt.

It was at this point that Tom Dawson was transported to Oz. From the interior of the ship a human voice announced: "I am Jimmy Hoffa. I am Jimmy Hoffa. I am Jimmy Hoffa, and I'm in this ship. I am . . ." and the voice was abruptly silenced and not heard again.

As each alien completed their part of the exam, they reentered the ship. The last two removed the headset from Dawson, then walked off ten feet and conferred. The aliens had appeared to communicate during the medical tests, continuously emitting a shrill, high-pitched sound that struck Dawson as gibberish. One of the females kept repeating a word that sounded like English to Dawson, "Jupiter."

Dawson thought the creatures were debating whether they should take him with them—perhaps Jimmy needed a playmate. For reasons known only to them, the aliens declined to "earthling-nap" Dawson. The leader "waved" at the man by crossing his open palm across his chest, then he and his companion boarded the ship. Within seconds the hatch closed and the ship quickly rose to seventy-five feet above the ground, then vanished soundlessly.

Man and animals were instantly released from whatever force had immobilized them. Dawson hastily secured his clothing and ran as quickly as he could to the Kolbie house, where Linda was working in the yard around 9:15 A.M.

Linda attempted to learn what had happened, but all Dawson could choke out was "spaceship." Fearing for his life, Mrs. Kolbie called an ambulance, which rushed Dawson to the local hospital.

Dawson recovered, but the experience still had him shaken days later. Despite experiencing the disbelief of others, he stuck to his story, saying: "I don't care what they say. This is the truth as I know it. I'm not crazy. The whole time it happened, my mind was alert. I knew what was happening. I have doubted since that it happened. I don't blame people who say I'm nuts. I've heard stories like this before and I've said the same thing. But I do know what I've seen. I do know what happened."

Personal Note. In late 1977 or early 1978 I telephoned Tom Dawson. One Saturday morning I drove to Pelham for an interview with the man. I

Tom Dawson, who said he was paralyzed by a UFO that landed near Pelham, points out the spot where the craft landed. Aliens, some of them nude, subjected him to a physical examination. Dawson said that while all this was going on, he heard Jimmy Hoffa calling for help from within the aircraft. (Courtesy of the Camilla Enterprise)

am not particularly proud of this, but I agreed to try and sell his story to the *National Enquirer* for ten thousand dollars. I also interviewed the Kolbies and the medics who had rushed Dawson to the hospital. The attending physician refused to comment (I didn't blame him). I believed Mr. Dawson's story. His neighbors and the medics testified that the man had been so terrified that they were convinced he could not have faked his reaction.

I contacted the *National Enquirer*'s UFO "bureau chief" (honest, they had a guy covering the flying saucer beat). However, without my knowledge, Mr. Dawson also called the *Enquirer*, which I felt undermined my efforts, and the matter was sucked into a tabloid black hole, as, apparently, was Jimmy Hoffa and my good sense.

OUR OWN ROSWELL (NEW MEXICO, NOT GEORGIA)
Did Georgia have its own UFO crash around 1977, or did an experimental stealth bomber fall from the sky? That was the story MUFON field investigator John C. Thompson attempted to unravel several years ago. While Thompson was checking out another UFO report, a police dispatcher in LaGrange told him about a relative who was a witness to a strange event.

Her name was Carolyn Shelnutt. Sometime in late 1977 or early 1978 she stepped out of her house near Corinth, in western Georgia, near sundown and glanced up to see a great, metallic boomerang flying toward the southeast at about one thousand miles an hour. After several seconds a brilliant flash came from the UFO and it immediately fell below the horizon.

Shelnutt ran into the house, hustled her three children into the car, and drove toward where the object had disappeared. At dusk she saw smoke

189

rising from the road off GA 100. In her excitement Shelnutt ran into a ditch. The family flagged down a car that alerted Shelnutt's husband, who operated a service station in Hogansville. Mr. Shelnutt arrived and pulled the car out of the ditch, and all returned home. Mrs. Shelnutt and the others then got in Mr. Shelnutt's truck and drove to New River Crossing. About one thousand feet to the west they observed several helicopters flying about at low altitude and sweeping the ground with spotlights. A pall of smoke obscured the area, and the oldest child thought he could see a fire.

Unfortunately, Thompson has found no one to corroborate the story, but other strange events have occurred around New River Crossing. Two years earlier, in the summer of 1975, two brothers on a hunting trip spotted a UFO flying erratically, apparently dodging a low-flying plane. The object, operating four miles from the "crash" site, was cigar-shaped and bright orange.

THE PAUSE THAT REFRESHES

At the same spot in 1980 another witness, a tool and die foreman, was parked beside U.S. 27 when he observed an enormous cigar-shaped UFO estimated to be six hundred feet long. It was taking on water from Potato Creek via a tube three feet in diameter. The craft emitted a blue glow similar to what "a tungsten-inert gas torch makes." It slipped sideways as the dark tube was retracted into a blue-lit compartment on one side, then the UFO passed over the witness at treetop level and "instantly accelerated."

Earlier, on May 28, 1977, the tool and die man was involved in a strange encounter involving a crashed helicopter. With his nephew, the man watched a helicopter scan the ground with searchlights. After watching it crash, the two men headed for the scene. Before reaching it, however, the tool and die man reported seeing a "cleared-off landing area and bivouac" packed with helicopters, military trucks and jeeps, tents, soldiers, and, most curious, civilians outfitted in "white decontamination suits complete with beehive-type headgear."

The pair found the heavily damaged chopper lying on its side in a gully. There was no evidence of the pilot, although bloody bandages were noticed nearby. The man shot several black and white photos of the chopper before men in decontamination suits and a soldier found them. When the soldiers shouted, "Grab that camera!" the two men ran into the woods and eluded pursuit.

Although the nephew confirms being chased by someone who wanted the film, he denied seeing the encampment or military personnel.

The helicopter was a civilian model, a Bell 206B, and the crash was documented by the National Safety Board in Washington, D.C., but the names of the pilot and the helicopter's owner were omitted from the report. What had the chopper been searching for?

This story just keeps giving. In January 1991, only a mile from the site of the 1977 helicopter crash, a twin-rotor CH-46 made an emergency landing, or a search, depending upon your personal level of paranoia. While the chopper was being repaired, a military helicopter joined it and soldiers established a perimeter around the scene. Reportedly, Heard County sheriff's deputies and the fire department were refused entry. A soldier manning the barricade, in an attempt to ease the tension, confided that the helicopter was "on a secret mission, and had a high-ranking official aboard." The chopper was on the ground several hours, then flew off between 10:00 and 11:00 P.M.

Another witness, who saw the helicopter at 10:00 A.M., rejected the idea of mechanical failure, saying the machine was low enough for him to have heard any engine problems. He maintained they were searching for something. Perhaps the military was probing for further wreckage of the crash of a UFO or top secret stealth bomber that allegedly occurred more than ten years ago.

ADVERTISING PAYS

For several days in late May 1978, several Atlanta-area residents reported UFO sightings. One woman claimed she was chased into a building at Candler and Glenwood in south DeKalb County. This UFO did not remain unidentified for long. The pilot of an advertising plane operating out of Conyers accepted responsibility for the sightings, explaining that the plane is often mistaken for a UFO. From a distance of two miles "the plane looks opaque," said Tim Moore. "I can see how it could confuse someone," particularly in hazy conditions.

OUR FIRST TRIANGLE

At 9:30 P.M. on December 23, 1978, a twenty-two-year-old senior airman stationed at Moody AFB in Valdosta was standing outside near the north end of the facility when he saw a "chevron- (presumably V-) shaped aircraft with no fuselage" pass by low overhead. Forty feet long, with rounded ends, it mounted two rows of semirecessed white lights on the bottom. It made a little noise, but not like any aircraft engines. The airman and a second witness were alarmed because the craft was heading toward a runway where F-4 Phantom jets were landing. It sailed majestically just above the traffic pattern, and perhaps it was invisible to the pilots because "the F-4s never aborted or broke from their landing approach."

PAGING DR. STRANGELOVE

Maybe it had something to do with the Armageddon Express, a train of twenty-two white cars, which rolled through downtown Jesup on the afternoon of May 4, 1984, presumably with a load of nuclear weapons.

Perhaps the UFOs had been scouting its route on the evening of April 26. That's when brothers Warren and Mike Purvis had loaded cabinets in their pickup truck in Screven (see "Ghost Lights") and were returning to Jesup on U.S. 82 at 8:10 P.M.

"What's that?" Mike asked, and Warren followed his gaze to a clearing between the highway and the railroad. He saw two bright lights low to the ground—the blinking red lights of a radio tower beyond were above it. As the lights zipped toward them the brothers said, "Helicopter." Then the object stopped and Warren accelerated toward it for a closer look. Suddenly, a "huge mass of lights," a second, round UFO materialized out of nowhere and "moved over the top of that other thing," according to Warren. The smaller UFO then entered the larger one.

"It was like a huge 747 hovering over a Volkswagen," Warren said. The second UFO was "a big 'un, I mean it was at least twenty stories tall."

The big UFO flew off toward Jesup and Warren gave pursuit, but the craft easily outdistanced him. The encounter had lasted ten minutes.

Either it was a secret government project, Warren thought, "or something mighty strange is happening."

Hundreds of UFO sightings followed, the calls flooding the Jesup police department, the Wayne County sheriff's office, and radio station WLOP, where Al Harper called the situation "very mysterious." He fielded scores of reports and noted that "their accounts are essentially the same." Among the witnesses was a deputy sheriff and reliable citizens from every walk of life.

The sightings were made across Wayne County—Jesup, Rayonier, Screven, and Midray Springs—primarily on May 25, 26, and 27, just after dark. In Screven, Ray Poppell and his family were watching two large objects hover above the tree line across a field. "All of a sudden the field in front of our house got real bright, like it was on fire," Poppell said. "I went to the door and saw these two objects shaped like big Ws with lights on every point."

On the evening of May 25, Robert Thorton was summoned outside by his mother and stepfather to see a UFO. He thought they were kidding, "But I looked up and it was all different colors." The rotating lights seemed to be attached to a stationary object. At one point during the forty-five-minute observation, Thorton's stepfather blinked a flashlight at the UFO to "signal" it. The reaction was a pair of brilliant lights "so bright you could see them shining on the tops of pine trees across the road," Thorton testified.

"I think it turned out to be a weather balloon or something like that," Wayne County sheriff Jim Poindexter later said of the UFOs. Not hardly, sheriff.

Certainly unrelated, but amusing nonetheless, was an object found by a child beneath his porch that resembled the neck of a sea monster. The child's mother took the growth to the local Georgia extension service office, where Jim Fountain announced that it was a mushroom, deformed by its efforts to reach sunlight.

UP CLOSE AND PERSONAL IN SCREVEN COUNTY

Frank and Wanda Alcorn had recently returned to Screven County, located in rural eastern Georgia, after years of living in the metro Atlanta suburb of Clarkston, where Frank had been a police officer. He had taken a job as deputy sheriff in neighboring Effingham County and the family was renovating an old house on Hershel Bazemore Road. It was located a short distance from Wanda's brother, Emerson Scott, near Newington and the Savannah River, five miles from Sylvania.

After the Alcorns and Scotts had enjoyed a family cookout at a nearby pond on Monday, July 12, 1987, the Alcorns arrived at home about 9:45 P.M.

"We pulled in to our driveway with our kids, Lee and Tracy," said Frank, "and sitting out in the field beside the house was this huge craft, clustered with lights."

The car's headlights flashed across the object as it sat in the field beside a barn.

"What the hell is that?" Frank exclaimed, killing the engine and stepping out of the car for a better view.

"We didn't hear a sound," Wanda added. "It was an incredible sight."

She heard no sound from helicopter blades in the still air, nor did she detect the jet or prop engine noises usually associated with airplanes. Wanda noted an absence of wings and a tail on the object, and described it as "shaped like a huge cylinder, dark yet metallic, shaped like a tank on a gas truck. And it had three large red lights with a cluster of white lights underneath."

After being observed for two minutes on the ground, the UFO slowly began to rise to a height of ten feet, then hovered a short time. It moved in the direction of a highway and rose again, just clearing the trees and power lines. The Alcorns heard a short, low zipping sound and the craft suddenly accelerated away over the trees and disappeared.

The field, which bordered the Alcorns' house on three sides and was covered with waist-high grass, was searched by the family the following morning. They located three large depressions in the soil arranged in a straight line about one hundred yards from the house.

The Alcorns staked off the area to preserve the scene until more qualified researchers arrived. Two weeks later the grass, which had turned yellow, finally began to spring back up.

Local radio station WSYL publicized the spectacular sightings, and by dusk the following day the road leading to the Alcorn house was crowded with carloads of the curious. The Alcorn family was sitting on the back porch at 9:45 P.M., when apparently the same UFO descended from the heavens and hovered over a field behind their home. The object slowly drifted around their house and nearly settled down at the same spot as the previous night before departing in the same flashy fashion. The Alcorns heard gawkers in several cars shouting excitedly, "Did you see it? Did you see it?" Witnesses included a deputy sheriff and a paramedic.

Wanda Alcorn, Margie Scott, and Wanda's mother spotted the same craft as they were returning home from church. Margie, driving, attempted to follow the object to the Alcorn house but the UFO outpaced her. She arrived at home to find the ship hovering over the trees and described it as bright, with red and white lights.

"It was close enough and bright enough that it blocked out my sight of the trees," Margie stated.

There were many witnesses, between forty and sixty, to Tuesday night's show. Nearby, Mac and Shirley Mahaffey, owners and operators of WSYL in Sylvania, observed it for two minutes cruising majestically over the woods a quarter-mile from Poor Robin Ferry. Their description of an enormous ship with the same light pattern and zipping sound matched the one seen by the Alcorns.

The Mahaffeys, joined by Dee Morgan and Philip Boston, who also saw Tuesday's show, and Louise Johnson and her children, Joyce and Chris, saw a UFO at a much higher altitude on Wednesday. That phenomenon, which came to be known as "dancing lights" and "dancing offshoots," was seen by many on Thursday and Friday as well.

Mark Rodeghier, scientific director of the Center for UFO Studies (CUFOS) in Chicago, was intrigued by the sightings but doubted that UFOs would return to the same location two nights running. He also believed people were confusing celestial bodies for the dancing lights.

"Typically, UFOs do not return again," he stated. "What they are seeing now is likely not a UFO. They are mistaking one for bright stars and planets."

Wanda Alcorn and others were indignant over this explanation.

"They're telling me that what happened the second night didn't happen? They're saying that I don't know the difference between stars and what I saw. That's a bunch of bull. Stars do not dip down into the trees, lighting up the woods. We're not a bunch of loonies. We know what a star looks like, but these weren't stars."

The Georgia News Network spread word of the strange events throughout the state, and UPI alerted the nation. Mrs. Alcorn grew hoarse from talking to reporters across the country and the curious who phoned continually.

Meanwhile, the sightings continued. On Thursday morning Sharon Sheppard was taking her son Richard into the Jackson School when he asked, "Mama, what is that?" and pointed toward the sky above the playground.

Looking, she spotted a silver cylinder hovering nearby at low altitude.

"It was clustered with brilliant lights, even though this was during the daytime," she related. "It had no wings, and it made no noise."

Shirley Mahaffey and husband Mac detected a new wrinkle in the phenomenon exactly a week after the sightings began. About a mile from the Alcorns' house they saw a craft with two brilliant white lights on each end and three or more dimmer lights spaced between them. It was silent and disappeared to the northeast at an "incredible speed."

THE LUNATIC FRINGE

Most people assume that the possibility of UFOs being intergalactic, interdimensional, or temporal transportation devices is weird enough, but often the appearance of an ordinary "spaceship" is only the beginning of weirdness. The Alcorns learned this lesson on July 21, when two men claiming to be representatives of the Mutual UFO Network (MUFON), a legitimate and respected organization headquartered in Seguin, Texas, showed up unannounced.

Only one identified himself, and he only as "Frank." According to Wanda the family was warned that aliens might move into the neighborhood and attempt to befriend the Alcorns. The men asked if any strangers had been spotted recently. Wanda said they went on to make comments more bizarre than that. They wanted further information about the sightings and inquired about recent illnesses among family members. Besides the UFOs, they inquired if any unusual events had occurred to them. They asked endless questions, proposed a number of theories, and offered a lengthy list of UFO literature for the family to read.

RIN TIN CENTARIAN

When asked if any strange animals had arrived soon after the UFOs, Mrs. Alcorn jokingly replied, "Well, to be honest, a beautiful black dog had shown up shortly after the sightings. It didn't have a collar or anything, but you could tell it had been well taken care of. So I jokingly mentioned the dog." One man was soon peering into the dog's mouth, ears, and eyes with a flashlight, then fell on his knees and shouted, "Speak! Speak! Speak!" The dog made no reply, not a bark, whine, or growl, which I suppose could be taken as evidence of alien possession.

Frank and his associate took soil and grass samples from the landing site, and departed without any explanations of their actions. Taken in total, this seemed like a friendlier version of the "men in black" who were reported to have plagued UFO sighters in the 1950s.

"They did a number on me and my family," Wanda concluded. "We were okay and coping with it until they came." Wanda called the men "strange" and said the meeting left her "unnerved" and "truly scared." The visit caused the family to lose sleep.

"The crazies are crawling out of the woodwork," an exhausted Wanda said. "It's getting to where you don't know who you are talking to, friend or enemy."

Cars by the hundreds lined both sides of the roads for miles leading to the Alcorns' house. Strangers camped in their field, including one little old lady who spent three days. Some called from around the world to request personal interviews. College students wanted to write their thesis about the phenomenon. Many people have written letters soliciting information or forwarding their own theories and literature, some of it "very weird stuff," from astronomers, scientists, ministers, cultists, spiritual healers—in short, the whole gamut of weirdness.

Mahaffey filed a complaint with MUFON, alleging that it released information to the creepy duo. MUFON's national director, Walt Andrus, replied that the men were conducting private research and were not associated with his organization.

On July 24 a man reported a sighting at the Savannah River near U.S. 301 to the Screven County Sheriff's Office. His UFO, egg-shaped and larger than a helicopter, alternated a band of green light at the base with an orange-colored band. It hovered for a short time, then moved silently at treetop level across the sky near the man's home.

Dr. Julius Benton, a Savannah astronomer and investigator for the Center for UFO Studies in Chicago, visited Sylvania on July 26. He was reticent in interviews, citing his "sensitive government work," but said his research would be shared with MUFON and other organizations. He declined to discuss his investigation and refused to examine the landing site while journalists were present.

After Dr. Benton departed, so did interest in the case. Things settled into a semblance of normality in quiet Screven County.

When asked if military activity at nearby Fort Stewart might have been responsible for the sightings, a base public affairs specialist, Dean Wohlgemuth, said, "We almost never conduct exercises off post." Whatever was seen in Screven County, "it certainly wasn't from Fort Stewart."

"At times the highway outside our house looked like a runway," Mrs. Alcorn said three years later. "We had people lined up for miles waiting to see whatever it was.

"We never said it was an alien spacecraft or anything like that. All we said was we saw something. We still don't know what it was."

BLOOD-SUCKING ALIEN PARASITES!

A wave of UFO sightings began in Madison County at 8:00 P.M. in mid-March 1989, when Jerry Haley and his daughter pulled into their driveway off of GA 98. Haley first spotted what he thought was a car in the yard, but then brilliant white lights seemed to shoot straight down his driveway. He stopped his car as the lights vanished. In wonder, Haley stepped out of the car and scrutinized a huge airship with white, green, and red lights circulating around the bottom, which sailed silently over him.

"It was an L-shaped thing," Jerry said. "I actually thought it was going to run into us. It was huge. You could put an airplane in it."

An identical object appeared over the Athens Auto Wrecking yard on U.S. 29 on the afternoon of March 22. Callie Atewine, wife of owner William, who was away, and three employees watched a giant, brilliantly lighted L-shaped object appear and disappear three times behind a wooded area.

On the following day William collected sixteen ticks, bloated with blood, near the site where the UFO had appeared. They were turned over to Burton Evans, an entomologist with the University of Georgia Extension Service. He found each tick to be a female and explained that when filled with blood, they detach from the host, lay eggs, and die.

"It is unusual to find numerous adult ticks in one location," Evans stated. He suggested that the ticks were from the three dogs or one mule (Frances?) Atewine kept in his compound.

"But the dogs never lie there," Atewine said, and the mule was locked up elsewhere. Atewine discovered thirteen additional blood-saturated ticks in the same location on April 11, but no UFOs were spotted.

Mrs. H. M. Hubbard reported the last sighting at midnight on April 2 when she, her husband, and their daughter watched two UFOs through binoculars. She said they were the size of small buildings maneuvering over the Diamond Hill community for forty-five minutes. The objects, silent like the other UFOs, were round, with red, blue, and green lights.

The L shape is similar to the giant triangular, boomerang, horseshoe, and V-shaped UFOs that plagued Europe in the 1980s and Georgia in the 1990s.

ONIONHEAD

While a single visit to Vidalia will convince travelers that the onion is truly God there, in the early 1990s a phenomenon persisted that caused residents to raise their eyes from the rich soil and gaze into the heavens.

It started with a roar one night in mid-February 1991, when a woman sighted four UFOs. All were twenty-two feet in diameter, with red and white flashing lights, and they hovered soundlessly at eight hundred feet.

She summoned police officers to a Wal-Mart near the airport, but they saw nothing. However, Gerry Richardson, disc jockey at radio station WVOP, fielded more than twenty UFO-sighting reports. The elusive craft had apparently left Wal-Mart for the communities of Uvalda and Charlotte. In neighboring Montgomery County, a caller reported observing two UFOs heading for Hazlehurst and two flying back toward Vidalia.

Vidalia police lieutenant Paige McNeese drove to the airport, where he watched what he thought were two high-flying airplanes. While he watched, a third craft raced through the night sky at a high rate of speed. He considered it another airplane, but admitted, "It was probably the fastest airplane I have ever seen in my life."

It was obviously sweeps week in Atlanta, for TV stations WXIA Channel 11 and WAGA Channel 5 sent a van and helicopter, respectively.

The UFO circus had actually started in Vidalia three weeks earlier when Ricky Monroe, a minister and UFO investigator, informed the *Vidalia Advance* that unidentified objects had followed him. He saw another over the Vidalia post office. The newspaper had investigated UFO "photos" Monroe claimed to possess, but found they were line drawings.

Monroe continued to be a controversial character in Toombs County, which he described "as a hot spot for UFOs." A year later he claimed to have made thirteen sightings of UFOs, including one that landed in a Montgomery County field planted with pine seedlings, which commenced to grow at a greatly accelerated rate. Ricky and wife Amanda said UFOs danced in the sky, took soil and water samples, and shot red lasers at cars. They also believed that "shape-shifters" were operating in the area.

Asked the motivation of the aliens, Monroe thought they might have been monitoring area military installations or taking power from Plant Hatch, a nuclear-powered, electricity-generating facility located twenty miles away.

In June 1992 Monroe claimed that an alien named Altrex materialized in his living room and took him aboard a UFO "scout ship." Monroe was flown to Florida, where an underground installation was toured. Another secret base, located in southeast Georgia, was examined during the three-and-a-half-hour expedition. The aliens told him that there were seventy species of aliens currently on earth.

Another year passed before Vidalia was struck by a new wave of UFO sightings. In a four-hour period one night in March 1993, more than fifty sightings (but no glass onions) were reported to MUFON, an organization that Monroe served as local director.

"They've come in all shapes and sizes," Monroe stated. "We have sightings of triangular shapes, the classic disc shape with a dome top, cigar-shaped, every shape imaginable."

SOMEWHERE OVER THE RAINBOW

Joye J. Pugh holds a doctorate in educational administration (as a teacher I'll try not to hold that against her) and lives with her businessman husband, Mel, outside Douglas in southern Georgia. At 5:30 P.M. on November 13, 1991, a clear, cold evening, they had left home when she noticed the setting sun reflecting off a silver metallic object hovering in the sky. After they stopped to observe it, a beam of pure white light was emitted from the front of the disc-shaped UFO. The beam, arched like a rainbow, suddenly retracted after a few seconds and repeated the cycle several times. As the beam shone, an identical UFO appeared. It was "almost like the

In 1973 and 1975 the fields and woods of southwest Georgia were the favorite Georgia visiting spots for UFOs. Most of the observers were law-enforcement personnel. This spot is in Mitchell County.

craft divided into two craft," she wrote, with the beam in the center. After the light withdrew into the original UFO, the "copy" sprinted across the sky at tremendous speed, pursued by the first, and both glowed pure white in the darkening sky.

The couple resumed their trip, but Joye never took her eyes off the UFOs. Mel dropped Joye at her mother's house on Bay Meadows Estates Lake, five miles west of Douglas. Her mother provided binoculars, and they and Joye's grandmother watched the display from a deck overlooking the water. Joye called the Douglas Airport, seven miles distant, where the director was also observing the display. Moody Air Force Base in Valdosta told Joye that all their planes were grounded, nothing registered on their radar, and they had no explanation for the objects.

The silent, twin discs circled the lake side by side, traveling very slowly away from the observers, but racing back at high speed. As the crafts maneuvered, sparks flew off them like static electricity. Joye thought the term "cat and mouse games" applied to their behavior.

EVERYBODY CONGA!

The witnesses then heard "the sound of aircraft" from the northeast. Looking in that direction, they saw a formation of perfect triangles flying in a two-by-two-by-two configuration, closed up wingtip-to-wingtip and zigzagging. Half the bottoms of the triangles were covered by rows of red lights, the other half contained rows of green lights. All roared like F-16s landing. These six triangles took station behind the two discs and followed them in their circuit of the lake. After several revolutions, the triangles scattered and stopped at different points around the horizon. For a time one triangle would race toward the discs, then return to its original position. The triangles eventually flew out of sight in various directions as the discs continued their revolutions, then headed northeast, from where the triangles had appeared.

TAKE US TO OUR LEADERS

In 1991 Ed Komarek, a forty-four-year-old Thomasville land investor, cofounded Operation Right to Know (ORTK), an international group numbering about two hundred. He believes the U.S. government and other nations are concealing evidence that sentient beings in spacecraft have regularly visited earth for half a century. The organization considers this to be a massive global "Watergate."

"There are millions of sightings, videotapes, and twenty thousand pages of the government's own documents showing UFOs are real," Komarek stated in 1994. "What we are trying to do is get the people to inquire and investigate and get to know that this is real and is going to have a big impact on them in the future."

BULL SESSIONS

Komarek's interest in UFOs started with philosophical discussions he had in college. "It just wasn't a world that seemed to have a future for me, that I was really interested in. Why are we having children if there's no more to life than just business and sex?" he wondered.

ORTK pressures the government to reveal hard, documented evidence that will concretely prove the existence of alien intercourse with earth. This will be accomplished by "public, political action," ORTK's Web site states, including "demonstrations, picket lines, marches, rallies, lobbying, political theater, speak-outs, vigils, and other forms of creative and legal activities." Their targets are "U.S. executive branch agencies, private corporations involved in the cover-up, the press, and members of Congress."

The organization probed former Georgia senator Sam Nunn's participation in the massive cover-up with a demonstration at his Atlanta office. Nunn was chosen because of his chairmanship of the powerful Senate armed services committee, which gave him access to and influence over sensitive UFO documents, the group claimed.

ACT SANE FOR THE CAMERAS

Before the action commenced, Komarek warned participants against sensationalism. "If you're an abductee, talk in kind of general terms. Don't get too specific, something that might be kind of ridiculed. People who have sightings—you gotta realize that the public is not sure UFOs are real."

To a reporter, Komarek said, "We're in a political war for the public's right to know. We must break down the wall of ridicule that has been built up over fifty years."

Picket signs at the event proclaimed: "Tell the Truth about UFOs, Senator Nunn," and "UFOs Are Real and the Government Knows It!"

"Every president, as soon as they're in office, is briefed on UFOs," said Robin Quail, a participant and Atlanta resident who had personally seen two UFOs, one in Alabama in 1970, the second in Atlanta in 1979. "It's the highest secret the government has." The government has also taken steps to prepare for the inevitable. "Every fire department in the country has been furnished with a booklet on exactly which procedures to handle" when the UFOs arrive, she claimed. "Now every police department, too."

The *Macon Telepath* (*graph*, sorry) *& News* jumped on this assertion, calling area fire and police agencies. "I want to find out where my manual is at," said Chief Warring Doles at Central State Hospital in Milledgeville. Despite his long career in fire fighting, which started in 1961, "I haven't seen one," he stated. Warner Robins fire chief Larry West laughed and said, "I missed my copy," and then wondered why the fire department would have the manual. "I've never heard of it," said Macon police chief James Avera.

"I'm a normal person," said one demonstrator, Tricia McCannon. The Atlanta resident, who saw a UFO twenty years earlier while driving between Atlanta and Florida, claims that the government and big business are deliberately introducing aliens and UFOs into advertisements for all manner of products to accustom us to the reality of UFOs. That way, when the real aliens arrive, we won't panic. "The government's gotten in bed with the money people . . . so you and I won't jump out of buildings," she claimed.

In a letter to Jim Thomas, a Columbus television reporter who investigated UFOs, Sam Nunn denied "personal knowledge" of spacecraft in the possession of the U.S. government or any secret government groups which

201

handle truly illegal (but now simply undocumented) aliens (but then, he would deny it, right? Right?).

Komarek acknowledged that the UFO community is split between factions that concentrate on hard, documented sightings of unusual phenomenon, and others who endorse abductions, contactees, and the like. Government documents would lend considerable credibility to the field.

"We have to break down the wall of ridicule and denial built up around UFO issues," Komarek said in mid-October 1995, at the National UFO Conference, held in Atlanta. "It's a political war, folks. If you want to get the truth out, you've got to write your congressman and take on political activity."

JUST CHECK THE ALIEN PARTY

Komarek took his beliefs one gutsy step further that November when he announced his admittedly low-budget candidacy for the U.S. House of Representatives, running for the Second District congressional seat held by Sanford Bishop (D-Columbus). ORTK cofounder Mike Jamieson had also planned a congressional campaign in California, but finances forced him to drop out. He claimed that Congress had forsaken its oversight duties by neglecting to reveal the government's knowledge of aliens.

"If members of Congress like Sanford Bishop don't have the backbone to dig out the truth about the UFO cover-up because of potential ridicule surrounding the subject," said Komarek, "then Mike (Jamieson) and I will get into Congress and do it ourselves."

Komarek hit the stump in Valdosta, saying, "The two greatest issues facing the human race today are overpopulation that results in environmental degradation and the impact of alien, space-faring civilizations on earth societies."

Komarek's candidacy was a "further assault upon the wall of denial and ridicule surrounding the UFO subject," he concluded.

In addition to investigating aliens, Komarek promised to campaign on agricultural issues. He opposed NAFTA, saying it forced farmers to compete against cheap foreign competition, and also believed that corporations were squeezing the farmers. He promised to reform county land use regulations that are "excessive and irresponsible."

Not everyone took Komarek's campaign seriously. An article in the *Americus Times-Recorder* read, "Candidate Wants Shields Down On UFO Cover-Up."

Ah, a prophet in his own farmland.

THE LOST CONTINENT OF MOO: OUR COWLESS MUTILATION, OR, OH, DEER

I swear to you that I exhausted every possible source to find a cattle mutilation of our very own, but to no avail. The best substitute I located is a white-tailed deer, and various cats and dogs, but those are more likely the act of sick individuals rather than paranormal manifestations.

I understand your frustration (and please don't fake one just for me), but not far from Georgia, in northern Alabama, is Fyffe, atop fertile Sand Mountain, which has a cattle mutilation track record to match any in the country.

Their first was discovered on October 20, 1992, when a cow was found with its entire milk sac removed in a neat, oval incision. There was no blood on the animal or ground.

Six months later the total was thirty in Marshall and DeKalb Counties, nine in the first week of February 1993. No blood was found at any site, and despite the muddy conditions of many pastures, no footprints, tire tracks, or any other markings were found near the carcasses. Certain parts of the cows were removed with surgical precision, and in a number of cases evidence of high temperatures, hundreds of degrees, was found at the incisions. Sex organs were removed from male and female cattle alike, and the rectum often cleanly cored out, without leaving blood or other body fluids. Eyes and ears, sometimes both, were removed, tongues were cut out deep into the throat, and jaws stripped to the bone. Most wounds were perfectly oval, the cuts precise and clean. Some cows were drained of blood.

Explanations put forward always include animal attacks (which would leave blood and ripped, ragged flesh), and satanic cults and bored college students (who have never been suspected or charged), and of course UFOs. An odd feature of cattle mutilations is the frequent presence of unmarked black helicopters before and after attacks. The mystery choppers are often seen and heard in Alabama, and associated with UFO sightings in west-central Georgia.

Cattle mutilations started in 1963 and have been noted in forty-eight states. From 1969 to 1993, ten thousand instances of bovine butchery were reported nationally, with identical characteristics. No one has ever been charged or prosecuted in a single case.

Now for our deer mutilation. The white-tailed deer, frozen stiff after a cold night, was spotted in a pasture visible from GA 372 by C. Leigh Culver and an associate. It was 7:30 A.M. on February 9, 1995, five miles east of Ballground in Cherokee County. The genitalia and rectum had been excised, leaving the body cavity with a "cored-out" look. The right eye had been removed, the tongue taken off deep in the oropharynx, and the jaw was cut down to the mandible and teeth. A hole was in the chest, the surrounding hair removed in a counterclockwise manner. There was no blood on the ground.

When the investigators returned later in the day to retrieve the carcass for autopsy, it had vanished. The landowner and his neighbors had no knowledge of the disappearance.

LIGHTS IN THE PINEY WOODS

A new ring in the Georgia UFO circus opened three years ago along the Ocmulgee River around McRae in the southeastern part of the state. The sightings started in February 1997, in the Jeff Davis County–Hazlehurst area. According to a policeman, many people have since seen them on thirty different occasions. Lights hover, cluster together, and are joined by lights that zoom in at many times the speed of an airliner, and exhibit high acceleration. Through a high-powered scope, one witness observed a structure in the midst of a green haze. The policeman said that many witnesses were hesitant to openly acknowledge their sightings.

One police officer swears that he has frequently seen unexplainable phenomenon in the sky while fishing on the river and on late-night patrols of rural areas. In February or March of 1997 the officer was driving home after his shift ended at 5:20 A.M., when he saw a bright, basketball-sized globe in the sky. He stopped at two houses and rousted relatives to observe the UFO. Through a rifle scope they determined that it was a bright white light surrounded by a green glow. It appeared to be as close as half a mile.

On August 22 the officer and his brother, also in law enforcement, were fishing on the Ocmulgee when they spotted a bright, white-orange UFO three times larger than a star. A second, similar UFO joined the first, and fifteen minutes after that a third flew across the sky at a tremendous rate of speed and disappeared when it reached the others. A fourth and fifth light soon imitated the third. A sixth object, the size of an aspirin and giving off green and orange light, then joined the other two. The brothers continued to watch as one UFO disappeared behind the tree line, then reappeared with a spotlight.

This activity attracted the personal attention of a former police chief and MUFON and the International Society for UFO Research (ISUR) investigator Walter T. Sheets, who spent the night of September 13 at a high spot with a good view of the region. While driving on U.S. 23 near McRae he spotted the lights of a small aircraft and a patch of clouds near it. Suddenly, a brilliant ray of light, thick as a full moon, the length described as "both hands held side by side at arm's length," and colored a bluish purple tinged "with yellow-orange at the edges," lanced out toward the plane. After two or three seconds the light "clicked" off as abruptly as it had started. Sheets described the color as pure like "an artist's palette or an animated effect." The plane flew on undisturbed. Ironically, Sheets's stakeout, which ended at 6:00 A.M., produced no further sightings.

204

During the winter of 1999 John Thompson interviewed a seventy-seven-year-old woman and her daughter who witnessed a fat, planelike UFO with a short, stubby tail and swept-back wings. The craft had appeared at 11:00 P.M. during the summer of 1997 near Moultrie. The silent, car-sized object was only a hundred feet away and twenty feet above a cotton field during their twenty-minute sighting. One bluish-gray-green light projected from the UFO, then retracted.

In April 1998 an elderly woman living on an isolated farm on Moultrie-Culbertson Road in rural Colquitt County was awakened at 2:00 A.M. by her dog. She took the dog outside to the end of her driveway and spotted a bluish gray, V-shaped UFO hovering silently and motionless at just above eye level above a large pasture. She said it resembled a giant glider, with narrow, thick, swept-back wings and a tail on the rear, but had no canopy or landing gear. "Transfixed," the woman said, she watched as six car headlight-like lights emerged from an invisible opening and slowly floated around the UFO at treetop level, turning and twisting and always circling around the craft. The lights reentered after fifteen minutes, and the witness reentered her house to keep watch through a window. Her dog had remained at her side throughout the encounter but seemed "indifferent" and made no sound.

HIGH WEIRDNESS

This really weird sighting was submitted to the National UFO Reporting Center. At 6:00 A.M. on May 4, 1998, a family in Moultrie was subjected to a shape-shifting UFO. According to the report, the object "kept changing shapes, and spinning slowly," casting bright, waving lights in every direction. The silver object "kept lighting up with neon colors" and passed over the house before landing in a field behind it. During the sighting, "stuff like the forks in the kitchen were standing on end, my son's four-wheeler engine cut off, the air conditioner cut off and would turn back on until it left," stated the mother of the family. Their television set "started flipping through the channels," and a radio likewise explored frequencies by itself as house lights flashed on and off. A neighbor who saw the UFO attempted to videotape the object, but his camera refused to work until after the incident had ended.

At 10:00 P.M. on May 18, 1998, a man driving to work in Douglas spotted "a big copper-colored sphere" which "split into two then four then eight" till the UFOs numbered at least sixteen. "Every time they split, they did so under each other, like an X pattern falling from the sky." The UFOs then assumed a V formation and "took off at a very fast burst of speed."

A NORTH GEORGIA CORRIDOR?

A leading citizen and respected businessman in Murray County lives near Chatsworth in an impressive home perched twenty-eight hundred feet up the side of a mountain. Expansive views of valleys and mountains to the north, south, and east add to the ambiance. The formidable Cohutta Mountains, a rugged wilderness composed of two hundred thousand acres, are to the north and east, and there are views of Tennessee and Alabama. Since late summer of 1995 the man has seen numerous UFOs. The first was a hovering disc shaped like a teardrop that had a bubble, presumably a cockpit, on the top. Colored like dull aluminum, a dark hole opened in its side and an "icicle" of energy or rays projected and spread out a distance of one hundred feet. Unidentified lights traveling at high rates of speed appeared and disappeared. During the summer of 1997 a half moon appeared. In late 1997 and early 1998 a dark, thick-bodied and very bent boomerang or triangle appeared. White and red lights were along the bottom edge of the tractor-trailer-sized object.

At 9:30 P.M. on August 8, 1998, the businessman was sitting on his deck watching the skies when he spied a yellow orb as it penetrated an eight-thousand-foot cloud cover and hovered at thirty-eight hundred feet half a mile to a mile distant. The yellow glow intensified in concentric circles around a small, dark donut in the center. In sight for ten seconds, it was the size of a basketball held at arm's length and had the intensity of a full moon. It abruptly vanished.

Four researchers, Tom and Barbara Sheets and Amy Seville—all ISUR field investigators—and Mark Ausmus, a board member, set up surveillance at the site on the night of August 22, 1998. They placed chairs facing the northeast at the recommendation of the owner, who had seen the most activity in that direction. At 11:00 P.M. Ausmus and Tom Sheets spotted a yellowish light with a reddish tint, twice the size of Jupiter and brighter, appear over the Cohutta Mountains. It quickly disappeared behind the distant ridges with a "wiggling motion."

The UFOs returned at 9:30 P.M. on September 28, 1999, when a glowing, bright white object shaped like an octagon, with additional octagonal structures within, making it look like a honeycomb, was seen by a motorist ascending the mountain. Described as the size of a softball held at arm's length, it hovered for a few seconds a quarter mile above the peak of Fort Mountain.

On the same day, a man in East Ellijay, thirteen miles to the east, spotted an intense bright white light in the sky. Two days later he awoke early in the morning and saw the same object, one and a half times the size of the moon, hovering over the community for fifteen minutes. While moving forty degrees across the sky it expelled nearly twenty small "sparkly, prismlike objects." Another resident revealed that such occurrences had been noted for six months.

The Chatsworth businessman spotted another UFO at 10:30 P.M. on October 16, 1999. The sky was clear and calm when the glowing orange sphere appeared about a mile distant.

These mountains are accustomed to mystery. Fort Mountain rests upon its highest peak, and the face on the gravestone is nearby.

SMILE, YOU'RE ON UFO CAMERA

Just after midnight of November 4, 1998, a Dalton resident captured on videotape a large glowing orb one-quarter the size of a full moon. The hovering, slightly elongated UFO emitted various colors. MUFON is analyzing the footage.

At dusk on April 16, 1999, a group of adults at a ranch near Cloudland watched half a dozen UFOs, each the size of a small pill and colored green and red, dart about the sky, executing unusual maneuvers at speeds ranging from slow to extremely fast. The woman who reported the sighting, west of Chatsworth, said such objects appeared frequently.

At 9:00 P.M. on November 18, 1995, a UFO shaped like an arrowhead hovered at treetop level and shone a cone-shaped beam into a backyard along Davis Ridge Road in Ringgold. The craft, measuring forty by twenty-five feet and mounting a light on each corner, projected the beam from its center. A man and his family spotted the object from their car. They stopped in the center of the road and got out to watch the UFO, which was only eighty feet off the ground and a hundred yards distant. Apparently in response to the observation, the silent craft doused the beam and slowly got underway, making no more than five miles per hour. It drifted over the car and flew west, with the car in pursuit until the object disappeared behind a ridge. The incident lasted fifteen minutes.

A purported photograph of a UFO appeared on the Internet in 1997. It shows a toplike UFO hanging in the sky over a mountain landscape. The photo was taken by Lee Cross near Ringgold.

Another resident of Ringgold made four sightings of a round UFO with white, blue, green, and reddish orange lights in a two-week period. The UFOs were usually accompanied by smaller, similarly colored objects that circled the primary. One night in early November 1999, the man had seen one of the lights and was talking about it outside on a cordless phone when the UFO made a return appearance, apparently turning off his phone and outside light, although his neighbors were unaffected. Inside, the stereo, VCR, and television, which had been turned off, were on, but no music was coming from the stereo and there was no picture on the tube, although it had sound.

Another UFO apparently disliked cell phones. At 10:25 P.M. on November 9, 1999, a man was driving over the mountains from Blue Ridge to Dahlonega when he "saw a very bright large green fireball" streak from east to west, leaving a red tail behind it. The UFO was the size of one and a half moons. His phone was lying on the passenger seat being recharged by an adapter, but when the UFO appeared the phone cut off. After repeated attempts the phone finally was able to be turned back on.

During the evening of December 22, 1999, a strange light was seen over Blairsville. It was also observed the following morning from before sunrise to 7:45 A.M. MUFON member Carroll Watts watched through binoculars as it sped erratically across the sky at great speed. It had red, green, and blue lights that shimmered and changed colors rapidly. Smaller objects left the larger craft, then shortly returned. Another resident saw a bright light flying back and forth across the sky at 9:00 P.M. on December 26.

A huge, deafening UFO appeared at 1:00 A.M. on October 8, 1997, to two deputy sheriffs parked at a church on GA 23 north of Lula, near Gainesville. The rectangular craft rose above trees eight hundred yards away and moved silently toward them. Seconds later the men were shocked by a thunderous roar as it passed three hundred to five hundred feet above them and raced off at great speed with flames erupting from the rear. One deputy was in the process of taping a call and the sounds of the UFO were captured.

The deputies immediately investigated the location from which the UFO had appeared and found a small valley occupied by cattle stunned by the craft's passage. One officer concluded, "It was a low-level military bomber flying the contour of the hills at night for practice missions at very high speed. The slow and silent approach was probably caused by the perception of an object coming at close to supersonic speed and flying over."

Of course, it could have been a giant UFO screaming across the countryside. However, as I write this, officials at Robins Air Force Base are attempting to obtain permission to operate just that kind of mission across northern Georgia.

ISUR field investigator Terry W. Kimbrell speculates that this new corridor would be a natural avenue for military training. Plus, it "would make sense that . . . something else is using these routes to make runs to stay hidden in these Eastern Mountain ranges. In the last two years there's been a lot of reports coming out of the area . . ." Noting the frequency of reports, George Flier says they "may indicate bases are hidden in the mountains . . ."

The region of Sand Mountain, Alabama, not far from Murray County, has provided many UFO reports in recent years and has one of the most concentrated incidents of cattle mutilations in the country. A number of UFO sightings have also been reported in the mountains of western North

Carolina and around Chattanooga. Several investigators have proposed that this is another corridor of anomalous phenomena like one in western Georgia (see chapter 9). The route traverses some of the most rugged mountains in eastern America.

THE SAVANNAH CONNECTION
Savannah has also seen a resurgence in UFO sightings in recent years. It started with a V-shaped craft seen on February 15, 1989.

At 5:30 A.M. on September 9, 1996, a woman who lived on the top floor of a Savannah hotel, with windows facing the South Carolina marsh, was lying in bed when she "suddenly became aware—that something was beginning to pass over the hotel from south to north. At first I saw just the lip, then more and more" as it floated slowly past the windows. "It was round and lit from beneath or within with white lights, not uniform in brightness, but some spots brighter than others." Although it was a disc shape, she thought, "It looked like a tentacle-less jelly fish—because it was sort of translucent appearing." As the UFO cleared the hotel by a few hundred feet, the woman found her voice and startled her husband, an executive with the hotel, from sleep. As he came to the window the UFO "absolutely streaked away" in seconds. Hubby saw red and white lights receding into the distance.

It was 1:35 A.M. on April 3, 1997, when a man driving to work at Gulfstream Aerospace near the Savannah airport spotted what he thought was an aircraft approaching for a landing. The plane, no more than a thousand feet high and traveling north, had "a shiny polished metallic appearance" and was the size of a Learjet or large jet fighter, but the man realized that at four hundred to five hundred miles per hour, the craft was traveling too fast for landing. The silent object flew past the runway, turned sharply left, and disappeared toward Savannah. The witness noted that the fuselage was domed or more rounded than an airplane and had "short stubby wings or none at all." It had no props or exhaust. The man was an expert on aircraft from his work at Gulfstream, but he had "never seen an aircraft of this type before."

A man in Pooler was gassing up at 8:00 P.M. on May 30, 1997, when he saw "a huge green fireball or ball of light" that flew at a tremendous rate of speed across half the sky in four seconds. Silent and ball-shaped, he said it "did not look like any shooting star."

A family on Wilmington Island scored the next several sightings in the Savannah area. At 6:00 P.M. on March 10, 1998, a man spotted a triangle with one white and two green steady lights. It floated effortlessly past the house at an altitude of five hundred feet, making no sound before disappearing over trees to the south. He was familiar with military planes from nearby Hunter Field, and felt this UFO was "taking advantage" of the location. He also stated that UFOs had been seen previously in the area.

UFOs made a return appearance to Wilmington Island on January 1, 1999, at 5:15 P.M. On this occasion, a clear, beautiful evening, the man was observing the contrails of commercial traffic over his house when he spotted a plane low enough to distinguish the four engines. About four plane lengths away from it and off its left wing was a bright, pencil-point ball of light pacing the plane. Only the light left no contrail in the sky.

Several weeks later, at 7:45 P.M. on January 29, the man was returning from Savannah and approaching the Spencer Gray Bridge when he observed "a triangle flying low and as big as two houses" flying west. As he passed beneath the craft "the light pattern changed to a rotation of white lights" and formed a disc shape. The witness stopped his car and got out, but could hear no sound.

DRY RUN

A December 14, 1998, Internet posting from Scott Colborn to the organization Citizens Against UFO Secrecy related the "unprecedented" number of UFO sightings in Georgia to a story related by, admittedly, a reputable acquaintance of a reputable acquaintance. The reputable acquaintance once removed is an air force member who "is part of a team of individuals whose job it is to go to the crash sites of alien craft. Once there, they are to secure the area, remove the craft, all debris, occupants, etc., and return the area to as natural a setting as they can, and then leave" (just like they did in the X-Files movie).

Except when needed, the members of this IMF (Impossible Mission Force, should you choose to accept it, Mr. Phelps) are stationed at separate bases. On November 29, 1998, this agent received orders to fly to Atlanta on December 1. Upon arrival, he was immediately sent home. The RA (reputable acquaintance) felt this was a "dry run for rehearsal" because "superiors wanted to know how long it would take the team to get to Georgia from their different locations." Apparently, a future event is anticipated for the Big Peach.

This incident may be related to a strange sighting in Warsaw, Indiana, located eighty-five miles from Chicago. On August 1, 1999, two readers of the Internet column UFO Roundup were eating breakfast at the American Table when they spotted a striking van parked next door at a Days Inn. The full-sized, solid-white vehicle had a lavish array of high-tech communications and detection equipment on top, including the "rotating dish of a radar," which was in motion. On the side was the logo, "UFO Intercept," with UFO Roundup's Web address of UFOINFO, the parent site, beneath it. It also had a Georgia license plate.

Joseph Trainor, editor of *Roundup*, and John Hayes, webmaster of UFOINFO, had no knowledge of such a van. John thinks it was just a fanatical fan, while Joseph speculated that it was "a surveillance van of the Bureau of Alcohol, Tobacco, and Firearms (ATF) in UFO drag." *UFO Roundup* fans have since kept a sharp eye out for the van and it has been sighted several times, but without the Georgia tag, in Lake Charles, Louisiana, in October 1999, and in Tucson, Arizona, in February 2000.

6

Psychic Phenomena

THE SURRENCY HORROR

Allen Powell Surrency, born February 7, 1825, was one of twenty-five children born into a Terrell County family. After he married Wealthia Roberson, the couple settled in her home in Appling County. He purchased considerable land in an area of pine forests and swamps, and constructed a sawmill. Surrency served as Appling County's sheriff, state representative, and tax collector. When the Macon & Brunswick Railroad arrived in 1870, the community became Station No. 6, later to be named Surrency in honor of its most distinguished citizen. Surrency constructed a store beside the rails, served as an agent for the line, and used his residence as a boardinghouse.

"There be more things in heaven and earth, Horatio, than are dreamed of in your philosophy." So the *Macon Telegraph* quoted Shakespeare on Monday, October 21, 1872, as an introduction to press accounts of extensive paranormal activities at Surrency. The paper reported that for two or three days, following Thursday, October 17, "occurrences of so strange a character as to induce . . . people to believe that supernatural influences were at work" had occurred, and had "kept up, without cessation, ever since."

An unnamed gentleman traveling to Macon stopped at Surrency and asked the proprietor "if he had any ghosts about him." Surrency referred him to his wife, who replied his curiosity would be satisfied in a few minutes. While waiting, she displayed a pile of fragmented china and knickknacks "which had been thrown down and broken, without any visible agency being engaged in the work of destruction," the correspondent stated.

As they talked, a "lumbering" noise was heard in an adjoining room. Asked about the disturbance, Mrs. Surrency said, "Another brick (has) been thrown into the room," the latest of "a large number" that had arrived throughout the day.

As the intrepid investigator and others approached that room, "something whizzed by their ears and fell with a crash behind them." They

Surrency is proud of its spooky past, as evidenced by this city limit sign. The house burned decades ago, but a painting of it hangs in city hall and locals still sight a spook light.

turned and found a shattered barroom glass that had been "thrown through the door with such force that the heavy bottom of the glass penetrated so far into the floor that it required some force to wrench it out."

After another "heavy fall" directed them to another room, they found that a smoothing iron had been removed from a trunk and deposited in the middle of the floor.

Mr. Surrency revealed that he had gone to bed at 3:00 A.M. on October 20, "but bricks fell around him so thick and fast that sleep was impossible. Out of two full sets of crockery in the house but two pieces remain whole."

These supernatural shenanigans occurred every few minutes throughout the day and night, without interruption, the investigators were assured, and "the family have not been able to sleep during the time, and are beginning to look greatly worn out."

The bricks were thrown into rooms perfectly closed up, with windows shut and latched. The onlookers were "perfectly mystified," the newspaper stated, although they believed "some human agency" was responsible and would be detected by further investigation.

ENLIGHTENED GEORGIA?
Other interested men had traveled to Surrency, the report continued, and further facts would be forthcoming. The paper lamented that "at this late day of the nineteenth century, there should occur in the civilized State of Georgia manifestations" of supernatural origin.

On Sunday evening, October 20, a conductor on the Atlantic & Gulf Railroad reached Savannah and announced that the extraordinary happenings had erupted on October 17 when, according to the *Savannah Morning News*, "a large stick of wood was thrown through the closed window," while the family ate dinner. The log struck the floor with such force that the whole house shuddered. Not only was the window shut, but those present did not believe that a man could heft so large a timber from the ground and up to window level.

The Surrencys investigated and found nothing unusual, other than the teleported timber. They had scarcely sat down again when "a tumbler and a cup and saucer were dashed from the table and broken right before the eyes of the astonished and frightened families." Additional objects were tossed about the room, and bricks and other things continued to fall to the floor, apparently materializing through the closed window.

Hearing accounts of the incidents, local people flocked to the Surrency home and "were astonished and bewildered" by the activity. A railroad agent at Surrency initially doubted the reports, but he was soon convinced that the family played no part in the acts.

The populace of Brunswick were so interested by the mystery that a special train, bearing eighty to one hundred people, left Monday, October 21, to witness "the singular sights" at Surrency. A number of intrigued citizens had also departed Savannah that night for the Surrencys' place. The Savannah paper anticipated that "affidavits will be made by reliable parties" who had investigated the occurrences and found "no human agency . . . visible in the proceedings." Those stories further fueled the controversy.

AN AMBIDEXTROUS POLTERGEIST

These events "could go on in different parts of the house at the same time," often in broad daylight and "inside the house and over the yard at the same moment, and with articles of an altogether different size and nature," the account continued.

The *Morning News* was informed that the Surrencys had abandoned the house, it "becoming really dangerous to remain there on account of the constant hurling of stones, etc., through the windows."

On October 22 the *Macon Telegraph & Messenger* stated that the reports it had received were "so incredible . . . that it was very difficult to give them full credit." To arrive at the truth, the paper dispatched reporter Peter Lindenstruth, accompanied by two other Macon residents, James Campbell and a Mr. Mason, to Surrency on Saturday night, October 19. They arrived before dawn, about 4:00 A.M. on Sunday morning, entered the parlor, built up the fire, and waited.

ANOTHER BRICK IN THE HOUSE

Lindenstruth described Surrency as lying 126 miles from Macon and about sixty from Brunswick and the coast. The town consisted of a railroad station house, two stores, and the Surrencys' house, a two-story structure covered in weatherboards. The main portion of the house contained four rooms on the first floor and four on the second. An ell running from the back contained a kitchen and a dining room. Lindenstruth went outside for wood, and upon returning "heard a heavy thud" on the floor of a neighboring room. He initially thought it was a family member up and about, but "subsequent events" convinced him it was the first brick of the day. As they waited in the still darkness, they heard "an occasional rapping about the house." Twice it sounded like "some heavy body had fallen."

Surrency arose at daybreak and welcomed his new guests, then openly described what had happened and submitted a report of the phenomenon's activity, which he had written on October 17. The missive answered a number of questions about the origins of the phenomenon.

At 9:00 Thursday night, October 17, Surrency had returned home after traveling to Station 7½.

"I found my family and some of my neighbors—among them Rev. Benjamin Blitch, Col. D. M. Roberts, my brother, and several others whom I consider men of truth, very much excited," Surrency wrote. "In a few minutes after my arrival at home, I saw the glass tumblers begin to slide off the slab and the crockery to fall upon the floor and break. The books began to tumble from their shelves to the floor, while brickbats, billets of wood, smoothing-irons, biscuits, potatoes, tin-pans, water buckets, pitchers, etc., began to fall in different parts of my house. Nearly all of my crockery and glasses have been broken."

Surrency, who stated that he had lived there "for twenty years unmolested," labeled the events "a strange freak of nature." He estimated the number of people who had witnessed the phenomenon as seventy-five to one hundred.

Just before sunset Friday in the front room "the family were greatly alarmed by sticks of wood flying into the house and falling about the floor from directions they could tell nothing about," Lindenstruth wrote, "and without any human agency they could see or find out. The wood would fall before being seen, and what made the mystery still more mysterious, the room into which the wood was falling had all its doors and windows closed."

Surrency, his wife, their two grown daughters, Reverend Blitch, and Colonel Roberts witnessed all of this activity. Blitch left, "and all remained awake the whole night. Notwithstanding the windows and doors were tightly closed, and no opening left in any portion of the house, these brick-bats continued to fall, but although sometimes just missing, not one struck any person."

Soon after the brick campaign started, bottles, vases, and other glass-ware commenced "jumping" from their accustomed places and shattering on the floor.

This is the only known photo of the Surrency House, which burned nearly eighty years ago. (Courtesy of the H. D. Tippins family)

After a few hours' peace, the activity commenced again on Saturday afternoon, October 19. Family members, joined by most of their neighbors, "watched every nook and corner of the house to detect, and if possible, to unravel, the mystery. But so quickly would pitchers, tumblers, books, and other articles jump from their positions and dash to the floor the eye could not follow, and broken fragments were the first things seen, except in one instance, and that was a pan of water and some books; they were seen to start.

"Chairs, shoes, and clothing were tumbled about the house, as if the hand of a veritable witch or unseen devil was present." However, the journalist considered the most "inexplicable incident" to be "the escape of a lot of ordinary clothes hooks from a locked bureau drawer. They also fell on the floor, the drawer remaining tightly closed." After 8:30 P.M., nothing unusual occurred until morning.

After relating these tales, Surrency stepped up to the old family clock and was relating how rapidly the hands had traveled around the dial when the ghosts were about, on the previous day. All eyes were turned to it and much to their astonishment the hands commenced running around at the rate of about five hours a minute. It was suggested that a large magnet was secreted beneath the house, but the correspondent's pocket watch was unaffected. Lindenstruth "set the clock right, when it continued to keep correct time up to the time he left."

Things were quiet until 11:43 A.M., "when the performances reopened by a pair of scissors jumping from the table to the floor. At that time Lindenstruth was sitting in a chair when, without the slightest premonition, a large brickbat fell with great force right beside him, breaking in two. He immediately picked up a piece of it and handed it to Mason, and both found it hot. Then taking up the other piece he tried two or three times to break it by throwing it on the floor, but failed."

Lindenstruth placed the piece on a windowsill, intending to take it home with him. Returning to his seat, "he was again startled by the piece he had placed on the windowsill falling at his feet, once more breaking into two pieces."

Dinner was then served, with the Surrency family and a number of guests crowding around a large table. "Soon after being seated, an ear of corn, apparently from the ceiling overhead, fell between" Campbell and Mrs. Surrency, and "striking the floor with great force it broke in two, scattering the grains all around the room. Later in the day another ear of corn fell in another room, striking near Mrs. Burns, a Northern lady, who at the time had an infant in her arms."

While eating supper, a crash announced paranormal activity in an adjacent room. The reporter instantly entered the room, finding no trace of a person and the windows closed and locked, but a pitcher had been thrown from a stand and shattered.

Events continued at a rapid pace. A book was ejected onto the floor from a bookcase, an umbrella slid from a dressing table onto the floor, three ears of corn fell, one at a time and at different places on the dining room floor, each incident separated by several minutes, and a vial and a tin cup hit the floor. The Macon reporter emphasized that he did not include other "freaks" that occurred during the day outside of his immediate presence.

MANNA?

"Little piles of sugar totally unlike anything of the kind then used by the family were found upon the floor of the residence," the reporter continued. "In one of these a few pins and a steel pen were found. There were various other incidents of this totally incomprehensible mystery related to and seen by our reporters, but enough have already been given."

By this point word of the mysterious events in Surrency had spread. On Sunday afternoon the Macon & Brunswick Railroad responded to public demand by dispatching a special train which reached No. 7 at 3:00 P.M. with seventy-five curious gawkers. The haint apparently did not appreciate the expanded audience. No paranormal manifestations occurred until most left on a train one hour later.

Surrency's family planned to leave the house that day for twenty-four hours, hoping that several volunteers could solve the mystery, if that was possible.

The reporter found each member of the family honest and patient. He also stressed that Surrency was "a gentleman of most excellent character in his community . . . one of the leading men in his county, a quiet and good citizen" who owned an extensive farm.

When Lindenstruth's party left, people were still arriving from all directions.

On October 24 the *Macon Enterprise* reported that "passengers, conductors, and officers" of the Macon & Brunswick continued to arrive in Macon announcing even greater excitement in Surrency.

The Surrencys were "thoroughly worn out" from the spook and the huge crowds descending upon their home. Also, "Their household furniture has been ruined or is every day being destroyed by an unseen power."

PORTABLE PORK

Conductor H. H. Sharpe swore to the most mysterious event. On October 23 six to eight men and women were relaxing in the parlor when a hog slowly entered the room, walked to the center of the room, turned in a circle, then made for another room. All followed the portable porker. "Whilst some were in the room, some in the door, but all intently watching what it would do, it instantly vanished like a vapor or an apparition, leaving its audience stupefied with horror, with no one able to tell how it escaped. The windows were down and no means whatever open for escape."

SCOTTY, A BOTTLE OF WHISKEY, AND THE TRANSPORTER

An old salt named Burns, presumably husband to the woman with the baby, and who was said to have sailed around the world numerous times, arrived "to unravel the mystery." Rather than chase poltergeists around the house, he chose to concentrate on one object—the smoothing iron. He sat and watched the iron for hours, but it did nothing. As he longed mentally for a drink, a bottle of whiskey fell beside him. Burns "picked it up and helped himself, set it down and continued to eye the iron. It did not move, but the bottle left as mysteriously as it appeared."

On October 22 W. C. Remshart wrote a report from Jesup to relate his experiences on Sunday, October 20, in the company of J. W. Brothers,

219

superintendent of the Atlantic & Gulf Railroad, and D. M. Mitchell, a company agent. It originally appeared in the *Blackshear Georgian* and was reprinted in the *Savannah Morning News* on October 28. Several bricks and chamber pots fell, but the witnesses did not see them in motion and were "inclined to believe that they were thrown by some person."

Remshart returned Monday night and remained through Tuesday night, October 22. After dark Tuesday Remshart informed Surrency that he "saw nothing that could not have been thrown by some living person." The phenomenon apparently accepted that as a challenge. Minutes later Mrs. Surrency entered the parlor and informed the men that "Every one would have to leave the kitchen, as things were falling there at such a rate that it would be dangerous to remain."

In the kitchen Remshart saw a number of items that had fallen. While inspecting the scene, the party heard objects falling in the parlor. Remshart watched Mrs. Surrency cut a piece of meat on the table, then turn to the stove. As she returned to the table, several family members and a servant entered the room with the cut meat, which had fallen into the center of the parlor. No one else had been present in the kitchen.

On October 24 the Macon papers printed the story of "a Macon gentleman," a skeptic on the subject of ghosts, who traveled to Surrency to "solve the matter." Arriving at 3:00 A.M. one morning, he found the moon down and pines blocking out starlight. Owls hooted, fireflies flitted about, and bullfrogs called from the swamp. When the train left, the man started for the Surrency house "when all at once an apparition appeared very near him, upon the railroad track."

Terrified, his hair standing on end, the disbeliever took flight along the railroad bed. Following a five-mile sprint, "the hideous specter" on his heels, this character heard, "Wake up here. Didn't you say you wanted to get off at No. 6?"

"No, I'll be damned if I did," he told the conductor. "I'm going to Jesup." He then took a bottle from his satchel and had a long drink.

The *Savannah Morning News* dispatched its own correspondent to Surrency for "an intelligent, correct and interesting account of the late wonderful phenomenal manifestations" at Surrency. The reporter returned on October 28, and his report appeared the next day. He had arrived at 11:30 P.M. on Saturday, impressed with the ordinary scene, "one of the last places that I would suppose a spirit would choose to locate its ghastly pranks of legerdemain."

The comfortable, old-fashioned house was surrounded by cypress ponds, the land low and covered with saw palmetto. The family had retired, but the reporter found young men gathered around the fireplace in the parlor and spent the night swapping jokes and ghost stories. In the morning Surrency related the story of the clock, which hung on a wall in the parlor, which "had ever been characterized for the correctness of its time. Suddenly with a weird, buzzing noise, the hands began to move around with exceedingly rapid motion, the hour hand exactly five minutes ahead of the minute hand. In this singular position they continued to move for seventeen minutes, in which time it had described five hours, and each time it arrived at the twelve o'clock mark it would pause and strike, though with the greatest irregularity. Sometimes it would strike one hour for another, such as twelve for one, &c., and at the end of the five hours ceased its wild movements." That was the timepiece reset by Lindenstruth, "and ever since has kept its usual correct time."

As the phenomenon continued, then ceased, many wondered about the origin of this mystery and speculated on its source. The Express Messenger locomotive of the Macon & Brunswick Railroad arrived on Thursday, October 24, with a belief, published in the *Brunswick Appeal*, suggesting that a daughter of the Surrencys' "is an unconscious medium," this based on "the fact that she left the house and visited a neighbor where the spirits appeared, leaving as she left." However, the question was asked, if she was the source, "Who can explain why the spirits have never before appeared?"

MY DARLING CLEMENTINE

On October 28 the *Macon Enterprise* proposed that a seventeen-year-old daughter of the Surrencys', Clementine, was the "medium." A reporter attempted to interview the "beautiful and modest young lady," but she was attending church. He settled for a conversation with a Mr. Patterson, into whose house, two miles distant, Miss Surrency had been sent on the advice of Surrency and family friends. The party was cordially received with "sugar cane, and a recital of all the strange occurrences. He was a truthful gentleman and we believe his report."

According to the account, A. P. Surrency had traveled to No. 7 on Thursday, October 17, and was scheduled to return that evening. About dark, with the train overdue, an anxious Clementine walked to the railroad to search the gathering night for the locomotive's light.

"While looking in the direction of the train towards Macon," the *Enterprise* stated, "she saw something in the shape of a man, dressed in white, coming towards her. Being frightened she ran to the house, but did not reach it before a lightwood knot fell within a few feet of her. This was followed by a shower of wood and a few brickbats." Further, the apparition had vanished although there were no obstructions to her vision. As Clementine sat on the front steps, a Savannah reporter noted, "Other things similar to this first fell around her in very rapid succession, and in quite close proximity, none striking her. They all came from the direction

221

whence she had seen the apparition." Clementine retreated into the house, and as she passed from the parlor to the kitchen, witnesses "could distinctly hear things similar to those described, falling in the yard and against the end of the house, apparently moving in the direction of the kitchen. By the time she had gained the entrance, brickbats, bottles, etc., were falling in thick profusion on every side. The gentlemen present were called, and diligent search made, though no one could be seen, yet those missiles were falling around. It then got among the pots on the stove, threw them off, overturned the coffeepot, threw crockery, knives, &c., about the floor, and entered the house, where similar actions took place. Books, glasses, and other things were scattered about the floor."

A farmhand was sent to investigate, but he "ran back, for fear of being struck by the falling bits of wood." Believing pranksters were showering her home with sticks, Mrs. Surrency ventured forth "and she, too, saw the wood falling in every direction. It then ceased outside and began to show itself in the house." Surrency's younger brother Hampton was summoned and also witnessed the events.

Suspecting that Clementine might be precipitating the mayhem, she and Mrs. Surrency were sent to stay with the Pattersons during the week. When they left, paranormal activity ceased at home, but when they reached the Patterson house "the strange things began to occur there. A wash pan was on the water shelf nearly full of water, and while Mr. P. was about five steps from it, fell at his feet, spilling the water. Chairs would tip over, shoes would fall about, etc." After a few hours Mrs. Surrency returned home alone, arriving about dusk and inducing the frightening events to commence there again. The problems at the Pattersons' home had ceased with her departure. A number of witnesses saw Clementine at the Pattersons', while psychic activity continued at the Surrencys'.

The *Savannah News* concluded: "These strange things have never happened except where Mrs. Surrency was present, and always ceased when she left; and it is very clear, assuming it to be from a supernatural source, that she is the medium through which it acted."

The *Enterprise* also rejected Clementine as the source, for she was absent from home while paranormal activity occurred there. Another suspect was a young black servant girl, but she had been sent on errands while the experiences continued. The only female present throughout all the events was Mrs. Surrency. "This conclusion may be hasty and ill-founded," the paper allowed, but after all of its inquiries, "this is our solution."

The popular fad of spiritualism was also rejected by Clementine and Mr. Surrency, who "has always been a strong opponent of the doctrine of spiritualism in any form. He is a plain, practical farmer, a well-to-do and popular citizen, and has an excellent name among his neighbors, many of whom we met at his house, and all of the railroad employees with whom we spoke seem to vie with each other in heaping praise upon himself and wife," wrote the Savannah reporter, whose pen name was Saint Bernard. The correspondent emphasized that Surrency was never suspected of a hoax, and, apparently more important in Georgia in the 1870s, "was a staunch Democrat" and a subscriber to the *Morning News*.

A. P. Surrency did deny the teleporting hog story and the one about Burns and the frisky liquor bottle. His wife confirmed that "she had lost several dozen pieces of crockery, glassware, china," and had only a small saucer remaining, "which she had for six different times seen removed mysteriously and by an unseen power, from one part of the house to another, without being broken."

The *Savannah News* team concluded with "sincere thanks to Mr. Surrency and family for their untiring attentions and kindness during our brief stay. The many questions were met by prompt and cheerful answers, and each seemed to aid the other in all those little kindnesses that go to make life and business pleasant."

The investigative team departed Surrency at 11:00 P.M. on October 27, "feeling satisfied that the cause of the mysterious doings lies in some supernatural agency." They extended "hearty thanks" to the Surrency and Patterson families, and to the Brunswick line conductor, Captain Jarvis, "a gentlemanly and an efficient officer."

"Surrency, farewell!"

The last psychic phenomenon occurred Friday night, October 31 (When else but Halloween?), "and we hope they will never occur again." The last reporters again praised Surrency, who "throws his doors open for everybody, and if visitors continue he will be eaten out of house and home. His heart is entirely too large."

As is true with most supernatural stories of this kind, the Surrency saga died as suddenly as it had started. Apparently, the ghostly manifestations ceased for good.

Three years later, in August 1875, an article in the *Warrenton Clipper* claimed to have identified the person responsible for the phenomenon. A servant girl was said to have been seen actually throwing bricks around the house. Further, she was reported to have been arrested (charges unspecified) and confessed to responsibility for all the mysterious occurrences at the Surrency house to reputable authorities in Bartow County. This "debunking" story was "extensively copied by the papers throughout the country," an Eastman paper declared. That paper pointed out that no single human being could have carried out all the mayhem attributed to the force at Surrency. Also, the Eastman paper made inquiries and declared that "Mr. Surrency had no Negro girl in his employ who is now in Bartow County."

A. P. Surrency died on January 7, 1877, and was buried in Overstreet Cemetery.

Unfortunately, at his death Surrency was deeply in debt due to a depression, which caused hardship for his family. Wealthia later married J. F. Thigpen. She died on July 12, 1899.

Serious world-class weirdness occurred at the Surrency home for a week or so in October, 1872. However, the worst was yet to come—in the form of what people later claimed to have occurred there. Take it all with a salt lick.

REVISIONIST SURRENCY

Elaboration on real events started in 1929 with an article written by Rev. J. W. Tinley, pastor of a Methodist Church in Rochelle, Georgia. Twenty years earlier, in 1909, he had talked with A. P. Surrency's brother Hampton about the events at Surrency, which had occurred thirty-seven years earlier. Therefore, the "facts" presented in the *Atlanta Journal Magazine* section are based on the memories of an elderly man speaking thirty-seven years after the events occurred, and the memories of a man writing down what he was verbally told twenty years before. Now you know why I'm skeptical, and why you should be too.

According to Hampton-Tinley Memories, Ltd., the supernatural events apparently started a day earlier than previously thought, before Clementine's experience. One night, "as some of the boys were coming home a shower of dead leaves and trash fell over them. They thought somebody was trying to scare them, and yelled back for the folks to quit getting their clothes dirty. Just then another shower of trash dropped down on the boys. They ran into the shrubbery looking for the person who had thrown the stuff, but did not find a sign of a living thing." Emphasis on living, I'm sure.

Summoned by Mrs. Surrency after all hell had broken loose on the following evening, Hampton ran home fearing someone was ill or injured. Upon entering the living room he found the family standing across the room from the fireplace.

"Hamp," Mrs. Surrency said, "we can't keep that piece of wood on the fire!"

"It was an unexpected and startling remark," Hamp was quoted as saying. "Nevertheless, I went over to the hearth and looked at the stick of firewood. It was an ordinary split of oak, and seemed incapable of trickery. I picked it up and tossed it into the fireplace. But no sooner had it touched the andirons than it bounded back at my feet. I tried laying it back into the fire, but it hopped over the high firelogs again. Then I placed it gently on the irons, but no sooner had I removed my hands than it again jumped out. I gave up trying to refuel the fire, and my sister-in-law pointed to the door. 'See if you can close it, Hamp,' she said. 'We can't.' I pushed the door shut and heard the latch click, but when I removed my hand from the knob, the portal flew open and struck the wall with a loud bang. I tried again with the same success. Then I took the key from the nail on the wall and locked the door, but no sooner had I removed the key than I heard the bolt click back, and the door was thrown open so violently it shook the whole house when it swung back against the wall. This was repeated several times, and then we decided to leave the door open, although the weather was really too cool for so much fresh air."

Strange events continued the next morning. Hamp said, "As we were at breakfast, the dishes suddenly hopped off the table and fell in a broken mass upon the floor. This trick was repeated many times in the days that followed. So many dishes were broken that my brother bought tinware, which was unbreakable, to cut down on the expense. Even then, the food was ruined, and an awful mess was made on the floor for the womenfolks to clean up. And frequently they had to prepare the meal twice, when food was dumped off the table before we had eaten."

The family searched everywhere for an ordinary explanation for the puzzling acts, but had to accept "the strange doings as being the work of a real ghost."

"We might all be sitting in a room, when a brick would crash against the wall and thus to the floor. This was disconcerting, as we were never sure that the ghost's aim was accurate enough to miss us all. However, nobody was ever injured in any of the pranks. The ghost seemed harmless, but mischievous."

Contrary to contemporary accounts, Hamp claimed that the force got "a special delight out of entertaining a large audience. Watching the queer manifestations got to be a regular diversion" for residents and visitors.

Hamp dismissed the possibility of human perpetrators, saying, "I don't believe there was anybody in town smart enough to perform everything that ghost did." He also rejected conventional wisdom by claiming that his sister-in-law could not have been responsible because "We saw them when she herself was away visiting."

Hampton-Tinley added two additional stories to the mythology that is Surrency. To protect items he particularly treasured, Hamp placed them in an outhouse. However, "he had hardly stepped inside the door before the things were dumped upon the floor behind him." A visiting teacher wedged her shoes between the mattresses at bedtime so the ghost would not appropriate them during the night. Next morning the shoes were gone and did not return until a week later, when they appeared in the center of the room.

But what about the fate of the ghost, Reverend Tinley asked?

"That also is a mystery. We might almost say that it was killed by too much popularity. People came from everywhere to see it. The railroad

225

advertised its presence, and ran special trains at tourist rates to bring visitors to Surrency. The village was small, and hotel accommodations were not sufficient to care for such large crowds. My brother realized the danger, and knew that it would ruin him, as he was a very hospitable man who made every effort to assure comfort to the multitudes that came. So he decided to move to another farm he owned six miles out in the country. The ghost didn't go with him, nor was it seen again at the big house. It appeared to have vanished as suddenly and mysteriously as it had come."

A second article in the *Atlanta Journal Magazine* on August 15, 1940, introduced more myths to the story. Written by Madolyn Surrency Roberts, apparently a woman with some family connection, she described platters filled with ham and biscuits being whisked out the window by unseen forces on the first morning of the phenomenon. On another morning their cook, Sarah, watched a coffeepot turn itself upside down on the stove, followed by a frying pan filled with meat. After Sarah removed a pan of biscuits from the oven "the pan promptly sailed out the window . . . the family was obliged to live on canned food for days, and even then they did not dare take their hands off the cheese and crackers or canned meat for fear the food would be smashed against the wall or go sailing out the window."

Another corrupted story seems to stem from one denied by Mr. Surrency. In this one Captain Burns (he of the magic whiskey bottle) is conductor of a train. "One day, just as the passenger train stopped in front of the Surrency home, everyone left the train except the conductor, Captain Burns, who remained in one of the coaches. To his horror, a huge cross tie whizzed through the window of the train, narrowly missing Captain Burns's head and passing through the opposite window, where it landed on the ground and stood upright like a fence post."

Ghost writer Nancy Roberts does the Surrency legend a serious disservice in her 1988 book *The Haunted South*. She calls A. P. Surrency by the name of Millard, and his wife, Ann. In her version the supernatural incidents began in June 1872 and continued until 1877. The unsubstantiated first encounter involves "Ann," not Clementine. In it a pitcher, washstand bowl, china soap dish, and glasses rock and roll before being dashed to pieces in her bedroom. Next, two windows close of their own accord, then rise, and repeat faster and faster until panes shatter. Shades of Uri Geller, Roberts has forks and spoons being bent and even broken by invisible forces.

Supernatural activity is first confined to Ann's bedroom and the dining room. Children suffered broken bones and other serious injuries as heavy wardrobes and bureaus toppled over on them. Clementine had a problem with motivated furniture. Tables and chairs she touched would follow her throughout the house, up and down stairs, and into the gardens. At times all the furniture in a room would stage "a weird, maniacal kind of dance, whirling here and there for as long as five minutes at a time" in her presence. Phantom hands tugged Clementine's hair, covers were snatched off her bed, and one morning she was levitated just before the bed turned itself over. Ms. Roberts's entity "delighted in mussing up newly made beds."

Apparently, new stories enter the records every time a reporter stumbles across the story and interviews area residents about stories they have heard handed down over the past 130 years. Later accounts, for example, have plows furrowing the earth and brooms sweeping with no human effort. There are now accounts of insane laughter, sorrowful weeping, and bloodcurdling screams. Glowing red lights are reportedly seen in the sky above the railroad near the old Surrency House, and residents today speak of the Surrency Ghost Light. Writers place the end of the ghostly manifestations in 1877 apparently because Surrency died that year, but there are no records of continued activity after late October 1872.

Speaking of Surrency, although he was considered a saint in life, ugly rumors erupted in the century after his death. There are now stories about his occult power—reportedly, he once ran a broom straw or a twig through his head without bleeding. Other legends have Surrency murdering a farmer who once owned the land and then hiding the body in a bedroom trunk, or killing a railroad worker outside the house, and it was one of their ghosts that caused all the trouble. Another called Surrency a "sick, sadistic fellow possessed with sorcery-like talents." Hershel Tillman, a witness to the burning of the Surrency House, said cryptically, "That thing haunted Old Man Surrency until the day he died. But when he was buried, the haunting stopped."

The Surrency House burned on a Sunday morning in 1921 or 1925, according to various accounts. One witness swore that smoke from the old wooden building formed the image of a man with a long flowing cape—which resembled Surrency before his death!

Could there be a scientific explanation for the Surrency Horror, or is the following story just a geological coincidence? In the early 1980s geologists were looking for a "suture" where North America and Africa collided 500 million years ago, an event which formed the Appalachian Mountains. About 180 million years ago, the continents pulled apart, leaving a chunk of North Africa embedded in North America beneath Florida and South Carolina. Scientists found their suture running in a wide, gentle arc from Brunswick to Americus and the border with Alabama.

NINE MILES DEEP
During this scientific testing, which consisted of beaming sound waves deep underground and recording the reflections back to the surface, an anomaly turned up precisely under Surrency and nine miles deep. It is

called the Surrency Bright Spot—bright because it reflects sound waves. The curiosity is shaped like a contact lens two miles in diameter. What does it consist of? Apparently, some type of fluid, probably water, but perhaps a liquefied gas like methane, carbon dioxide, or even liquid helium, but probably not oil. At that depth its temperature would be almost five hundred degrees Fahrenheit, and geologists had previously thought fluids could not exist at such a depth "due to the intense heat and pressure," said Dr. Larry Brown of Cornell University, who admits that scientists "don't have a good idea what the formation is composed of." This discovery "would upset a lot of scientific theories as it is theoretically impossible for water or other fluids to exist at such a great depth. . . ." Brown, director of the Consortium for Continental Reflective Profiling, is developing the first accurate chart of the earth's mantle, which extends to twenty miles below the surface. He said the Surrency Bright Spot is "big and we've never seen anything like it before," anywhere in the world.

Stanford Tillman, Surrency's mayor at the time the discovery was made public in 1987, commented: "It might have something to do with Surrency's ghost. If this town is known for anything, it's for the ghost . . . A lot of us also suspect that the goings-on had something to do with unusual magnetic activities in our area. The discovery of this formation is very exciting to me."

Personally, I prefer a supernatural explanation for the events at Surrency, which ranks as one of America's greatest ghost stories, on a par with the infamous Bell Witch case in Tennessee, and certainly far more credible than the events that inspired *Poltergeist: The Multi-Media Event*. Forget you ever heard about the *Blair Witch Project*.

Vanguard Sciences of Texas raises a point, which never occurred to me but should have. During the 1950s science fiction bled over into Altantan studies and produced the Hollow Earth Theory, advocated primarily by writers Richard Shaver and Ray Palmer. They proposed that a civilization based on various vanished races from the surface had taken residence inside the earth. Many caves and tunnels led deep within the earth from various places, particularly the American southeast. Perhaps the Bright Spot is an entrance to the Hollow Earth or an energy source for it. There are also evil people down there called the Dero who use machines to project rays that affect our minds, cause levitation, or even teleport people (abduction madness). And, of course, this would explain the mysterious events in Surrency so many years ago.

HOUSE OF BLOOD

As of 1987 Minnie and William Winston had been married forty-four years. For the previous twenty-two years, they had rented a six-room, red-brick home at the corner of Fountain Drive and Morris Street in southwest Atlanta.

It was just before midnight on September 8 when Minnie, seventy-seven, stepped out of the shower and found the bathroom floor covered with splotches of blood. Mrs. Winston immediately ran to the bedroom and woke her seventy-nine-year-old husband, saying, "Come look at all this red stuff coming out of the floor."

She claimed not to be frightened by the unusual sight, "because I didn't know where it was coming from. It didn't look like blood and it didn't smell like blood."

Spots of blood, ranging in size from a dime to a silver dollar, were found on the floor and lower walls in the bathroom, bedroom, kitchen, basement, and every hall. The substance was also located under a television and in narrow, nearly inaccessible crawl spaces in the basement.

"We've never had anything like this happen before," Mrs. Winston said, adding that it was the first time they had ever called the police for any reason.

Homicide detective Steve Cartwright agreed with Mrs. Winston, saying that in his ten years of service, "I've never seen anything like this." He called it "an extremely strange situation." However, there was no evidence that a "crime had been committed."

"I'm guessing it was an animal," stated homicide detective Richard Price. "Hope that's all it was," but it wasn't. William said the couple had no pets, and there were no rats, mice, or roaches in the house.

Police were not terribly concerned about the matter because William, retired from the National Screen Service Company, spent most of his time in bed attached to a dialysis machine, which cleanses the blood of people suffering from kidney failure.

However, Mr. Winston seemed to reject his blood as the solution to the mystery. "I don't know what the stuff is. My wife is upset because she doesn't know where it came from. Me, I'm not bothered by it because I'm in bad enough shape as it is."

The "bleeding house" immediately captured the fancy of Atlanta, drawing crowds from across the metro area. Prying visitors became such a problem that police declared the house a crime scene to prohibit inquiring minds from trespassing.

THE MATCHLESS GAME

On September 10 it was learned that the blood type of the house was O, and William was A. No match. By the following day the Winstons' family physician revealed that Minnie's blood was also type A.

Atlanta homicide detectives grew frustrated as their work progressed. "We will continue a routine investigation," stated homicide commander,

Lt. Horace Walker, "and if we find that no crime was committed, we're through with it. As we see it now, there has been no crime." The fact that the Winstons' son, William Jr., was a burglary detective with the Atlanta police bureau guaranteed a thorough investigation.

Detective Price stated, "We're still trying to figure out where the blood came from. There were no new leads but we plan to check with the state crime lab today about other possibilities." However, there was friction between Atlanta police and the state crime lab.

IF THE SPLOTCHES FIT—

Police handling of the bloody evidence came under immediate criticism. Believing a wounded animal might have deposited the splotches, police sent fresh samples to Grady Memorial Hospital to determine if it was human or animal blood. Only then, thirteen hours after Mrs. Winston called police, was the state crime lab notified.

Crime lab director Larry Howard stated that they could have learned much more—sex, race, traces of drugs or alcohol—more easily from fresh blood.

"We are usually the first people called in by the police," complained crime lab forensic serologist Ted Staples.

The only semirelevant fact discovered by the crime lab was that it "looked like the blood was projected out of something or shaken off something." Out or off of what was never ascertained.

"I still don't believe it's human blood," Minnie declared. "I don't care what the police say."

As the police investigation continued, public and media interest intensified. The offices of the *Atlanta Journal Constitution*, radio and television stations, and the police department were flooded with inquiries from across the Atlanta area and as far away as California and New York.

"Are the walls of that house really bleeding?" people generally asked.

"We were swamped with calls," admitted police spokesman Charles Cook. "This place was a madhouse. Some people wanted to know if the radio stations were joking. Now they know it isn't a joke."

The Winstons found themselves besieged in their home by throngs of curious, nosy spectators. One local said, "This place was humming with cars and police, just wanting to know what all the fuss was about."

"The phone rang all night," Mrs. Winston complained. "I'm fed up with it." No new blood had appeared, but its origin remained a mystery. Mrs. Winston declared that she did not want to have anything to do with the controversy. "People are coming out here to see it and troubling us. I haven't had any sleep today and I probably won't get any tonight."

The passage of another day left the Winstons even testier than before. From inside the house Winnie was heard to shout, "What they've said about all this is lies! Just leave us alone!" From the bedroom William yelled, "There's no blood in this house! Now get away from here!"

One intrepid reporter who gained entrance found spots of blood on the floor and lower walls of the living room, and a quarter-sized splotch on the back door.

These Fortean, paranormal mysteries usually just slowly fade away, and such was the case with Atlanta's bleeding house. The homicide bureau and the state crime lab never identified the source of the blood nor did they detect any indication of a hoax or criminal activity. "It troubles me that we don't have any answer," crime lab director Howard summed up.

BRINGING OUT THE DEAD

THE FACE ON THE GRAVESTONE

Smith Treadwell moved to Murray County in 1840. He married Polly Mobley, and the couple had two children while living in Tunnel Hill. After Polly's death in 1851, Smith, with his first wife's advance permission, married her sister Betsy, a union that provided eight additional offspring.

Treadwell prospered in north Georgia, purchasing additional land in Floyd, Cass (present-day Bartow), Whitfield, and Terrell Counties. During the Civil War, Treadwell wisely moved his family to a Terrell County plantation, far from the war ravaging northern Georgia. Although too old for active service, Treadwell volunteered for duty and served as a prison guard at Andersonville.

In 1865 Treadwell moved to a two-story colonial home in Spring Place. There he built and operated several water-powered wheat and corn mills. He died on February 20, 1893, and was buried in a cemetery on his property. Soon after a marble monument was placed at the grave, the fun began. Streaks appeared on the stone, the markings forming a pattern resembling Smith Treadwell.

THE FIRST POLAROID

"I helped bury Mr. Treadwell," former slave Levi Branham wrote in *My Life and Travels*. "Within a year I noticed the picture. I think it resembles him very much. It seems to me that the picture becomes plainer every day."

The *Dalton Daily Citizen News* reported: "The face on the tombstone . . . is a wonderful likeness of the man who is buried beneath it. The marks in the marble outline the face in a remarkable way."

The Photograph Monument once topped the grave of Smith Treadwell, a former Murray County resident. The monument has been vandalized and stolen, and it is now in storage. Treadwell's descendants are tired of the controversy.

Although a few relatives argued that the portrait did not resemble photographs of Treadwell, a face had undeniably appeared on the stone. Over the years occasional publicity would send hundreds of people on a journey to see this marble marvel for themselves. Visitors pestered owners of the property with questions and generally made nuisances of themselves.

A question soon arose—had the picture manifested itself because Treadwell was a good man or an evil one? Those who had known Smith Treadwell considered him an honest, decent man, but legends erupted. Treadwell had murdered his wife, a popular story maintained. He was widely but falsely accused of being a bootlegger. Treadwell was also alleged to have been generally mean and dishonest. A. P. Surrency had received similar treatment.

In the 1930s the Smith Treadwell monument was featured in "Ripley's Believe It or Not." A sketch of the monument and its mysterious face was accompanied by this description: "The Tombstone Portrait—Spring Place, Georgia. A few years after the death of Smith Treadwell, an exact likeness of him appeared on his gravestone."

After Ripley provided this national exposure, curious travelers bothered the property owner at all hours, and vandals damaged the cemetery. It was almost a sense of relief that greeted the theft of the gravestone in 1951. Years later it was found in Mill Creek near Dalton, but Treadwell's descendants elected not to remount the stone.

HELL'S NIGHT LIGHTS: GHOST LIGHTS, SPOOK LIGHTS, AND WILL O' THE WISP

A number of rural communities across Georgia have stories of a ghost light, spook light, or mystery light. Many of them seem related to tales of engineers, conductors, or signalmen, all of whom were decapitated.

THE SCREVEN SPOOK LIGHT

Perhaps Georgia's most famous ghost light is that of Screven, located in Wayne County in southeastern Georgia. Its renown originated with an *Atlanta Journal* article that was reprinted in *Info Journal*, a noted Fortean magazine.

Just before Halloween in 1982, *Journal* writer John Vardeman visited the railroad tracks where a dirt road crosses at Milligan's Crossing. The lane runs through flat, sandy, isolated territory where nights get really dark. Locals informed Vardeman that the light most commonly appeared late at night, particularly after a rain and following the passage of a train. A common description is of "a glowing clear-white ball that floats and swings side to side along the tracks, its light often flashing bright, then dimming," Vardeman related.

"The ghost light has provided a lot of fun for those of us who grew up here," stated Donald Waldron, a carpenter. "There aren't too many things to do for entertainment in Screven."

Local groups once sponsored hayrides to the area. On one such jaunt a personal close encounter with the glowing orb convinced Waldron to consider the phenomenon in a different light.

"We've had scientists come down here to look at it, but nothing ever came out of it," said Andy Lastinger, Screven's fire chief. "I don't think anyone will ever really know what it is. There's definitely something there—and we've just come to live with it."

"Years ago, a group of us were watching the light come and go," no more than ten feet away, revealed JoAnn Surrency(!). "That scared me more than any other night I had watched it. I screamed and ran."

Jim Henry Bennett, like many residents, had heard stories of the light from his father and grandfather. On many of his nocturnal observations, he thought a train was approaching.

"We would listen and wait, but there was never a sound," he recalled, "and the train never came."

Railroad workers confirm that the light is not associated with rail signals or machinery.

Most of Screven's 850 residents had seen the light at one time or another, and all had heard stories of it. Explanations abound. Elderly Witsell Griffin, who lived just yards from the rail line, said, "There must be ten thousand tales explaining the ghost light."

The favorite theory is that it is the spirit of a railroad flagman on the Seaboard Coast Line who was decapitated in an accident between Screven and Jesup. The bobbing light is reputedly the lantern he swings in search of his head—although how he could know to look for it without a brain escapes me—I suppose his not knowing any better explains why he returns every night to resume the effort.

Here is the truth of the local train wreck. Late on the afternoon of February 19, 1884, a southbound train on the Savannah, Florida, & Western Railroad overshot the place where it was to stop at Screven Station and collided with a northbound train waiting on a siding. Fortunately, the only injury occurred to the man apparently responsible for the accident, an Engineer Ford. His leg was caught between the engine and tender, crushing the bones from the ankle to the knee. Hearing of the accident, Ford's father and brother, both physicians in Waycross, hurried to the scene. They amputated the leg midway between knee and thigh, but the engineer died several days later in Waycross on February 21, 1884. He did, however, die with his head still attached to his body.

The light is also postulated to be the ghost of a man who died during construction of the railroad and was buried along the tracks following the Civil War. However, many natives insist that the light predates the Civil War by a number of decades.

If one rejects a supernatural explanation for the spook light's origin, there are two common "scientific" theories. The first is that it is "swamp" or "marsh" gas, produced by decaying organic material in local wetlands. While that phenomenon undoubtedly explains the occasional inexplicable night light, I doubt that it is a dependable source of continuing reports. If it is a reasonable solution, then why are there not a hundred thousand regularly scheduled ghostly glows in Georgia? Countless parts of this state are swampy!

The other typical explanation is that the lights of Jesup or the lights of cars from nearby highways are reflected by atmospheric conditions.

In late June 1998, my son Paul and I traveled to Screven to check out their ghost light. Every citizen we talked to had personal observations to relate, although no one seems to watch for the phenomenon anymore—apparently, modern life has gotten so busy we have no time left for mysteries. After watching *Godzilla* (speaking of a horrible phenomenon) at the drive-in outside Jesup, we ventured to the lonely crossing just before midnight. Paul and I spotted a light we could not explain down the tracks to the east, but we otherwise failed to experience a dramatic sighting.

THE HEARD COUNTY LIGHT

Another ghost light with a respectable pedigree is found in Heard County, five miles south of Franklin and a mile and a half west of U.S. 27 at an old home site called the Spearman Place. It debuted to regional fame after an article describing it ran in the *LaGrange Daily News* on September 4, 1962. As often happens with this phenomenon, when the story spreads, frequently in the fall of the year, the site becomes immensely popular for a few days around Halloween. Then the novelty wears off. On one Sunday night in 1962, 150 cars jammed the narrow road, a number easily surpassed on Friday and Saturday nights. People waited for the spook light to appear, debated its origin, and argued over its history.

Standing in the yard of the Spearman Place, one could look north toward Franklin into a bottomland 150 yards away. At different times during the night, the glowing orb would appear for a few seconds before disappearing.

Joe Davis had been aware of the mystery for forty years. For fifteen of those years he had occupied a house near the Spearman property. He stated that "On any given night I could stand in my yard and see this glow."

On hot, dry nights, it was the size of a baseball; on cloudy, rainy nights it was "bigger, about the size of a train light. It would glow about three minutes and disappear. In a few minutes, I could see it at a spot a little distance from the first glow."

Elusiveness is a primary trait of spook lights.

Asked if the existence of the floating fluke bothered him, Davis replied, "No, but I often wondered what caused the thing. I never showed it to any outsiders, and nothing much was ever said about it until now."

Other residents, including David G. Daniel, who lived near the light bright site, knew nothing of the phenomenon until it became a cause celebré in the area.

Heard County sheriff Virgil Bledsoe had his own, albeit common theory. "I think it is caused by reflections of car headlights coming from heavily traveled U.S. 27," Bledsoe said. Marsh gases were also proposed as an explanation for the apparition.

Two rival local folktales have a man being hung from a big oak tree in the yard of the house, and women being shot nearby. The lights are said to be the "corpse candles" of one of these misguided souls.

A daughter of the aforementioned Joe Davis, Sallie Timmerman, rejected the headlight suggestion, saying, "I have seen this light many times through the years, and I don't think cars cause it. It is too hilly, and the trees are too thick in this area."

A granddaughter of Davis, teenager Mary Ann Pike, added, "I saw this glow many times as a little girl when I visited my grandfather. He would show me the light," so to speak, but she also discounted the ghost stories associated with the event. Pike noted that outsiders were more concerned about the phenomenon than locals accustomed to it.

A NATIVE AMERICAN LIGHT

Cherokee Chief Red Bird lived in what is now northern Dalton. His home was at Hamilton Springs, and he loved to compete at the horse track he laid out along Thornton Avenue. While racing recklessly one day, he was thrown from his horse and shortly died from his injuries. His grave, near his home, is now covered by the railroad. A ghost light attributed to Chief Red Bird is occasionally seen bobbing above the tracks.

THE CAMDEN LIGHT

A ghost light in Camden County originated with a lover killed by a jealous husband. The victim was buried at the end of Crum Hammock. For years lightwood markers indicated the grave, but its occupant was unknown. Over the decades many people have been frightened there at night by a light that approaches and passes them, continuing on into the darkness.

A ghost light, the spirit of a young bride who never slept without a candle burning because she feared the darkness, floats across the grounds of Christ Church on Georgia's Saint Simon's Island.

HAUNTED UTOPIA

At various times in America's history, "utopian" societies have flourished. One was the Ruskin Colony, a socialist enterprise that developed five miles west of Waycross. It followed the philosophy of John Ruskin of England, who emphasized self-reliance and discipline, honesty and hard work. Capitalism and competition would be replaced by a cooperative enterprise that sought social and economic opportunity for all.

The community originated in 1898, when nine families from the American Settlers Association in Indiana and Ohio moved to Duke, a small sawmill town. Families owned their houses and land, but worked cooperatively. Within a year they had constructed homes, a depot, and a post office, and had 760 acres under cultivation. They were joined a year later by refugees of a failed utopian society in Tennessee.

The colony's population topped out at a little over three hundred. The community prospered with a sawmill, planning mill, photography studio, and factories for brooms, suspenders, shoes, and coffee. They constructed a school and library, had their own justice of the peace, and welcomed local workers. Within the colony they used a script substitute for money that was accepted by Waycross banks. The *Coming Nation*, their newspaper, was mailed to subscribers around the world. The colonists instituted a twelve-year school long before the state did, sponsored a light opera company, held debates and lectures, brought in guest artists, and constructed a dancing pavilion. Many members gathered in a communal dining room to eat food from their own kitchen and bakery. Their products were sold across the region.

Utopias never seem to work. Rumors circulated within the colony about financial improprieties, and outsiders talked darkly about atheistic Yankees who practiced free love. A rainy winter in 1901–1902 caused many deaths, and a fire consumed the printing press, dining room, bakery, and kitchen, and, later, a two-story commissary. Colonists made charges of discrepancies in work hours and types of work assigned. Two days before the colony's books were to be audited, the records burned and money disappeared. One member of the board of directors died mysteriously, one decamped to California, and enraged colonists threw a third down a staircase.

The colonists abandoned Ware County for Indiana and Ohio, and even faraway New Zealand and Australia. The colony disappeared under vegetation and Ruskin survives only as a name place beside the railroad. A ghost light is frequently seen by those who venture through deep woods to the Ruskin Cemetery.

A HEADLESS GHOST

Another Ware County ghost light tradition, this one dating to the 1930s, owes its existence to the railroad. A man fishing along the tracks at

Henson Creek, near Manor, fell asleep one night with the rails as his pillow. A train appeared, sounding its whistle frantically, but there was no response. Steel wheels kept on rolling, and the fisher person was high-landered.

Now for a twist. The legend is that the body can be seen walking the rails at night swinging a phantom lantern in search of its head. Kevin Dial claims that his grandfather went in search of the "shade" one night. Sure enough, it approached, solid white and six feet tall, walking directly toward Gramps, who fired a futile shot before fleeing.

FAITHFUL SLAVE STORY

Cogsdell is not listed in authoritative *Georgia Place Names*, but Barbara Duffey says a ghost light haunts a crossroads near the vanished community. It is a typical story. Rich plantation owner went off to fight for the Confederacy. Believing he would soon be home, the man instructed his faithful slave to stand at the crossroads every night to guide him through the wilderness to his home. The owner never returned, but the faithful slave dutifully carried his torch until his own death, thirty years later. *Even today*, dear friends, travelers see a mysterious light hovering above the intersection.

MARY, THE WANDERER

Saint Simons Island can claim two ghost lights. In *Georgia Ghosts* Nancy Roberts tells of young Mary MacRae, left orphaned by disease on her immigrant journey from Scotland. She was taken in by the Demere family, which lived at Mulberry Grove Plantation. Mary fell in love with the Demeres' son, Raymond, who fought with his strict father just as a hurricane was brewing and set out in a small boat for Brunswick or Darien. Mary lit a lantern and headed for the dock to await Raymond's return. Both Raymond and Mary disappeared into the ocean, never to return. On stormy nights you might see a light wandering along the beach, forever searching for Raymond. Some say she rides a white stallion along the roads on her quest. Various versions of this and the following tale are told on Saint Simons.

THE CANDLE IN THE GRAVEYARD

The story is also told of a young woman desperately afraid of the dark. She molded hundreds of beeswax candles so that she would never spend a second in darkness. Of course she died young, and her devoted husband kept a candle burning every night on her grave in beautiful Christ Church Cemetery. Long after his death a supernatural candle burns eternally on the grave. It has been seen countless times in the churchyard at night floating among the graves.

HENRY COUNTY SEES THE LIGHT

Henry County's train wreck legend dates to June 23, 1900. It had rained virtually every day for more than three weeks, and four inches had fallen in the previous twenty-four hours. Floodwaters had eaten away a thirty-foot-high brick and granite culvert over Camp Creek, a mile and a half north of McDonough. At 9:30 P.M., No. 7, with Engineer J. T. Sullivan and conductor W. A. Barclay and thirty-eight passengers, headed north on the Southern Railroad line. The train thundered down a steep, mile-long downgrade and crashed into the ravine. Thirty-one people died in the shattered wreck, including the engineer and conductor. A ghost light is occasionally spotted in the area.

Off Padgett Road near Starr's Mill in Fayette County is the Old Hanging Ground. During a lynching circa 1900 a potential hangee escaped and hanged the landowner, known to folklore only as Old Man Padgett, from a railroad bridge. Although the line has been abandoned for some time, people hear train sounds and see ghostly figures on the tracks. Reportedly, Padgett is still seeking his killer.

GHOST LIGHTS AND HELLHOUNDS

Gravediggers near Bainbridge were often given several days' notice of deaths around New Enterprise Freewill Baptist Church Cemetery. Residents who occasionally sighted a ball of fire hovering above the grounds of the graveyard realized that a death was always imminent.

The graveyard was reportedly haunted and/or guarded by a "hellhound," a large black dog with a bloodcurdling howl. The creature never left tracks, even after being seen crossing a wet, freshly plowed field.

Such creatures are typical of paranormal activity. Another, though not associated with a ghost light, has been seen around a cemetery at the Tucker-Newsome Place in Madison County. If anyone intruded on the grounds, the great dog would materialize and bark until they left.

During the 1930s a derelict named Wee Willy fell asleep on the railroad tracks along Cleveland Avenue in Athens. A locomotive either smashed his head to jelly or decapitated him, and Willy was interred headless in the pauper's plot in the old Athens Cemetery. People have seen his head, wailing and shrieking, floating beside the rails in search of his body.

Another railroad spook light story falls into the realm of folklore for it does not designate place, time, or name. Lawrence C. Stanley wrote a number of books detailing the legends of north Georgia. In one, a railroad crossed a river valley on a long, high trestle. Because floods threw logjams at the bridge supports with considerable force, a small building was erected at the northern end of the span, where a signalman watched the bridge during bad weather. Just before the tracks crossed the trestle, they passed through a high, steep ridge in a mile-long tunnel that curved halfway through its length. An engine's headlight did not illuminate the span until the train was halfway through the tunnel. If there was a problem, the signalman raised a red lantern and the train was shunted to a siding before the trestle.

The signalman, who had served here faithfully for many years, was well known by all the engineers, conductors, firemen, and brakemen on the line. They shouted his name and blew their whistles as they passed his lonely post.

One night when the river was flooded, a northbound train entered the siding and watched for a scheduled southbound express to pass. The train's engineer chatted with the signalman, kidding him "about how old he was. The old man laughed and said he was still young and hoped to remain on this job for many more years."

Two nights later, when the engineer made a return run, the river had risen even more. As he made the curve in the tunnel, the engineer "saw the old signalman run out from the little building, with his red lantern in his hand, and he began to swing the lantern back and forth across the track in an urgent signal to slow down."

The crew desperately applied the brakes. The signalman dove off the track as the train screeched to a halt, and did not reappear. Inspection revealed the bridge was fine. Puzzled, the engineer continued to the next junction, twenty-five miles distant. There the engineer complained and asked what caused the signalman to flag him down.

"There was nothing the matter with the bridge or track so far as we know," the railroad agent responded. "Besides, the old signalman did not flag you down tonight."

"I did see him," the engineer retorted angrily. "The signal he made meant for me to slow down and proceed with caution. What do you mean when you say I did not see him, and that there was no signal?"

The stationmaster replied: "You did not see old John tonight. He stepped in front of a northbound train about ten o'clock last night, and was instantly killed. His body is lying in state in a funeral parlor about two blocks from this station."

TAYLOR COUNTY SHOULD SEE THE LIGHT

If any stretch of rail should be haunted, it would be at the Taylor County community of Reynolds. Early on a spring morning in 1908, No. 1055, a Central of Georgia engine hauling freight from Columbus to Macon, pulled onto a siding there to allow No. 4, a passenger train running from Macon to Columbus, to pass. A block from the tracks, stationmaster Eugene E. Hodges followed the sounds as the engine detached from its cars and pulled onto the main line to take on water from the tank. By sound Hodges knew something was amiss. He roused his wife Frances, eight months pregnant with their ninth child, and told her the engineer was putting cold water into an overly heated boiler. The explosion occurred before he could leave the house.

All that remained on the tracks were the wheels of the locomotive—the engine had been blasted into a street one block away. The engineer was dead, headless, his fireman dying. As alarmed townspeople rushed to the scene, Frances Hodges realized the No. 4 train was due and would wreck on the debris. She lit a lantern and hustled up the rails, waving the light frantically. The engineer of No. 4, seeing the signal as he barreled through the Flint River swamp, stopped in time.

Nor does the tale end there. The dead engineer's head was nowhere to be found despite an extensive search, and his funeral was to be held the following day in Macon. A head would somewhat comfort the family. Fortunately, a heavy rain had started a leak in the roof of J. N. Bryan's store in Reynolds. When repairmen scaled the building, they found the AWOL head. It was rushed via train to Macon in time for its funeral. Perhaps the ghost is absent because the head was found.

Frances Hodges delivered a girl named after her. The daughter wrote this story in the *History of Reynolds*.

Another potentially good spot for a railroad ghost light is the bridge over the Alabaha River a mile east of Blackshear on GA 82. On Saint Patrick's Day, March 17, 1888, No. 37 crossed the thirty-seven-foot-high trestle on the Savannah, Florida, & Western Railroad, but the tender and six cars collapsed with the bridge into the wreck. Dozens were injured, a number killed.

Another possibility would be the railroad bridge at Stone Creek in Twiggs County, where a passenger train wrecked on February 29, 1896. Half an hour later a freight train smashed into the rear of the first, killing three trainmen. A unique note to this case is that it was the result of criminal mischief. Twiggs County residents Thomas Shaw and Warren Criswell had removed spikes from the roadbed. Their wives had traveled to Macon that day to shop, and if the women were maimed or killed, Shaw and Criswell would collect money from the railroad. Shaw also planned to marry another woman. The wives were unharmed, but Shaw and Criswell received life sentences for the deaths of the three men.

THE HAUNTED PILLAR, OR THE PILLAR OF PROPHECY

Motorists and pedestrians who pass the corner of Fifth and Broad Streets in downtown Augusta invariably notice the lone column standing on the southwestern corner. The artifact, two feet in diameter and ten feet in height, is composed of brick covered with concrete. It is the "Haunted Pillar," and there are many who believe death awaits any who touch it. Eerie events are said to occur around it.

The pillar is all that remains of the Market, two large sheds about two hundred feet long and one hundred feet wide that once occupied the center of Broad Street from 1830 until 1878. Known as the Upper and Lower Markets, the citizens of Augusta flocked there daily to purchase food from farmers, grocers, and butchers.

In the late 1800s an itinerant evangelist visited the city (although a less-authoritative source lists the year as 1829). The eccentric preacher was described as an elderly, white-haired, stately looking man whose

clear voice was "incisive even to the piercing of the human heart," one witness declared. It is variously argued that no church would host his services or that he disdained them. Again, the story varies, that he preached in the Lower Market for some time or that the managers refused him permission to speak or that he was run out of town by disbelievers. Whatever the circumstances, this Old Testament–style speaker proclaimed that a storm would soon destroy the Market, either for his being denied permission to speak there, or to punish the people of Augusta for their transgressions, or simply to prove that he was a prophet of God. Take your pick— that's the great thing about folklore, you can choose your own story. Only

Augusta's Haunted Pillar is all that remains of the city market, cursed when a traveling preacher was either denied permission to speak or run out of town.

the southwestern column would survive the storm, the preacher declared, and anyone who attempted to move it would be killed.

The prediction/curse came to fruition at 1:10 A.M. on February 8, 1878, when a tornado touched down in Augusta. It remained on the ground for half a mile, tearing a two-hundred-foot-wide swath through Augusta from Ellis to Market. Two people were killed and several houses were knocked down. The Lower Market was "totally destroyed," noted the *Augusta Chronicle & Constitutionalist*, leaving "a mass of ruins, timbers broken, and masonry piled in utter confusion." It was reported that the Market bell rang a single time before the destruction commenced.

Perhaps prophecy was fulfilled, but in reality the curse did not kick in until later, for the city council elected to rebuild the Market on its original site. The surviving pillar was carefully moved to the corner of Fifth and Broad, which is where the legend of its being haunted/cursed began.

Early in 1879 Theodore Eye, whose Lavasseur & Eye firm was a grocer, paid workmen fifty dollars to move the column across the street. They rigged cables and had started the moving process when a mischievous boy lit a big firecracker then got away. The shaken workers reportedly abandoned the effort and by some accounts vacated the city permanently.

Reportedly, when the street was later widened, two workmen who attempted to move the pillar were struck by lightning or otherwise caused to die. Another version has a bulldozer operator dying of a heart attack while advancing against the column (this one is reminiscent of Trahlyta's Grave). However, a man who managed a liquor store across the street for fifty years denied the story, saying the pillar had "been moved (without injury to workers) several times because it was too close to the street."

It does seem at least to be haunted. Late at night visitors near the column have reported hearing whispered conversations between phantoms and the footsteps of invisible beings pacing alongside them. When contacted by a reporter on the Halloween beat, local police revealed that eleven traffic accidents had occurred at the intersection between January and October one year, so perhaps the pillar has an effect on cars or their operators—or perhaps careless drivers eyeing the column caused their own accidents. The pillar seems to attract its own bad luck—it twice has been struck by lightning and been hit by an errant car.

The pillar remains a great tourist draw in the historic city, attracting individuals, buses, and walking tours. At times it seems to receive more publicity than the Masters Golf Tournament. On December 12, 1996, the Haunted Pillar received its own historical marker.

ALL WE NEED IS A MIRACLE, OR TWO

O, HOLY PASTA

On April 9, 1991, Pizza Hut launched a promotional campaign in northeast Atlanta for spaghetti. A giant poster depicting a steaming helping of pasta was plastered onto twenty billboards in the area of I-85 and I-285.

Two weeks later Joyce Simpson was praying about a decision she had to make in her life as she filled her car with gas at a Texaco station on Memorial Drive at Village Square Street in DeKalb County. Should she remain in her church choir or become a professional singer? She beseeched God for an answer, asking for a sign. Feeling compelled to glance up, she saw the Pizza Hut billboard across the street.

ON TOP OF SPAGHETTI

"I saw Christ's face," Simpson said. Her shadowy image of Jesus, contained in strands of spaghetti hanging from a fork, had deep-set eyes, a beard, and a crown of thorns.

Joyce Simpson had her answer. She stayed with the choir and also spread the Gospel. Soon the parking lots of a gas station, Jiffy Lube, and steak restaurant were overrun by the faithful or merely curious. A church bus containing sixty parishioners stopped for a look and people drove in from across the metro area—and farther. Television camera crews broadcast live from the site.

Many people saw Jesus. Lewis Grizzard saw tennis star Bjorn Borg. Others detected Jim Morrison and Willie Nelson. "It's hilarious," said Debbie Payton. "I think you can find anything if you look for it."

Colleen Nowak, with the advertising company that handled local Pizza Hut advertising, said, "Unless Jesus looks like a Muppet . . ." She didn't see it.

The photo was a stock shot provided by Pizza Hut headquarters in Wichita, Kansas. It had been used on many previous occasions with no reports of supernatural manifestations. Roger Rydell, media spokesman for Pizza Hut central, assured the public that no subliminal message had been intended.

The billboards, leased for thirty days, were soon replaced with less-inspiring fare.

THE JESUS TREE

A gnarled, battered tree in the front yard of Margaret Richardson's Columbus home became the center of a controversy in spring 1994. Richardson had long considered the tree strange, but in mid-April a passerby stopped and said she had seen the face of Jesus on it the night before. That night Richardson looked for herself. She also saw what she thought was the face of Christ, formed by shadows and light and the rough texture of the bark.

Within days heavy traffic choked North Lumpkin Road as fifteen hundred to two thousand people a night swarmed over Richardson's yard, trampling flowers and grass and requiring the presence of police for crowd control. Some nights the street was barricaded and yellow police tape stretched across her lawn.

The exodus began soon after dusk and continued until well after midnight. Visitors not only saw an image of Jesus, they were soon interpreting and arguing over additional appearances of Jesus on the tree, plus the Virgin Mary, a lamb, and a calf. Some saw nothing at all. One skeptic grumbled, "It's like a waste of taxpayer money for the police to baby-sit a tree."

Richardson was quite gracious about the uproar and welcomed pilgrims from across Georgia and Alabama. "If it's Jesus," she said, "I'm glad to have it in my yard. If it's Jesus, He can stay right there."

Unfortunately, in early May, a vandal sprayed black paint across the tree where the images were seen, but the faithful continued their pilgrimages.

Before being vandalized, this part of a tree in Columbus displayed an image of Jesus.

THE HOUSE OF THE RISING SON? Benny and Lucy Tillman have lived together along an isolated Wheeler County road, twelve miles from Alamo, for more than thirty years. Today they alternate occupying an old two-story house and a mobile home placed atop a hill behind the house. They were in the trailer about 11:00 P.M. on January 22, 2000, when Benny was disturbed by the barking of his dogs, Bigfeet and Pee Wee. He went outside and saw nothing in the direction the dogs were facing. "Then something told me to look the other way, at the house," Benny said. "And that's when I saw it."

"It" was a startling, traditional image of Jesus projected against the side of the house by the glow of a security light filtered through a gnarled

In January and February 2000, thousands of people flocked to a house located in rural Wheeler County where the shadow of a face, which many thought to be that of Jesus, was projected by a security light through the branches of a tree. Check out the upper-left quadrant of the photo to the left of the window and just above the shadow of a thick branch. (Photo by Paul Miles)

chinaberry tree. Presumably, it was a new revelation because no one had ever noticed it before. The family soon discovered that shaking the branches of the tree did not motivate a flicker from the image.

"I think it's a sign from God, a warning to get your house in order," Lucy said.

The giant image is of a face from the crown of the head to the chin. One eye is eerily realistic, and the face thickly bearded. Some viewers saw the image immediately, while others had to have it traced out for them, and a few never saw the apparition that stared out from the shadows.

Word spread slowly through the community for a few days, generating up to two hundred visitors a night. That number exploded when the *Macon Telegraph* printed a front-page story about the phenomenon on February 4. Nearly six hundred people came on Friday night, a thousand on Saturday night, and hundreds more over the following week. The weather turned unseasonably cold for the area, with sleet and rain, but that did not deter the crowds. Benny Tillman Jr., one of the Tillmans' three sons, made it his duty to keep a hot fire burning in a metal barrel, which was soon replaced with a blazing bonfire, where pilgrims gratefully warmed themselves.

Early visitors came from around the county, then surrounding counties. As the image's fame spread, people showed up at all hours from as far away as Texas. The Tillmans kept late hours to graciously accommodate all who wanted to see this apparent miracle, and they made up their lack of sleep with catnaps during the day.

"I can't do anything about it, so I might as well welcome them all," Lucy said. Some even arrived during the day, when there was nothing to see. "I walked outside one day—and there were three women sitting on the bench in the yard, just singing," she said.

"Some people have said this is a sign just for me," Lucy stated, "but if that was so, other eyes couldn't see it. I can't explain it, and I can't interpret it, but as I've told each and every one who's come, they're welcome to be here."

A number of preachers came to see the image, Lucy said, and "They say it's a sign, but they can't explain it nor interpret it."

"It's a sign," said Wendell Whitehead. "He (Jesus) said he would send a sign near the end of the world. I believe it."

The Tillmans are lifelong residents of Wheeler County, respected citizens whose married sons and several grandchildren all live nearby. They attend Pleasant Hill Church of God. Not a word was uttered of a possible hoax or deception of any kind.

The day after the image hit the print and television media in Macon, I shouted "Road Trip!" and packed wife Earline and children Paul and

Melanie into the Blazer. We drove through the darkening evening and reached the site, several miles down a narrow rural road, around 8:00 P.M. on a Saturday night. Traffic was bumper to bumper and numbers of parked cars and pickup trucks lined both sides of the lane while people streamed toward the yard. The image was immediately visible to all of us when we first saw the house.

We joined the throngs in the yard, picking our way around cars, bushes, and assorted rubble. Hundreds were present but it was as quiet as church during a prayer. Everyone was reverent and spoke in hushed tones. Dozens snapped photographs or trained their video cameras on the sight while speaking quietly for the microphone. Parents with children, young people, couples of all ages, and the elderly stood in awe before the image. Blacks and whites mixed, sharing a religious experience. Earline noticed several older women dressed in their Sunday finest despite the frigid wind. "They've come to church," she said quietly.

Most made out the portrait of Jesus easily enough, but some in the crowd were finding greater detail. They tried to show others images of Mary, the infant Jesus, a lamb, and other figures. I couldn't see them, and while I don't doubt that the vision on the wall could have depicted Jesus, I saw the picture of a specific Confederate general, Nathan Bedford Forrest. However, as Robbie Browning had previously said of that contention, "I don't think a Confederate soldier could do that." Good point. We, and all our newfound brothers and sisters, left awed by the experience.

Less than two weeks after the phenomenon started, it came to an abrupt halt. A five-year-old girl walking down the road near the Tillmans' property ran into a passing car, breaking her leg. A legal adviser then informed the family that they could be held liable if someone were hurt on their land. Local police provided yellow tape to rope off the yard, and the security light was turned out, dousing the image.

GOD VOTES REPUBLICAN

Mike Crotts, a Conyers millionaire who owns real estate and insurance companies, entered the political arena in 1988 by challenging incumbent state senator Harrill Dawkins for the Seventeenth District seat. Crotts lost, but tried again in 1990. Completing a heated debate with Dawkins on October 9, three weeks before the election, Crotts walked outside the office of his press secretary and collapsed on the sidewalk. His heart had stopped. Medics and a nurse saw him fall and immediately attempted to restart his heart with cardiopulmonary resuscitation and electric shocks. They were unsuccessful as the ambulance rushed Crotts to Rockdale Hospital. There his heart was revived, but Crotts remained unconscious for five days.

Crotts's wife Phyllis was initially told that her husband was dead. After he was transferred to Emory University Hospital on the following day, she was informed that he would suffer brain damage. Phyllis refused to accept the diagnosis. Four days later she grabbed Mike's ankles and commanded, "Michael, get back in your body in the name of Jesus," and at that moment he woke up. The Crotts were Christians, but they had rejected the notion of faith healing until then. "I had to go down that road to find out it is real," Mike said.

Of course Crotts lost the election of 1990, but in 1992, fully recovered, he again ran for the Georgia senate, opposing developer J. T. Williams. Of his near-death experience two years earlier, Crotts said, "Quite frankly, I didn't want to come back. It changed my perspective on death. It's no different than walking from one room to another."

Crotts had experienced a deep spiritual encounter during the time he was in cardiac arrest. He and his wife discussed sharing the story, but for several years he would only speak of it when invited by churches. However, in December 1993, the couple appeared on the Trinity Broadcasting Network, a Christian cable channel, and described the experience on an hour-long show.

HEAVENLAND

Crotts claimed that he was dead for thirty-four minutes, from the time he collapsed to the time he was revived at the hospital. "I saw where we're going," he said, "and it's magnificent. It's wonderful. It's a place we'll enjoy."

Crotts found himself walking across a beautiful meadow with a pure, clear brook running through it. The sky was a vivid blue, and on the horizon was a beautiful light. He felt drawn to the light but a companion, whom he believed was the Holy Spirit, said he could not go just yet. He had to return to life and continue running for public office.

"God is placing key people in political areas," Crotts stated.

Crotts knew some would be skeptical about his account, yet he received positive feedback from most people. Dawkins, who twice defeated Crotts, believed many people in the district did not buy the story.

At Emory, Dr. Ziyad Ghazzal, who had no connection with the case, discounted the thirty-four-minute "death." He stated flatly that there is "no way" someone could recover from such an episode. However, if CPR was supplied, and it was, and the heart periodically regained normal rhythm, survival was possible. Ghazzal had heard of accounts like that of Crotts, but said he "always wondered if it happened when we brought the patient back, not during the time when the heart was stopped."

Crotts was not bothered by the controversy. "I'm not on a conversion trip," he said. "I'm sure there might be some people that are skeptical. That's fine. That's their right."

MIRACLE MOM

"I know I was dead for a few minutes," Tamara Higgins said two weeks after she was apparently lifeless for fifteen minutes on March 8, 1998. Higgins, a twenty-seven-year-old kindergarten teacher, and her husband Chris had just picked up their eleven-month-old daughter Lindsey from the nursery at Woodstock Baptist Church. They had attended the 8:00 A.M. service, and it was now shortly after 9:30 A.M. With little warning, Higgins fell face-first on the floor. Her heart had stopped beating. "She had no pulse and no heartbeat," Chris said. "Her ears had already turned blue."

Chris, a former lifeguard, immediately administered CPR while someone ran into the church service that had just started. A doctor, nurse, emergency medical technician, and two paramedics rushed out as Pastor Johnny Hurt asked the thirty-two hundred worshipers to get down on their knees and pray.

Higgins had no pulse for a quarter of an hour. When paramedic Jonathon Oliver hooked her up to a defibrillator, it took four jolts to bring her back to life.

"In five years, I've never seen anyone come back like that," Oliver marveled. "I believe God had his hand in that."

Dr. Beechan agreed, saying he had seen nothing like it in fourteen years of practice. "While I was performing CPR," Beechan said, "it was a great comfort to know there were three thousand people in there praying."

After a week in the hospital, Higgins was released. A tiny defibrillator was implanted in her chest in case her heart ever stopped again. In the hospital a second miracle was discovered. Blood work revealed that Higgins was pregnant.

Two weeks after she "died," Higgins returned to the church, which she and Chris had visited five times and had just decided to join. They thanked the congregation for the medical miracle they believe was worked through fervent prayer.

"I believe deep in my heart it is the prayers that saved me," Higgins stated.

"The story itself is a story of faith and belief and the power of prayer. The power of prayer is real. People can believe it if they want to."

GOD IN HIS CORNER

In November 1996, Atlanta's Evander Holyfield was a bet to lose his boxing match against Mike Tyson by 25-to-1 odds. Holyfield, adored by fans, had been an erratic heavyweight champion twice before, but managed to lose the belts in disappointing fights. He called it quits in the middle of one fight, then dropped out of the sport due to heart problems. Skeptics were legion when Holyfield later announced that a minister had divinely healed him after contributing to the man's mission.

249

Holyfield's comeback was not a pretty sight. He barely defeated several poor fighters until he "earned" the right to challenge "Iron Mike," the indestructible bully that fans loved to hate. On the evening of November 9, 1996, there were those who thought Holyfield might sustain serious physical damage in the fight.

Holyfield started the bout well, but said that he was confused, concentrating mainly on avoiding Tyson's hammer blows. Then he found a way to focus. Returning to his corner after an early round, he started talking to God, in tongues.

"I'd be over there speaking in tongues," Holyfield said, "and they (his cornermen) would say to me, 'What was that?' I'd tell them, 'I ain't talking to you, bro.'"

Holyfield explained that by "doing that, I was ending my confusion. I was talking directly to God spiritually about what he wanted me to do."

For a while Holyfield's handlers thought he had been knocked silly by Tyson's fists, but they soon realized the truth.

"They got to the point where I'd come back over there, and they'd yell, 'Pray on. Pray, Brother. Pray.' They didn't exactly know what I was doing, but with three rounds left, it was like they could see that it was working."

Holyfield fought each round better than the last. Absorbing all the punishment Tyson could administer, Holyfield knocked the champion down, leaving him wobbling across the ring on rubber legs, face bloodied and an eye swelling.

Early on, the Las Vegas crowd started a loud chant, "Holyfield! Holyfield! Holyfield!"

After ten rounds and thirty-seven seconds, the referee declared a technical knockout and stopped the fight. Evander Holyfield, supposedly washed up at age thirty-four, had become only the second man to win the heavyweight boxing title three times.

"It goes to show you," Holyfield said the following morning, "that God is good."

A MIRACULOUS RAINY NIGHT IN GEORGIA

Believe it or not, Mable was the name of a church that once existed in Camden County and later doubled as a post office. A century or more ago, the wooden structure, which stood on Hazzards Neck, was in immediate danger of destruction by a raging forest fire sweeping inexorably toward it. Every resident of the rural hamlet raced to fight the fire, except one man who entered the church, prostrated himself, and prayed desperately for showers of blessings. So earnest were his entreaties that those futilely attempting to stem the blaze heard his voice ringing in the rafters, beseeching the Lord for a rain or a shift in the wind. A downpour shortly drenched the area, extinguishing the fire.

A HARD RAIN IS GONNA FALL
When Ezekiel and Mary Jane Stafford settled on the banks of the Altamaha River in Tattnall County in 1825, their nearest neighbor lived six miles away. Despite the distance, Mrs. Stafford felt a burden for the spiritual needs of the area and started holding prayer meetings in different houses. Ezekiel was an "infidel," as it was uncharitably said at the time, but he often accompanied his wife on her treks through the piney wilderness. During one journey a forest fire had erupted and spread quickly through the deep bed of dry needles. Many houses were endangered and no available human agency could stay the conflagration, but Mary Jane fell to her knees and entreated with the Lord. A heavy storm soon unleashed its fury on the pines and extinguished the fire. As a result of this miracle, Ezekiel was converted, which some thought was the greater miracle.

YOU KNEW WHAT THIS SECTION WAS GOING TO BE ABOUT—PREMONITIONS AND DREAMS THAT MOSTLY CAME TRUE

FLYING THE UNFRIENDLY SKIES
In December 1988, Velisa Smith was a twenty-one-year-old Clark College senior studying in Europe. Longing to spend Christmas at home, she planned on accompanying her roommate Pamela Herbert. The two friends and others planned to fly back to the states on Pam Am Flight 103 on December 21. But when the reservations clerk asked her when she wished to fly, "something told me to book it for December 19. When the lady asked what day I wanted, December 19 came out of my mouth. Prior to this, I had some dreams . . . I kept smelling death in the air." Smith was fearful on her flight, concerned that something would happen. She landed safely, but her vision became reality two days later. On December 21 a terrorist bomb knocked Pan Am Flight 103 out of the sky over Lockerbie, Scotland, killing all aboard. Velisa Smith's premonition had saved her life.

A DOUBLE HEADER
Roswell resident John Robinson's life was saved in Vietnam when a "voice" advised him to take a different flight than the one he was booked to fly. He did, and the first plane crashed, killing everyone on it.

Fast-forward to the home front, twenty years later. In 1987 Robinson and his four-year-old son were swimming in a friend's pool.

"I was way down at the other end of the pool, talking," Robinson said. "All of a sudden, I heard a voice, and it was very emphatic, clear as a bell, as if someone was talking to me. I swam to the other end, and my son, who couldn't swim, had slipped off an inner tube and fell to the bottom. If I hadn't come, he'd have drowned.

"There's a lot we don't understand. But there's no doubt in my mind that what saved David was supernatural."

A VIDEO FAREWELL
Near Christmas 1987, Linda Kimsey of Loganville was attending a family reunion when she felt a powerful need to record the party because a person there would not survive the year. Kimsey was overwhelmed by "this urge, a real need, to find this video camera. It was like somebody was standing behind me, saying, 'You need to do this.' It wasn't a verbal voice; I could sense it more than hear it. I think it was the Lord."

Linda found the video camera and made a tape of the gathering. She was later glad that she had.

"I got a strong impression it was my daddy. And sure enough, he died in February. It wasn't a fluke, because I'd thought it might be my grandmother, who was in ill health. Things have happened all my life I couldn't explain."

MR. BEN
Ben W. Fortson was one of the most beloved men in Georgia history. Although crippled for life from a traffic accident when he was twenty-five, he became Georgia's secretary of state and held that post for thirty years, until his death at the age of seventy-four on May 19, 1979. Hundreds of friends attended his funeral, and the entire state mourned his passing.

As the funeral arrangements were being made, Fortson's driver, Frank Cook, revealed that "Mr. Ben" had been aware of his impending death only hours before it occurred. Cook drove the secretary to speaking engagements throughout the state, and every week Fortson returned to his hometown of Washington to visit with and purchase groceries for his 101-year-old mother-in-law, Annie Cade.

"He promised his wife when she died that he would look after her mother until the day he died, and he did," Cook said.

The last visit was on May 18. Although his wife was buried in historic Resthaven Cemetery in Washington, Fortson rarely visited her grave, which had a double headstone with his name already carved on it.

"We make this trip every week," Cook continued, "and he hardly ever stops here. But this time he told me to drive in and we stopped at the grave. He told me, 'All you have to do is put a date on here and bury me.'"

Fortson returned to Atlanta and died early the following morning. He is buried beside his devoted wife in Resthaven.

BROTHERLY LOVE

On May 26, 1990, thirteen-year-old Joshua Krieger left home on his racing bike to test a new speedometer. At 6:30 P.M. a car struck the boy near the intersection of Thomas Road and Split Rail Road in Clayton County, then raced away.

Although Ben Fortson, Georgia's long-serving secretary of state, rarely visited his wife's grave, the day before his death he stopped here, pointed to the blank date of death on his side of the stone and told his driver that all they had to do was fill in the date.

As Joshua's half-brother, Geoff Rickerson, rode his bike to search for the overdue youth, "He just saw him dead," in his mind, Mrs. Krieger said. Joshua was found half a mile from home. He was pronounced dead at Clayton General Hospital.

PSYCHIC TIP NO. 1: DON'T PREDICT SOMETHING THAT MIGHT LOOK LIKE A CRIME YOU COMMITTED, OR KARMA COMEDIAN

"I've been shown the karma that's attached to this house," Susan Lee Stacy, a thirty-eight-year-old hairstylist, wrote of her Duluth home to a friend. "It will burn even if I don't set it on fire."

The vision assured her that she would then own a house in Florida which "is beautiful and it even has an in-ground pool."

In the spring of 1989 Stacy was two months behind in mortgage payments and had sold off furniture to make past payments. On May 9 the house burned but not by supernatural means. Stacy was soon arrested and charged with pouring flammable liquid on a rug near her furnace and water heater.

A jury did not buy Stacy's Karmac the Magnificent act. After ten hours of deliberation, jurors found the woman guilty of arson. As Stacy collapsed at the defense table and cried loudly, Superior Court Judge James A. Henderson sentenced her to five years in prison and an additional five years' probation.

"I was left baffled by her explanation of the fire" and the letter, said assistant district attorney Keith Miles (no relation to the author). "She was a difficult person to cross-examine."

DEVIL WITH A BLUE DRESS

A newspaper account from Statesboro in early December 1933 described Mrs. Mike Scarboro's illness and confinement to bed. On Sunday she asked about a stranger standing in the room—a woman wearing a blue dress with white dots. Although assured no one was there, Mrs. Scarboro saw the same person several times.

On the following Wednesday Mrs. Scarboro's son Fred arrived from Houston, Texas, with his wife and children, whom the mother had never seen.

"That is the woman I've been telling you about," Mrs. Scarboro said, pointing at her daughter-in-law, "the woman wearing a blue dress." She was standing in the exact spot as the vision woman.

IS IT PARANOIA, OR ARE THEY REALLY OUT TO GET YOU?

Eric Rider became known as a reclusive millionaire with unusual beliefs after moving to Lake Rabun in 1985. Rider believed in UFOs and New Age ideas, and he settled in north Georgia because it had become somewhat of a center for people like him. He also held some very conservative beliefs, among them an opposition to the United Nations, a desire to return the country to the gold standard, and the repeal of income tax laws.

Rider was so convinced that he would be murdered by organized crime—specifically Florida drug dealers—that he set up a $250,000 fund to be used to find his killer. It turned out to be a good idea, because in January 1989, Rider and his ninety-two-year-old mother were both killed execution style.

Attorney Randy Shepherd administered the fund, which paid for a private detective and trips for local policemen to travel to Texas and Florida in their investigation. Only seventy thousand dollars had been expended by 1992 when Jack Douglas Dinning was arrested. He was tried the following year on two counts of malice murder, two counts of armed robbery, and one count of burglary. Convicted, he was condemned to four consecutive life sentences. Dinning, while not associated with organized crime, was a drug addict from Florida. The remainder of the fund was left to Liberty Lobby, a conservative political organization.

"The irony of this case was that Eric Rider thought he would be killed by drug people from Florida," said district attorney Mike Crawford. "He was murdered by a man from Florida, who was a doper."

SUDDEN DEATH

"I don't want to play for ten years in the NBA and die of a heart attack at age forty."

Thus spoke Pistol Pete Maravich of the Atlanta Hawks to sports reporter Andy Nuzzo in 1974. Fourteen years later, in early January 1988, the Pistol died suddenly of a heart attack. He was forty years old. He had played in the National Basketball Association for ten years.

Maravich had practically been born with a basketball in his hands. As a child he dribbled a basketball while riding in a car, a ball in his hand (presumably, *he* wasn't the one driving), and sitting in aisle seats at the movies.

He played three seasons at Louisiana State University under his father, Press, scoring 3,667 points and averaging 44.2 points a game, which was ten points more than the runner-up. His yearly scoring totals ranked first, fourth, and fifth in NCAA history, and he was three times an All-American.

Entering the NBA as the third pick in 1970, Maravich spent his first four years with the Atlanta Hawks. His two-million-dollar contract, a record for a rookie, caused considerable fan resentment. He averaged 24.2 points a game as a pro, scored sixty-eight points against the New York Knicks on February 25, 1977, and was an NBA All-Star five times. Six years after retiring from the game, the Pistol was inducted into professional basketball's Naismith Hall of Fame.

The world of professional basketball, shocked by Maravich's death, had nothing but praise for his phenomenal talents. Maravich was "the greatest ball handler who ever played the game," said former Hawks coach Cotton Fitzsimmons. "Nobody could handle the ball like Pistol did." Fitzsimmons considered him "one of the greatest showmen ever."

"He could dribble two basketballs at one time," said former teammate and UCLA basketball coach Walt Hazzard, "spin basketballs on both hands. He knew all the tricks."

On January 1, 1988, Pistol Pete Maravich was participating in a half-court, pickup basketball game with friends at a Church of the Nazarene in Pasadena, California. He told Gary Lydick that he had not played basketball in a year, since an NBA Legends game. "I need to do this more often," Maravich told Lydick. "I'm feeling good."

Maravich turned away and immediately collapsed. He never regained consciousness and was pronounced dead at 9:24 A.M. at St. Luke's Hospital.

"It's a tragedy," Fitzsimmons said, "but he died doing something he loved."

STICKS AND STONES

Judy Smail suffered a sudden and horrible death on August 26, 1990. While riding with her family on I-20 in Douglas County, a twenty-five-pound rock was thrown from an overpass and crashed through the windshield onto her.

"She had a premonition that something was going to happen to her," said Judy's mother-in-law, Laurine Holcomb. "One of her daughters said she felt all week that something was going to happen to her."

Two teenagers, including a classmate of Judy's daughter, were arrested, convicted, and sentenced to long prison terms for the crime.

255

PHOTOGRAPHS AND MEMORIES
"I hope that you all will like this picture and want to keep it forever and even fall asleep and dream about it. Remember to always cherish this and don't lose this if something happens to me. Peace Out. Love Always, Twyla Carter."

Miss Carter, seventeen, wrote these words on the back of a photograph of herself that sat in the living room of her mother not long before the teenager disappeared on July 19, 1997. Her skeletal remains were found eight months later, a bullet hole in the back of the skull. The investigation continues.

NAG, NAG, NAG
Americans were settled in Charlton County, but the Okefenokee Swamp was controlled by Seminole Indians who occasionally made forays against isolated dwellings, killing settlers and burning their cabins. One day a wife demanded that her husband transport their family to Fort Alert at Trader's Hill, where a detachment of soldiers had erected a crude stockade. The husband was reluctant to make the six-mile trek through the wilderness, but his wife was insistent. She "just felt" that Indians would attack their isolated home and destroy it and them. The husband grumbled that there were no indications of an attack, and argued that the Seminoles had not ventured out of the swamp recently. However, he acceded to his wife's premonition and they left for the fort before dusk.

That night a party of fifty Seminoles did visit their home. They stole or destroyed all their property and set fire to the cabin.

REVENGE OF THE TOMAHAWK CHOP
Some time around 1820 Benjamin Willis was constructing a water wheel for a gristmill near the Ocmulgee River, forty miles from his home near Dakota. One night he dreamed that a party of Indians were slaughtering his family—he "heard" their screams.

Willis walked home as quickly as he could, only to find every member of his family brutally murdered. Their graves are said to be in the cemetery at Dakota.

THE GREAT WASHINGTON FIRE
In August 1837 Capt. Lewis Brown took his ailing wife from their Washington home to see Dr. Durham, whose office was thirty miles away near Scull Shoals. On the night of August 25 Mrs. Brown awoke from a dream in great agitation and described to her husband "a very vivid dream that Washington had burned," related the *Chronicles of Wilkes County*. "It made a great impression on her and she described in detail where the fire began

and where it ended," the story continued. Mrs. Brown fell asleep again and had the same dream. On the following day Mr. Brown sat beside the road and asked travelers for news from Washington. Late in the day a man said, "Washington was burned up last night."

The inferno had raged for three hours and destroyed thirty buildings. The fire started and ended exactly as Mrs. Brown had described it, igniting in a kitchen near the square and being stopped by two brick structures.

DEAD DAMN YANKEES

In late spring 1864, Federal soldier Rice Bull was advancing with his unit on Dallas, Georgia, where they had a leisurely dinner while engineers bridged Pumpkinvine Creek. As Bull attempted to relax, his good friend Sgt. James Cummings sat down. Wise noticed that Cummings, usually affable, was "melancholy and sad." Cummings confessed to a belief that he would not survive their next battle. Bull attempted to reassure his friend, explaining that occasionally they all experienced a premonition of death, which always failed to materialize. Cummings insisted that death was near, but it would be in the service of his country, and since he was a Christian he had no fear for his future.

When the bridge was finished, the company marched on to a crossroads called New Hope Church. By morning Northerners would dub it the "Hell Hole." The Federals ran into a storm of rifle fire and batteries of artillery that pumped vicious charges of canister into their advancing lines. Bull's colonel was killed, and the men took shelter behind a slight ridge as night arrived and nature erupted with a furious thunderstorm. Men pressed close to the sodden earth, more fearful of Rebel fire than of drowning in the pools of water that formed around them. Bull heard one soldier call to an officer, "Now, Captain, if you will just give the order, we will swim over and tackle the Johnnies."

Around 10:00 P.M. the shooting slackened, but isolated picket fire still punctured the night. Cummings had gone to ground near Bull, but now he stood up, drawing a harsh whisper from Bull: "Jim, you know there are orders not to fire; why do you stand and expose yourself?"

"I don't think there is any more danger in standing here than lying in the mud. I have had enough of that," he explained.

No more than a minute later Bull heard a noise like a hammer hitting a tree. He looked up to see Cummings fall heavily to the ground, a bullet through his forehead. His premonition had come true.

UNCLE AARON'S STORY

Another Union invader was Theodore Upson, a literate private who recorded his experiences in a diary, which was published in 1943. Upson's regiment was involved in one of the few real battles that occurred during William Sherman's infamous march to Savannah in November 1864. While bypassing Macon, Sherman left a blocking force of fifteen hundred men and two cannon at Griswold to prevent Confederate troops from interfering with his passage. A thirty-seven-hundred-man force of Georgia militia, mainly young boys and old men with no military experience and led by a drunken general who disobeyed orders to avoid combat, encountered the Federals. Upson's men slaughtered the attacking Georgians from behind barricades. Southern casualties exceeded five hundred; Northern losses totaled ninety-two, with only thirteen killed.

One of the dead was an older enlisted man fondly called "Uncle Aaron" by his younger messmates. The night before the battle, Upson found Aaron Wolford "greatly depressed, something unusual for him." Upson asked what was wrong, and with no evidence of impending fighting, Wolford confided that he had experienced a premonition of his own death.

"I felt that I have not long to live," Wolford stated, "and when I am gone I want you to promise me that you will take charge of my things. Send them to my wife and write to her all about me."

Wolford rejected Upson's reassuring words, "sure his time was nearly out." At the height of the battle Wolford took a bullet in his head.

"I put my hand on him and spoke his name," Upson recorded, "but he was gone where I hope there are no wars, no sudden partings. That night after the Johnnies had gone, we buried our dead. We had no coffins, but I could not bear to think of putting my old friend into his grave in that way. I remembered that at a house a short distance away I had seen a hollow log of about the right length and size. We got it, split it in halves, put one in the grave dug in the sandy soil, put his lifeless body in it, covered it with the other half, filled up the grave and by the light of a fire we had built with the rails, marked with a piece of lumber pencil his name, Company, and Regiment."

Upson then sat down to write Wolford's widow. Enclosing the little money Wolford had on him, his watch, and "a well-worn Testament," Upson described "what a good man" Wolford had been, "how brave and faithful to duty he was." Thinking of his dead friend and the wife and eight children he had left behind, Upson's tears smudged the wet ink on the paper. "I hope they will realize what a grand soul he had," Upson thought.

ON THE CONFEDERATE SIDE
CARRY ME HOME TO MOTHER
Dr. John Jones, chaplain of the Georgia state senate, often told the story of Jethro Jackson of Griffin, whose eighteen-year-old son was killed at Resaca during the Civil War. His comrades buried him in a rough pine coffin made of wood taken from a bridge.

Two years later Jackson journeyed to Resaca to bring his boy home. Although given explicit directions by his son's comrades, a day-long search proved fruitless. With heavy heart Jackson returned home.

Several nights later Jackson dreamed that his son appeared at his bedside and said, "Father, I am buried under a mound which was thrown up by the Yankees after I was killed. You will know the mound when you see it by the pokeberry bushes growing upon it. Go and take me up and carry me home to Mother."

Jackson immediately returned to Resaca with one of his son's comrades. They quickly found the grave, beneath a mound with pokeberries growing over it. The identity of the body was confirmed by the name marked on the clothing.

Another person who experienced an unusual premonition was Col. Warren Atkin, who had been Speaker of the Georgia House of Representatives before entering the Confederate army. On February 8, 1865, he had a vision in which his oldest son was lying beneath a tree on a sidewalk in front of his house in Elberton, a pool of blood spreading around his body. In this vision or dream, Atkin ran to the boy and found him unconscious, with blood streaming from his right ear. Starting from sleep, Atkin immediately attempted to telegraph his home, but within minutes he received a letter from his wife assuring him that all was well on the home front. Unfortunately, two days later the son Atkin had seen in his vision fell from a horse beneath the tree and struck the sidewalk. A neighbor ran to the boy's side and found his condition as Atkin had earlier prophesied. The child died on the following day, although Atkin did not learn of the event for three weeks.

HITS AND MISSES

John B. Gordon was a Georgian who went into the Civil War with no military training and ended it a corps commander. He would later become governor of Georgia and a U.S. senator. During the war he had firsthand experiences with premonitions that came true. Col. Tennant Lomax, a friend from Alabama, approached Gordon one morning as battle loomed and said, "Give me your hand, Gordon, and let me bid you good-bye. I am going to be killed in this battle. I shall be dead in half an hour."

Gordon vainly attempted to convince Lomax that nothing evil would befall him, but his friend was calmly convinced of his fate. He rode away with a smile on his face. Within the time period specified, a bullet had killed Lomax.

The saddest premonition for Gordon occurred when his younger brother, Col. Augustus Gordon, rode up to him in the Wilderness battle and quietly told him, "My hour has come."

Gordon tried to reassure his twenty-one-year-old brother, but the colonel replied firmly. "You need not doubt me. I will be at my post. But this is our last meeting." Minutes later the younger Gordon was leading his men in a desperate counterattack when a Union battery fired and a canister ball tore into his heart. Grief-stricken, the elder Gordon continued to lead his men into battle.

Gordon revealed that he had once experienced a premonition of death, what he called "an unbidden, unwelcome calculation of changes," while fighting in the Shenandoah Valley. He had been ordered to storm a Federal fort situated on a high ridge at dawn. As the sun set, Gordon watched light glitter on the enemy cannon and bayonets, and thought of the long, open field his men would have to traverse to reach the bastion. He didn't believe his unit would be able to take the objective, and was appalled to think of the horrendous casualties the men would suffer in the effort. Near dawn he took up pencil and paper and wrote a final letter to his wife, then gave it to his quartermaster and requested its delivery if he fell. Gordon tells the remainder of the story:

"Mounting my horse, my men now ready, I spoke to them briefly and encouraged them to go with me into the fort. Before the dawn we were moving and soon ascending the long slope. At every moment I expected the storm of shell and ball that would end many a life, my own among them; but on we swept, and into the fort, to find not a soldier there! It had been evacuated during the night."

BATROY

This might not be precisely prescience but perhaps ESP or some other human agency most of us do not have access to. Roy Bradley of Washington was blind but could give directions with uncanny accuracy. He was able to tell a person's height by shaking their hands, and he knew exactly how far someone stood from him. Bradley was also a math whiz, solving difficult problems in his head. Locals believed he had ESP or radar. Asked his activity as a sighted saint in heaven, he replied, "I want to spend a long, long time enjoying the Atlanta Cyclorama." A man after my own heart.

NO GRASS GROWING OVER THEIR FEET

Lumpkin County has a Gallows Hollow located on a hill two miles southwest of Dahlonega along Aurora Road, where a cemetery is located. Hamilton Sneed and a man called Jones were hanged in a nearby ravine and buried at Gallows Hollow in the mid-1800s. A prevalent legend held that trees never grew above the condemned men's graves. One of Dahlonega's most reputable men, a Sunday School superintendent, was dispatched to check out the report. His observations confirmed the old legend—a forest grew thickly around the graves, but not one limb extended over the graves, leaving an open space to the sky.

IT'S ONLY WEIRD GEORGIA ROCK AND ROLL

IN MEMORY OF THE ALLMAN BROTHERS

After the Allman Brothers moved to Macon in 1969, they rented a house on College Street and lived communally. Often, late at night, they would walk to historic Rose Hill Cemetery and make their way down the hill to a peaceful, grassy plot near the railroad and Ocmulgee River. There, amid the tombstones, they smoked marijuana, drank wine, and jammed acoustically through the night.

One classic Allman Brothers instrumental was inspired by a bizarre dream Duane Allman experienced one night at a Holiday Inn. In the dream Jimi Hendrix described a new song to Allman, then played it out on a sink faucet. Waking up, Allman took his guitar and played the tune, which became "Little Martha." During their rambles at Rose Hill, the Allman Brothers had discovered the grave of Martha Ellis, a girl who had died at the age of twelve in 1896. A four-foot statue of the sad-looking child, who holds a rose in one hand, marks the tomb.

After a concert in Nashville on the night of October 29, 1970, Allman consumed a large quantity of opium. When band members could not wake him the next morning, they noticed he had difficulty breathing, and his lips and fingers had turned blue. An ambulance rushed Allman to the hospital, where the emergency room doctor told the band, "We'll do what we can, but there's not much hope. He's pretty far gone."

Bassist Berry Oakley was particularly close to Allman and pleaded to the heavens, "Please, just give him one more year. Whatever there is up there, please, just one more year."

One hour later the doctor returned with good news. Allman would live.

October 29, 1971, was a joyful day for the Allman Brothers. A big birthday celebration had been arranged for Linda Oakley, Berry's wife. Allman leaped on his big Harley-Davidson motorcycle and sped across Macon on Hill Crest Avenue to the party. As he approached the intersection with Bartlett at 5:44 P.M., he swerved to avoid a flatbed truck hauling lumber, which had stopped in the road. Allman clipped the truck and came off the bike. The impact knocked his helmet off and the heavy chopper landed on top of him, then skidded for ninety feet before slamming into a curb.

Allman was knocked unconscious. Twice he stopped breathing in the ambulance en route to the Medical Center of Central Georgia. Emergency surgery revealed a collapsed chest and extensive internal injuries, and there were probably also head injuries. Nothing could be done for Allman, who died that night at 8:40 P.M.

It was Macon's most memorable funeral, held at Snow's Chapel. The Allman Brothers, Dr. John, Delaney and Bonnie Bramlett, and others jammed, playing "In Memory of Elizabeth Reed," another instrumental title taken from a headstone in Rose Hill, and singing "Will the Circle Be Unbroken?"

Those who knew the Allman Brothers recalled that Berry Oakley had developed a death wish after Allman died. He had become preoccupied with a song called "Hellhound on My Trail," written by blues great Robert Johnson. Oakley seemed to believe the hellhound had killed his friend and was now after him. He ate little and his weight dropped to 145 pounds. Oakley also became enamored of motorcycles, although he did not ride well.

On November 11, 1972, Oakley and a friend were riding their cycles down Napier Avenue. He was going too fast to take a curve near Inverness Avenue, and his Triumph slammed into a city bus. Oakley was thrown from the bike, which landed on top of him sixty feet from the point of the collision.

Oakley was initially knocked out, but shortly regained consciousness. He "talked coherent and seemed all right," a friend recalled, although he was bleeding from his nose and mouth. Oakley refused to go to the hospital and insisted on returning to the communal Allman house. He soon became delirious and the Brothers' road crew carried him to a car and rushed him to the hospital. His skull had been fractured and he was hemorrhaging. At 3:40 P.M. Berry Oakley died.

Fans from around the world make pilgrimages to Rose Hill Cemetery in Macon, where the grave of Duane Allman can be found. Many leave touching tributes.

The similarities of the two deaths have long been recognized. The band-mates were killed almost exactly a year apart in motorcycle accidents that occurred within one thousand yards of each other and on parallel streets. Allman had crossed Inverness before the accident at the intersection with Bartlett. Oakley crossed Bartlett and hit the bus at the intersection with Inverness. Allman, Oakley, the truck driver, and the bus driver had all been twenty-four years old.

Allman Brother Butch Truck believed this was more than coincidence. He also noted that Allman died a year after his drug overdose in Nashville. "I mean, it was *to the day* a year," he told Scott Freeman, author of *Midnight Riders.* "And a year and two weeks after that was when Oakley got into his wreck."

Allman's wife Donna had yet to bury her husband, whose body was in cold storage. Ironically, she had recently returned to Macon to determine where he should be buried. She and Linda Oakley decided to bury Allman and Oakley side by side at their beloved Rose Hill.

The graves are near the railroad, not far from the Ocmulgee. A Les Paul guitar is inscribed on Allman's stone; a Fender base decorates Oakley's. Instead of "Died," Oakley's stone reads, "Set Free." Another inscription reads, "Help my brother's boat across, and, lo! Thine own has reached the shore!"

Band members, fearing they had been cursed, expected additional deaths. In a Doonesbury cartoon strip banished from the *Macon Telegraph & News,* Garry Trudeau had character "Uncle Duke" speculate that perhaps the band was breaking up through attrition. Nearly thirty years along, the remaining Brothers survive and prosper and occasionally perform together in various incarnations. As stated on Berry Oakley's grave, "And the Road Goes on Forever."

IT'S THE END OF THE WORLD AS MICHAEL STIPE KNOWS IT

Michael Stipe, front man for REM, Athens' most famous band, told a *Rolling Stone* reporter that before earthquakes occur, evidently anywhere in North America, he knows about it.

"I usually get headaches when an earthquake happens," he said.

After a severe quake in Mexico City, "I was on my back for three days, really bad," Stipe stated. He missed a 6.1 earthquake in California and swore that it "was the first time since I became aware of it that there's been an earthquake anywhere in the continent and I didn't know about it ahead of time."

This extraordinary ability apparently started as a youth in the Peach State.

"My parents' farm is right on a fault line in Georgia," he said.

SITTING ON THE DOCK OF THE WISCONSIN DEATH TRIANGLE

In the September 26, 1990, edition of the *Milwaukee Weekly*, Jim Euken attempted to relate the deaths of three legends of rock and roll. In February 1957, Buddy Holly's plane crashed near Clear Lake, Iowa. In 1967 a plane carrying Macon music great Otis Redding crashed into Lake Mendota near Madison, Wisconsin. And in 1990 Stevie Ray Vaughan's helicopter crashed near Lake Geneva in Wisconsin. The accidents occurred within 225 miles of each other.

First, Euken noted that the birthdays of Holly and Redding were only two days apart (Okay, they were separated by five years, but why quibble?). Each of the flights passed over or occurred near dense concentrations of effigy mounds constructed by American Indians hundreds of years ago. Euken wondered: "Perhaps the effigy mound configurations somehow entered into a complex of time-timing-timelessness and of the possibility of cosmic factors understood only by the inhabitants thousands of years ago. Perhaps they aligned the mounds to focus subtle energies and the musical energy generated by the stars and their fans disrupted the burials associated with the mounds."

Another interesting coincidence was the fact that Les Paul, who developed the first electric guitar, lived near Waukesha, Wisconsin. A study of his invention and many of the effigy mounds reveal startling similarities. These curious mounds feature long necks and the bodies are divided into two symmetrical bulges to represent the creature's limbs. This same configuration is shared by electric guitars. Euken suggests these ancient constructions influenced guitar design.

Otis Redding died near a huge, 640-foot-long effigy mound, and elsewhere in the state of Wisconsin is Aztlan, a Mississippian temple mound complex, easily the northernmost settlement of that culture. Every resident of central Georgia is aware of Ocmulgee, a classic Mississippian site preserved as a national park at Macon.

Is there a relationship between the demise of three rock 'n' roll greats, or is this a coincidence or mere flights of fantasy (sorry)? You decide.

CIVIL (WAR) DISOBEDIENCE

A CONFEDERATE SPIRIT IDENTIFIES HIMSELF

It was one of dozens of rearguard actions that took place in the spring of 1864 in northern Georgia. Union general William T. Sherman's superior numbers would threaten to lap around Confederate general Joseph E. Johnston's flanks, and the Southerners would be forced to retreat again. Troops were left behind to slow the Federal advance, and if lucky enough they escaped to rejoin the main body of troops. In late May two men never returned. Killed along the railroad tracks at Adairsville, their bodies were consigned to the earth there, unidentified. The graves became a local landmark, lovingly tended by residents and railroad workers, who often wondered who the men had been.

Eventually, Mrs. Alice B. Howard asked the same question in a strange setting. It was around 1939 and Mrs. Howard had joined hands with others gathered for a table-tapping séance.

"Well, it started tapping," Mrs. Howard reported many years later. "We had a way worked out for the table to spell with an alphabet, and we got the name Jack Kirby and that he was one of the soldiers buried near the tracks. (The tapper) named Tice Furrow, too."

Mrs. Howard says she "didn't believe in that sort of thing, but it happened." She later learned that a letter had been found on one of the bodies and preserved. It had been addressed to T. W. Furrow. Mrs. Howard located another letter, written by one soldier serving in Georgia to another, which revealed that "something dire happened to Jack Kirby and Tice Furrow" at Adairsville.

Mrs. Howard then contacted the National Archives, seeking information about the two soldiers. Furrow was on record, but there were so many J. Kirbys that identifying one specific individual proved impossible.

More than 110 years after they were placed unidentified in lonely graves, Tice Furrow and Jack Kirby received a military funeral in Adairsville's city cemetery. They identified themselves in a table-tapping séance, and research proved their identities.

Mrs. Howard continued her research and located a relative of Furrow, Carson Furrow, in Norfolk, Virginia. They "were able to find out that Tice Furrow and Jack Kirby had been neighbors and went off to war together," Mrs. Howard said. "That's good enough for me." Both men had belonged to Company I, Fourth Regiment of Volunteer Infantry.

On the basis of this evidence, the federal government prepared an official headstone for Furrow. Mrs. Howard ordered an identical stone made for

Kirby, and the pair were reinterred in East View Cemetery at Adairsville on May 1, 1974. Despite a drenching thunderstorm, dozens of people, including Mrs. Howard, Georgia secretary of state Ben Fortson, a U.S. representative, and a Georgia state representative, attended the graveside ceremony near the 110th anniversary of the men's deaths. The graves are on opposite sides of a narrow road that meanders through the hilltop site. On Confederate Memorial Day, tiny Confederate flags are placed at both gravestones.

This remains one of my favorite stories, primarily because it was the first weird story I wrote for profit. It was published in *Fate* magazine in 1975, and I received a check for forty whole dollars.

ROBERT TOOMBS AND THE DISSOLUTION OF THE UNION
Georgia has seen few figures as controversial as Robert Toombs, a character of the turbulent mid-nineteenth century. Perhaps the weirdest story has Toombs breakfasting in Washington, D.C., with fellow senator John C. Calhoun in 1850. Calhoun, a prominent advocate of secession, was a militant war hawk and fire-eater. The former vice president's appearance was so haggard that Toombs expressed concern for his health.

Calhoun proceeded to tell a strange story. The previous evening, as he sat in his room writing, a confident stranger, his face concealed by a cloak, appeared and took a seat. The phantom asked Calhoun what he was writing. It was a document of secession, Calhoun replied. The menacing vision then asked for Calhoun's right hand. As the stranger arose the cloak fell away and his true character was revealed. It was a spectral George Washington, clad in his military uniform. The ghostly apparition grasped Calhoun's hand and asked if he would use the paper to dissolve the Union.

When Calhoun affirmed that he would if necessary, a black spot suddenly appeared on the back of his hand. Washington then declared that a similar sign marked Benedict Arnold "in the next world." Calhoun then awoke, and found the black spot still on the back of his right hand. He showed Toombs the mark. Calhoun died within the year. I personally don't give much credence to this story, probably because I haven't located the original source.

As for Toombs, he had been expelled from Franklin College (now the University of Georgia) in 1828 for riotous behavior. Legend has him returning at commencement and speaking so eloquently beneath a tree between Demosthenian Hall and the Chapel that the graduation ceremonies in the Chapel were vacated as all gathered to hear Toombs speak.

Toombs became one of the most influential citizens in Georgia history. He served in Georgia's House of Representatives, the United States House of Representatives and Senate, and as a general and secretary of state for the Confederacy. He was also a successful lawyer and planter.

The spirit of Robert Toombs, expelled in life due to his boisterous behavior, haunts Demosthenian Hall at the University of Georgia. When Toombs died, an oak tree beside the building was struck by lightning.

Legend further states that at the moment of his death one stormy night in 1885, the magnificent oak tree, called "Toombs's Oak," was struck by lightning. The dead tree toppled over in 1908 and was cut up into highly prized sacred relics for UGA grads. Visit the marker, erected by the state in 1985, where the tree stood for good luck.

The validity of these stories is open to question. One Clarke County historian maintains that Henry W. Grady, the famed Georgia newsman, invented the entire affair.

Demosthenian Hall housed the literary society, one of Toombs's favorite institutions on campus. Legend has it that a Confederate officer, perhaps Toombs himself, haunts the building, his ghostly act including footsteps heard in the empty building, doors opening, lampshades spinning by themselves, and cold spots in the structure.

PSYCHIC LASSIE, OR A SHAGGY DOG STORY

In the spring of 1933 a woman returned to her home in Statesboro with two-month-old collie puppies. She drove eight miles into the country and allowed a friend to choose a puppy, then presented the second, named Rig, to a friend in town. For the following six months Rig remained happily at home, but two days after his owner left for a visit, on Christmas Eve, Rig ran away from home. His owner was distraught until a telephone call came from the friend in the country. Rig had been to that farm only once, as a small puppy, but he had walked there and was visiting his brother for Christmas.

7

Abductions, Alien Intruders, and the Shadows of Night

As a youngster I was enthralled by abduction tales, particularly that of Betty and Barney Hill, brilliantly related in John G. Fuller's *The Interrupted Journey*. I was also titillated by accounts of Antonio Villas Boas's erotic abduction in Brazil. At the time those incidents were rare and unique.

The abduction phenomenon had become so serious that in late March 1993, 150 mental health professionals met in the Tara Hall conference room of the Sheraton Atlanta Airport for what was billed as "A Workshop on Unusual Personal Experiences." Its purpose was to teach psychologists, psychoanalysts, and therapists how to treat patients who believe they had been abducted. "Mr. Abduction" himself, Budd Hopkins, appeared to lecture on warning signs of abductions.

A 1991 Roper Poll found that 3 percent of Americans had experienced characteristics of abduction: 1. Seen unusual lights or balls of light; 2. Experienced a hour or more of missing time; 3. Woke up paralyzed with strange beings in the room; 4. Found unusual scars on their bodies. I did the math (actually, my gifted son Paul crunched the numbers for me) and the grand total is 8.1 million Americans who might have been abducted.

Today some "authorities" claim that millions of abductions have occurred—a number so outrageous that a significant portion of the reasonable UFO community is presently questioning the reality of the experience in general.

Personally, I would give greater credence to Tom Dawson's Jimmy Hoffa story over most modern abduction tales seemingly pumped out in mass production by Abductions R Us.

The first Georgia abduction case I came across occurred on December 15, 1971, in Forsyth County. A woman was kidnapped by aliens and given a physical examination that left marks on her body, including blisters and burns. She also experienced backaches, nightmares, and insomnia, and her eyes became sensitive to light.

269

On June 15, 1973, sixteen-year-old Kate Mansfield fled her house as her parents argued, and she went for a drive at 9:00 P.M. She was on rural GA 155 near Panola Mountain in Henry County when her engine died. While noticing a glow in the woods, she frantically but unsuccessfully attempted to restart the car. Suddenly, an unusual being was standing in front of her. In Kate's conscious memory, she started the car and drove forward to hear a "bump" as if she had run over a pedestrian. For some time she lived in fear that police officers would come to arrest her for hit and run, or even manslaughter.

Under hypnotic regression by UFO investigator C. Leigh Culver twenty years later, Kate realized that the creature was a typical Alien Gray about five feet tall, with a long head and elongated eyes. The being took her from the car and escorted her to a UFO located where she had seen the glow. Several Grays were hard at work placing local rocks and plants in square metal boxes. They ignored her (SOS, I suppose they thought).

Kate entered a small examination room that was round, gray, and musty. After she was stripped and laid on a table, her body was probed by an alien who, as usual, paid close attention to her genitals. The Gray stepped out for a moment to allow Kate to dress (sudden modesty?). Then the original alien returned her to the car, looked into her eyes, and instructed her "not to remember."

Suddenly, Kate was conscious. She turned the ignition key and drove forward over two speed bumps placed before a stop sign. She immediately turned around and returned home, frightened and confused, having forgotten everything but the approach of the creature and her starting the car, a common characteristic of abductees.

UNCLE MARTIN?, OR THE SIX-MILLION-DOLLAR, PISTOL-PACKIN' ALIEN
At 10:00 P.M. during the early summer of 1974 or 1975, a man in Troup County heard a "whirring" sound as he passed under I-85 near Hogg Mountain Road. Emerging from the overpass, he spotted a large circular UFO, 150 feet in diameter, with revolving red lights that seemed in sequence with the sound, pacing his car for a distance. Initially moving at ten to fifteen miles per hour, the object ascended to avoid trees several times, then returned to an altitude of one hundred feet above the ground. The UFO then greatly increased its speed and disappeared.

Returning his attention to the highway, the man noticed standing beside the pavement a four-foot creature covered from head to toe in a skintight silver "wetsuit" which covered even his hands and fingers. On each side of its head were antennae, ten to twelve inches in length. Around the waist was a belt that resembled a holster. Frightened, the man accelerated to sixty-five miles per hour. The alien not only kept ahead of the car, it widened the space between them from forty to one hundred feet. After a ten-second encounter, the creature scrambled into dense bushes and the motorist kept going.

The witness was a respected member of his community. A Georgia state trooper who had known him for thirty years said he accepted the story simply on the man's word.

GREMLINS

In Franklin at 10:30 P.M. on March 19, 1995, a married couple were talking in bed when the woman saw a small white light on the bedroom ceiling. She then looked at the window and saw a strange creature pop up. She described it as similar to a character from the *Gremlins* movies. It was three to three and a half feet tall, with pointed foxlike ears, yellow eyes, and brown skin. A sketch she later drew showed a robot face with large ears, a small mouth, big round eyes, and a pointed crown on each side of the head. After twenty seconds the apparition disappeared.

The woman calmly informed her husband that there was an alien in the window. As he raised up to peer out, the woman said, "It's too late, he's not there now."

The husband thought it was a joke, but the wife insisted she was serious, then added, "They don't like you. They don't want you to see them. We need to go to sleep. They want us to sleep."

The husband got out of bed, peeked out the window, then suggested they get the children. "No," she replied, "leave the children in their rooms—they're not going to hurt them. But they don't like you."

The husband later stated that he thought another person, not his wife, was speaking. Normally, she would have been extremely concerned by such a threatening situation, but instead she soon fell asleep.

This frightening mind-control episode lasted about fifteen minutes. While speaking to an investigator, the woman, thumbing through a book, pointed out a drawing of aliens who attacked an isolated farmhouse near Hopkinsville, Kentucky, in 1955. There is obviously more to this story that may emerge with further investigation.

PARADISE LOST BY THE DASHBOARD LIGHT

Georgia's most thoroughly studied abductee seems to be Mark James, a thirty-five-year-old painter with a happy marriage to Janet and a four-year-old son, Allen, who also seems to have experienced the same phenomenon since age two.

It was 8:30 P.M. around June 23, 1981, when eighteen-year-old Mark and a girlfriend, Linda, parked on a cul-de-sac at Martins Crossing near Stone Mountain. They climbed into the back of his Chevy Vega to make out.

Fifteen years later C. Leigh Culver placed Mark under regression hypnosis to aid in his recollection of the experience. The teenagers had barely settled in when Mark looked up and noticed that a light was approaching the car.

"Let's get out of here!" he shouted, but the car would not start and apparently the girl panicked. "Linda, shut up!" he shouted.

The light grew brighter and he heard a "thick sound" that resonated. Next, he spotted six figures approaching who opened the locked door. "They are taking me out of the car," he continued. "I have to go."

The couple exited the hatchback to find the area illuminated as bright as daylight. Mark was concerned about Linda, who had "this really stupid look on her face."

As they entered the UFO, Mark described passing into a dark room, where he felt like liquid. "You become a liquid," he explained. "You're liquid." Perhaps a force field or semipermeable barrier protected the entrance. He experienced an identical sensation when exiting the craft. "Liquid. I feel like I'm just completely liquid. Nothing solid," he said.

Mark and Linda were escorted through the liquid and a bright, "almost pulsating" yellow light. An alien stood on each side of Mark, holding his arms.

The next portion of the vessel was cold, dimly lit, and musty, "like under a house." They walked down a big ramp, made of cold metal, the walls smooth and colored blue green.

When the ramp curved he lost sight of Linda and saw a large machine, fifty feet long and tall as a man, which hummed like a transformer. Metal plates projected from it, and a doorway was cut into it. Through this entrance he saw an extensive room dimly lit by a circular light in the ceiling and filled with tables, each occupied by humans.

The aliens instructed Mark to sit in a booth barely wide enough to accommodate him. It was rounded on the top and, although he thought it might be metal, the material gave when he sat on it. The booth was "to keep you out of the way," he explained.

All the humans Mark could see "have that same look that Linda had on her face." Some were strapped down. Apparently others were waiting in the booths, and Mark watched as pairs of aliens escorted first a man, then a pregnant woman, to tables.

"It's a big room," he recalled. "Lots of tables. Lots of aliens. There are people on them . . . as far as I can see."

Many of the humans were moaning and the room smelled "like dirty clothes."

When Mark's turn came he was required to remove his clothing and lie on the table, where he was paralyzed. An alien tapped his body, starting with his feet and moving up to his head. They bent his legs and seemed amused because one knee kept "popping." As they examined his genitals, Mark whispered, "I wish they would leave me alone."

A LIGHTER SHADE OF PALE

As the "physical" progressed, a female alien arrived. She was a head taller than the others, with a larger, more "bulbous-shaped head," and big eyes like her colleagues. She had no ears and her slit mouth never opened. Her skin was a lighter gray than the males, almost transparent. Hands with four long "elastic" fingers, without nails, were on the end of long arms. Mark described the males as "clumsy," with "herky-jerky" movements, while the female was far more graceful. None of the creatures wore clothes, and external genitalia were absent.

The female moved close to Mark's face. "She is caring," he felt. "Sympathetic. She is trying to calm me down. She's right in my face. She is telling me that I have no reason to fear them. That I am needed. They do not intend to harm us. They just need me," for "genetics and for future events," he continued. Mark detected a "sense of caring, even loving," from her.

"You must remember," she "thought" to him. "It is important." She then spoke the word "Ebola" repeatedly, years before the disease was commonly known. He learned that the disease would be hard to contain. "She's telling me the future," he thought, for "when I am old."

The female Gray then produced a crystal device on the end of a wand that glowed ever brighter. She touched his forehead and his mind "just exploded like a bright light."

This memory frightened Mark out of his regression and a second appointment was made for nineteen days later. At that time he was anxious, but ready to discover what had so distressed him.

APOCALYPSE THEN

When the wand touched his forehead, Mark experienced a bright light, then, "Warmth, my whole body is warm." He was standing on a highway bridge in Atlanta, but noticed a discrepancy on the highway, which he realized was I-20. The cars "are all going in one direction" on both sides of the road, he noted. "They are leaving the city. There are people on foot, carrying things and running, they've leaving. There are people crying," Mark said. "It's like they're all running from something." The young man paused, then uttered, "Oh, Lord, Lord have mercy!" and he started crying. "They blew it up! They blew it up! They nuked it!" In his mind Mark saw a nuclear bomb as it "came down from the sky" and left a "big mushroom cloud over Atlanta."

"Everybody's gone!" he cried. "It's all gone."

Abruptly, the scene in Mark's mind changed from Armageddon to pastoral. He, Janet, and their son Allen were having a picnic in a field along the Chattahoochee River. Researcher Culver described Mark's scene as "pure idyllic joy and happiness." He believes the aliens were "studying Mark's emotional reaction to the scenes, which ranged from one extreme to another." Although son Allen was two when this session occurred, he was six in the tableau, picking flowers and then giving his father "a big hug." "I love being with Janet and Allen," Mark said under hypnosis. "It's so good!"

Suddenly, reality returned and the female alien was in Mark's face. Although he was upset by his experience, she "says that they're almost through with what they need."

A male Gray appeared on Mark's left with a device in his hand that ended in a tiny ball, smaller than a BB, which was painfully inserted into his left ear. When Culver asked why they did this, Mark replied, "So that they can find me," the alien said. Find him they would.

Mark examined all of the room that he could see. He estimated that it was sixty to seventy feet wide, the ceiling twelve to thirteen feet high, highest in the center, and sloping down at the ends. Perhaps as an attempt to pacify the abductees, there was a "skylight" directly overhead through which stars shone brightly. Mark noted again the moaning and dirty-clothes odor.

Mark described a disturbing incident in which he saw a baby carried off in a glass vessel filled with amber-colored liquid and containing three attached hoses. He felt the baby, with a small body but big head, was not normal. The infant was transported to the humming wall and laid in a box that was "absorbed into the wall."

The two males soon returned and manipulated his penis, perhaps inserting something in it. He was then allowed to get up, when he again noted the people. "Oh, God! They've all got blank expressions on their faces. Some look horrified. Everybody is naked."

Two tables away, three aliens worked on the pregnant woman, two males in her genital area and the female "in her face," apparently inflicting emotional distress. He noticed tables without humans that held different types of instruments.

TIME IS MONEY

Finished with Mark, the aliens rushed him to don his clothing and led him out of the UFO. At this time he observed two symbols in the corridor. One was composed of four dots—three forming a triangle and the last in the center. The other was composed of a circle enclosing a jellyfish-like figure and adorned with three finlike projections.

Mark walked down the ramp to the "liquid room." Outside the craft he said, "I can see the car, we're way up high. The car looks small, really small."

The alien placed Mark in the driver's seat, and Linda, already in the car, was in the back seat. They sat there for several minutes after the aliens left until Mark woke up.

"Got to go, we've got to get out of here," he said. The engine started and Mark thought he had "to go away from that helicopter. Maybe if we get away maybe they won't follow us."

Mark then returned to the real world of being a teenager. It was 10:00 P.M. "Bummer," he thought, "I'm going to get my butt chewed out by her dad for getting her home late. Linda's dad is real strict."

Mark did get chewed out and went to bed "pissed off" at Linda's father. He awakened hungry and with no memory of the abduction.

In the years since, Mark developed chronic problems in his left ear, but there is an even more chilling addition to the story. Mark and Janet married in 1992, and Allen was born two years later. At age two, when Allen saw a book cover depicting an Alien Gray, he declared that similar creatures occasionally entered his room at night.

A week after the abduction, about 9:00 P.M. on June 23, 1981, Mark was playing basketball with a girl in his neighborhood named Jan when they spotted a "stranger lurking in the woods." Mark sent the girl for help and felt a compulsion "to walk into the woods" and "be checked out," although "Jan is telling me not to go."

Short Mort

Among the trees Mark found a diminutive creature "wearing a really large hat" and a black trench coat that "doesn't hang on him very good." He was skinny, and long arms extended below the sleeves of the coat. It was in fact an Alien Gray. Time for a checkup.

"He's got something in his hand and he's holding it up to my face." It was circular and had a "little black thing in the center of it," Mark said. The device was held up to his right temple and eye. Mark felt the creature was taking a "reading" and felt "little pulses." He was then told to leave.

Mark remembered finding no one in the woods, and when he exited he was exhausted.

This sounds like a classic man-in-black entity, although those were human of some kind.

Mark apparently led an active social life as a teenager. Two months after the abduction he had arranged a secret meeting with a girl named Michelle. She agreed to sneak out of her home and rendezvous with him behind an empty house.

The clandestine mission accomplished, they sat and held hands next to sliding glass doors in the vacant structure. Suddenly, they saw a giant, three-fingered hand pressed against the glass and then "eyes behind the hand."

THIS WON'T HURT A BIT

The teenagers were immobilized, Michelle with the traditional "blank" look on her face. The creature that opened the door and stepped out wore no clothing and had a long, needlelike device in his hand. He turned Mark's head, then inserted the instrument into his ear. The procedure hurt and Mark heard a "pop." When the device was removed, the tiny BB-like ball was on the end of the probe. The alien pricked one of Mark's fingers, then returned his head to its previous position. Close up, Mark detected the "dirty clothes" odor from the UFO. The alien departed through a gate in the backyard.

When the teens regained mobility, Michelle asked, "What was that? What was somebody doing in that house?" Frightened and with no memory of the encounter, Mark said, "We just need to get out of here. Let's call this off and go home." They did.

In 1996 Culver contacted Michael Norris, a friend who is a Norcross writer and UFO investigator, and said: "We have to meet immediately." When Norris asked why, Culver responded curtly, "Not over the phone."

Meeting at a restaurant, Culver informed his friend that three uniformed American military officials had accosted Mark in his bedroom. If he did not cease his hypnosis therapy, they threatened to hurt his son. Mark was terrified.

Culver convinced Mark to undergo another session and the "truth" came out. Military personnel were never involved in the case. As Norris wrote: "The entities that have visited him so many times before were promoting a lie in his mind."

This incident led Norris to discuss another abduction case in the July 1996 issue of *Georgia Sky Watch*. Norris had worked with "David" for two years, and Culver for a longer period of time. Described as "highly intelligent and rational," David related an episode which occurred on September 12, 1994. He awoke at 2:00 A.M., glanced at his clock, and fell asleep. Next morning he felt a deep pain in the abdomen and noticed a faint bruise appearing. After several days the bruise had grown to an ugly reddish purple and formed a perfect equilateral triangle. The pain remained, and he recalled a strange dream from that night.

When Culver placed David under hypnosis he remembered waking at 2:00 A.M. to find Grays surrounding him. These typical aliens, small, with large black eyes in their large bald heads, had four-fingered hands attached to long arms, and were accompanied by "little monks," five-foot beings wearing cloaks. "They don't want me talking about this!" David said when asked to describe the new aliens. "They look like some of the Easter Island figures," he said. "Very, very long features. Very stout," and colored grayish brown.

The aliens rolled him over and floated him through his backyard and into a semicircular room in a triangular UFO. Glowing floor, ceiling, and wall panels provided illumination to the dark, metallic gray space. He felt no support beneath him, and looked up to see "very strange equipment" over him. Perhaps sensing his apprehension, he was told, "That's not for you, don't worry."

Far more disturbing were the body parts that he saw in the room. Some of the parts looked human—a black man's leg and foot, for example—but, thankfully, most seemed to be of alien creatures—an arm, part of a back, and a leg and a foot. An alien hand had been dissected, displaying a type of muscle and tissue different from humans. Some parts he described as "very stout" or "massive," "very convoluted flesh." He made out at least three different species of aliens, and thought of the chamber as "some sort of anatomy lab." He could not tell if the shadowy figures in the background were models or specimens. Strangely, the aliens "don't seem to mind" his curiosity about that, he realized.

"This is strange stuff!" he said of the parts. One chunk resembled "a large cabbage leaf" frayed on the edges, where he thought he saw muscle tissue. It was colored "a rich purple" with green down the center and white on the edges, and displayed on metal to which it "electrostatically clings."

While he speculated, the aliens appeared to be conducting urgent emergency surgery on him. "There is something very wrong with me," he said. The aliens were worried, "showing me images of myself . . . dead . . . with blood coming out of my mouth."

Naturally enough, David wondered what was going on. He felt "like something is being pulled . . . open. Like my abdominal area is being stretched." He was very hot and felt dull pain. "They don't want me to see anything." I don't wonder.

David reported being "paralyzed . . . motionless. It's like I'm stuck to a large magnet . . ." He continued feeling stretched and hot, but a hand was laid across his forehead, covering his eyes, and the pain was blocked. "It's just a weird feeling," he said, and bright, "like looking at the sun through closed eyes."

The surgery apparently finished, David was taken to another chamber—a recovery room?

The lead alien had "cracky . . . really rough" skin and said, "You're going to be okay now."

David explained that aboard the ship he was trying to remember what happened, but the aliens "don't want you remembering. It interferes with their work." The aliens have informed him that they "can't explain" their purpose. "We're not allowed." The creatures are "not here to help us with that . . ."

Norris had questions: Were they repairing David? What were the parts? "Are we just part of some advanced science project?" While admitting that "these individual stories sound ludicrous," together "an ultimate agenda is perhaps revealed," Norris concluded.

Judging from the facts revealed by studies of thousands of abductions and the abductees he has worked with over a six-year period, Norris believes humanity is "part of an ongoing project with a higher intelligence." He wonders why "have we been chosen for this? Why have they come? Will our future be shaped by these experiences?"

GO TOWARD THE LIGHT

During the early summer of 1985 a twenty-six-year-old artist and her husband were sleeping at her mother's home in Valley, Alabama, just across the Chattahoochee River from West Point, when she awakened at 1:30 A.M. to find the bedroom lit brighter than day by a huge white light. She sat up, then stood beside the bed and was frozen in place. At that instant she was levitated six inches above the floor and slowly "towed" toward the center of the light at the far end of the room. The short journey required fifteen minutes, during which she believed her body "had no weight or was real light."

Inside the light she encountered a seven-foot creature with unusually long arms and burnt or wrinkled skin, similar to Freddie Krueger's face. The brownish-gray-colored figure was hairless, appeared sexless, and had two oval openings where eyes should be, although the woman saw no eyeballs, mouth, or ears.

The woman immediately blacked out. Regaining consciousness, she was returned to her bed as she had exited. Unfrozen and in a cold sweat, she saw it was 5:00 A.M.—two and a half hours were missing. The husband knew nothing about the incident.

Five years before this experience the witness had seen a tire-sized ball of fire in a different bedroom in the house. On several occasions, in company with her husband, she had spotted UFOs in the night sky floating over power lines near their home. She has since witnessed two "cloud" UFOs. She has also developed depression and entertained suicidal thoughts. Her art has also changed—she paints and sculpts a number of dragons and petrified dinosaurs. She believes the heads of her wildlife paintings "move" to different positions from where she painted them.

REPEAT BUSINESS

Casual observers of the UFO phenomenon generally believe that most UFO sightings are a one-time occurrence. Repeated experiences by a single individual are often viewed with suspicion of a hoax or mental imbalance. However, UFOs exist in a queer universe, and their behavior is rarely rational.

At 10:00 P.M. on February 27, 1991, a woman and her teenage son were driving on GA 190 near Pine Mountain when she spotted yellow lights through the trees. Pulling over, they both got out of the car and watched the lights grow larger until they cleared the trees and passed one hundred feet directly overhead and at less than five miles per hour.

The UFO was a dark triangle, seventy to one hundred feet to a side with three round, nonblinking yellow lights, each five to ten feet in diameter. It continued in a straight and level path and disappeared over a ridge.

Three hours later, at 1:00 A.M. on February 28, the woman awoke to sounds of someone crawling beneath her porch, where she was asleep, and into the crawl space under her home. Then a "female electronic voice" from beneath the house called her neighbor's name. Attempting to stand up, she found herself frozen. She recalls saying out loud, "God is their father also," then she fell asleep until morning.

FOOTPRINTS IN THE SAND, ER, CLAY

The woman crawled under the porch to find numerous shoe prints, a single odd handprint, and "drag marks" impressed in moist clay. The shoe prints were eight and a half inches long, twelve and a quarter inches long, and three and a half inches long. Within these prints were two marks—wavy lines and targetlike circles. The woman felt there were three different types of shoe prints represented. The small handprint, estimated as the size of a two-year-old's, had a thumb and six fingers for a grand total of seven digits. Also imprinted in the soft clay were coil-like impressions and assorted markings. The prints extended beneath the house to a point where the overhead was only three feet high.

The woman's teenage son also saw the marks and videotaped them, then made sketches.

During the next year gray mushrooms suddenly flourished under the house where they had never grown before, and have not reappeared since. The woman thought that perhaps aliens had planted them there.

A UFO appeared to the mother and son again on March 4, 1991, when they spotted a large yellowish white ball. They ran to their car to follow it. At the entrance to Roosevelt State Park, a popular place for UFO sightings, they reacquired the target and the boy videotaped it. Jeff Sainio, photo analyst for MUFON, examined the tape and said it might be Venus, although the witnesses claim that the tape suggests it was larger than the planet.

UNARMED ALIENS

A family of four was camping along the Flint River in west central Georgia on August 31, 1991. At 11:30 P.M. the father was awakened by what he interpreted as "animal grunting noises" outside. He climbed out of his sleeping bag and stepped outside the tent to investigate. He was stunned to see only four feet away from him a nine-foot-tall alien clad in a "pearly white robe." The entity had no arms, and his bare feet were floating four feet above the ground. The man's shouts awakened his wife, who stepped outside only to be frozen in place as her husband, similarly paralyzed, was "towed" by the floating alien. He could not even move his eyes.

The man was towed into a silver sphere, more than one hundred feet in diameter, and floating twenty to thirty feet off the ground. A large door set in the craft slid in to admit the abductor and abductee. Alien and victim passed through a thirty-five-foot-long hallway and entered a brightly lighted "large information center" crammed with monitor-less computers and bright flashing lights tended by up to twenty aliens.

The procession continued into an examination room, where the man was laid on a long black table. Eight to ten aliens looked him over (we can safely assume they did not lay a hand on him; finger neither) but did not insert or remove anything. The man noted that the interior of the object was too large for the size vessel he had seen, a claim made by abductees as far back as the fairy folk age.

When the exam concluded a few minutes later, the original alien towed the man outside and placed him beside his wife, at which point they both regained mobility. The couple watched as a "jet engine" fired up from the bottom of the sphere, and it rocketed away at great speed. The showy exit burned a two-hundred-yard circle into the ground. Four years later John Thompson found many burn spots at the site, but countless people had since camped and fished there, hopelessly contaminating any remaining evidence.

The couple's children slept through the episode, and the wife refuses to speak about it. The man has refused hypnotic regression, but has started seeing a psychiatrist. He claims a subsequent abduction, and the creatures have promised another visit—a prospect that frightens him.

PILLOW TALK

A woman who prefers to remain anonymous has described several strange encounters to Tom Sheets, a former police chief who investigates UFO activity out of Fayetteville, where the witness lives. She awoke between 7:00 and 8:00 A.M. in January 1995, after her husband had left for work, to see two diminutive aliens perched on her husband's pillow. She presumed one to be male and the other female, and both were the size of six-year-old children. One had crinkled or dry beige skin, large round eyes, and short, dark hair. Both were clad in neutral-colored garments. She raised an arm to touch them, but her arm fell back down. She glanced away for a moment, and the figures vanished.

A year and a half later, around January 1, 1996, she woke during the night and saw a small being scamper away from her, across her husband, and to the foot of the bed without movement from the mattress. The creature moved to the floor and joined at least three other creatures that huddled against the wall on her husband's side of the bed, watching her. The woman could not move or speak, just observe the beings by the illumination from a VCR light.

The humanoid creatures were five feet tall, with skinny limbs, gray skin, small mouths, large eyes, thin limbs, a reverse teardrop head, and a face also shaped like a teardrop. The odd part of the story (what has our society developed into when the presence of four Alien Grays is considered "normal"?) was their dress-black Panama hats and dark cloaks. She noticed neither smell nor sound during the experience.

The witness apparently fell asleep again. In the morning her husband was ignorant of the incident, but the couple found orange-brown stains on the bedroom carpet and a sheet. A burn the shape of a commando dagger blade was preserved.

The woman had seen a UFO as a child and may have been abducted when a teenager. She and her husband are well educated and worked in the aerospace industry during its glory days. Both are well respected in their community. Sheets found the fifty-five-year-old woman intelligent, articulate, forthright, and well read, with no reason to attempt a hoax. Her description of shy, skittish aliens is certainly unique. Maybe it was an alien kindergarten field trip.

ASSEMBLY-LINE ABDUCTIONS

At 2:00 A.M. during the early winter of 1997, a LaGrange resident claimed three dark silver figures, four and a half to five feet tall, walked through his bedroom wall and froze him in place. They exited the same way, according to the witness. He thought the aliens, who had what looked like ceramic skin without seams or wrinkles, were energy creatures. He could not make out facial details because they were distorted, like "looking at coins in a deep pool of water." The humanoids had arms and legs, but the hands were shaped like clubs, with webbed fingers. He could see muscles and bones in their bodies.

Outside, the man observed the outline of an enormous saucer "dark-light" along the edge. He estimated it was more than seventeen hundred feet long and that it hovered a hundred to 150 feet above the trees. Part of the craft extended into his backyard. The victim and aliens were instantly transported inside, where it felt as if there was no gravity. The interior of the craft was illuminated like daylight "in the middle of a three-million-acre farm," which we can take to mean real bright.

The interior of the vast ship resembled a modern factory packed with tables as far as he could see. Many aliens and machines with long arms were working on a number of humans. After the man was placed on one of the examination tables, a probe whacked his right front calf, then he was rotated and thumped on his left buttock, while a mechanical arm seized the crown of his head.

"You could hear a pin drop" inside the craft, the man said, although the moving machines made some sound and the creatures spoke low in a language he did not understand. The humans were quiet.

Next thing the man knew he woke up at 10:00 A.M.—four and a half hours past his usual rising time and late for work. He found a perfect quarter-size circle on his right thigh where the skin had peeled. It was red and hurt and looked like a "catfish skinner and a compass" had made it. A large, painful bruise decorated his left butt cheek, and a scab had formed on the crown of his head. He also "felt hot inside all over." Without the scars, he would not have believed the incident had occurred.

The man was awed by his experience, declaring that the alien "technology is beyond anything we've got."

DAMN BROTHER, I DON'T THINK I'D HAVE TOLD THAT
(A TRIBUTE TO LEWIS GRIZZARD)

"An alien had sex with me," a man wrote the National UFO Reporting Center. The incident occurred on the night of July 1, 1997, in Fort Benning. The man awoke to find "two alien-looking creatures at the foot of my bed." They were typical Alien Grays. The man was immobilized and felt no fear as he "knew their purpose and was shamefully looking forward to the encounter." He was concerned that his wife would awaken, but the aliens let him know that she would not. Apparently, the Grays were familiar with human males and "told" him "that 'this' would not take long." The man then did the dirty with the creatures.

A FAMILY AFFAIR

A Stockbridge family seems to be stalked by aliens. On December 29, 1999, a mother and her thirteen-year-old son discovered beings in their respective bedrooms. The woman was at work on January 3, 2000, when her sixteen-year-old daughter called, crying over a similar encounter. Her alien was surprised that she had awakened. When it touched her, she "suddenly received a visual image in her mind of a craft and five beings in the backyard." Mom has experienced the visitations all her life and was aware of previous incidents involving her daughter, but hearing of the son's experiences was a surprise. He explained "that was why he always slept under his bed and in the closet as a kid."

DARK SHADOWS

Dedicated Georgia UFO researcher John Thompson does not believe in "this abduction madness . . . I don't believe hardly any, if anyone at all, has ever been *physically* abducted," he stated. Thompson attributes this popular phenomenon to the "Shadows," or dimensional interterrestrial beings (INTs). He believes they have existed for hundreds of years, perhaps "since the Indians arrived." Based on 120 personal investigations and hundreds of witness interviews, Thompson is convinced that the Shadows "are frequently visiting homes." Described as five to five and a half feet in height, they are dark and shadowy, their faces "almost always hidden," but their arms and legs visible. Some witnesses report "blazing red eyes and four long, animal-like claws" on each hand. They are often described as "being darker than dark," or "a shadow of a human."

These denizens of the netherworld have the ability to move through walls. Shadows vanish when they know people are observing them. They are often seen standing beside baby cribs, which harkens back hundreds of years to tales of the "Little People" in Europe and many other ancient cultures. People wake up at night and find Shadows sitting on them "in their beds trying to suffocate them." They feel no fear when they awake although the entity is staring at them—however, the victims quake with fright after it disappears. These characteristics are strongly reminiscent of succubi activity.

About 2:00 A.M. on May 5, 1992, a man in west-central Georgia woke up and saw a shadowy figure standing over his one-year-old son's crib. The stocky apparition stood no more than five feet in height, wore a long black cape and a wide cap with a "teepee"-like peak which seemed attached to the cape. For no good reason the top of the cone hat could not be seen, nor were arms or facial features visible.

The Shadow walked across the room in front of the man's bed and disappeared through the wall. The witness felt no apprehension during the encounter and was not surprised at the bizarre method of departure. During the ten-second incident the man thought, "There goes the Shadow of Death." He immediately got up to check the baby, but nothing was amiss.

The father went back to bed and awoke an hour before dawn from a nightmare, in which he had picked the boy up to find him shot in the head—a large-caliber bullet had flattened out on his forehead, but the round had not penetrated very far into the head. "It's okay," he thought, "he's going to live."

The man thought about the eerie encounter and dream for two days before relating them to his wife—she had slept soundly through that night. She discounted the incident, but the husband wondered if this was a warning from God about danger to their son.

At 6:10 P.M. on May 8 the man came home from work to find his wife racing down the drive honking her horn. She slammed on the brakes, rolled down her window, and shouted, "Get in! He's dying!"

Jumping into the car, the man found his son lying on the passenger seat, not breathing. He was turning blue and his eyes were rolled back. The infant seemed dead, but the father gave the boy mouth-to-mouth resuscitation as his wife raced for the hospital at one hundred miles per hour, recklessly weaving through traffic.

At the emergency room the boy was given oxygen and his body draped in wet towels. Doctors explained that a high fever had induced a seizure. The child recovered, but suffered a radical personality change from sweet to irritable and agitated. A year later his hair started falling out and continued to do so for a year. However, his personality and hair have since returned to normal.

Perhaps the INTs had brought a warning, but they have not departed. Other family members have seen shadowy apparitions passing through walls—in one case two brothers saw one creature with four claws on each hand step out of a hall wall and pass a hand through the chest of one of the boys, who felt no sensation at all.

On another night the family heard a loud, gunshot-like bang in the house. Later that evening a white light was seen dancing on the ceiling of the room occupied by the afflicted child. UFOs have been sighted from the premises, TVs are activated at high volume, inexplicable noises are heard, and electricity surges and cuts off for no reason.

HAINTS AND AINTS

It was 9:30 P.M. on November 4, 1995, as a man driving on Salem Road in Troup County topped a hill and spotted 5-5, "shadowlike" beings dashing about in the middle of the pavement about 250 feet away. He hit his brakes and high beams and glanced down away from the figures. When he looked up again, all of the entities had vanished. The man drove slowly for a while, examining the roadside closely for the creatures, but they had gone. Frightened, he continued home.

284

The man initially thought the figures were deer (my brother, who lives in the area, averages about one hit-and-run deer encounter every three years). Upon closer reflection, the things were remembered to be humanoid in shape, but resembled the shadow of a person standing in daylight. They appeared to be a stocky six feet tall with a vague triangular shape. He saw no arms, just legs. John Thompson suggests they are Alien Grays draped in dark-hooded cloaks. Traditionally, they might be what the country folk call "haints."

On another occasion a driver on Salem Road not only spotted the Shadows, but also hit one—or sorta hit one. The Shadow suddenly appeared in the cab of the truck, but instantly disappeared. The witness called the figure "darker than dark."

MOTHER MARY

One night in August 1996, a woman was sleeping with her six-year-old granddaughter who frequently suffered nosebleeds. Hearing the child cough, the woman saw her bleeding unusually heavy and sneezing blood. The grandmother cleaned the girl and stemmed the flow, then put the girl to bed again.

About fifteen minutes later the woman glanced at the girl and saw a tall "angel" standing over her from the opposite side of the bed. The angel, clad in a long white robe, had very blonde, curly hair, and disappeared after thirty seconds.

Another quarter hour passed. When the grandmother checked on the child again the entity was again standing over her, this time with a multicolored Afghan-like spread, decorated with a unique "pear-stem" pattern on it, held in her outstretched hands. It appeared that she was going to wrap the child in it. After ninety seconds the angel became aware of the grandmother's scrutiny and vanished instantly.

The room had been lit by a small lamp and a television set, which enabled the woman to twice get a good look at the being. She was insistent that it disappeared while clearly in view. The woman was not frightened by the encounter, believing the being was there to help her granddaughter.

At about the same time another strange event was recorded when local residents found a "split-open hog with no guts" dangling off a bridge.

Another INT incident manifested itself in LaGrange on October 29, 1998. A man was alone in his house at 9:45 P.M. when he noticed a "girl," about four feet in height but featureless and dark, standing less than twenty feet away. In the two seconds that they stared at each other, he noted she wore a flowing dress nearly the color of the face, and her shoulder-length hair seemed to flow into her clothing. Thompson suggests she was clad in the traditional INT hooded cloak. The apparition then "floated away."

Two hours later the man spotted "a blue cast" shining from under his daughter's bedroom door. He rushed in, but the light had vanished.

The man and his wife had heard phantom footsteps walking about the house and unintelligible conversation for four months before these incidents. Their daughter's television set would also turn itself on during the night (they're hereeeeeeeee).

On October 30 the husband awoke feeling he was suffocating and found an invisible entity sitting on his chest. The foot of the bed also levitated off the floor, and his hair seemed wet. Somehow returning to sleep, he dreamed that the "grim reaper" was standing at the foot of the bed. Both husband and wife have observed "shadow" figures roaming through the house.

During the early morning hours of November 6 the man left a tape recorder running and recording as he slept. A sound like a shotgun firing roused him from sleep, but a search of the house and yard produced nothing tangible. However, the tape recorder captured two explosions and the barely audible conversation. Such sounds and voices are commonly related to various paranormal manifestations. The family, which believes the activity is demonic or supernatural, considered moving.

John Thompson believes the presence of INTs "has frightening and unknown implications" for humanity and "more logically explains the abduction phenomenon." It definitely answers a prime question regarding abductions—how are millions of people physically levitated out of houses and cars and into spacecraft for considerable periods of time and never missed? It also provides a reason why most of those UFOs and all of the cars and empty beds are not noticed.

Thompson charges that those who perpetuate the alien-abduction theory have not investigated such cases, have a monetary interest in a book or other related project, are "biased, wish(ing) to remain politically correct in the UFO camp," or are "hopelessly naive." He finds the existence of UFOs proven by "tens of thousands of credible" reports made by an "amazing number of impressive and reliable witnesses, but "no proof that extraterrestrials are kidnapping people." He believes that over "90 percent of this (abduction) business is dimensional" which is "why there is never, never any physical proof."

While acknowledging the "abduction threat," he believes it "does not involve physically abducting people." He considers it a "captive mental process" and wonders why "the INTs are coming back repeatedly to the same people." He assumes it is for a logical reason, and the effect is to leave people "with thought-processing manipulation or mind-altering programs . . . the dumbing down of our species certainly cannot be ruled out" because Thompson sees humans as "a growing threat to the INTs." He says the Shadows are "conditioning mankind for their own sinister purposes" and seem to be "mind conditioning" us.

"Abductions are the actual mechanism for how evil is imported into our bodies," Thompson claimed. He believes "the actual emplacement of evil by abductions appears to be happening. Fortunately the conditioning by INTs does not often take or can be warded off with the assistance of God . . . . But as long as there is 'an opening,' the INTs probe. This is why the INTs continue to come back for many visits throughout the abductee's life." The abductors, who "are not creatures of the flesh, . . . are and have been negatively effecting mankind's mental evolution." Thompson suggested that perhaps teens who slaughter classmates at school are under such influences.

Thompson compares our focusing on physical abductions to crossing a busy highway without looking for cars. "We are getting hit repeatedly!" he said. "I personally believe many of our leaders in American life have been 'contaminated'" (which would certainly explain a lot).

Thompson believes "that our religious leaders should be researching and warning" the country. Two weeks before Thompson made these declarations, George Filer had reported that the level of UFO, abduction, and ghost activity seemed to have grown, particularly in Georgia. "Religious organizations are reporting an increase in demonic-like activity," he wrote. Filer sees "a startling relationship" between modern supernatural events and those of the Middle Ages. In the past churches took these accounts seriously and exorcised demons—today we think aliens are responsible.

"We could be dealing with several different phenomena that are visitors to people's homes," he wrote, and related the story of a woman in New Jersey who was apparently raped by an invisible entity. The victim had ugly black bruises as evidence. She had awakened when she suddenly fell to the bed after being levitated off the mattress and saw "a luminescent scary form."

The creatures involved in recent UFO and other paranormal activity "seem to come from another world, a realm beyond our physical world." These "stories fit the old incubus and succubus legends." There is an obvious relationship between those and the breeding experiments reported in many abduction tales.

Filer later wrote that he receives "a steady stream of these type reports, mostly from Georgia and New Jersey," which are often accompanied by "scratches, bruises, and damage to sexual organs, etc. The church has believed in these accounts for hundreds of years. Perhaps we are watching the modern version of the same attacks. Perhaps these are the fallen angels also described in historical documents."

Thompson cites the lack of "physical proof to prove" abductions and a lack of witnesses "seeing a person being kidnapped into a physical spacecraft." However, he does believe that "millions, knowingly or unknowingly, have experienced symptoms that suggest they were abduction victims." Thompson's research has proven that very few people who report entities also saw a "physical spacecraft." They may have seen UFOs on occasions before or after the entity appearance, but not connected with the creatures. He thinks the reality of the INT threat "will turn many folk's stomachs."

"When there is *never* any physical evidence of substance, how can you not consider mental projections or hologram-like images being projected into the victims' minds?" Thompson writes. He states that physical effects like bruises "could be created by mental actions."

In an article posted on ISUR's outstanding Web site, Thompson asks if extraterrestrials "are behind abductions, why aren't millions of bewildered spouses calling local law-enforcement agencies to report that their loved ones have suddenly disappeared and are presumed kidnapped? Why are there not stranded cars and trucks all over America's highways—their drivers gone? . . . Nobody is missing from their beds or cars; it is only mind tricks played by the Innerterrestrials."

Thompson believes that INTs, often called "haints, shadows, witches, demons, grays, fairies, gnomes, goblins, ghosts, reptiles, or whatever" do not care if people see them because they "cannot be touched, nor can they touch a human." Many witnesses report that "the entities stick their clawed hands through their bodies with no resultant physical harm."

"UFO sightings and abductions are two distinct and separate phenomenons," Thompson concluded. "It has definitely been an enormous mistake to downplay the similarities between bedroom abductions and demonic activity," he stated, and believes "99.9 percent of all entity sightings do not involve UFOs or extraterrestrials."

"Make no mistake they are an alien species—but not one of the flesh," Thompson continued, but they are "dimensional creatures" who "are spiritually abducting . . . many victims seemingly everywhere."

The million or more estimated abductees present a logistical nightmare for aliens—a capital investment "involving thousands of spaceships." A very unlikely scenario.

Thompson explained that UFO research was an old-fashioned endeavor involving gathering evidence, largely in the form of testimony, and attempts to substantiate witness accounts until September 19, 1961, when Betty and Barney Hill were apparently abducted. Their story came out under regressive hypnosis, now often referred to as hypnotherapy, and in the following years thousands of recovered memories of abductions, examinations by aliens, and breeding experiments surfaced. Researchers accepted hypnosis as "a quick truth serum that often eliminated the necessity of independent witnesses and background checks of the alleged abductees." We assumed they had to be relating truthful facts, and "the lack of supporting physical evidence" bothered no one. Investigators developed the theory of "screen memories" that aliens purportedly used to "switch off" the memories of abductees and other witnesses in order to "conceal their sinister space kidnappings."

However, dedicated researchers soon found "many aspects of the abduction experience . . . troubling," Thompson said. "There seemed to be considerable overlap into what in the past had only been referred to as paranormal activity." Abductees heard explosions and other strange noises in their houses, and "small balls of light floating on their ceilings" or "strange green or blue flashes popping inside their homes." In bed, "they have terrifying nightmares." Awake, they glimpsed "shadows" near their beds. More disturbingly, the entities often appeared "near the beds of their infants, toddlers, or children" and entered and disappeared through walls. These frightening experiences did not cause fear because, Thompson wrote, mind control "is induced to calm the abductees."

A number of researchers and innumerable followers of weird phenomena are hostile toward this idea, but Thompson is not dissuaded. "I feel I am doing groundbreaking research," he maintained. "I also believe much of what I say will be eventually proven.

"Sometimes INTs and ETs play on the same 'fields' but their objectives are different, and with the extraterrestrials, their motivations unknown," Thompson proposes. Scientists should study physical UFOs, Thompson says, while "religious leaders . . . should be investigating 'abductions.'" He believes ministers should warn their congregations about the INT threat and purpose, alerting "parents that their children are vulnerable to mind-conditioning or, worse, 'dumbing-down' attempts by Interterrestrials."

MEET JOE BLACK

People reporting INT encounters generally report one of two different types of entities—the Panama hat guy or a Gray. In Dallas, Georgia, a Panama-hatted creature showed itself to a middle-aged woman whose husband had been ill for some time. The husband died several days later, leaving her to believe it was the "Angel of Death." A twenty-three-year-old woman in LaGrange saw the Mad Hatter but thought it resembled her grandmother, long deceased. Both these women realized that their intruders were not aliens, but evil, supernatural entities. A nineteen-year-old male college student in LaGrange saw a hatless Panama-style creature. The appearance made him think of a dead friend and he too realized the nature of the apparition and vanquished it by calling on God for help. The twenty-three-year-old woman, who saw her INT twice, ten years apart, has a family history of such encounters. Her grandmother had seen such an entity, as had her brother, who even encountered them in prison, and a niece, but "none have seen the same exact entities."

Soon after Thompson released his conclusions, a Florida researcher, Wes Clark, affiliated with MUFON and the CE-4 Research Group, took it further, writing, "The abductees we work with have had great success in stopping abductions by calling for help from Jesus." He found that the biblical book of Acts "has many parallels with the present-day, UFO-abduction phenomena. We are not trying to tell anyone what they should believe, we are reporting what our cases have proved . . . It's amazing how few things have changed in the enemy's tactics."

Thompson talked with Clark and seemed initially skeptical, but has since interviewed people who reported the same thing. One Georgia woman had been jumped in her home by an INT that she thought intended to "suffocate her." When she cried out, "Jesus! Jesus! Save me!" the entity vanished and never returned. A man was struggling with a dark, big-eyed Gray in a lucid dream when he shouted, "Jesus is my Savior!" The Gray and related activity in the house stopped. All members of a third family had been having similar nightmares until a man observed his dog barking and leaping, apparently at an unseen creature on a bed. He was able to "exorcise" the trouble from his home.

Thompson was dumbfounded by the simplicity of this "cure." He acknowledged a long-recognized connection "between abductions and paranormal activity" and found that "This is compelling proof that abductions have nothing to do with space kidnappings. If high-tech ETs are behind the abduction madness, why would one's belief in God stop abductions cold?" Appeals to the Lord would stop "earthbound evils," Thompson continued, "so why would they halt highly advanced and technologically sophisticated ETs from abducting?"

Some twenty years ago I abandoned the field of weirdness for a more socially acceptable area of journalism (Civil War history). The last article I wrote for UFO magazines mirrored these late developments in ufology. Please understand that I am not claiming credit for the theory. That honor belongs to the great UFO researcher Jacques Vallee in his groundbreaking book *Passport to Magnolia* and expanded in the writings of John Keel. This theory was largely ignored by mainstream ufology until recently, as more investigators became frustrated at finding themselves making no progress toward solving the UFO mystery. As the *X-Files'* Fox Mulder once said, "All the evidence to the contrary is not entirely dissuasive."

THE EYE OF THE BEHOLDER

This news from the art world probably eluded you, but a new genre is "alien art," composed by abductees/contactees. David Huggins's experiences with aliens started years ago in Georgia. In a review of abduction art, the *New York Times* said Huggins "paints graphic and disturbing images from a lifetime of supposed encounters, including babies fathered on alien mothers. The women have the bodies of *Playboy* centerfolds and the familiar gray alien heads with sloe eyes." The *Times* referred to Huggins as "another self-described abductee."

According to the *Los Angeles Times*, Huggins, "who asserts that he's had sex with numerous pointy-chinned alien women and fathered their almond-eyed alien babies, supplies the figurative canvasses he painted to document the encounters initiated by an 'insect being.'

"The insect being, which resembles a praying mantis, would bring (alien) women to my apartment, and we'd have intercourse. He put me in a paralyzed state and I'd lay in my bed not being able to move. Then the women would melt me, I'd reach my climax, and, well, then they would get up and leave."

After one alien woman mentioned that he had fathered hybrid children, Huggins asked to see them. "I laid on my bed and passed out, and the next thing I knew is that I'm wherever they are, with the babies."

Here in the real world, Huggins worked for Merrill Lynch & Co., in New York City.

A TRUE CONFESSION

When I started researching this book I decided to end my history of Georgia UFOs with the line: "I don't do abductions. You must have *some* standards."

Having criticized *Abduction Nation*, I must relate the following. I attempted early on to exploit the phenomenon. It was about 1980, and I tell myself that it was the week I had four wisdom teeth cut out and was taking narcotics. Truth is, it was January and I had spent three brain-numbing days watching my students take long semester tests. In that context, I composed the only short story of my adult life.

With appropriate shame I admit that it was intended for confession magazines. I plead temporary insanity. The gist of the tale is that a woman wakes up one night to find herself being assaulted by an invisible entity. Of course, no one believes her tale, but nine months later . . . Rosemary's alien. To my chagrin, I must report that it was so wretched that none of the confession rags I submitted it to bothered to reply, even with rejection slips. I finally figured it out, though—I was ahead of my time. Happens to all visionaries.

8

Unique People

We have just begun to explore the mysteries of the mind and human potential generally. What lurks in that unused 90 percent of the human brain? Were our past ancestors telepathic, and do those abilities lie fallow? Can we heal ourselves or others? Do we have the power to perceive events removed from us, divine the future, or communicate with the dead? And what the hell was Lulu Hurst, spiritualist, master of mechanics, or petite Russian weight lifter? These may be the last questions that we manage to answer, if we ever do.

LULU HURST: GEORGIA'S GIRL WONDER

Lulu Hurst was born in 1869 in lovely Collard Valley, just outside Cedartown. One grandfather was considered a biblical whiz who concentrated on prophesies—one could only imagine his embarrassment had he lived to 1932—the date he had selected for the battle of Armageddon. Lulu's parents hailed from Tennessee, where her father, William E. Hurst, was remembered as "a gallant Confederate soldier," the highest praise that could be lavished upon a Southern man following the war. Her mother was a graduate of Mary Sharp College.

The family moved to Cedartown for Lulu's early education, then returned to a farm in the country. On September 18, 1883, fourteen-year-old Lulu and her cousin Lora were sleeping during a severe electrical storm when a "quick, muffled popping sound" was first heard emanating from her pillow before spreading to different parts of the room. A thorough search by the entire family could not locate the source of the sound, which frightened them all.

The noise started again the following night, with the added feature of a mysterious force pulling young Lulu's hair. Soon she noticed that tables and her bed would tap on the floor when she placed her hands on the furniture. Then she discovered that it would rap out answers in response to questions; one rap meant yes; two signified no.

293

Next, hickory nuts flew off nearby trees and whizzed into her upstairs room, clothing sailed through the house and draped itself across picture frames, hats teleported from bureau drawers to cabinets in other rooms, crockery flew off tables, and collected minerals took flight and spread across the floor.

MOVERS AND SHAKERS

Then fate intervened and Lulu discovered her stagecraft. No person or combination of persons could budge a chair on which Lulu laid her hands. While another person held an umbrella, Lulu's touch caused it to suddenly fly apart. Holding a walking cane or billiard cue, Lulu could drag the strongest men around who also had a grasp on it.

Neighbors came in droves to watch Lulu demonstrate her powers, and rumors spread that she could will people to death. After city people started trekking out to the country for demonstrations, her parents, reportedly initially opposed to placing Lulu on the stage for profit, allowed her to perform in Cedartown. She also took on a manager, Paul M. Atkinson, whom she had met in Madison. Before you could say, "Roll the presses!" the neighboring community of Rome demanded a show. Lulu acquiesced, attended by her parents and Paul, the Manager. The reticence of Lulu's parents seemed to evaporate when they received offers of a hundred dollars a night for their daughter's services.

Henry Grady, famed editor of the *Atlanta Constitution*, heard of Lulu's antics and dispatched ace reporter Josiah Carter to privately preview her act. A glowing review solicited an offer from DeGiues Opera House in Atlanta. She appeared in late January 1884 as "Miss Lulu Hurst, the Electric Girl," and was sandwiched between minstrel shows. After up to three men, sometimes totaling five hundred pounds, would pile upon a wooden chair, Lulu would place her hands on the back of the chair and induce it to rise six inches off the floor.

Men, individually and in groups, would grasp a cane and brace themselves for the storm to come. Little Lulu would step forward and grab the cane, then drag the men back and forth across the stage and often fling them into the footlights or the audience.

Men would similarly take hold of an umbrella. At Lulu's touch the umbrella started to wrestle the participants around the stage before turning inside out and flying to pieces.

The men who participated in her stunts were always local volunteers, and no matter what mayhem befell them, others eagerly pressed forward to take their chances. Spectators considered it great sport.

Woman-child Lulu performed in a black velvet dress with a gold necklace, and her shoulder-length hair was gathered in the back by a pretty

PRICE $1.00

LULU HURST

(THE GEORGIA WONDER)

Writes her Autobiography and for the first time

EXPLAINS AND DEMONSTRATES

The Great Secret

OF HER MARVELOUS POWER.

A Death Blow to Spiritualism and Superstition of every kind. A new and unparalleled Revelation of the forces that puzzled and mystified the entire Continent. Full Page Illustrations.

COPYRIGHTED.   ALL RIGHTS RESERVED.

Published and for Sale by PSYCHIC RESEARCH CO.

TIMES-HERALD BUILDING, CHICAGO.

Who Reads the Book can Acquire the Power.

All of the illustrations in this chapter of Lulu Hurst's acts are from either her autobiography Lulu Hurst: The Georgia Wonder, *or Frank Leslie's* Illustrated Newspaper, *page 361, dated July 26, 1884.*

295

pink ribbon. Throughout each act she laughed and giggled with such merriment that she was often called "the Laughing Lulu Hurst."

In one audience was Henry Grady, who was captivated by the girl's charm. After Lulu staged a private demonstration for the editor the next day, the *Constitution* followed her career with alacrity. Although Lulu and her entourage emphasized that her talent was mechanical, Grady always considered it supernatural.

Also present that night was Hoke Smith, a future U.S. senator from Georgia and member of President Grover Cleveland's cabinet. Believing Lulu a fraud, he volunteered for the chair, but refused to follow Lulu's instructions. Frustrated, she stalked off the stage and would not return until Smith departed.

Lulu next performed in Chattanooga, then toured Georgia for four months. Papers like the *Gibson Enterprise* loved her, stating Lulu had

"recently developed very remarkable power as a spiritualist, or electrician." Conversely, the *Athens Weekly Banner-Watchman*, citing Smith's shenanigans, said Lulu "turns out to be a first-class humbug."

Manager Paul was ringmaster at Lulu's performances, introducing her and reciting drama and comedy between acts. He was often billed as "Professor Atkinson, the Elocutionist."

THE POWER BEHIND THE THROWN

The source of Lulu's "Power," as she called it, was a constant topic of specu-

Lulu Hurst

lation. Her father strongly denied spiritualism as the source and stated that his daughter had great quantities of electricity in her body. The *Greensboro Herald* agreed, citing "animal-magnetism" and "animal-electricity." Of course, the editor also believed that the electricity in a human body could be used to light gas jets by merely pointing a finger.

One editor in Athens, Larry Gantt, was converted by her performance there. He even swallowed Mr. Hurst's claims that while lying in bed Lulu could "think a song in her mind, while any part of the bed or room to which she directs her attention will at once give forth the music distinct enough to be heard all over the house" and "make the bed whistle, sing, groan, etc." Mr. Hurst loved nothing better than messing with people's minds.

Gantt was seemingly enchanted by the "animal-magnetism" he saw in Lulu's eyes, writing, "They are literally the windows of the soul, and seem to mesmerize you." He felt a desire to "gaze again and again" into them. Gantt climbed onstage to participate in the umbrella stunt. "So taking out a life insurance policy," he wrote, "and lining our raiment with volumes of congressional literature, we marched on the stage with the desperation of a martyr to science." Taking hold of the umbrella, "we felt like we were trying to hold down a flash of lightning."

In Lulu's act, "break a leg" was a serious possibility.

Another participant, described as three-hundred-pound "Captain Bradeen, the Jumbo of Athens," was also vanquished, later stating: "I have wrestled with a grizzly bear in the mountains of North Carolina, I have had boxing matches with cyclones in Georgia, and laughed in the face of a Texas blizzard, but the electric maid of Collardtown lays in the shade anything I have ever tackled. I am dumb with amazement."

May 1884 was Lulu's most spectacular month to date as she played Macon, Augusta, and Savannah. The Lulu Show had now developed a genius promotional technique. Before public performances in a new city, a private exhibition was provided for newspaper reporters and editors, scientists, local government leaders, and doctors and lawyers. News accounts then related Lulu's tricks and the prominent citizens she had victimized.

In Macon the faculty of Mercer University and their wives requested a private show. Among those present were president Archibald J. Battle and professors Joseph E. Willet, John B. Brantley, and Vincent T. Sanford. All were humbled by Lulu's prowess. The participants came away convinced her Power was not muscular, but electric, magnetic, or spiritual.

In Macon Lulu was described as five feet, six and a half inches in height, and weighing 120 pounds, a "stout, healthy, ruddy-complexioned girl of sixteen summers," the "perfect picture of health," and a "tall, well-formed brunette, with rosy cheeks, dark eyes, and chestnut curls."

THE POWER WAS WITH HER

The *Augusta Chronicle & Sentinel* touted Lulu as "the Amazing Wonder of the Nineteenth Century." Her private audience before the faculty and students of the medical college astounded and perplexed those learned men.

Next stop was Savannah, where "The Magnetical Electrical Georgia Girl," according to the *Savannah Morning News*, performed in the Pulaski House for a former U.S. senator, the city's mayor, and officials of the Georgia Historical Society. Lulu's "many remarkable and unaccountable endowments" were lauded, an account read, her Power "something more than mere physical force, which is beyond the ability to explain."

When Lulu stopped on the street and asked why several people were watching her intently, the reply was that sparks flew from her feet.

Lulu's mischievous father had become an accomplished storyteller, convincing a Savannah reporter that in Louisville she had induced a bed to rise up off the floor and move around the room without a touch from the girl.

During her Georgia travels, Lulu's fame spread nationwide and Sanford Cohen arranged a series of performances outside the state. In June Lulu appeared in Charleston, first enticing the staff of its medical college. "There was not a man in this distinguished and learned array who could explain the mysterious phenomenon," reported the *Charleston News and Courier*.

Lulu continued on to Washington, D.C., as "the Georgia Wonder and Phenomenon of the nineteenth century." There she enthralled members of the U.S. Congress. Former Georgia governor, U.S. senator, and renown Confederate general John B. Gordon was among the volunteers at the private demonstration. As Lulu said, "He who rarely beat a retreat before the bravest armies (was sent) flying before this power in the most demoralizing fashion." Lulu's Athens patron, Larry Gantt, claimed that the teenager had "danced half a dozen leading congressmen and correspondents all over the room."

A TRUE SOUTHERN BELL(E)

Lulu's performances were so impressive that Alexander Graham Bell invited her to his home, where she demonstrated her feats before noted astronomer and inventor William Harkness, geologist John Wesley Powell, astronomer-mathematician Simon Newcomb, and many other famed scientists of the day. She repeated the performance at the Volta Laboratory.

Newcomb missed an initial session, but was told Lulu could cause "objects to move as if acted on by powerful forces without any muscular action on her part." A description of her act "by a select circle of educated men" intrigued Newcomb.

THE SCULLY THEORY

These learned men devised several scientific tests of Lulu's Power. She stood on scales while lifting a two-hundred-pound man sitting in a chair. Inexplicably, the scales only registered an additional forty pounds. However, Newcomb believed that such a force could "throw him off his balance, and make a new adjustment necessary. The motion given by the performer to the rod was not a regular one, which could be anticipated and guarded against, but a series of jerks, first in one direction, and then in another; so that it was impossible for the holder to brave himself against them: consequently, by a force which might not have exceeded forty pounds, he was put through a series of most undignified contortions," and defeated.

After Lulu performed the trick "a great number of times," Newcomb concluded she controlled the chair with pressure delivered by the ball of her hand. He and others believed the trick became easier for Lulu to control as the number of men perched in the chair increased. Forget the added weight, they averred, the trick "was no concert of action among the four muscular holders, more than that each one tried to keep the chair still by resisting any force which he felt it to exert. A few jerks in various directions by the performer led them to begin resisting her motion by pulling the chair first this way and then that. It was of course impossible for any one holder to tell whether the motion came from the performer or from his companions. The result was, that they all began to wrench desperately against each other until the chair came to pieces."

After a strenuous exercise, Lulu's pulse was found "but little above normal." While she demonstrated "the absence of any sign of physical exertion," a male participant "was blowing like a porpoise."

When Newcomb shook Lulu's hand, he "felt like moving the arm of the giant," giving him the "impression that she had a much better muscular development than would have been supposed."

Lulu next produced a hat that Newcomb said she held by the balls of her thumbs and resulted in "the hat (being) gently attracted upwards as if by electricity."

When Newcomb grasped a staff firmly with both hands in the center, Lulu placed the palms of her hand and her extended thumbs against the end of the pole. Newcomb suffered the fate of all former contenders but claimed to have solved the trick after a repetition, claiming that Lulu "began with a delicate touch of the staff" but "changed the position of her hands every moment; sometimes seizing the staff with a firm grip, and that it never moved in any direction unless her hands were in such a position that she could move it in that direction by ordinary pressure." He estimated the force at about forty pounds.

When the experiments were completed, Newcomb concluded that Lulu's Power was mere physical strength. However, "the exhibition is perfectly honest," he admitted, "there is no trickery or pretense, or any endeavor at concealment." The fact that witnesses assumed "because Miss Lulu begins by touching the articles deftly with her fingers, she never takes them with a firm grip" is self-delusion "without any effort on the performer's part to cause that illusion," he wrote.

When a reporter asked Newcomb why Lulu exhibited no sign of exertion, the scientist stated, "I cannot explain it. I leave that for psychologists to do."

SUPER GIRL

Newcomb wrote about the Power in the prestigious scientific journal *Science*. He again emphasized that Lulu's act was honest, but maintained his belief that somehow she cleverly maneuvered the participants into adding their strength to the tricks. He lamely wrote that "the absurd simplicity" of the act gave it "vitality." He said Lulu's only trick was "in distracting the observer's attention at the critical moment," meaning that those watching the act saw Lulu merely touching objects, so they never realized that she was grabbing them firmly. Still, there was that pesky matter of no exertion displayed on her part.

Newcomb felt it "only just to mention the perfect frankness with which the most thorough investigation of the case was permitted by those having the exhibition in charge. There was no darkening of rooms, no concealing hands under tables, no fear that spirits would refuse to come at the bidding of a skeptic, no trickery of any sort. The opportunities for observation were entirely unrestricted." Lulu willingly repeated tricks until the scientists believed they had found an explanation.

Lulu and her handlers were never reluctant to perform under any circumstances and never ducked a scientific examination, factors that gained for her considerable respect across the country.

Science shortly published a rebuttal written by R. W. Shufeldt, whose close examination of Lulu and her act discounted the earlier conclusions. Shufeldt found the girl "plump rather than muscular," her muscles "*not* unusually developed . . . rather the reverse." He found that the staff "gyrated rapidly about its long axis, obliging me to quit my hold." In the hat trick he was to lift the object from Lulu's flat hands, but the hat "was only removed after considerable force was exerted, and then came away with a crackling noise, as if charged with electricity." Finally, he discounted Newcomb's chair theory and said that Lulu had lifted a two-hundred-pound man simply by placing her palms on the uprights of the chair "*without any* contraction of the muscles" of her arms "or increase of pulse or respiratory effort" or any other sign of exertion.

In D.C. Lulu told a reporter that while she was unable to explain her Power, she was convinced it was not supernatural in origin. She also said her only inconvenience in everyday life was an inability to carry an umbrella because it would be torn from her grasp.

When Lulu toured the Treasury Building, officials feared that Lulu might somehow spirit away their gold.

After appearing in Baltimore, Lulu was booked for New York City in July by Charles Frohman, who in D.C. had grabbed Lulu's pool stick and was "circling the stage at a rate of speed which . . . would make an uncommonly brilliant sprint runner."

Lulu owned the Big Apple. News articles heralded her arrival days in advance and the hype never diminished until long after her departure. With seats as expensive as one dollar, she performed every night, with occasional matinees, from July 7 until July 19. Every element of New York crowded the theater, including ten-year-old Winston Churchill, in attendance with his grandfather; Roscoe Conkling, corrupt U.S. senator and presidential candidate; Union general Daniel Sickles, who nearly lost the battle of Gettysburg for the Union; and many others.

GIRLS JUST WANNA HAVE FUN
A reporter described Lulu one night as "a finely developed girl, with an interesting, but scarcely pretty, face (no Southern gentleman, he), and she

continually laughed and chatted with the gentlemen while exhibiting her power over them."

Another found her "a powerfully built country girl, about five feet, ten inches in height, with black hair worn loosely over her shoulders, dark eyes, and a full, round, fresh-looking face, not expressive of any great intelligence (how could she, being from the South?), however. She was dressed in a suit of black, and an enormous gold chain was about her neck. She speaks with a strong Southern accent, as do her parents (the shame!)."

SHOP TILL YOU DROP

Lulu treated herself to a lovely wardrobe, reportedly spending two thousand dollars on dresses in the city.

One of Lulu's private shows in New York City was for the city's actors and actresses. One actress attempted the chair trick and was "ignominiously upset," shooting across the stage, but "was rescued uninjured and marveled much."

"I felt an uncommon force bear me down," she said. "Just see, I am trembling all over."

The New York Star reported that when the actress volunteered for the cue act, "the Wonder laughed—a sure sign that she meant business." She did. Afterward, the victim stated, "Why, it's wonderful. I don't know what has happened. It was like a flash of lightning followed by a thunderbolt. It's a mercy I'm alive; I don't want any more of it. I have had a great curiosity to test this power, but I am now fully satisfied. It is indeed the most wonderful thing I ever saw."

Lulu also gave special performances for women only so that "the ladies will have an opportunity to fully test the power of Miss Hurst," who soon laid "stout matrons on their backs."

At one show, one hundred proud, fit members of athletic clubs arrived en masse, twenty of their number manfully volunteering to challenge Lulu's Power. In short order, they "retired from the stage after the performance covered with perspiration and confusion. The Georgia girl who had tossed them about like so many jackstraws, was perfectly cool and not in the least tired."

The "simple, unassuming girl" did "not look anything smart enough to attempt to impose on a New York audience," but did. She continually ran her hands through her bangs and laughed throughout, "a rather low, seemingly hysterical chuckle; quiet but audible all over the house."

Throughout every performance in each city, Paul Atkinson was the front man and "certainly allows the curious skeptics to make all the investigations they desire to," wondered the press. Dozens of the athletes crowded around Lulu during the performance, but discovered no evidence of trickery.

Look Deeply into My Eyes . . .

On another night, a mesmerist named William H. Wiggins took the stage. Gazing into Wiggins's eyes, Lulu "almost chuckled herself into hysterics." Sitting in the infamous chair and still challenging Lulu with his hypnotic eyes, Lulu "gave the chair a twist, and Mr. Wiggins turned a double-back somersault over it, made two complete revolutions, and brought up on his back . . . while the vast audience got right up on its hind legs and went frantic with delight, and cheered and screamed and howled with overpowering mirth."

After participating in the magic umbrella trick, a reporter was "bathed in perspiration" while "Miss Hurst looked as cool as a cucumber." Another victim declared, "She's the one to knock Sullivan out," a reference to the legendary boxing champion. A reporter wrote that Lulu could "not raise an umbrella while on the street without the mysterious force turning it inside out or performing some other antic."

Lulu's worst night in show business started well: "Miss Hurst began to chuckle, the chair began to whirl around the stage, and the spectators began to roar and shout. Mr. Hill clung to his seat and was bounced around in a very ridiculous fashion. After a while he got up and tried to press the chair to the floor. He struggled like a cart horse, but the large, white hands of the phenomenon baffled him."

Then Dr. W. E. Forest, who claimed he could replicate her acts, came onstage in a belligerent mood. After he refused to do as Lulu directed, all hell broke loose.

"Men in the top gallery took off their coats and vests and howled like demons at the people below. The women screamed for fair play to the girl on the stage, surrounded as she was by a small mob of excited men, who were wrangling and gesticulating like brokers . . . Men in the orchestra chairs shouted for peace, but no one paid any attention to them. A dozen talked at once. Miss Hurst sat down by her mother just outside the scene, and looked on in perfect amazement."

Sanford Cohen gave Forest the hook and threatened to stop the show. Lulu resumed her act, while a doctor who took her pulse stalked the stage wondering, "Surprising! Surprising!" Lulu was cool, but "her hands which were white and moist, burned like hot cakes."

Arguments raged throughout the city over the origin of Lulu's Power, or whether it was a mysterious power or trickery. Newspapers fueled the controversy, which was debated by tens of thousands.

There's a Sucker Born . . .

"She claims to be an 'electric girl' purely," Frank Leslie's *Illustrated Newspaper* stated, while Lulu's father told the *New York Tribune*, "It's a psychic force." A woman cattily commented that "She is more masculine than any wearer of petticoats ought to be." The *Tribune* stated that if real, "the phenomenon demand scientific study," belonging "in the region of nerve force, a region far too little explored." Some argued that she mesmerized participants into throwing themselves around the stage. A *New York Times* headline read: "The Performances Not So Much to Be Wondered at as the Gullibility of the Audience." Many felt her patrons were willingly deceived, "a phenomenon of stupidity," the *Times* thundered, which should "show how willingly people will be fooled, and with what cheerful asininity they will heap on their deceivers."

However, *Leslie's* observed, Lulu managed "to outwrestle athletes, outwit scientists, and outstrip trained actresses in that practical drawing power which attracts the shy and elusive dollar to the box office."

The Hursts and "the perpetual smile," as the *Times* described Paul the Manager, now continued to Boston, where boxer John L. Lewis, perhaps wisely (*Lewis KO'd by Georgia Girl!*), declined an invitation to participate onstage. Before another all-female audience, a woman, believing Paul was the source of Lulu's Power, demanded that he withdraw. Upset, Lulu flubbed her next trick, then left the stage. The Power soon returned, and after she performed the trick backstage with her parents, Lulu returned to the stage and challenged the lady. If the woman would participate in an act, Paul would leave. The woman accepted, and Lulu threw her violently about the stage. Paul returned in time to catch the woman before she would have taken a dangerous fall, and commented, "I now hope, Madam, you can understand why it is necessary for a man to be on the stage."

The *Boston Transcript* wrote that Lulu's "performances are marvelous, whether they proceed from muscularity, psychic force, magnetism or trickery; and whatever may be her secret power, she is well worth investigating by everybody."

Lulu toured Massachusetts, Rhode Island, Connecticut, New Jersey, and New York again. The wealthy, sophisticated crowd at Newport, Rhode Island, were too dignified to volunteer their participation. Eventually some did, with the usual results. When an earthquake shook the East Coast, people wondered, "Did Lulu Hurst do that?"

Lulu returned home in August 1884, changed in some respects by the experiences she had encountered. "She has been transformed from a country lass into a citified belle," the *Dade County Weekly Times*, surely authoritative in such matters, wrote. "She was dressed in the height of fashion, being attired in a handsome black brocaded silk, exquisitely trimmed. A jaunty traveling hat sat back on her head, exposing a profusion of the latest style of waving bangs. She wore an elegant pair of diamond earrings and a large solitaire glistened on the index finger of her left hand."

After a short rest in Polk County, Lulu trekked cross-continent to San Francisco on a tour arranged by Charles Frohman. In the pre-exhibition demonstration, newsmen, entertainers, and the city's elite watched as three volunteers "danced everything from the 'Hula-hula' to the Boston 'dip'; strained their muscles until their bulging eyes could have been knocked off with a club, and still the recalcitrant chair remained in midair and the discomforted trio retired in perspiration and abasement."

Despite Lulu's being struck by the chair during one performance, the *San Francisco Chronicle* stated, "Probably the most puzzled concourse of people that ever left a public building in this city . . ." departed the performance.

HURSTAMANIA!

Shows in Sacramento and Oakland followed. At the latter a newspaper declared that "Hurstamania" ruled. "A Town full of Lulucondriacs Monkeying with Broomsticks, Umbrellas, and Kitchen Chairs," a headline declared.

The Lulu Tour continued through Nebraska, Idaho, Montana, Wyoming, and Colorado, where in Denver a city alderman boldly claimed he could duplicate Lulu's entire act. Paul called him on it, betting $500 against the alderman's $250. The politician failed onstage to the accompaniment of considerable abuse from the audience.

After Denver, Lulu played Kansas, Missouri, Texas, Illinois, Wisconsin, Ohio, and Indiana, then rested in Cedar Valley for Christmas before tackling Chicago. There she added to her act, holding a billiard cue horizontally in both hands while standing on one foot. The object was for one or more people to push her off balance. All takers failed.

A nasty incident occurred when the Hurst party refused to allow a black volunteer to participate. The event cast a negative light over the Chicago stand, and reviewers were less enthusiastic than in other cities. Part of her performance was attributed to "trickery and muscular strength." On the last night two men who claimed the ability to duplicate Lulu's effort attempted to brawl onstage until Lulu's father intervened.

The campaign continued in Milwaukee, then traveled south to New Orleans. Afterward Lulu returned home and only performed once more outside Georgia, appearing in Athens, Greensboro, and Atlanta, where Gantt wrote that success had not spoiled the young lady.

"You see the same, fresh, modest winsome face, and sparkling, majestic eyes, that have gone so far in opening the public heart for her successful career. She has not been spoiled by sight-seeing or rendered vain by flattery . . . She is certainly one of the most attractive ladies we ever met, there is something peculiarly fascinating about her."

Lulu asked Gantt to the stage, but he was hesitant after the earlier experience.

"But when she turned those magnetic eyes upon us full of some wonderful drawing power, we could resist no longer, and with the resignation of a martyr pranced to the front. Miss Lulu whispered to us that she had her own power under better control than at first, and would handle us tenderly and with care. We grasped the chair, closed our eyes, braced our muscles, and sent up a prayer for safety.

"Miss Lulu gently rested one of her soft hands upon a round, and in about two seconds' time we felt ourselves giving away all over, and an uncontrollable desire to travel. Whether we held on to the chair, or the chair held on to us, will be an unsolved mystery to our dying day. Anyhow we were finally joined together as a pair of Siamese twins and that inanimate piece of wood and white-oak splits began to wheel us around the stage in a regular old-fashioned breakdown. It swung corners with us, promenaded all, backed to places, and, in fact, did everything except change partners, a termination we so earnestly longed for. The chair tried to throw us over the footlights, rammed us between the scenes, and at last was making way with us for a side window when Atkinson whispered in our ear not to let the chair loose. Let it loose! Why we would have given half of our wealth to have been able to let it loose. The chair clung to us closer than a brother, . . . At last Miss Lulu seemed to take pity on us and removing her hands the spell was broken."

In Greensboro, a local "scientist" said Lulu's Power was only an "application of mechanical laws . . . a certain advantage obtained by position." A man also caused an umbrella to fall apart from a trick. Traveling to Conyers, Lulu encountered three girls who claimed to have her ability and an explanation. Of course they had neither.

Back in Atlanta, a flamboyant horse trainer named W. N. Webster took the stage. Described as "a fierce-looking man, tall, raw-boned, with a big mustache, plain clothes, and boots outside his pantaloons," the crowd enthusiastically chanted, "Boots! Boots! Boots!" But the chair soon mastered him, and he claimed no man on earth could have controlled that maddening piece of furniture. An umbrella gyrated so violently that it tore a hole in the scenery.

LULU IN THE HIGHEST

At that point a disturbed woman stood up in the audience and shouted, "Glory to God! Glory to God! Woman rules the world! Oh, God bless Lula Hurst, for she has set woman free!" She was intercepted rushing the stage and shouting, "Glory to God! The Great Jehovah! I'll go to Lula Hurst! I'll come to you, Lula! I'll go to Lula Hurst! God bless you, Lula! God bless you!" The spectacle upset Lulu, who became ill and canceled her next appearance.

After two successful shows at Knoxville, Tennessee, Lulu abruptly told her parents that she would never perform again. Stunned, they offered a number of arguments against her decision. Her career had just begun, and there were lucrative offers for a world tour. Lulu stood firm, writing twelve years later that she did not want "to be looked upon as some abnormal quasi-supernatural sort of a being." She rejected the philosophy of spiritualism that was sweeping the nation and feared that her abilities were fueling superstitious belief. Lulu also stated a desire to finish her education, and that was the end of it.

After two years and a triumphant transcontinental tour, with soap, tobacco, and cigars bearing her name, Lulu retired permanently from the stage. She had certainly fulfilled the oldest entertainment axiom, "Leave 'em wanting more."

Lulu enrolled in Shorter College in Rome, near her home, to study music. The Hurst family returned to Cedar Valley, and Mrs. Hurst told a reporter that Lulu was "more fond of home than ever." She also denied persistent rumors that Lulu had lost her Power.

There had been endless speculation about Lulu's relationship with Paul Atkinson. They denied rumors of love and even a secret marriage while traveling across America, but after two years of study Lulu withdrew from Shorter in December 1886 and returned home to arrange her wedding to Paul, "a quiet affair" held on February 8, 1887, in Cedar Valley, an event that solicited considerable interest from the nation's newspapers. As one observed, Lulu's many male stage victims were "preparing resolutions of condolence to the happy groom; and insurance companies have issued circulars making policies forfeitable when death comes from electric causes. Alas, poor Paul!"

Ten years later, in 1897, Lulu published her memoirs with this long-winded title: *Lulu Hurst (the Georgia Wonder) Writes Her Autobiography and for the First Time Explains and Demonstrates the Great Secret of her Marvelous Power. A Death Blow to Spiritualism and Superstition of Every Kind. A New and Unparalleled Revelation of the Forces That Puzzled and Mystified the Entire Continent* (whew!). Published by Psychic Research Company of Rome, it confidently proclaimed, "Who Reads the Book Can Acquire the Power."

The treatise was equal parts about her stage life and an explanation of the Power. Lulu had given her fame and Power considerable thought since leaving the stage. She awoke one morning in 1895 with insight into the mystery and started writing. The book leaves most readers unsatisfied. She claimed the disturbing experiences at her Cedar Valley home that launched her career were her own childhood pranks. As to the matter of her "Power of Force," it was neither psychic nor spiritualistic nor electrical nor magnetic, but simple physical force manipulating natural laws—the fulcrum, lever, pulley, etc., by which she was able to redirect forces generated against her, the exact things the scientists charged years earlier. Anyone could replicate the tricks, she claimed.

Lulu's writing smacked of show business, proclaiming, in the third person even, "For two years or more she astonished the nation, and then disappeared as suddenly as she had come . . . she flashed athwart the sky of this continent like some weird, supernal meteor, whose nature and mission no one could divine, and, having overwhelmed this hemisphere with consternation and mystery, she suddenly disappeared from the wondering gaze of all, leaving no light behind her to illuminate the deep, dark secret of her marvelous power! . . . College professors, doctors of medicine, scientific investigators, common sense business men, one and all pronounced her wonderful 'Force' and its phenomena to be inexplicable and unfathomable."

One of the more interesting aspects of the book are photographs in which Lulu demonstrates the chair, umbrella, and pool cue tricks.

IT'S THE PEACHES

The void created by Lulu's retirement was instantly filled by others. A near neighbor, Mattie Lee Price of Bartow County, one year younger than Lulu, swore that her power manifested itself at Christmas 1883 during a table-rapping party. After Lulu's father labeled the ninety-pound, fourteen-year-old "a fraud," a Georgia editor said, "She does the same astonishing things that Miss Hurst does." The *New York Times* wrote: "This one is only fifteen years old, but, in addition to Lulu's tricks, her manager alleges that she will twist hickory sticks to pieces in her hands. After her the public may expect a child of ten who will tie a crowbar in a knot, and then a baby of five to lift the end of a freight car. Georgia is prolific, and it is alleged that every girl over twelve years of age in the State is about to start in business as a wonder."

And indeed Mattie Lee was not the last. "Lulu Hursts are springing up in all parts of Georgia," a state paper noted in April 1885. Milledgeville produced a ninety-pound wonder, Dixie Haygood, who was said to lift one thousand pounds. Her manager attempted unsuccessfully to arrange a contest with Lulu. Mrs. C. F. Coleman performed at the YMCA in Atlanta, while Mattie Pound of Macon performed privately, probably because she used dreams to tell fortunes, but she was also alleged to have been a mind reader. "Lulu Hurst and her imitators are utterly eclipsed by this Georgia wonder, because there is no trickery in what she does and because her feats are so remarkable," the *Macon Evening News* declared.

Lulu Hurst spent the last fifty years of her life quietly raising a family in this house in beautiful Madison.

Although she was never identified and never performed, Commerce (then Harmony Grove) laid claim to a woman superior to Lulu, who was "as brimful of electricity as a telephone battery." Her touch caused chairs to fly "around promiscuously."

Performing in New York was a Connecticut girl, and several frauds toured the nation as Lulu—then left town with the receipts before the shows started.

Even if Lulu had merely applied mechanical principles, it means that a Georgia girl, barely a teenager, invented and developed a much-copied and enjoyed entertainment genre. If a humbug, then she deceived hundreds of scientists and thousands of common folks and mystified a nation. By retiring early, completely, and enigmatically, Lulu made herself a legend, still famous 120 years later.

In her brief two-year career, Lulu earned fifty thousand to a hundred thousand dollars, which equates to well over a million dollars by modern standards. It paid off the mortgages on the Hurst properties in Polk County and funded a lavish lifestyle. "While Lulu was lifting around editors, senators, governors and congressmen, she certainly lifted the mortgage off our home, too," her father admitted. A descendant maintained that "Her father had financial difficulty and that she had prayed for power to get them back on their feet."

Lulu and Paul spent most of their married life in Madison, Paul's hometown. The Atkinson family lived at 433 South Main Street in Madison, the house now called the Atkinson-Duffy House.

Their first child, Grady, born on December 28, 1889, was named for *Atlanta Constitution* editor Henry Grady, who had died earlier in the week. Paul Atkinson admired the newsman so much that he wrote a check to start a fund that resulted in the erection of a statue to Grady in downtown Atlanta. A second son, Paul, was born, and Lulu raised the children of her sister, Mamie Alice Hurst Craddock, who had died. It is also believed that the family helped raise or educate the children of two other families. Both sons attended the University of Georgia before returning to Madison to start their own families and work in agriculture and medicine.

Lulu was greatly loved in Madison, where she was known for her charity work. She apparently discouraged discussion of her theatrical career, preferring to be known only as "Miss Lulu," an excellent wife and mother, and a pillar of the community.

Besides initiating the Grady statue, Paul also owned three panoramic paintings (cycloramas) depicting famous Civil War battles, including the famous one preserved in Atlanta, which he displayed across the country. After two of the giant paintings were destroyed in separate incidents, one by tornado, the other by fire, Paul sold the Atlanta panorama, which was eventually donated to the city of Atlanta. The following story is almost certainly a fabrication, but bears repeating. Purportedly angry with scenes of retreating Confederates pursued by victorious Federals in the Battle of Atlanta, Lulu insisted that the fleeing soldiers be repainted in blue and the pursuers in gray.

Of course, Lulu's legend continued to grow despite, or because of, her self-imposed exile from the public eye. In Madison it was alleged that she once helped motivate a train stalled on the tracks. Another tale claims that when fire threatened her home, she hefted a huge trunk of mementos and trotted outside with it. It was said that when her son Grady suffered from terrible headaches, Lulu had but to lay her hand on his forehead and the pain would cease.

Paul, born September 18, 1858, died in 1931 at the age of seventy-three. Lulu lived a long pleasant life in Madison, dying nineteen years later on May 13, 1950, aged eighty-one. They are buried in the Madison city cemetery. The Hursts' homeplace in Collard Valley near Cedartown was destroyed by a fire of mysterious origin in 1978.

TRY AS YOU MAY, TRY AS YOU MIGHT, THE EVIL DEED WILL SEE THE LIGHT

In 1948 John Wallace and his family ruled Meriwether County like a fiefdom. They did what they pleased and nobody dared cross them.

Wilson Turner had sharecropped for Wallace for three and a half years, working one hundred of Wallace's two thousand acres as a tenant farmer and running liquor from Wallace's extensive moonshine industry. After proving Wallace wrong about a 'shine operation, Wallace beat Turner and ran him off the land. To retaliate, Turner foolishly stole two of Wallace's prized cows. He was jailed in Carroll County, then transferred to corrupt Meriwether. On April 20 a trustee released Turner, explaining that the sheriff did not have sufficient evidence to hold him.

After his release Turner ran to his truck, which held only a gallon or so of gasoline—when he was arrested the tank had been full. Turner quickly started for home, but he saw Wallace and three other armed men waiting for him on the courthouse square in Greenville. Turner quickly turned around and fled for Coweta County.

After crossing the county line Turner pulled into a restaurant parking lot shouting for help. Wallace and another man grabbed Turner and dragged him to their car. Angered by Turner's fierce resistance, Wallace raised a sawed-off shotgun into the air with both hands and crashed it down on Turner's head with such force that the stock shattered. The impact killed Turner and caused the gun to discharge.

Believing he had gotten away with murder, Wallace tossed Turner's body down an abandoned well on his vast property and threw a fifty-pound stone on top of it. By the following day he knew that Coweta County sheriff Lamar Potts, an honest and relentless lawman, was after him. Wallace tried to locate the well, but it was lost in fields reclaimed by vegetation.

This brings us to Mayhayley Lancaster, who many people thought was a witch. For as long as anyone could remember she had predicted people's futures, helped locate lost or stolen valuables, and cast spells. She was apparently able to conjure up visions by watching the flames in her fireplace and falling into a deep sleep. In this state the spirits advised her.

Mayhayley lived with her elderly, widowed sister, Sallie, in an 1830s-era cabin in the wilds of Heard County, thirty miles from Greenville and ten miles north of Franklin. Mayhayley was eccentric—she always wore a World War I army cap, a memento of her dead brother; old-fashioned, high-buttoned shoes; and a long woolen skirt. She had one artificial eye. A pack of thirty-seven dogs guarded the cabin and slept among forty bales of cotton, a payment for timber cut from her land long ago, scattered across the yard.

A week earlier Wallace had visited Mayhayley in an effort to locate his cows. After paying her a dollar and a dime, she informed him that Turner had stolen the two animals and that he would be caught and one cow recovered.

Wallace returned to the eerie woman when he failed to relocate Turner's body. After looking into the fire, Mayhayley turned to Wallace and demanded, according to noted author Margaret Anne Barnes, "You killed him anyway, didn't you?" She angrily reminded Wallace that she had told him not to kill Turner. "Danger! Death! Destruction!" she thundered.

Mayhayley knew the body was in a well deep in the woods. She predicted that with help the well could be relocated, but added, "Soon others will be looking," and, worse, "The evil deed will see the light."

After consulting the fire again, she chanted, "Run, run, the trouble's begun. They'll get you, too, before it's all done."

Who will get me? Wallace asked.

"A man who is brave, a man who is true, a man who is just as determined as you."

Wallace enlisted the aid of two of his tenants, borrowed a pickup truck, and rounded up rope, a bucket, burlap sacks, two cords of pinewood, and two five-gallon milk cans filled with gasoline. After a night of searching, the well was located. A rope was looped around the body and it was dragged to the surface. The men wrapped the body in burlap and tied it with rope, then cut down a small pine and slipped it between the ropes. They carried the body several miles from the well.

Wallace considered burying the body, but concluded that Mayhayley would "know" and expose him. The only option was to destroy the body. The corpse was secured to a horse and hauled across a swamp and creek to a moonshine pit twelve feet long, six feet wide, and two feet deep. Wallace stacked the two cords of wood in the depression, then laid Turner's body on top. The gasoline was poured on the pyre and Wallace lit a match. A huge blast shook the woods as sixty-foot flames charred nearby trees.

The fire burned through the night. In the morning Wallace sent the tenants back with feed sacks and a shovel. The pit was scraped to bare earth, the ashes thrown into a creek. In Georgia there is no murder case without a body.

State patrol sergeant J. C. Otwell and Georgia Bureau of Investigation (GBI) agent Jim Hillin learned that Wallace had consulted with Mayhayley. Informed at midnight, Potts, the sheriff, immediately directed the pair to interview the psychic. "Hell, Sheriff," Otwell snickered, "I heard she was a witch."

Potts explained that Mayhayley's appearance and manner disguised an intelligent and law-abiding woman.

"You're not going to believe this," Otwell told Hillin, "but the sheriff ordered us to go see that fortune-teller right now."

Uneasily, the two lawmen disturbed Mayhayley's rest. When told that they were there concerning a murder, Mayhayley screamed, scaring the officers and setting her mangy pack of hounds into a chorus of baying.

ORACLE OF THE AGES

Mayhayley revealed that Wallace had seen her twice—once to find lost cows, and the second to find a lost body. She had told him how to find each. Asked how she knew, Mayhayley replied, "I'm an oracle of the ages. I was born with this power."

When they asked what Wallace had done with the body, Mayhayley demanded her pay, a dollar and a dime.

Why that sum? Hillin inquired.

"A dollar for me. A dime for the dogs."

Mayhayley took out a deck of cards and placed it on a stool in front of the fire. She asked Hillin to cut the deck, which left the king of spades revealed.

"Death!" she shouted.

"Whose?" Hillin asked.

ROADKILL PROPHECY

Mayhayley announced that his outburst had frightened away the spirits, and she would have to utilize the hair from the back leg of a possum (honest; you can't make this stuff up).

Mayhayley removed hair from a snuff can, placed them on her tongue, then spit into the fire. She stared intently into the flames, rocking back and forth and chanting, "Water, fire, water, fire."

Otwell wanted to leave, believing Mayhayley had fallen asleep.

"She's not asleep," commented Miss Sallie from the darkness. "She's having a séance with the spirits." Sallie peeked out the window, then continued, "The moon looks right. She shouldn't have any trouble tonight."

GOOD RECEPTION

Mayhayley suddenly started in her chair. "I see a terrible fire," she said. Asked where the body was, Mayhayley replied, "Gone from its hiding place . . . men, horses, a truck, fire." The old woman then slumped in her chair.

"She needs to rest," Miss Sallie said. "Wrestling with the spirits is a very tiring job."

"I think she's nuts," commented Otwell, but Sheriff Potts was excited. Mayhayley's testimony indicated that Wallace had located the body and tried to conceal it. He explained that the local prosecutor, Luther Wyatt, had used the witch woman as a source of information for years. Criminals regularly went to Mayhayley to ask if they would be caught, in effect confessing their crimes to her. Wyatt would then send someone to talk to Mayhayley. "She gives them a reading and spills the whole story," Potts explained.

Encouraged, Potts began a massive search of Wallace's vast property holdings. The abandoned well, the cremation site, and human remains were soon located. Heavy rains, which would have destroyed much of the evidence, had been predicted for days, but held off until the moment the evidence had been collected.

Mayhayley Lancaster, seer extraordinaire and star witness at one of Georgia's most celebrated trials, practicing her arcane trade. (Courtesy of Heard County Historical Society)

On the first day of Wallace's trial, Mayhayley startled the crowd by appearing in a bright red dress adorned with black dragons and a Shriner's hat. Miss Sallie was also in attendance, every inch covered by black dress, gloves, and hat.

Mayhayley would not be called to testify immediately, so she asked Potts, "You won't mind if I do a little business, will you?"

Potts laughed. "As long as you don't set up shop in the courthouse."

Walking out to the courthouse square, Mayhayley was surrounded by customers. The first man announced that he had bet $370, all he had, that Wallace would not come to trial. Would he win the bet? he asked.

"A fool's way is a fool's pay," she replied.

Mayhayley was the last witness of the day. She described simply Wallace's two visits to her, his requests, and her responses. She told of seeing the body in the well and the green flies that circled it, and the body being moved.

Wallace's attorney, A. L. Henson, attempted to discredit Mayhayley's testimony, but she parried every attempt with intelligence and wit. When he challenged Mayhayley to predict his future, she snapped, "You may get what Turner got." There were no further questions.

TURNER'S LOT

Talking to reporters after the court adjourned for the day, Henson declared: "Not since the seventeenth century has the testimony of a witch been allowed in a court of law."

The trial went downhill from there for Wallace, who did himself irreparable harm by making a daylong statement that strained the credulity of all present.

Near the end, Wallace demanded that his lawyer find a way to "get that damned witch and her spook sister out of here. Every time I look up, I see Mayhayley's glass eye staring at me. She's trying to cast a spell."

Wallace was convicted of murder and sentenced to death by electrocution. Despite a number of delays due to appeals, Wallace was executed on November 3, 1950, one of the first times in Georgia history that a powerful, prominent citizen was executed for killing a lowly tenant farmer.

As he filed the first appeal for Wallace, Henson declared, "The prosecution resorted to everything from sorcery to science."

"I see either life or the electric chair for John Wallace," Mayhayley had assured the late Celestine Sibley, the *Atlanta Constitution* reporter who covered the sensational trial. It was her interviews and descriptions of Mayhayley that made the psychic a national figure.

When asked about the outcome of Wallace's appeals, Mayhayley smiled and said, "I don't want to influence the judge's mind by telling what's going to happen."

Margaret Ann Barnes wrote a best-selling book about this unique trial, *Murder in Coweta County*. Her celebrated account was made into a critically acclaimed television movie that starred Johnny Cash as Sheriff Potts and June Carter Cash, Johnny's wife, as Mayhayley. Andy Griffith, known for portraying a small-town sheriff with a heart of gold, portrayed the evil Wallace.

The trial had garnered national attention and made Mayhayley a celebrity. People from across the United States begged for readings via mail, telephone, and in person. On weekends traffic jammed the primitive dirt road leading to her cabin. Mayhayley raised her rate to two dollars and a dime and Miss Sallie made considerable sums by selling refreshments to those waiting for their turn with Mayhayley. Distrusting banks, they kept the money in mattresses.

Mayhayley's life was a colorful legend long before the Wallace trial. She was born on October 18, 1875, and lived most of her life in the hand-hewn log cabin with its fieldstone chimney her family had owned for a century. She started telling fortunes at age twelve, although her parents would not allow it in the house. She purchased the cabin after her father's death.

Mayhayley was tall and slender. At a time when women wore dresses to their ankles, Mayhayley's fine dresses, often silk, exposed her knees. She favored fancy hats with large bows over her reddish-brown hair, multiple rings, and large hoop earrings. Gold-rimmed spectacles, customarily worn perched near the end of her nose, allowed her to see from her one good eye.

Mayhayley was feisty, one of the smartest and richest citizens of Heard County. She accumulated her fortune through hard work, frugality, and fortune-telling. Mayhayley owned rental property, operated several businesses in Franklin, and had livestock. She and Sallie grew a few acres of corn and cotton and a garden for personal consumption, plowing the ground with mule and ox.

In 1922 and 1926 Mayhayley ran for the thirty-seventh senatorial district of Georgia, which encompassed Heard, Troup, and Carroll Counties, but lost both elections. Her declaration sounded deceptively literate, "made after receiving solicitations and promises of support from many of my partial friends and voters who know me and my qualifications. I am a native of Heard County and my education and life work has thrown me in contact with the farmers, laborers, and business people of the entire state . . . Being a real 'Dirt Farmer' and having lived all my life on the farm, I understand the needs of the farmers as well as the interests of the other classes. If elected I shall render a faithful service and endeavor to prove a profitable servant of the entire public."

Her platform called for better public education, elimination of the poll tax, improved roads and reduction of vehicle taxes, strictly regulated banks, lower penalties for moonshining and violation of fish and game laws, expansion of jury lists, "keeping prison cells of Georgia sanitary," and a lowering of doctor's birthing fees from twenty-five dollars to fifteen.

Rev. Zane D. Chambers stated that after Mayhayley's death, the sheriff and other law-enforcement agents searched the property and three houses she lived in, finding "money under every loose board, in every knothole," and many other sites. "It filled two cotton baskets and three croaker sacks," he said. Apparently, she had not paid taxes on much of her fortune, "and the government got most of it."

It was said that Mayhayley once refused to give one man a reading. That man was killed in a traffic accident on his way home. Another woman was turned away because her companion did not believe in Mayhayley's power.

Young couples would arrive to ask if they would marry, and singles came to ask who they would wed, and all wanted to know the number of children they would have. Pregnant women came regularly to determine the sex of their unborn children. She could "see" the location of lost rings or hunting dogs and stolen property and money. People from Atlanta came for the numbers they should play, "and if they played that number continually for several days, would often win," Reverend Chambers wrote. He also recalled instances when Mayhayley instructed a farmer what he had to do to prevent a rash of deaths among his cattle.

316

Mayhayley told Celestine Sibley, "I've got some learnin'. I taught school. I passed the bar in Carrollton and could practice law, but seeing the future is my art."

Of her "art," Mayhayley said, "It's not a learned gift, it's a borned gift."

Her claim to be a lawyer is probably bogus, although local legend holds that the first law books in Heard County were hers. Under the pen name Uncle Sam, Mayhayley wrote a column for the *Franklin News & Banner* about her part of the county. In one column she claimed to have been awarded a life scholarship (whatever that means) from the American Law School. She did teach at Red Oak.

Mayhayley Lancaster is buried beside her beloved sister, brother, and parents. When I visited the graveyard, someone had left four quarters and a dime on a stone at the end of the family plot. That was the price for a reading by Mahayley—a dollar for her and a dime for her pack of dogs.

Every Sunday Mayhayley and Sallie walked three miles to Caney Head Methodist Church, near Roosterville. Although they often arrived late, they trooped to the front pew, accompanied by several of their pack, who slept beneath the seats. On the way to services they picked wild flowers, and later placed the bouquet on their parents' graves. Mayhayley died on May 22, 1955, at age seventy-nine. Sister Sallie lived another nine years, dying on October 14, 1964. Both are buried in the cemetery at the family church. Over the years, vandals, reportedly college students, chipped pieces off Mayhayley's stone to sell as souvenirs, although tragedy allegedly befell the vandals. Legend has a teenager killed in a car crash after disturbing the grave, and others have reportedly suffered bad luck. The stone was eventually donated to the Heard County Historical Society and the church placed a new one. Engraved on both are a Bible verse chosen by Mayhayley, John 7:5: "For neither did his Brethren believe in him."

Mayhayley's legend looms large in Heard County to this day. Locals claim that she was the county's richest citizen, largest business, and best tourist draw.

THE LATE MADAM BELL

"What you see for others you cannot always see for yourself," psychic Mother Margaret said after Atlanta's most public psychic drowned in 1999. Madam Bell, also known as Judy Marks and Dina Adams, was born on December 3, 1944, in Stockton, California. After her wedding to Bill Marks in a family-arranged marriage, the couple moved to Atlanta, where they had two sons and a daughter.

Bell "always had a gift," a daughter-in-law said. "She always had visions; she could see things nobody else saw."

Bell moved her home and business to Cheshire Bridge Road in 1980. The street was named for Hezekiah Cheshire, a Confederate soldier who died in 1876. Bell encountered his ghost soon after she moved in.

"He is a good spirit, a warm spirit, generous—not cold at all," Bell said. "He sat on the sofa. I have a good feeling about him. We spoke and he seemed happy. He seemed pleased with what is happening on his street."

Bell was not the only odd person in the neighborhood. Just down the street Murray "Doc" Silver Jr. ran a baseball card shop. In 1983 he had helped a former wife of Jerry Lee Lewis, now an Atlanta resident, write *Great Balls of Fire*, a best-selling book made into a wretched movie. His next book, about the "murder" of Elvis Presley, interested no publishers, so Silver went into the sports memorabilia business.

"You couldn't invent the weird stuff that happens in this store," Silver said. "There's a crazy energy that's unlike anywhere else."

During the summer of 1993 a self-proclaimed New Orleans witch entered his store, ripped up a number of San Francisco Giants cards, and cursed the team. "Not long after, the Giants fell out of the lead," Silver noted. "Too bad she didn't come back and do it to Philadelphia," which defeated the Braves.

A prominent Atlanta chef initially feared that Bell's gaudy establishment, two doors down, would drive off his customers. However, "After awhile I told people that the wedding couple could go over there and find out if the marriage was going to work before they came to see me," he joked.

"I see big things for this street," Bell once prophesied in her usual upbeat fashion. "It's going to be a miracle mile."

Bell prospered in the psychic business, opening three locations in Gwinnett and Fulton Counties from headquarters on Cheshire, where a neon sign proclaimed, "Tells past, present, and future." Late-night television commercials touted her ability to advise troubled lovers, and billboards featured an outstretched palm and a royal flush—Bell's symbol. She employed other psychics, who continued the business after her death.

Bell read thousands of palms over thirty years. She once claimed five new walk-in clients a day in the building where she lived and worked. "This is my home," Bell said.

When Bell failed to return home during the early hours of June 22, 1999, her family reported her missing at 3:00 A.M. Five hours later a jogger found her floating facedown in a shallow reflecting pool at the Buckhead Ritz-Carlton. There was no evidence of foul play. Her purse, stuffed with cash destined for a night deposit, was found on a bench, her shoes were placed neatly on the grass, and her new Mercedes 500-S was parked nearby. Police speculate that she had gone wading and fell in the five-foot-deep pool. Police ruled her tragic death an accident.

"I don't know what she was doing up there," said daughter Debbie Bell, who had a role in the family enterprise. "I think it was a meditational place for her. She loved to be around water, that was her peace time."

BELL WEATHERS

In 1987 Bell read palms, a crystal ball, and tarot cards at an Arthritis Foundation benefit at the Ritz-Carlton. Considering that each participant paid $125, her predictions promised prosperity. When *Georgia Economou* revealed Bell's prediction that she would be "successful, very successful," another participant exclaimed, "She told me the same thing!" Imagine!

Novelist Stuart Woods was told that his career was "going to go very well," although he expressed disappointment because she did not supply him with a title for his next book.

"I see a lot of problems ahead in the Congress," Bell announced for 1996. It would have been a surprise if that prediction hadn't occurred, but she then made the mistake of getting specific. "A lot of confusion, conflict, and pressure," she said. "It won't stop for two years. It's too late for Mr. Clinton to be elected again. He sent people to war. He did what was right, but it won't help him in the election."

Considering that Atlanta was hosting the Olympics, her final thought was certainly safe: "Atlanta will do well in 1996. I see a very prosperous year ahead."

Days before the Super Bowl in 1999, Bell was asked if the Atlanta Falcons would prevail.

"I'm speaking with the angel right now," Bell said. "She says it will be something great. The Falcons are very good and powerful and are headed to something very new and powerful. They are going to win. Who are they playing? The Indians or something?"

The Broncos, she was informed.

"Yeah? The Broncos are very powerful. I'm getting some vibrations that (the Falcons) are going to win by seven points. They'll win by seven points in the first game, but they'll stop being so good in the second or third game."

It was then explained that the Super Bowl consists of one game, with four quarters.

"Okay. It will be in the fourth quarter. I'm not into the game, but my husband is going." Certainly, the signs looked good. It was the thirty-third Super Bowl and the thirty-third year of the Falcons' existence. Furthering the string of threes and its divisibles, the Super Bowl had been started in '66, and the year was '99. Of course, Atlanta was crushed, 34-19.

WHAT WOULD PERRY MASON THINK?

Atlanta police officer J. M. Oglesby Jr. claimed that sixteen-year-old David Samples pulled a knife on him just before sunup on August 1, 1984, forcing the patrolman to fire his pistol. The Cabbagetown resident died from five gunshot wounds. Oglesby was cleared by the police department, but a civil suit filed by Samples's parents dragged on for over five years.

Several days before a verdict in the civil case was delivered, *Atlanta Journal Constitution* writer Michele Hiskey reported on a man in the employ of Jeffery L. Sakas, the Samples's attorney. His name was Bob Plummer, and he was a psychic. Each day he entered the courtroom, spent twenty seconds finding his altered state, and prayed for two "spirit guides" to place him "inside the circle of white light." Plummer was then ready to work—reading the auras of witnesses, lawyers, the judge, and jury members—which allowed him to divine their thoughts and emotions. Auras, colored glows that surround all things according to some, let the psychic decide which witness to call or avoid, whether the judge would allow certain evidence, and when witnesses were lying. During the proceedings Plummer passed this information on to Sakas.

SHE'S A RAINBOW (ROLLING STONES)

Green means deceit. Light blue denotes calm; dark blue distress. Yellow indicates mental illness or drug use, and red physical illness. The aura of a stressful individual hangs tight against their body.

"If anyone lies, a gray halo with red shoots from around their head," said the fifty-three-year-old psychic. "The first time I saw a lawyer lie in court, I couldn't believe it."

Federal judge Orinda D. Evans was aware of the psychic's presence, but it was a surprise to Oglesby's attorney, W. Roy Mays III, who said, "I'm rather complimented that they think they need a psychic in this case. I guess if someone can look into folks' minds, you can get them to do it in the courtroom."

One might justifiably ask, what was Sakas's motivation? He responded, "When the stakes become very high, each side is going to be looking for an edge. Then you might find more people like Bob in the courtroom . . . We have an arsenal of tools, and he's one of them."

How Do You Itemize a Psychic's Services?

The unlikely duo of Plummer and Sakas originated over a decade earlier when they met in a softball league. Ten years later Plummer suggested that his services might assist the lawyer.

"I thought he had to be nuts," was Sakas's initial response. "But he said he could size up a person on a rapid basis, and that's what you need in selecting a jury."

As a Southern Baptist, Sakas rejected the idea that Plummer was a psychic. He preferred to believe that his friend is "supersensitive" to the emotions of others.

"He has a gift, and what he calls himself is really not important," Sakas said, doing a good imitation of a lawyer.

Aura Phonics?

Plummer said his psychic ability had been revealed only a few years earlier, when the pastor of a Scientology Church in Florida clued him to an earlier life as a preacher and requested that he prophesy for members of the congregation. He honed his skill in aura interpretation and turned pro after a fellow guild member accurately predicted the death of Plummer's son. "That pre-information helped me handle my son's death," Plummer said.

Mary E. Pratt, executive director of the New Age Information Network, based in Atlanta, believed this was the first instance of a psychic being used in a courtroom. She approved, claiming that a "psychic is almost like a lie detector."

Plummer believes that "A day will come when there will be a psychic sitting in every courtroom. And maybe two competing with each other." (Hell's bells, let's pick a jury made up entirely of psychics and achieve true justice.)

Plummer claimed that anyone can utilize their psychic powers by calling on their guardian angels and focusing on their first feelings toward people. "Men call it a gut reaction," he explained. "Women call it intuition. The difference is listening to it and trusting it."

Plummer worked with businesses, advising them about mergers, new product lines, and hiring. He had plans to establish a network of three hundred psychics for use in locating missing children.

Plummer claimed to know the outcome of the civil suit, but would not reveal it. His team lost the case the following day. He also flubbed a prominent missing person's case. A week after Julie Love was reported missing, her family asked Plummer to help locate her. He led police to some woods near Stone Mountain, but they found nothing. In October 1989, Love's body was found in northwest Atlanta, far from his prediction. But did Plummer admit defeat? Of course not. "I still think her body was moved," he maintained. "The aura was so strong in Stone Mountain I thought I'd step on her."

SPIRIT WORLD

SEE ME, TOUCH ME, HEAL ME

The tiny Macon County community of Ideal yielded Georgia's greatest faith healer, the *Macon Telegraph* stated in 1939. Lonnie Taylor, who had two months of formal education and operated a four-hundred-acre farm, had always considered himself a preacher called by God. However, he "refused to bind myself to the regulations of my church creed," Taylor said, and as a result received limited opportunity to preach his hellfire messages and was never ordained.

Taylor's life seemed ended during the winter of 1935. At the age of fifty-five, he was confined to bed for forty-nine days by a serious illness. However, on that last day two angels that "didn't have any clothes on, had wings, but looked sort of hazy all over," appeared in his sick room. They bore good tidings for Taylor. "They approached my bed and told me that God wanted me to live and continue to preach, but I wouldn't need any Bible or hymn book. They said I had been a chosen vessel since my birth and that I would be given another weapon—the power to heal the sick. Hereafter I was to preach to one man as though he was a congregation."

After receiving the message, Taylor decided that he should obey the Bible's admonition to cut off the sinful parts of his body and called for wife Florence to fetch a butcher knife. Thankfully, "when the knife arrived the angels told him God would be willing to overlook the evil parts," the *Telegraph* reporter wrote.

Taylor followed his divine instructions. Four years later he had seen thirty-five thousand patients and claimed success in every case save for three notable exceptions. Saturdays brought about sixty afflicted people, and Sundays up to 150 people, who rode in cars, trucks, chartered buses, and wagons down the rutted, narrow, dirt track to Taylor's home. His reputation spread throughout Georgia and many other states.

Taylor took on every comer, no matter how trivial or desperate their conditions, from colds to cancer. He offered visitors one hundred unsolicited testimonials written by all kinds of folks—the barely literate to those educated at universities.

The Holy Spirit instructed Taylor to gradually heal the sick in three sessions. "It is the Spirit's ruling that I cure the afflicted gradually. So I give them three separate treatments, one for the Father, one for the Son, and one for the Holy Spirit." On three occasions Taylor rejected the Spirit's admonition and attempted to heal the sick all at once. In each case the patients "fell out and died on me in five or ten minutes."

On one occasion, feeling particularly powerful, Taylor lined up twenty-five supplicants and walked down the line, briefly laying on hands and "relieving the suffering of all."

Taylor charged no fee for his clients' healing, but did expect a gift at some time. However, he likened the response to Jesus healing the ten lepers, saying, "only one returned to thank him."

Accused of reading crystal balls, Taylor stoutly denied it. "Telling fortunes belongs to the devil," he said emphatically.

FROM GOVERNMENT ARCHIVES

During the Great Depression the U.S. government hired many people who otherwise would have been unemployed. This number included all manner of artists and writers, who fanned out across the country to record the nations' folklore. On March 6 and 7, 1939, Grace McCune interviewed Nick Waller, who lived on Tabernacle Street in Athens. Waller was a successful black farmer and a locally respected preacher-prophet. McCune's transcript is preserved in the *American Life Histories Manuscripts* from the Federal Writer's Program, which functioned between 1936 and 1940.

"They said I was always a very peculiar sort of a chap even when I was just a little tike," Waller said. "I was always asking questions. I was gifted with some kind of a strange power, but it was sometime before I could really understand this strange and wonderful power. Fact is, I don't understand it now. But things just come to me. I can see them and tell folks for it is just like a vision."

ELI'S COMING

"I have been wonderful blest for God gives me these visions so that I can help folks and I have been so thankful, but Mistress, war is coming. I know it is, 'cause I had the same vision before the World War. I has seed the people gatherin' together and marchin' in crowds, and the Bible full-filling its teachins', for it says, 'There shall be wars and rumors of war,' and the war that's comin' fast is goin' to be bad 'cause folks is worse'n ways than they were in the last war. I has had visions and predicted for our governors."

His claim of predicting for governors cannot be substantiated, but Waller called World War II six months before it started in Europe, and two and a half years before the United States was drawn into it.

PSYCHIC MALPRACTICE
A bizarre murder case played out in Macon in late March 1946, when Beulah Brown took a knife and stabbed Mary Calhoun, a coworker at Southern Crate and Veneer Company, ten times. Brown freely admitted that she had killed Calhoun, but only because the woman had bewitched her.

"I had pains in my joints and side and all over, and I had a breaking out on my head," she said. "It was from a spell Calhoun put on me. I told her right after Christmas to take it off, but she said she didn't know anything about it. I told her again today (March 28) and she still said she didn't do it, but I know she did."

Calhoun probably had nothing to do with casting an evil spell on Brown, who had been treated for syphilis for a year. That undoubtedly accounted for her ailments, although she claimed to have suffered from the witching for ten years. So what motivated Brown? A local psychic.

Madame Deas (Peggy Pearl Harris) told Brown that a woman named Mary had bewitched her. Madame Deas and a second area psychic, Ozie Haralson, gave Brown potions to ward off the evil spell. Apparently, their cures failed to work. Deas and Haralson were arrested and charged with practicing (or mediuming) without a license.

Thirty years later Haralson was still in the psychic business. A *Macon Telegraph & News* article published on June 17, 1978, quoted the man as receiving forty to fifty calls a day from around the country. He also answered about eighty letters a week from people seeking his help.

JESUS CHRIST, SUPERPSYCHIC
Active in the Methodist church, Haralson saw no conflict between Christianity and his psychic sideline, saying, "The greatest psychic was our Lord Jesus Christ. I possess only a fraction of the power he had."

ENOUGH TO WONDER
Psychic James van Praagh was touting a new book in May 1998, when *Atlanta Journal Constitution* staff writer Bill Hendrick sat for a reading. Hendrick considered himself a skeptic before and after the session, but Praagh made him wonder. The psychic said that Hendrick's great grandfather's

name was Jim, a fact which the reporter had forgotten. Praagh said Hendrick's father was attempting to communicate with him, but it was his first attempt and "he might not know how to do it." Hendrick was shocked to realize it was the second anniversary of his father's death. Praagh told Hendrick that his grandfather was concerned about the hardwood floors in his house, which he and his wife had been restoring. Praagh finished by saying that Hendrick's grandmother had called his grandfather "Poppy." Hendrick was certain that was incorrect, but after consulting with a sister, aunt, and his mother, he learned it was correct. Not earthshaking information certainly, but food for thought.

THE SHOTGUN APPROACH

Are psychics ever wrong? Damnbetcha, all the time, but they, like doctors, prefer to bury their mistakes. Law-enforcement officers have spent thousands of hours beating the bushes while following a psychic's lead, and the families of missing persons have spent untold sums of money on consultations which never panned out.

For instance, in 1992 Charles T. White was accused of murdering Randy Beck. Beck was known to have visited White before the murder, blood was found in his home, and White's father told police that his son had confessed to slitting Beck's throat while resisting a sexual assault. Despite these facts, the prosecution felt shaky because there was no body. Psychics sent police searching along GA 400, but nothing was found. White was convicted, but police continued following tips from the public, including a number from psychics. One karmac wrote that the body would be found lying against the fence of a factory on a slight hill beside a minor road that paralleled GA 400.

"We get a lot of these kinds of things that are just too far out and not likely to be true," said Gwinnett County district attorney Daniel J. Porter, "but this one was just too specific to pass up." Nothing was found.

Atlanta psychic John Twombly predicted that 1992 might bring the crash of an alien spaceship, and the United States and several other national governments would acknowledge the reality of UFOs. Neither happened, although he also predicted bad weather around the world, including floods and drought in the United States—a prediction difficult to miss in such a vast land.

In 1991 Hazel Wood's prediction that Miss Georgia USA, Tamara Rhoads, would finish first or runner-up in the Miss USA pageant came a cropper.

A rather embarrassing episode occurred in April 1993, when the city of Chamblee decided to cancel a Psychic Affair, which had been a monthly event for a year. A group of psychics had met in the city's civic center, paying a rental fee of $350 for each day. When a citizen complained of "fortune-telling" being conducted on city property, city attorney Joe Fowler checked local ordinances. There it was, at least thirty-five years old, a statute which outlawed "the business of palmistry, fortune-telling, crystal reading, or predicting future occurrences."

That type law was "fairly common," said Ed Sumner, attorney for the Georgia Municipal Association. "Especially in the twenties and thirties citizens passed laws severely restricting fortune-telling."

"I think it's an archaic rule," asserted John Twombly, whose turban accented his long black beard at the last affair. He used tarot cards and zodiac signs to advise his customers. "I think Chamblee is enlightened. I'm almost blown away that they even have rules against it."

Organizer Mary Pratt was "surprised. They clearly knew what we were doing. The police let me in each time and locked up when I was through."

At the last fair twenty-five psychics had paid fifty dollars each and serviced up to two hundred clients for ten dollars apiece. Crystals and jewelry were sold, and a photographer captured auras on film.

None of the psychics saw the end of their enterprise coming. Ironically, the night before the final affair, the Georgia Skeptics organization had met at the civic center. Perhaps they hexed the psychics.

PSYCHIC, WIN THYSELF

When the Big Game lottery pot hit $160 million in early April 1999, Atlanta psychic Victoria Weston felt she had to play—she lost. "I got two or three of the numbers right," she said. Many clients ask her to determine the winning numbers, but it doesn't work. Why? "My readings are clouded by people's wishful thinking," she said. "Maybe they aren't supposed to win."

Weston doubts she'll play again, saying, "I like to earn my money the old-fashioned way. By predicting futures" (at seventy-five dollars an hour, no less).

SECRETS OF THE TRADE

Some psychics only work personally, one on one with customers, reading palms or touching hands, consulting crystals as well as traditional crystal balls, tarot cards, and other devices. Other psychics operate long distance, over the phone, or through the mail with photos and samples of handwriting. Clients are generally concerned with their love lives, pregnancy, legal issues, finances, family, careers, and other personal problems.

"A reading helps to relieve their minds and lets them get on with other things in their lives," said DeKalb County psychic Carol Carpenter.

Carpenter believes the gift is genetic—her mother and father had psychic abilities, as do her two children and six grandchildren.

"Everyone is psychic to a certain degree," which might be called intuition, she maintained. "Psychic ability is something that is nurtured, not learned." The bottom line for her is, "Most people are frightened of the unknown," and they come to her for information.

She tells first-timers not to speak as she holds their hand, allowing psychic images to grow vivid and voices to become louder.

"I don't have to meet a person in order to read them," she says. "I can pick up on their vibrations from their handwriting or from a picture."

Carpenter does not tell customers everything, but attempts to determine "how much information a person can handle. I don't handle death when I see it—people don't need to know everything. If it's something they can change, I'll tell them."

A Rose Is a Rose

Mrs. Rose of Stockbridge, Henry County's only palm reader with a business license, interviewed in 1999, claimed her great-grandparents "saw I had the gift, the knowledge to read people's spirits." She was two, and the talent had been inherited from Native American ancestors.

"Everybody has a spirit or an aura that I can physically see," she said. "Everyone has different colors revolving around them that I can read using crystals." Palm readings cost twenty dollars, detailed crystal readings up to one hundred dollars. Palms allow her to "read so much . . . a person's lifeline and information about their health and emotions." She also holds crystals in her palm and interprets "feelings and vibrations."

The industry has been hurt by the estimated seventeen thousand psychics who work via the Internet, and the immensely popular and heavily advertised phone services. She also feels they give genuine psychics like herself a bad name. "All they tell you is general stuff, things you already know about yourself. They don't make any revelations or anything. How can you read a person over the phone?"

In past times people knew where to find a local psychic. In Pike County a century ago there was the "fortune-teller of Pine Mountain" who located lost items and counseled lovers. Princess Pizada did the same from Buzzard Mountain in her nine-by-seven-foot hut, at least until she was converted during a summer revival. She claimed divine providence served her well. The great tornado of 1893 uprooted trees all around her humble home but spared it damage.

Bulloch County newspapers on January 21, 1932, revealed that a fortune-teller had located the body of T. J. Finch, who had drowned four days earlier. The man had fallen out of a boat while fishing on the Ogeechee River, and a three-day search had proven fruitless. The psychic was then called in and "pointed out the spot where the body could be found."

The Mitchell County psychic was R. W. Posey, known as the "Mystery Man" after he arrived from Canada in 1890. He baffled many by determining where lost and stolen items could be found, and where murderers and their victims were located. Posey died in 1904, but his son set up shop in Moultrie, where he earned a national reputation.

From Cherokee County came a story of a man who could "stop blood, or heal serious wounds" by the exercise of some necromantic act. A local conjure could teach mothers how to heal various infant afflictions, but one condition was a pledge never to reveal the healer's secrets.

VERY SPECIAL PEOPLE

Once known as freaks and geeks, individuals with curious physical attributes have formed a union and lobbied for the title "special people." Some consider the days of circus sideshows to be long vanished and good riddance, but the display of these people was once considered great sport.

HEAVYWEIGHT DIVISION

William J. Cobb put his weight to productive use. Born in Georgia in 1926, he became a professional wrestler under the moniker "Happy Humphrey." At 802 pounds in 1962, he had only to sit on opponents to win matches.

Cobb's appetite was prodigious. He once ate nineteen pounds of catfish within an hour, and consumed three or four loaves of bread with meals.

It should be no surprise that Cobb's health was poor. He was only six feet tall, and no human heart could pump enough oxygen to supply a man his size. Cobb needed to stop and rest after taking only a few steps.

Fortunately, Cobb had enormous willpower. Through a careful diet he lowered his weight to 644 pounds. At that point he volunteered to participate in a study sponsored by the Eugene Talmadge Memorial Hospital Obesity Clinic in Augusta. Cobb was placed on a thousand-calorie-a-day diet, but, considering his condition, physical exercise was forbidden. Every eight weeks his diet was changed from high protein to high fat and then to high carbohydrates. When he left the hospital eighty-three weeks later, Cobb weighed 232 pounds. His waist had shrunk from 101 inches to forty-four. He could no longer participate in his former profession, but had gained a chance to live a normal life and reach old age.

One of Georgia's earliest fat residents was Sterne Simmons of Lincoln County. His gravestone, in the family cemetery nine miles north of Linton near Honora, records his birth date, August 22, 1824, death date, August 25, 1853 (he lived twenty-nine years), and his weight, 650 pounds. Many exaggerated tales were told of his ravenous appetite, and his prosperous family had a special, reinforced buggy made for him. The morbid curious (that would be us) flocked from miles around to see the fat man, but he did not willingly display himself. He never married and lived with his folks. On the day he was buried, the door facings of his house had to be removed so the body could be extracted.

THE PINHEADS
In circus circles, one particular type of exhibition freak is the pinhead. Such a human has a small skull and a receding hairline. Known to medical science as a microcephalus, those afflicted are generally mentally retarded to some degree.

During the 1920s America's most famous pinheads were a brother and sister from Georgia. Known as Pipo, the boy, and Zipo, the girl, their intelligence was estimated at one and a half and five years, respectively.

Pipo and Zipo were discovered by Sam Wagner, who wanted to display them at the World Sideshow Circus at Coney Island. They were reluctant to leave their native South, so Wagner persuaded New York City mayor Jimmy Walker to involve the mayor of the siblings' hometown. The pinheads were induced to travel to New York, where they were initially so self-conscious that they covered their pointed heads with their arms. Wagner eventually convinced the pair to exhibit their peculiar "gift" with great pride.

During the Great Depression the two earned seventy-five dollars a week. They wintered at home in Georgia and owned a car, although one hopes they did not personally drive it.

THREE-LEGGED WILLIE
Not a freak, but a curiosity, was Robert McAlpin Williamson, born in Wilkes County in 1806. At age fourteen Williamson was afflicted by what was called "white swelling," which forced his right leg to turn up at an angle at the knee. He was outfitted with a wooden peg leg and got around fine, but as he stumped about on a leg and a peg, the afflicted leg stuck out. Local Indians dubbed him Three-Legged Willie, and the moniker stuck.

While recuperating, Williamson studied law and passed the bar at age nineteen. One year later, following a duel resulting from an affair of the heart, Three-Legged Willie fled to Texas. There he became known as the Patrick Henry of Texas, fighting for Texas independence and enjoying a long political and judicial career. His Texas gravestone recognizes him as the famed "Three-Legged Willie."

PRETZEL LOGIC (STEELY DAN)
Talbot County produced a noted contortionist, Charles Lumpkin, born in 1839. On February 7, 1889, the *LaGrange Reporter* stated that the fifty-year-old man "is as supple as an active boy . . . He can stand on one foot

and put the other on top of his head, and when sitting he can put both feet on top of his head.

"He can place a comb among his toes and comb his hair with either foot. He can stand with either foot reversed so that either heel will be squarely in front of his body, and can stand laplegged and jump twenty feet in three jumps."

Lumpkin was also recognized for his "considerable jaw power. He has been known to bite the blade of a pocket knife in two."

Despite his talents, Lumpkin never performed publicly, nor did he drink, swear, or consume coffee. These latter attributes may have been his most notable accomplishments.

THE HOLY GRAIL

In 1905 a Bulloch County newspaper reported that two of its citizens were on the brink of perfecting perpetual motion machines. After tinkering for some months, Benjamin H. Olliff "now believes he has the problem solved. We understand that it works by a pressure process, and those who have seen it say it is a go."

N. V. B. Foss had also been addressing the problem, but found "he has more confidence in (Olliff's) than in his own and will go ahead and assist Mr. Olliff in making his plan a success."

At the time the U.S. government had offered ten thousand dollars to the person who perfected a perpetual motion machine, and untold wealth would be the inventor's to command. Obviously, it has yet to be perfected.

9

UFOs: The Troup-Heard Corridor, the World's Most Active UFO Theater

MEET MR. UFO

John C. Thompson was a marine before attending the University of Tennessee, where he majored in geology. He worked as a uranium geochemical prospector, a petroleum engineer, and a sales engineer, and he has operated an insurance agency in LaGrange since 1981. He lives in rural Liberty Hill with his wife and five children.

Thompson was a skeptic regarding UFOs until less than a decade ago, when he and his family had a dramatic sighting of an unexplained object. He joined MUFON the following year and began active investigations a year after that, mostly of sightings in Troup and Heard Counties. Over a two-year period Thompson has recorded over one hundred formal cases, and 150 additional verbal investigations. He found half of all reported sightings are of Venus, the brightest planet which is perceived "as a round, white disc hanging in the air" at its closest approach to earth. About 10 percent of sightings cannot be explained, and that leaves a "handful of really solid cases" unidentified. Thompson firmly believes there is "an extraterrestrial component" in the UFO mystery. He is a former president of Georgia MUFON, and is a founding member of ISUR.

WELCOME TO THE THC

Thompson describes the THC (Troup-Heard Corridor) as an area in the piedmont of west-central Georgia and east-central Alabama with "a long history of UFO sightings and paranormal activity." It measures 120 miles from east to west, and seventy miles from north to south, a rural area of hard rock covered by extensively forested hills. It includes the counties of

331

The mountains of northeast Georgia, shown near Chatsworth, seem to be a corridor for UFOs. Bigfoot has been seen in this vast wilderness area, and ancient artifacts such as Fort Mountain are also found here.

Troup, Heard, Harris, Meriwether, Upson, and Talbot, and seems to funnel UFOs toward Atlanta. Although there is aircraft radar coverage in Atlanta and Columbus, located one hundred miles apart, UFOs are typically seen below two thousand feet, which is beneath detection range.

Thompson has found that hilly areas "with a sparse population base and scanty radar coverage are where real UFOs are seen." He also believes that a fault line somehow attracts extraterrestrial craft. Located just below LaGrange, the line is "very noticeable" on satellite photos, a "long, straight line that separates the North American tectonic plate from the old African plate, which separated eons ago."

FROM THE ARCHIVES

The earliest UFO sighting in the THC was made by a man who had been a teenager in 1938 when it occurred in LaGrange. The daylight sighting featured a UFO as large as a modern aircraft that flew at one thousand miles per hour, "faster than anything he'd ever seen and made some erratic maneuvers" at an altitude of four thousand to five thousand feet.

In September 1952 a roofer in the Troup County community of Mountville spotted a huge saucer-shaped UFO, sporting a glowing blue and yellow bottom, hover ten feet above the ground. The object hissed as it stirred the grass beneath it. After twenty minutes the craft flew straight up into the sky and disappeared among the stars.

The following day a fleet of army helicopters swarmed over the site. Because the vehicles were a novelty at the time, they attracted a great deal of attention. After the choppers disappeared, the roofer, his brother, and others examined the site and found a "blackened circle of a quarter mile around—the same size as the giant UFO." Two days later the circle was still hot and seemed "cooked" rather than burned.

In the fall of 1963 a young housewife in LaGrange sighted a giant, football-shaped UFO composed of flashing lights that hovered twenty feet above the railroad tracks near Greenville Street. A railroad worker observed the same object two months later.

GEORGIA'S OWN BELGIAN WAFFLES—THE GIANT FLYING TRIANGLE
AND ITS VARIATIONS: THE DELTA-V, BOOMERANG, ARROWHEAD,
DIAMOND, AND HORSESHOE
The earliest reported sighting of this majestic craft in Georgia occurred at midnight on August 1, 1973, in Morrow. Described as a gray metallic triangle with rounded corners, it measured fifteen feet to a side and had mounted rows of white lights, bright as car headlights, on the sides.

A dramatic sighting of a unique UFO that might be considered a triangle occurred at 2:30 A.M. on November 7, 1984. A man described as a prominent political scientist and two-time Fulbright scholar, presumably a professor at West Georgia College, and his wife, also well educated, lived six miles west of Carrollton on Garrett Circle. The couple was disturbed by "deafening waves of sound" that they called "a ninety-decibel-level sound of electricity as with a giant generator, and waves and waves of deep bass undertones."

Awakened, they saw extremely bright lights through their windows and raced outside to the front yard, where they saw an object shaped like a "vertically flying oil rig or wide-width broadcast tower." It was 150 feet high and thirty feet wide, approaching from a forest one hundred yards away and making the slow pace of one to two miles an hour. The craft stopped spinning as it came into view and proceeded over them at no more than thirty feet "in a *vertical* flying position" and cleared the roof of the one-story home and a pecan tree by one to fifteen feet.

The UFO had about three dozen intensely bright, arclike lights, most of them brilliant white but a few red and all randomly distributed across the bottom of the object. The couple thought the material of the craft was "black mat invisible," for the lights revealed no physical object behind them.

One hundred feet behind the UFO were two or three "red translucent and free-floating globes" measuring ten to fifteen feet in diameter. The husband called them "directionally motivated soap bubbles" that "had no discernible content inside." They floated randomly and maintained the same distance from the primary object, but were not connected to it or each other.

The man paced along with the UFO through the backyard to a fence, only ten feet below the ship, for several minutes of the ten-minute sighting. "I could walk along with the craft across our yard slowly and keep up with it," for seventy yards, he wrote, ending at his backyard fence. He clearly saw the lights for several minutes from a position only twenty feet beneath it, but "hard as I tried, I could not see past the bright lights to a surface." He felt he could have struck the UFO with a thrown apple as it cast shadows while flying over the pecan tree.

The couple wisely refrained from discussing the objects until they had written separate accounts and made drawings of the UFO.

Half an hour after the aircraft passed, the sound of helicopters and airplane engines drew the couple outside again, where one-half mile away two black, low-flying military helicopters were scouring the ground with searchlight beams. They were accompanied by a slow, low-altitude, two-engine plane that circled a radius of one mile before following the path of the UFOs. Secretive helicopters have often been observed in the wake of Georgia UFOs.

THE AURORA GEORGIALIS

A tenuous connection may be drawn between the triangles and an object seen at 5:00 P.M. on May 10, 1992, by Glenn Emery, who was gardening outside his Stone Mountain home when a peculiar sound attracted his attention. Looking up, he spotted the largest aircraft he had ever seen. It had a large forward wing and twin engines that emitted an extremely loud, deep-pitched beating sound. It flew at an estimated altitude of ten thousand to fifteen thousand feet, higher and faster than the Hartsfield airliner traffic clearly visible to him, and it left no contrail.

Local airports and Dobbins Air Force Base pleaded ignorance of the craft, although they later announced that a Metropolitan Life blimp had been in the area.

William B. Scott, editor of *Aviation Weekly & Space Technology*, stated that Emery was probably the first person to sight an experimental, extremely high-speed and high-altitude space-spy plane developed by the U.S. government. Named *Aurora*, it allegedly has the capability of launching payloads into space. Previously, the plane had only been heard late at night above Nevada and California.

Mention of the mystery in the *Atlanta Constitution* on May 15 brought dozens of calls from people who had also seen an odd aircraft, but most thought it was a strange plane called a Beechcraft Starship—a fiberglass airplane that looks like "they're flying backward," said Peachtree-DeKalb Airport director Ted Orvold. One operated out of his facility.

Emery rejected this explanation, saying the Beechcraft was "about the size of the tail" of the aircraft he spotted.

In September editor Scott revealed that a man had spotted the experimental plane over California's Mojave Desert. His and Emery's description matched in every detail, he claimed.

I do not doubt what Emery reported, but a highly secret aircraft being tested at night over barren areas of the West certainly would not have been flown across the country and through a densely populated urban area in daylight. Perhaps it was a variation of our triangular UFO, or a "phantom" space-spy craft.

One of our most substantial flying triangles was sighted in June 1995, by a state trooper from the Manchester post. The officer was patrolling U.S. 80 in Talbot County at 10:00 P.M. when he spotted a "football-field-size" black triangle with large orange lights. As he watched the craft, it began to pulse, then spun rapidly and flew off almost instantaneously.

The startled trooper immediately pulled over the car in front of him to see if the driver had seen the UFO. He had, and the officer taped his description and called the incident into headquarters.

Other witnesses confirmed the story to UFO investigators, stating that the triangle initially moved at no more than a walk, then accelerated to a speed of several thousand miles per hour. The craft was so low and vast that it blocked out the sky above the viewers.

ALIENS IN THE SKY WITH DIAMONDS

A relative of the triangle is the diamond-shaped craft, which two families observed at 10:20 P.M. on July 19, 1995, in LaGrange. A grandmother was standing on her porch stairs when she sighted a red blinking light in the sky that suddenly sped up and raced away. She went inside, but returned five minutes later when she heard her children and grandchildren screaming from the porch. Granny found everyone pointing at a diamond configuration with bright center lights and greenish blue lights at two ends shining down. The object, the size of a minivan and "navy ship gray" in color, was at treetop level and just one hundred feet way. The UFO circled the house for ten minutes at fifteen to twenty miles per hour and approached to within fifty feet. The experience terrified the grandmother, who huddled behind a vehicle with a child while the object passed directly overhead. A total of six family members witnessed the spectacle.

Six minutes later and two blocks away two men saw a UFO with red and blue lights and a large central white light that alternately hovered and moved slowly at an altitude of about two thousand feet. One man spotted a triangular arrangement of "arms," like deployed landing gear, between the lights during the four-minute sighting. One witness from the original family encounter had also noticed this "protrusion."

In 1996 three witnesses had repeated sightings of a huge boomerang UFO in Alpharetta. Over a period of eight months, mother, sister, and grown daughter saw the craft both in daylight and at night. The size, depending on its distance from the observer, was estimated at 150 yards wide or larger.

At 7:30 P.M. on Halloween 1996, two boys out trick-or-treating in LaGrange saw a car-sized boomerang or horseshoe-shaped UFO with three large lights as intense as car headlights and twenty smaller lights. The front sported a blinking white light, and on each end was a yellow and a red light that remained steady. Rows of smaller white lights were located between the larger lights. The UFO was zigzagging at low speed five hundred feet directly above the witnesses, but made no noise. Over the next three minutes the UFO ascended and descended and sped up between zigzags.

EARTH LIGHTS

At 8:00 P.M. on February 7, 1997, a 2.0 Richter scale earthquake occurred beneath western Georgia, accompanied by a tremendous boom. At 9:00 P.M. a woman was talking outside her house with her sister-in-law and a teenager when she spotted three enormous soft white lights arranged in a triangle flying directly overhead at twenty miles per hour. Each light, four to six feet in diameter, resembled the moon. The lights moved in unison, two leading, at an altitude between five hundred and one thousand feet. From the woman's description of the minute-long sighting, John Thompson estimated its size at 150 to 200 feet on each side.

Ten minutes later a roughly similar craft was seen seventeen miles north in Franklin by a fifty-year-old woman, her sixteen-year-old daughter, and a fifty-nine-year-old relative. Their UFO had at least forty-five steady red, blue, white, and yellow lights. It had flown rapidly until nearing the witnesses, when it slowed to a walking pace, inducing one to flee indoors. As the silent craft passed directly overhead at treetop level the two remaining witnesses saw additional lights underneath.

Over the following months unusually shallow earth tremors were experienced across Heard County.

THE HERKY-JERKY UFO

At 11:30 P.M. on March 4, 1997, a couple who operated a horse ranch east of Canton in Cherokee County arrived home to find a large UFO hovering above the pines. As they watched, the triangle, or boomerang, descended within two hundred feet of their barn in a series of jerky motions. Except for a dull red light located at two points of the object, the craft was "darker than a shadow." It formed a V about 120 feet wide, but they could not tell if it was solid between the arms. After five minutes the craft drifted directly over the woman, who had gotten out to open a gate. According to the husband, the object disappeared "like a light bulb" being turned off.

Throughout the sighting there was absolute silence—no sound from fifty horses or geese, dogs, or cats. Later a developer dropped by and told the couple that several of his workers had seen an object the size of a football field over their land.

Researchers rated this encounter high on the strangeness scale because earlier that day the couple had experienced an undisclosed "strong coincidence" involving the idea of aliens. The shadowlike description of the object, its stop/go method of movement, and the absence of sound suggest the couple were in a state of altered consciousness.

Skip one month and return to LaGrange, where on April 18, 1997, between 12:45 and 4:00 A.M., two people were sitting on their front porch when a large V-shaped object, outlined by one hundred red, white, and yellow lights, came into sight. They thought it was seventy-five hundred to twenty thousand feet high and at least 185 feet to 200 yards across, depending on its altitude. The round, mostly white lights were an estimated twenty feet in diameter and pulsed, dimmed, and brightened in sequence. Neither witness saw a center fuselage. The soundless craft approached at a sedate pace but accelerated when overhead and quickly vanished from sight. The episode lasted half a minute.

It has been suggested that the triangle-shaped UFO is a top-secret aircraft being developed at Lockheed. That idea seems patently ridiculous to me. Why test secret aircraft in a metropolitan area numbering three million people? There is a reason Area 51 is located out west—there is plenty of desolate land and few inhabitants.

DIT DAH, DIT DAH

Two young men were driving near Peachtree-DeKalb Airport in Chamblee at 3:00 A.M. on July 18, 1997, when they spotted a black, triangular object hovering four hundred feet above a shopping center. They lost sight of it after twenty seconds, then found it again several minutes later, hovering 150 feet above the tree line. It was a huge light, soft, yellowish white, somewhat dull or organic and glowing like an underwater pool light, and blinking erratically, leading the men to believe it was signaling. Between the large lights were three smaller blue and red lights, much brighter and sharper than the others. They thought the craft, as big as a C-130 transport plane or two tractor-trailer trucks, was grayish black or dark blue in color. They also noted a cross-hatched pattern on the underside of the ship.

While they examined the enormous device, a second, identical UFO approached from behind it. The ships blinked their lights in sequence, apparently communicating. After a two-to-three-minute encounter, the second craft instantly accelerated to a fantastic speed, gained altitude, and disappeared, followed immediately by the original. Both witnesses said the objects were soundless, although one sensed a very low vibration. They drew sketches that resembled giant UFOs frequently observed over Belgium in the early 1980s. Apparent "signaling" has been detected on a number of occasions.

GIVING BIRTH

Next is an anomalous anomaly—a triangle with loud noise found outside the THC. At 6:30 P.M. on November 5, 1997, a thirteen-year-old boy in Hephzibah, near Augusta, was disturbed by a jet noise outside his home. Looking out his bedroom window, he spied a diamond-shaped UFO which, several seconds later, split into two triangular craft. The released portion reversed course and retraced the larger object's path while the original continued forward and disappeared over trees five seconds later. The sound had intensified as it approached, but decreased after the "launch." The objects mounted a number of red and white lights.

At 8:40 P.M. on December 5, 1997, a forty-five-year-old man was standing outside a friend's house two miles north of Franklin on GA 100 when he spotted five bright white lights arranged in a triangle. He believed the silent lights that passed directly over him at an altitude of about twenty-five hundred feet were two hundred feet in width. The UFO was in sight for fifteen seconds and traveled about two hundred miles per hour. Another triangle was sighted one mile away in February 1997. Several hundred yards distant is Rock Bridge Baptist Church, where a local psychic/abductee claims aliens have congregated for hundreds of years.

RACK 'EM UP

On March 30, 1998, two women in LaGrange observed a "cue ball rack" shape hover in the sky over LaGrange at 10:30 P.M. Ten to twenty-five large, white, steady lights constituted the UFO.

Additional triangle configurations were reported from LaGrange and Norcross in September 1998. On the fifth a man in LaGrange saw a silent object which was "extremely bright white and shaped like a boomerang" for a few seconds. The silent, minivan-sized object was only sixty yards from the witness, who saw "no fuselage, just the wing."

In Norcross at 8:00 P.M. on September 13, fourteen-year-old Marilyn Chen saw "a translucent, boomerang-shaped aircraft." The girl drew a picture of an object with "a very large wingspan," according to her mother, comparable to a Stealth bomber. Several hours later, at 10:56 P.M. in Heard County, "a large red pulsating light" was reported "'bobbing' along at one thousand feet." Four times the size of Venus, it alternately dimmed and brightened while a bluish-white light was described as steady and diffuse.

Near 10:00 P.M. of September 21 a married couple were driving home to Hiram on GA 92 when they spotted a large dark triangle with rounded edges and green lights. It seemed to follow them for five minutes, until they reached home. There they scanned the sky and discovered a number of unusual lights, mostly round, which alternately hovered and darted about. One spun on its axis, a green light on one side and a white one on the other producing a strobe effect. A basketball-sized light flew across the horizon. During these observations the couple heard a slight humming sound.

At 12:45 P.M. on September 27 a man in LaGrange spotted a dull-black triangle shape flying less than two thousand feet above the city. It was small enough to suggest a Stealth fighter or a delta-shaped missile drone.

On October 15, 1998, at 12:30 P.M., a husband and wife, reputable and government-employed, spotted a UFO shaped like an isosceles triangle flying near Kennesaw Mountain. Before vanishing it shifted shape to a disc.

At 4:25 A.M. on December 4, David Brown, a MUFON investigator, was approaching Snellville when he observed a bright light approaching. Soon the object, diamond-shaped with a white light at each point and a larger rotating red light in the center, passed 150 feet overhead at a speed of thirty to thirty-five miles per hour. The silent craft seemed to be the size of a compact car.

Later on December 4, Brown and another MUFON researcher, William Lester, interviewed four witnesses in the Douglasville-Hiram area—a family of two adults and two children—who had seen several different types of UFOs. They included an enormous black triangle outlined on the bottom by colored lights and a variety of "rings" that presented rotating colors, seen every night since November 28. Before leaving the area, Brown and Lester saw: 1. A cone-shaped UFO with a blue top and yellow bottom fly across the sky in five seconds; 2. A round blue object rotating around a black core; 3. A glowing red UFO that swept across from horizon to horizon. "Rings" continued to sweep across the sky until midnight.

These sightings had begun when the couple saw "jerking and swaying" lights in the sky. Through a telescope one resembled a "cell"—a nucleus contained within a dark ring which shifted to a spiral and flickered different colors. A number of the family's friends and relatives have seen the UFOs. During the appearances their dogs bark at the phenomenon and the electricity fluctuates.

A family in northern Troup County had a series of three encounters with triangular and rectangular UFOs in mid-March 1999. The incidents began on March 13 at 12:40 A.M., when a man lying in bed noticed a greenish blue light seeping through his blinds. Opening them, he found three greenish blue triangles "sitting" on a ridge half a mile away—one near the top of the elevation, the others lined up halfway down the slope. All appeared to be twenty by twenty-five feet in size, the longer sides parallel to the ground. After five seconds they vanished simultaneously.

At dusk two days later the same man spotted a brilliant white light above woods near his house. While walking toward the object he heard a "humming sound" that increased to the level of a small but roaring jet engine. Then a black triangle, five to seven feet across, flew slowly above his head at a height of twenty feet. At 7:50 P.M. he saw a red light streak from the woods straight into the sky.

Over the past two decades aviation magazines have reported a variety of "flying wing" aircraft under production, primarily stealth or small, unmanned reconnaissance drones, but none approach the size of the objects seen in Europe and Georgia. Also, as stated above, "secret" craft would not be tested in this part of the country, particularly close to metro Atlanta.

PARTICLE-BEAM WEAPONS, HOLY CLOUDS, LASER LAUNCHES, GIANT LUMINOUS UFOS, AND MEDIA HYSTERIA, OR ARE TEN THOUSAND LAGRANGE RESIDENTS AWAKE AT 2:00 A.M. ON A MONDAY MORNING? On the morning of July 15, 1997, syndicated radio personality Art Bell took calls from LaGrange residents who had experienced a wave of UFO sightings. However, the LaGrange police department stated that they had received no reports.

In Atlanta, Ian Ponnet, of radio station WGST, reported that on the night of July 13 a giant, V-shaped UFO covered with lights hovered ten thousand feet over LaGrange and was seen by a reported ten thousand witnesses. An investigation revealed that the actual sighting occurred at 2:00 A.M. on July 14. However, the V shape and ten thousand witnesses were two facts fabricated somewhere along the line.

The media jumped on the story but completely misinterpreted and misreported the incident, as far as John Thompson was concerned. It seems to have started on July 15, 1997, with a fax by a "Thomas Trent," an unidentified source self-described as a resident of the city. Inquiries poured into the LaGrange Police Department, the *LaGrange Daily News*, and local television station Channel 33, all of which had received no sighting reports.

Thompson investigated reports of witnesses in Cannonville who reportedly saw flashing lights and a "giant laser beam" while partying. Those reports never panned out, but a dogged investigation led Thompson to three real witnesses.

The primary witness to this phenomenon lives northwest of LaGrange. After 1:00 A.M. he sighted a tremendous flash followed by a luminous, disc-shaped object traveling at great speed from east to west, low on the horizon. This plasma discharge or aircraft displayed a skipping motion, at least four times, like a stop-action sequence, and disappeared between skips.

Thompson's witness believed the UFO was five to seven miles south of him, and was in sight for three seconds. Thompson estimated the size of the object at fifteen hundred feet to twenty-six hundred feet—an enormous craft—that flew across LaGrange and near Cannonville.

A second witness, near Abbotsford, nine miles west of LaGrange, woke up around 2:00 A.M. and noticed brilliant lightning that repeatedly illuminated his bedroom. He was baffled by the absence of thunder.

Finally, there was a report from a California woman visiting her sister-in-law in LaGrange. She also awoke around 2:00 A.M. and found her bedroom brilliantly illuminated. From a window she saw an intense beam of light stabbing to the ground.

Thompson believes he stumbled upon the reality of this incident when he read *Unconventional Flying Objects: A Scientific Analysis* by Paul Hill. The book described how UFOs accelerate by firing what observers call a laser beam but is actually an ionized field beam that hits the ground to push the UFO to acceleration.

Using Hill's "field engine," a UFO focuses its energy onto a narrow beam for propulsion. The generated field surrounds the spacecraft with an ionized zone that flares. At night, it "lights up like a neon light," bright blue and then white.

At 2:00 A.M. on July 14, 1997, Thompson thinks a gigantic UFO, unseen because of the ionized field, directed a beam at the ground to silently power up, then raced off west, leaving a lens-shaped, blue-and-white trail half a mile long. It covered five miles in two seconds, giving it an estimated speed of nine thousand miles an hour.

In November 1997, *Aviation Week & Space Technology* reported on research conducted by Professor Leik Myrabo with the U.S.A.F. Research Laboratory. Propulsion is produced by firing a laser that will break down air into plasma. A series of laser pulses will result in bursts of plasma that

UFOs have been seen frequently around Stone Mountain, shown here, and a smaller granite peak nearby in Henry County (Panola Mountain), and abductions have been reported. Some paranormal investigators believe such natural features represent "power points" that attract unusual phenomena.

341

produces thrust. We have not utilized such a system because of the enormous amount of energy it consumes, and also earth creatures could never survive such acceleration. However, this proposal certainly sounds like the great LaGrange UFO and the behavior of several other craft observed above Georgia. (Check out such a system used by aliens in *Footfall*, an excellent science-fiction novel by Larry Niven and Jerry Pournelle.)

"I now believe that a giant UFO is regularly penetrating airspace over the Troup-Heard Corridor . . ." Thompson has written. "Before starting away it creates a huge flash, as it kicks into high speed. When loitering it flies well below the twenty-five-hundred-foot radar ceiling so that the FAA in Atlanta and Columbus can't track it."

Thompson cites reports "centered on a disc-shaped object that ionizes the atmosphere around it. This flash seen just prior to acceleration definitely has something to do with this process. The craft looks 'energized' with the resultant plasma that envelops around it."

Thompson suggests it is elliptical in shape, appearing as a slender disc when seen on edge. "At other times it appears as the shape of an egg or plate. At night it appears white." Thompson also proposed that "the actual UFO is smaller and only has a large 'halo' around it when 'energized.'"

Radar ignores the object "due to the computer elimination of high-speed targets. The UFO picks areas to operate where radar coverage and the population are sparse. It loiters only at night and uses terrain such as ridges, valleys, and hills for concealment purposes to mask its profile from ground view. Observers above the UFO claim it appears completely dark when looking down on it."

Thompson has gathered reports from as far away as Korea of giant UFOs that "power up" just before they vanish. These "luminous lens-shaped UFOs are the real McCoy," he thinks. "The distinctive 'flash,' the high-speed departures, and sometimes their incredible size rules anything else out."

TAKEN FOR GRANITE

Thompson cites the work of Allen J. Giles, a state geologist, in offering a hypothesis for the prevalence of UFO activity in the region. The Georgia Geological Survey has discovered unusual specimens of quartz rock that "display a remarkable piezoelectric quality" never found before, Thompson wrote. "Rubbing two flat surfaces of the quartz samples together, they were able to create a soft glow where the rock interacted," an effect called *triboluminescence*. He proposes this as "the reason why so many alien craft are visiting the corridor, to acquire quartz that is easily energized." One abductee-contactee has informed Thompson that there are extraterrestrials who are "solely visiting this portion of the Piedmont for the many large granite outcrops and remoteness" it offers. The natural triboluminescence effect "may account for some local sightings," he wrote, but not the many close encounters reported in Georgia. Many residents have noticed steady, glowing green lights on and in the soil, which Thompson believes might be the result of biological or piezoelectric activity.

(This brings up another embarrassing revelation about my past. For a few months around 1980, I was on a tear selling a series of articles to lesser-quality tabloid magazines and low-rent paranormal mags such as *True UFOs* and *Beyond Reality*. The titles, as best I can remember them, were "UFOs Are Stealing Our Minerals," "UFOs Are Stealing Our Water," "UFOs Are Stealing Our Aircraft," and "UFOs Are Stealing Our Spacecraft," all of which had foundation in fact but still are not the sort of thing you put on your journalistic resume. I have since gone straight. Honest.)

A second theory—that this spectacular aerial event near LaGrange was a particle beam weapons test—came from Tom Mahood, an expert in engineering physics, whom Thompson met on the Web site of Glenn Campbell, the colorful Area 51 researcher. From the description of the light that extended to the ground from the air, Mahood thought the incident sounded like a particle beam. He claims that for twenty years the air force has had three 747s modified to carry the weapon.

GREAT HOLY CLOUDS, SPACEMAN

Either theory, laser propulsion or particle weapons testing, might account for a very weird incident observed from both the ground and the air at LaGrange. At dusk around the first Sunday in June 1997, eleven people saw "cloud holes" which they described as two perfectly round holes in dark clouds which hung over LaGrange for ten minutes. Light seemed to shine down through the holes. The witnesses did not believe they were observing a natural occurrence.

On June 24, 1997, a pilot identified as Jerry T was flying at five thousand feet, beneath a heavy layer of smooth overcast cover at eight thousand feet. He was five miles east of LaGrange when he spotted five holes in the clouds.

"The holes were perfectly round and approximately three hundred yards in size," he related. "Below each cloud was a residue of cloud that was very thin and transparent. It appeared to me that something punched downward, creating the hole and pushing some of the cloud vapor with it."

Jerry did not believe the cause was air turbulence because that would "cause the clouds to mix, erasing the hole."

Between 7:30 and 8:00 P.M. on January 8, 1998, witnesses reported an intense beam of light that stabbed down through heavy cloud cover to the ground in LaGrange.

These curious events have apparently occurred for over twenty years.

FLASH DANCES

At 4:00 A.M. on November 18, 1995, a man spotted a circular UFO, five feet in diameter, in front of a tree line 150 yards from his backyard in Franklin. Thirty-six hours later, at 4:00 P.M. on November 19, four members of his family were inside the home when a brilliant flash of light erupted from the same tree line and lit up the back of their house—this on a bright, clear day. The mother felt "electricity in the air" and thought lightning had struck their residence. Three sons were facing the flash, which they thought was bluish gray, darker than a camera flash but brighter. Even twenty-five feet from the nearest window, the witnesses were forced to blink from the intensity, and one boy saw a flattened, diamond-shaped UFO emerge from the flare and fly away. A line of windows extended across the top of the UFO. A search of the area where the light originated produced nothing.

At 7:05 P.M. on the next day, November 20, part of the family was driving two miles away when their attention was attracted by another brilliant flash. From the flare of light they saw a luminous disc emerge at a speed described as many times the rate of a jet fighter. The UFO, thirty feet in diameter, raced away at treetop level.

A BAND OF LIGHTS

The laser-launched craft seem to be elliptical, discs, ovals, saucers, and circles. An early saucer sighting occurred at 10:15 P.M. on July 1, 1969. A couple approaching the Chattahoochee River Bridge between Fredonia, Alabama, and LaGrange, spotted a circle of lights loitering about fifty feet above the treetops. Stopping to observe the phenomenon from a distance of thirty yards, they saw that the white lights did not blink and were definitely attached to a physical object. After a minute an identical UFO came up behind the first. The woman picked up a flashlight and leaned across her husband to shine it toward the flying objects. She said the light seemed to "get lost," like flashing a light straight up into the sky—and did not reflect off the surface. After a second her husband slapped the light away and anxiously told her to stop. At that same moment the UFOs drew apart and, one after the other, instantly accelerated to fantastic speeds and disappeared. The episode was so troubling that they waited twenty-nine years before reporting it.

FLYING SAUCERS FROM LALA LAND

At 9:45 P.M. on September 23, 1997, a special-education teacher and her fifteen-year-old daughter were driving near Northlake Mall in Tucker when they noticed a fat, oblong saucer hovering above a tree 120 feet away. They stopped and observed the object for three minutes, noting that it was the size of "five minivans laid side by side" and had a circle of four or five large, red, pulsating lights in a depressed area on the bottom. The saucer was colored dark gray and had smaller white lights along the rim. It finally rose up and darted across the road to the northwest. The two thought it odd that no streetlights along the road were working, and twice as they sat still their speedometer dial jumped all the way up.

The mother and daughter continued toward home and were on LaVista Road when the same UFO was seen hovering over trees in front of a church. The red lights had ceased pulsating, and either the outer rim was rotating around the center, the outer lights were circling the rim, or those lights were blinking in succession to suggest a rotation. The witnesses again stopped to watch, and a searchlight from a store opening drew their attention to a second, identical UFO that flew through the beam and approached the first craft. For five minutes mother and daughter thought the UFOs "appeared to be communicating." Frightened, they hurried for home. They found it odd that there was no traffic on LaVista, normally a heavily traveled route. They believe they saw "hieroglyphic" characters on the bottom of the craft and noted that the underside was darker than the top.

LIGHTS IN THE SKY AND ANIMAL MAGNETISM

On August 30, 1997, a worker at Dunson Mill in LaGrange took a break and wandered outside to a pond. Overhead he saw a large "whitish blue" UFO that grew into an oval or elliptical shape. Its speed increased, then diminished to about thirty-five miles per hour, and slowed even further. At a distance of fifteen hundred feet and an altitude of two thousand, it sped west "faster than a shooting star." The object was believed to be about thirty feet in diameter, and its speed ruled out both helicopters and airplanes as explanations. The witness thought it was a structure illuminated by a powerful light.

One hour later and about a mile distant, a couple were viewing the Callaway Clock Tower, a LaGrange landmark, when they spotted a stationary "neon-color yellow" light surrounded by a haze that disappeared a minute later. The couple reported that birds flying around the tower had started acting so crazy that they feared a Hitchcockian attack and retreated to their car.

At 5:30 P.M. on August 10, 1998, a thirty-one-year-old computer programmer at the University of Georgia was sunbathing on his porch when he spotted a metallic elliptical object flying across the sky. After several seconds it shot straight up and disappeared at incredible speed.

On September 25, 1998, at 1:30 P.M., a thirty-eight-year-old man was working on a house three miles west of Auburn, Alabama, when he spotted directly overhead an enormous UFO flying at great altitude and with enormous speed. Its altitude may have been seventy miles, its size four hundred to two thousand feet in length, and it covered a third of the horizon in two or three seconds. The craft was at least twice the height of any jet, and it had no wings. Thompson suggests that the sighting "may represent a rare daylight entrance of a giant UFO into the earth's atmosphere."

Late in 1998 the Atlanta area was deluged with reports of oval-shaped UFOs. At 5:30 A.M. on September 15 a Lithia Springs horticulturist was driving to work fifteen miles west of Atlanta when she spotted a large, domed UFO hovering over a ball field. The ship "was huge, approximately sixty plus feet in diameter and about two stories tall and brightly lit with rotating red, green and white lights," the woman said. Lowering her car window, she heard a "shirring" noise before the UFO instantly vanished.

MiracleGrow

Several days later the horticulturist and a friend found a scorched area where the UFO hovered. When four MUFON investigators checked the area—a baseball diamond in a park complex—the burns were gone, but in their place were new green shoots, a not-uncommon UFO aftereffect.

A man in Smyrna was working at his computer on November 12 at 3:30 A.M. when he glanced out a window and saw a brilliant glowing light hovering several hundred feet above the runway of Dobbins Air Force Base, less than two miles away. Walking outside, he found it impossible to discern a shape, but it was large at the bottom and glowing a bright white. For fifteen minutes the UFO drifted up to about fifteen hundred feet, descended, "bounced," turned dull red, and ascended, repeatedly. He compared the phenomenon to a child's sparkler.

At 9:30 P.M. on March 10, 1999, a horticulturist (yes, another horticulturist) driving on I-85 in Troup County saw a brilliant white ball cross above the highway in front of him. The Venus-sized UFO was flying twice as fast as the small jet airplane that followed thirty seconds later. Following the jet was a low-flying helicopter. The witness believed the jet and helicopter were chasing the UFO.

UFO Sightings Deciphered

In late October 1997 the U.S. Army revealed that for six years it had flown a UFO over Fort Benning in western Georgia, just south of Columbus. The donut-shaped Unmanned Aerial Vehicle, code-named CYPHER, mounts two sets of rotating blades in the center that allow it to hover for hours, and it emits a whirring sound. Built by Sikorsky Aircraft in Los Angeles, it is flown by a navigation computer similar to those mounted in cruise missiles. It can observe enemy positions and drop tear gas for crowd control. "It was just like a computer game," said a young soldier who operated it. However, this is not a likely source of UFO sightings in the corridor.

SOUTHERN BELLS, THIMBLES, BULLETS, SPHERES, EGGS, AND MOONS

At 2:30 P.M. on September 16, 1996, a man was repairing a pasture fence on his farm near Valley, Alabama, when his beagle "Spot" (at least it wasn't Snoopy) started to "bark like no dog I have ever seen before." Looking up, he saw "a large black object" hovering above trees on the horizon.

The man carried a thirty-five-millimeter camera for photographing wildlife, and he snapped away. He noted that the UFO "was making a high-pitched whistling sound," which he believed made Spot howl. The object slowly moved and hovered, then climbed four thousand feet straight up. "It didn't make a sound and it moved as fast as a lightning bolt," he claimed. After five minutes the craft "seemed to crumble in upon itself and vanish."

Ten minutes later three "black helicopters," devoid of identifying markings, "flew low to the ground for a few minutes then left."

The witness had the color print film developed and sent six prints to a radio station and a newspaper. The photos and a copy of the letter were dispatched to Jeff Sainio, a photography expert who specializes in analyzing UFO photos and video. Sainio is noted for conducting photo analysis for the *Sightings* TV program—I can only assume that this is an endorsement.

Enlargements of the photos reveal a capsule-shaped object similar to those used by NASA in the Mercury, Gemini, and Apollo space programs. The cone-shaped capsule is black to dark green in color, and, according to ISUR, "shows a black Teflon-like covered bottom and a flange or rim that goes around near the top of the unknown object."

Thompson cited several similar UFOs seen over Georgia in the past twenty-five years. In Atlanta a man had seen one UFO in 1971 which caused the engine in his pickup to stop. Earlier in 1996, in May and July, the object had been seen by witnesses in LaGrange, twenty miles from Valley.

Investigations led ISUR to conclude that the photos alone were not enough to prove "a genuine UFO." The negatives, which the witness retained, would have significantly increased the amount of evidence to be analyzed. Appeals in local media failed to motivate the anonymous photographer to forward the negatives.

ISUR also felt that the absence of military helicopters operating in the area from bases in Alabama and Georgia casts doubt on the legitimacy of the objects. However, and I suppose I am stepping out on the paranoid fringe here, if they were the infamous "black helicopters" so associated with cattle mutilations and a darling of the militias, the military would disavow their existence, or perhaps the "shadow government" prevented the military from having any knowledge of their operations.

SHARING THE SPOTLIGHT

At 8:30 P.M. on October 15, 1997, a twenty-nine-year-old woman was returning home from work in LaGrange to her farm home in Cannonville, a rural community near West Point Lake. She had noticed unusual aerial phenomenon in the skies twice before, and was attentive when she spotted a bright light she thought might be following her. She drove home to pick up her eighteen-year-old sister, and they drove in search of the UFO. The sisters spotted it along Bartley Road and followed the object for several miles at a slow, steady speed as the object slipped from side to side and crossed back and forth across the road a number of times at treetop level. They described the UFO as a triangular bell the size of a car or four full moons. A white light topped the craft, and two red lights were near the bottom. The UFO stopped to hover over a three-road intersection near Hogg Mountain, frequented by many UFOs, and then it abruptly streaked toward the women at an alarming speed. They quickly drove home, but soon gathered their nerve and set off again to locate the UFO, which they found hovering near Rosie Civers Road, and observed it for five minutes. When it slipped lower they returned home.

Between 7:00 and 8:00 P.M. on another night in October 1997, the younger sister was driving home when she saw a solid object the size of a large transfer truck and was outlined by a number of nonblinking lights. It hovered over fields, one hundred yards away.

On the night of October 18, 1997, a married couple saw a "slow-moving, strange blue flashing light" near Cannonville which "lit up a sizable portion of the sky for twenty minutes."

The bell class of UFOs popped up again in Cannonville at 11:00 P.M. on October 21, 1997, when a group of people sighted a "cone-shaped" UFO. It had a round bottom surrounded by a rotating, flashing circle of red lights. An intense, steady white light was perched atop the cone. A separate witness saw a thimble-shaped UFO flying across the sky faster than a jetliner. The full-moon-sized object hovered for five minutes over the tree line around an I-85 overpass, moving up and down about three-quarters of a mile away.

On March 22, 1997, at 4:00 P.M., a woman driving near the same area spotted two brilliant silver balls hovering in the air. She believed they were larger than a four-room house. One shot straight up and disappeared, as did the second one a moment later.

Sightings of moon-shaped UFOs, according to John Thompson, persisted for a year and a half in the Troup-Heard Corridor, making at least eight appearances. Thompson considers the moon-shaped UFOs to be a significant player in the THC. They often materialize as a hovering ball of white light so bright that witnesses initially mistake them for the moon until they realize there are two moons in the sky. Soon after the UFOs streak away at blinding speed.

At 2:30 P.M. on August 18, 1996, two men fishing on Lake West Point near LaGrange watched a large white sphere appear through fog about half a mile away and fifteen hundred feet above the water. It suddenly disappeared at the time another area man saw a similar UFO flying quickly across the sky.

An egg appeared to a man, his girlfriend, and her daughter at 7:45 P.M. on June 7, 1996, while they were boating on the Chattahoochee River near the U.S. 27 bridge. The silver, vertical egg, the size of a small cart, was one hundred yards away and fifty feet above the water. The three drifted and watched as the craft rolled over to a horizontal position, made a ninety-degree, clockwise turn, and started a slow, ten-mile-per-hour path low across the river and up a hill, where it just cleared a barn. Past Franklin it gained altitude, reversed direction toward the trio, and flew out of sight.

THAT NEW UFO SMELL

At 7:45 A.M. on November 18, 1995, a man getting a drink of water glanced out his kitchen window and spotted an unusual craft sitting atop a tree in his backyard, sixty yards away and forty-five feet in the air. The rust-red sphere, six feet in diameter, was covered with what resembled a ceramic surface, slightly dimpled like a golf ball and containing numerous black grains. He believed it had exactly duplicated the fall foliage of the surrounding trees. The man thought of the object as a fabricated metallic probe with a protective coating and said it looked like it "had just come fresh out of a factory."

On March 20, 1996, at 10:45 P.M., a sixteen-year-old boy was lying in bed when he noticed a bright red light penetrating the blinds over his windows and the family dog barking excitedly. Peering out, he saw a sphere, colored "rust red," hovering one hundred yards away and just above the trees. Walking outside, the young man saw that the car-sized, glowing ball was bouncing up and down and moving away.

At 3:00 A.M. on May 2, 1996, a man fishing in West Point Lake near the dam noticed a huge bright oval of white lights that sparkled purple and green. It hovered or glided sixty feet above the dam, lighting up the entire structure. One minute later the pulsing light silently moved off at fifteen miles per hour, then sped off as fast as lightning.

On September 21, 1997, eight high school students camping out near Liberty Hill saw an enormous white "meteor" the size of the moon race across the sky. Minutes later, a boy in a second group of students saw a white, disc-shaped UFO, apparently one thousand to fifteen hundred feet in diameter, hover, then race away.

A NEAR SNATCH

At 10:25 P.M. on August 27, 1992, the sky was dark and clear, the air warm and humid as a woman and her niece drove home from church in southern Heard County. They spotted what they thought was a low-flying plane—a really low-flying plane—at treetop level and even lower at times, flying through thick woods only one hundred to three hundred feet from them, paralleling their route. After five miles the UFO disappeared into the woods, but when their car crested a hill and entered the intersection of GA 219 and Bevin Road, the women found the craft waiting for them.

The craft, which hovered eight to ten feet above the pavement and seventy-five feet away, was fourteen to eighteen feet in diameter. The women felt that the UFO wanted them to drive under it, but instead the driver slammed on the brakes, jammed the convertible into reverse, then raced to the nearest house. The pair burst in, startling the residents. As the women scrambled out of the vehicle, the UFO flew over them and away, then immediately shot up and disappeared over the tree line. A seventeen-year-old son of the family had heard an unusual "whooshing" sound seconds before the intrusion. The owners of the house were convinced the two witnesses were genuinely terrified and believed they had seen a UFO. A neighbor of the family had seen the object over his backyard that evening, and his son had been chased by it on GA 219.

GETTING YOUR KICKS ON ROUTE 74

A near collision occurred forty miles to the east, in Upson County, on January 13, 1989, at 10:00 P.M. There was a cloudless sky when the driver of a minivan noticed a bright light approaching her as she drove on GA 74. She thought it was an oncoming car, but five minutes later she saw it was a UFO racing toward her at windshield level. The metallic object, fifteen to eighteen feet in diameter and four to five feet thick, had five intensely bright red, green, and blue lights the size of car headlights, and was spinning. At a distance of less than ten feet, the UFO veered off and disappeared.

IT FALLS TO PIECES

At 7:30 P.M. in late January or early February 1994, four witnesses—a mother and her three adult sons—stood outside their home in Troup County, where they spotted a very large, bright, and round white light about a mile away and twelve hundred feet in the air. After five minutes it split into four pieces. One son, a marine on leave, observed the action through binoculars and said the sections raced off in different directions at "blinding speed."

Seconds later, two jet fighters with twin tails, either F-15s or F-18s, roared through the exact position where the UFO had been. The family members all believed the UFO had acted deliberately to elude the jets. None had seen jets fly so low or fast before.

Fifteen minutes later, six to eight helicopters arrived at the same place where the UFO had been, presumably searching for it.

SEARCH AND RESCUE OR DESTROY

A final "moon" UFO was observed between Pine Mountain and Whitesville in Harris County at 7:00 P.M. on December 1, 1998, by a couple who saw a ball of light, much brighter than the moon and a quarter its size, at an altitude of two hundred feet for fifteen seconds.

The "huge bright ball," which reminded the woman of "looking at a giant spotlight in the sky," was twenty times brighter than the red and white lights of the helicopter that suddenly appeared. Two other helicopters and a small plane soon approached and she believed the four conventional aircraft were conducting an intense search for the UFO near ground level. The man, a former military and civilian pilot, had conducted similar searches in the past.

FLYING FUSES, FLATTENED BARBELLS, AND CIGARETTES, OR SOMETIMES A CIGAR IS JUST A UFO

Between February and March 1997, at about 2:00 P.M., a man described by John Thompson as a "retired official of significant prominence" with an indisputable reputation and credentials, was on his deck when he saw two identical UFOs. He described them as resembling a refrigerated container of Pillsbury cookie dough, a metal car fuse "with its middle all shiny," or "flattened barbells." The two objects, drifting less than a mile above a LaGrange neighborhood, formed an inverted V for several seconds, leading the man to think they were "communicating somehow." Then one raced away to the west "like a bullet." It returned at the same speed and again hovered with its mate for five seconds before speeding off again to the south. The witness called his thirty-four-year-old daughter outside to watch, and she arrived in time to view the reunion and final departure of the first UFO at an astounding speed. The other UFO began slowly flying northeast at about sixty to one hundred miles an hour. The man then shouted for his wife to come outside with a camera. She hurried from the house in time to see and snap one photo of the remaining UFO at its closest approach, almost directly overhead at four thousand to five thousand feet, before it disappeared behind trees. The first object had been in sight for ten seconds; the second one ninety seconds. The witnesses estimated their size as one to three car lengths, or fifteen to fifty feet.

The photo shows a linear object, darker in the middle and with a vertical stripe around the center that the family had not noticed. Jeff Sainio analyzed the photo for MUFON and determined that the image was not a hoax. He believed the object photographed had "no conventional explanation."

At 11:30 A.M. on August 2, 1995, a LaGrange woman telephoned John Thompson to describe two UFOs she had just observed. Five minutes earlier she had spotted a "bar" fly above her house and disappear into clouds. While she watched that spot, a saucer or "dishpan" UFO appeared.

Twenty minutes later Thompson received a call from the son of the initial caller who reported that the flying saucer was back and a crowd had gathered at East Pender Street and LaFayette Parkway. Stan Reese, who was preparing a UFO special for local TV Channel 33, found twenty people gawking at the sky and pointing heavenward. Reese was told the saucer had disappeared but the bar had returned. Ten minutes after Reese started filming Thompson arrived.

Thompson interviewed ten different witnesses. The round UFO, described as "two plates stuck together," had a round canopy on top and hovered for ten seconds. It appeared to follow the bar and both periodically disappeared, dashing in and out of clouds at speeds up to five hundred miles per hour and turning abruptly. The saucer UFO spun and cast out a light that had a "searchlight" intensity so bright it hurt the eyes of those who watched it. It also emitted several spinning, white-yellow round balls one-third the size of the "mother." Described as the size of a large car or small house, it was colored metallic gray. The bar was whitish silver.

Jeff Sainio could not conclusively analyze the film, but he thought it was "a funny-looking, fat white jet" related to the UFO. "Maybe a special government plane that monitors UFOs," he suggested, while admitting that was "pure speculation."

AMERICA'S STRANGEST HOME VIDEOS
In May 1997 a Christian TV station was filming a children's show when the cameraman spotted three unmarked helicopters. Knowing that a segment of his audience was interested in the mysterious aircraft, he focused on them. Viewing the film at the studio, a film technician spotted an unidentified object flying in and out of clouds behind the choppers. It appeared to be a white, tube-shaped object. According to Thompson, enhancement of the tape clearly revealed "a structured object moving in the background."

In early September 1995, glowing green balls were seen in three separate incidents by two different families. In each case they resembled a plane descending as if to land. Two minutes after an appearance by the UFO on September 14, a number of residents of Davis Road in LaGrange saw at least four helicopters flying at treetop level and sweeping searchlight beams along the ground before leaving several minutes later. Witnesses believed it was obvious that the choppers were searching for the UFO.

THE BLOB AND THE NON-PLANE AIRPLANE

At 2:00 P.M. on March 4, 1997, three people were driving on U.S. 27 a mile south of Franklin when the driver spotted a large, metallic, roughly oval or round "shiny blob" hovering in the sky a mile away. The object was lost to sight only to reappear several minutes later for a few seconds. When the UFO was sighted again several minutes later, all three men saw it for five seconds. During this time they observed a dark gray, oblong UFO, half the size of the blob. The driver, who thought the newcomer had wings, said it was flying at the speed of a twin-prop plane, about two hundred miles per hour, and was about the same size. All three believe the two unidentified objects appeared to be on a collision course at four to five thousand feet of altitude and just southeast of New River Bridge. As the two UFOs passed each other, both instantly disappeared.

LESS TAR

While a high school science teacher was waiting for his wife in a shopping center parking lot in Chamblee at 3:30 P.M. on June 3, 1997, he observed airplanes taking off and landing at Peachtree-DeKalb Airport, one mile distant. He spotted a brilliant white cylinder-cigarette-style UFO with rounded ends hovering between two clouds. After five minutes the object began to "dissolve" until it completely disappeared from view.

When Tom Sheets interviewed the air traffic controller on duty that day, he found her reluctant to speak, but the woman did admit that she "knew there were unusual things out there" that her friends had observed.

Two people driving on GA 18 in Harris County at 7:30 P.M. in late February 1996 saw a large cigar-shaped UFO—metallic silver in color and the size of a house or commercial airliner—fall from the sky only six hundred yards distant. Initially spotted at two thousand feet of altitude, it plunged straight down before stopping instantly only a hundred feet above the ground. After pausing a second, the craft sprinted away at a steep angle, "faster than lightning," the witness swore.

OPEN POD-BAY DOORS, HAL

At 10:30 P.M. in April 1995, a man driving on U.S. 27 between LaGrange and Franklin spotted an enormous cigar-shaped UFO that he estimated to be 250 to 300 feet long. The craft had rounded ends and a series of ten blinking white, green, and red lights. As the UFO sailed majestically past one hundred feet directly above him at a speed of twenty miles per hour, the motorist stopped and watched in awe. The flat bottom of the object was one hundred feet wide, and in the center of the dark, nonmetallic surface was an indentation of several feet that he thought might be a doorway that "could open up."

A LOAFING UFO

It was half past midnight in LaGrange on August 10, 1998, when a thirty-one-year-old man left his bed and started for the bathroom. Passing a window he noticed it was completely dark outside—the glow of a street light seventy feet away had always shone into his second-story apartment.

Peering out, he saw only gray darkness, no street or residential lights, moon, or stars. Concentrating, he saw that something was receding, and steady red and yellow lights, then an intense blue green fluorescent light appeared. Finally, at an estimated distance of ten yards he was able to see the entire object. It resembled a dark gray "loaf of bread" with red and yellow lights around the edge. The bottom was squared off, the sides straight, with a ridged top. The blue-green light shone from the center of the object. He thought the UFO had been sighted at a height of twenty feet, and it slowly rose to several hundred feet, no more than seventy feet away. After a twenty-second sighting, the craft accelerated so rapidly—many times faster than a jet, but slower than lightning—that it left a blurred trail behind. Perhaps this is the latest twist on cigars; otherwise it deserves a category of its own.

At noon on August 21, 1998, a retired teacher was driving on the Stone Mountain Freeway when he spotted a dull silver-gray UFO, shaped like a medicine capsule, almost directly overhead. During the six seconds it was in sight, he pegged its speed as faster than a commercial jet and estimated the altitude at several thousand feet. The outline revealed no wings, protuberances, or markings of any kind.

At 7:45 A.M. on October 24, 1998, a man was driving in Acworth when he sighted a cigar-shaped UFO floating through the sky at an altitude of twelve hundred feet. The size of a commercial jet fuselage, it had bluntly rounded ends and no wings. The bottom half was colored like a golden sun; the top metallic.

Mini-cylinders arrived on November 8 at 6:00 A.M. as a medical specialist drove to work in Atlanta from his home in Dahlonega. At the Dawson-Forsyth county line on GA 400 a fleet of thirty to forty cylinder-shaped objects, sixteen inches by six inches in size and bright as headlights, descended in front of his car and started to dance above the highway. This bizarre ballet continued for ten minutes as the flying oddities approached to within twenty feet of the vehicle and six feet above the pavement. While this unusual phenomenon continued, he saw six or seven round white lights, an inch and a half in diameter, maneuver just inside the cloud cover overhead "like bees swarming."

HOSTILE INTENT?

At 2:15 P.M. on March 6, 1994, two F-4 reconnaissance jets of the Alabama Air National Guard were racing low across rural Troup County when one was destroyed in a catastrophic explosion that killed one member of the two-man crew.

The plane was from the 106th Reconnaissance Squadron, 117th Reconnaissance Wing flying out of Birmingham. According to air force crash investigators, bad welds, dating to the assembly of one of the jet engines thirty years earlier, allowed a high-pressure combustion chamber to fail, which blew debris into a fuel cell, causing an intense midair explosion.

Capt. Tracy L. Gilbreath, the weapons systems operator, said the sudden emergency "blindsided" him. The pilot, Capt. John McDaniel, suddenly screamed a warning and then "everything happened so instantaneously," Gilbreath said. After a "bang" the men were thrown violently against the left side of the plane. Gilbreath's shoulder still hurt a month later, and his head swelled inside his helmet. At that time "the aircraft just dug in and stopped," Gilbreath continued. "I've never been slammed into a wall that fast before." He called the side forces "extraordinary."

Believing he was about to die, Gilbreath initiated a duel ejection sequence that rocketed his seat out of the plane. The pilot's ejection was delayed by seconds to prevent the chutes from entangling, but the plane was so low that McDaniel was still in the plane when it impacted the ground.

The company that manufactured the engine disagreed with the air force conclusion, but settled a suit out of court with McDaniel's widow and Gilbreath. A company investigator believed the entire jet had failed—not just the one engine. He believes McDaniel had "over-stressed" the plane with "crew-induced maneuvers." In other words, hotdogging.

Debris fell over an area of 1.2 miles. Security personnel from Robins Air Force Base, Dobbins Air Force Base, and two air national guard units in Georgia and Alabama cordoned off the entire area for a month. Combat engineers from LaGrange arrived first, followed by a UH-60 Blackhawk helicopter with eleven medical personnel from the 117th Tactical Hospital.

Gilbreath does not know what caused the catastrophe, and MUFON investigators believe he had seen no UFO or witnessed any unusual phenomenon. They found him candid and accommodating.

The company investigator reported that the air force allowed him to view some of the gun camera footage shot by the plane and saw nothing out of the ordinary. He also found no evidence that a projectile had struck the plane, and there were no fused electronics from an electromagnetic pulse.

Despite these facts, John Thompson and others are convinced that for some reason the air force and air national guard incorrectly reported the course flown by the planes. According to the official report, people who saw the planes should never have seen them from their position, including Thompson himself, and others who only heard the planes should have seen them.

Thompson heard the first jet and rushed to a window of his Liberty Hill study in time to see the second race past "alarmingly low and fast." Thompson's son saw the explosion seconds later and three-quarters of a mile away. The family watched as a dense cloud of smoke rose above the horizon.

Bill Thompson, no relation to John, is an experienced Heard County fireman and EMT who had been a lieutenant with the Chicago fire department. He was off duty and working in his cabinet shop near Potato Creek when he heard the two jets, a common sight in the area, where military aircraft frequently train. Glancing up, he saw the two F-4s flying five hundred miles an hour at treetop level. Also, just below the treetops in front of and accelerating away from the jets was a silver object he described as an "aluminum cigar canister with a screw-on cap," one-third or one-half the size of the following F-4s. John Thompson estimated its size as twenty-three feet long and five feet high. Several minutes later Bill Thompson heard the explosion of the jet. One emergency worker later told Bill that M-16–equipped soldiers were leaping off helicopters soon after the crash. Heard County deputies immediately sealed off the area.

Precisely two weeks before the crash, on February 20, 1994, six miles from Bill Thompson's sighting, John Thompson's family videotaped a UFO, the incident that led John into UFO research. Thompson had gone upstairs to check on his children when he saw "a bright stream of lights that looked like Christmas tree lights just sitting there, maybe a hundred feet off the ground." At one point the object made a "lunge at our house," Thompson recorded, then rapidly returned to its original position. It was of "gigantic proportions," and he thought it was one hundred yards to a quarter-mile wide, or "as big as a football field."

Near the end of the observation Thompson remembered to get his video camera, but he experienced difficulties with the device, which "kept shutting down." It was his "distinct impression . . . that the occupants of the UFO did not want him to film" it. After getting the gadget started, the camera, set on infinity, could not focus on the distant object in the darkness. After videotaping the UFO for a minute, the battery died. An "out-of-focus revolving white light" had been recorded. Five members of Thompson's family, he, his wife, and three children, continued watching the object for another twenty minutes, then went to bed. The sighting had lasted forty-five minutes.

Jeff Sainio, MUFON's staff photo analyst, was able to eliminate airplane lights as an explanation, and he was able to label the phenomenon a "genuine UFO." A retired physicist and camera expert who examined the footage ruled out reflection, refraction, or lens flare.

Four weeks after the F-4 incident, Thompson and his family again saw from their home six white, moon-shaped UFOs flying low—and slow— five miles per hour and about half a mile away over a cow pasture. Each object, ten feet in diameter, flew soundlessly in a loose single-file formation, at times flying through the forest toward the crash site. They moved "through trees to such an extent that it seemed inconceivable that they could maneuver as such!" wrote Thompson. The UFOs bobbed up and down, and the intervals varied during the ten minutes they were visible.

Fifteen days before the crash, a UFO investigator from Stockbridge shot a two-minute video of a white, oblong, cruise-missile-like object flying through clouds near Goat Rock Dam in Harris County, forty miles from Liberty Hill. According to Tim Chitwood, writing in an article for the January 21, 1997, *Columbus Ledger-Enquirer*, the cameraman told him, "he once was abducted by aliens who told him quartz is the key to the universe and a ringing bell is the only sound that can be heard in the spirit world. He also sees angels, and 'I got Jesus three times on videotape,' the man claimed."

GETTING PHYSICAL

HIT AND FLY

At 8:00 P.M. on Halloween night, October 31, 1986, a male city employee was driving on Ball Street in LaGrange when he spotted an approaching flying disc, fifteen feet in diameter, with blue, yellow, and orange lights on the edges. In the center was a larger white light that revolved and shone down. Before he could react, the object dived toward the road and struck the cab of his pickup truck, shattering the windshield and breaking the grille. The driver dove to the floorboard at impact and rose to watch the UFO fly away. He called the police, who decided the incident did not fit any category of accident case they were familiar with, and they refused to file a report. They suggested that vandals had thrown bricks at his truck. No alien traces, or brick bits, were found on the truck.

UNDIAGNOSED ABDUCTION?

Two women were driving ten miles west of LaGrange on GA 109 at 1:15 A.M. on April 26, 1993, when their car suddenly died. Looking around, they spotted a round UFO, ten to twelve feet in diameter, hovering only twenty feet above them. Multicolored lights framed the edge, but in the center was a large, bright, round light that gave off incredible heat. Perspiring heavily, the ladies rolled up the car windows in a vain attempt to escape the heat. One woman thought the craft "was trying to get" them. After ten to fifteen minutes, the car could be started and the women sped off as the UFO raced south.

At home the witnesses believed that a half to a full hour had passed rather than just fifteen minutes, which suggests a quickie abduction. The two women were left with an "ill" feeling, and one said her health was seriously affected for a period after the encounter. MRIs, CAT scans, and other medical tests revealed nothing.

A boyfriend of one of the women was home when they arrived late. He confirmed their excited state and revealed that while waxing the car one month later, extensive pieces of paint came off with little effort.

WE HAVE A WINNER

At 9:00 P.M. one night in July 1993, seven female church members and a male driver were in a church van driving from LaGrange to Anniston, Alabama, to play bingo. Near Wedowee on AL 431, a round, dull-yellow light the size of a small helicopter paced the van fifty to 150 feet away and as low as twelve feet above the ground. Two witnesses swear they saw the shape of a humanoid fetus within the light. After five miles, the UFO streaked into the sky and disappeared.

Two of the women, the only ones wearing glasses, believe a beam of some kind was projected into the van. Later that night and on the following morning, their eyes hurt and teared, and they had dark circles around their eyes which extended to their cheeks. One woman, who suffered migraine headaches for the following three weeks, claimed that before the encounter her eyes were blue—one has since turned green.

It was 11:00 P.M. on June 25, 1996, when a couple and their dog approached the Chattahoochee River bridge on GA 219 in Troup County. They saw a large, bright-red light five hundred feet above the ground that appeared to be stationary and increased to the size of a large car as they drew nearer. After an observation of two minutes, with the UFO 150 yards away, it departed at "the speed of lightning," the husband said.

On the following morning the couple noticed that their dog acted "crazy," like it did not know them. Soon after they gave the animal to a neighbor and it developed severe burns on its face and head, then disappeared. The female witness, then pregnant, and her baby have suffered persistent health problems, which she feels were caused by the UFO.

SOUND AND FURY, SIGNIFYING . . . UFOS, OR STUCK IN LOW DRIVE AGAIN (FAMILY JOKE)

The most entertaining aspect of the west Georgia sightings is its diversity—the phenomenon seems to constantly mutate and is often bizarre. In 1994 and 1995 the THC saw five separate instances of UFOs emitting loud, grinding noises.

The best example originated from Ragland Street in LaGrange. Just before dusk, about 8:00 P.M. on a weekend night in early September 1995, a family of four heard a heavy, irritating sound. It sounded like a helicopter, but one person thought it was so loud he feared a plane was crashing. Then the house began shaking.

Two people, the mother and her eighteen-year-old son, walked outside to investigate the commotion and immediately spotted the source—a giant silver bullet over the Troup County Seniors Center. The forty- to sixty-foot-long object was flying about sixty feet off the ground, faster than a dirigible but considerably slower than a jet, and sported no lights. Approaching within 150 feet of the two witnesses, the rumbling, grinding noise was deafening, shaking the ground and causing their ears to ache. Two people who remained inside "felt" the sounds, including a woman on the telephone who could not hear the other party during the incident, which lasted four to five minutes.

The other four bump-and-grind incidents occurred at night. Near Glenn an enormous UFO with one bright light flew behind a house. Described as "lumbering," it seemed to absorb all light and flew so slowly that a woman walking beneath it kept pace while it passed only a hundred feet above her.

In southern Troup County in late January 1994, a couple found one end of their house lit up like daylight at 1:00 A.M. The residence shook so much that they feared "a tornado was coming through." They awoke their two children and took shelter in the safest portion of the structure as the disturbance passed immediately above their house. When the father went outside, the light was extinguished and the noise stopped. He had flown in many helicopters in the army and was convinced this was not a chopper. A couple down the road had also been awakened at the same time by the audiovisual show.

A fourth incident occurred in November 1995, in southern Heard County, and the final appearance was near Standing Rock, Alabama, where the car a man was driving was shaken violently.

The sounds in these encounters were described as "a plane crash," "a tornado coming through," and "fifty helicopters landing on my house." In several instances objects vibrated on the tops of tables.

Similar incidents originated in Pennsylvania during the early 1990s when hundreds of witnesses heard and saw loud, slow-moving triangles or boomerangs in the sky, which are also common in the THC.

..- ..-. —- (THAT'S UFO IN MORSE CODE—I WAS A BOY SCOUT)

On the same day that the Valley photos were taken, September 16, 1996, a mother and her two daughters were driving near Heard County High School in Corinth at 8:30 P.M., when their attention was drawn to a strange cloud. Black and threatening, it was about two miles long and positioned five miles away and ten thousand feet high, sitting alone in a windless sky. The most fascinating feature about the cloud was an internal flashing that occurred at a steady pace, every fifteen to thirty seconds, and in a pattern that did not extend outside the cloud.

The three drove home and sat on their porch for half an hour observing the unique phenomenon. After a while a smaller cloud approached the first and began responding to the "signals."

The flashes were yellowish and pinkish orange in color, circled within the cloud and around its edges in a predictable sequence. The pattern started on one side of the cloud and spread along the perimeter. When Big Cloud flashed, Junior responded with a flash that originated on the corner closest to the larger cloud. Because there was no lightning and no thunder associated with the phenomenon, the mother was led to wonder whether the clouds concealed UFOs.

On December 25, 1996, the manager of a Hogansville store and one of his customers observed two lights, eight times brighter than any star in the sky and flashing red, green, and yellow colors, which remained parallel to each other for three minutes. One light then abruptly moved beside the other and they flashed together for a minute. At that point one left a dim streak and disappeared. The second continued blinking for five minutes, then left in a similar fashion.

BAR-CODING HOGG MOUNTAIN

In August 1996, "Lisa," who lives at the foot of Hogg Mountain, watched a triangular UFO "scan" the ridge with red rays that would turn on and sweep an area, then disappear, only to reappear and examine another area.

At 3:00 A.M. on October 15, 1997, a young man awoke and looked out a window to see a "drifting" bluish gray light the diameter of a pencil. As he watched, the light instantly turned and shone into his right eye. The light did not make the witness squint as he looked directly into it for a second. He "could not see around the edges" and the phenomenon reminded him of chalk. After looking away, he could not make himself look out the window again.

BOX LITES

Around 8:30 P.M. in mid-August 1995, a married couple driving south of LaGrange spotted a white light several hundred feet high shining a beam into a cow pasture half a mile away. They pulled over and saw that the light was encased in a dark "box." The beam, three feet wide, seemed to shift its point of origin every two seconds. When the boxed light grew more intense the beam stabbed down to the ground, and when the box light diminished, the beam seemed to shine up to the UFO from the ground. The projected light always came and went from the same spot, and was a very tight beam. The UFO appeared to be the size of the moon. After ten minutes the witnesses continued their journey.

Investigators found a local landowner who had seen a UFO over that pasture around 9:30 P.M. in mid-August 1995. It was a large white light with two red lights that hovered for half an hour, but no beam was involved.

Boris (The Spider, for Who Fans), or the Spiders from Mars (for David Bowie Fans)

Near the Georgia-Alabama line at 3:30 P.M. on July 7, 1997, a man driving on I-85 noticed a "fuzzy, spider-like UFO" high in the sky. It was black and the legs of the spider were folded back to the body.

Where and When to See a UFO in the THC

Thompson considers the THC one of the hottest sites in the world to view UFOs, and he offered tips on where and when to experience a sighting. Prime spots are the long shoreline of West Point Lake, Pine Mountain, particularly Roosevelt State Park, which offers a wonderful view of the area, and the Troup-Heard County line between Glenn and Corinth. Other sites include Cannonville, Stovall, Antioch, and Hogg Mountain in Troup County, Liberty Hill in Heard County, and crossings of waterways like New River and Potato Creek. Rural areas composed of "heavy forest, secluded fields, hills, dark hollows, and water" are UFO haunts, Thompson notes. Few sightings are made in densely populated areas. He recommends studying ridge lines and scrutinizing large leafy trees, because UFOs camouflage themselves. Also search the skies when there are loud rumbling sounds or mysterious explosions. If possible, hang out

UFOs have been seen frequently from overlooks atop Pine Mountain, in west-central Georgia.

361

with previous sighters of UFOs or abductees, who seem attuned to the presence of UFOs.

UFOs apparently avoid times when the most humans are on the prowl. Therefore, the most auspicious times are late Sunday or early Monday morning after 10:00 P.M., particularly from 1:00 to 4:00 A.M. Dark, moonless winter Sunday nights are best. Dusk to dawn also seem to be good times, as are clear nights, nights with little or no moonlight, several days before cold fronts arrive (snowbird aliens?), and before and after unusual weather patterns.

UFOs are still going strong. As of 1998, an estimated thirty-one million Americans believe in UFOs—about half that number have actually seen one. An *Atlanta Journal-Constitution* poll released on June 30, 1998, revealed that 57 percent of Southerners believe UFOs are real, with 53 percent convinced that aliens might have visited earth. That percentage is higher than the national average, a fact on which I hesitate to speculate. George Filer reported that in 1998, 290 UFO reports were received from across the United States, and Georgia had more than any other state— forty-three. Second-place New York had thirty-seven.

Besides John Thompson, another leader of Georgia's current UFO community is Tom Sheets, a Vietnam veteran who worked for twenty-five years as a homicide detective before becoming police chief of College Park. Sheets's interest in the phenomenon began as a student in the 1960s, when he observed through a telescope a "V-shaped formation of disc-like craft, traveling east to west, high in the sky, performing unusual and bizarre maneuvers." He has investigated hundreds of sightings.

Michael Hitt, a Roswell police officer, is MUFON Georgia's historian. He saw a UFO in 1967 during a family trip to Florida, where they watched a rocket launch from Cape Canaveral. The night before the launch, Hitt, with his sister, mother, and a grandmother, saw a "meteor" shoot across the sky, but then "it reversed, and reversed its course." In 1996, Hitt began compiling a list of all Georgia sightings since the historical area started in 1947. When compiled in chronological order, he hopes to identify trends and common denominators. So far he has discovered three hundred sightings between 1947 and 1987, including one hundred between August and October 1973, half of those by police officers. He has pored over hundreds of newspapers in libraries across the state. When he locates a UFO sighting, he checks papers from neighboring towns, a technique I have used for years. A total of eighty-one sightings have been reported by policemen, and eighteen by pilots. Fulton County leads Georgia with thirty-seven sighting reports.

10

Natural Wonders

Nature is a weird mother. Not every event is governed by its laws. At certain places, cars roll uphill and refuse to go downhill. Tornadoes are filled with fire, and lightning leaves patterns of vegetation on humans. Caves blow, then suck. Lakes fill, then empty of their own accord. Meteors, traditional and glazed, fall, and an extinct comet left us with celestial acne. There are years when winter never comes, and sometimes no light accompanies the day. We have great cracks in the ground and bald mountains from which the sounds of an eternal bowling game seem to emanate. Limestone sinks, giant stones rock, and rock cities seek tourists.

ROCK STEADY

Most people assume that the famous Rock City is located in Tennessee. Not so, for towering seventeen hundred feet above Chattanooga and the Tennessee River, atop scenic Lookout Mountain, Rock City stands a half-mile south of the Tennessee-Georgia border.

More than ten million people have visited Rock City since it opened in 1932. They stroll through ten acres of rock gardens and see Mushroom Rock, Needle's Eye, a tight spot named Fat Man's Squeeze, which is only one to three feet wide (but musclebound Paul Anderson, at one time the world's strongest man, made it through, and even more significantly, so did I), Grand Corridor, a cavelike attraction called Shelter Rock, a one-thousand-ton balanced rock, and the low Goblin's Underpass. At the end of the path visitors view seven states (with a bit of imagination) from Lover's Leap and Observation Point. Rock City even has a waterfall, but its magic might be diminished a bit by the knowledge that the water is piped in and turned off at night.

Every bit as interesting as the natural wonders is the hype Rock City has generated. During the Great Depression, crews traveled throughout the southeastern United States, offering to paint barns if farmers would allow them to include the message "See Rock City" on the roof. At one time nine hundred barns, extending from Maryland to Texas, bore this message. More than ten thousand birdhouses (one is preserved in the Smithsonian) with the same slogan were seen at virtually every motel and restaurant in this half of the country. Miniature versions can be bought at Rock City today.

SHAKING ROCK
The titanic upheavals of nature have produced other balanced rocks. "Shaking rocks" or "rocking stones" are a rare phenomenon that occurs when geologic forces deposit a large boulder on top of a second rock, with the first stone balanced perfectly with only one or two points touching the base. Such

The Shaking Rock at Lexington is one of at least three in Georgia. Geological forces placed a large stone atop another boulder with just a few points touching, allowing the top stone to be easily rocked.

a stone can be easily pushed or rocked on this axis. One, called Shaking Rock, is located a few blocks south of the Oglethorpe County Courthouse in Lexington. Children could once easily move the fifteen-ton boulder.

George R. Gilmer, a distinguished lawyer who served several terms as governor, state legislator, and United States congressman, discovered

A unique geological feature at Rock City near Chattanooga is the Turtle Rock.

Shaking Rock. In 1838 Gilmer's always-fragile health collapsed. While convalescing at home in Lexington, he scoured the countryside for minerals, Indian artifacts, and geological curiosities. During this time he began to develop the natural wonders where he had played as a child.

In his autobiography, Gilmer described the place where he found Shaking Rock, on a hilltop with a stream running along its base. "Masses of granite rocks, which have been divided by some great convulsion, are scattered about," he wrote, "the parts usually lying so near, and being so shaped for fitting into each other, that the most casual observer discovers that they were at one time united."

On this hill he found a rock "which rests upon two small points at its transverse ends so equally, that it is easily moved. A level space of several feet extends from this moveable rock to the precipice. The young people of the village assemble here to try the state of their hearts, by trying to set the rock in motion. As this is easily done, everyone over fifteen is found to be in love."

Gilmer decided that this mysterious spot should be a public park, so he bought the land to share its wonders with others. He laid out a walk from his home to the rock city and decorated it with flowers, grapevines, and fruit trees. The enchanted site was preserved and today Oglethorpe County maintains Shaking Rock Park.

The rocks are overwhelming in size, number, shape, and unique positions. There are perfectly flat boulders like Table Rock, which appears to have been sawed off even. An immense stone split cleanly down the middle with the halves lying three feet from each other is called the Squeeze. Giant rocks lie atop each other, leaving cavernlike spaces seven feet high beneath them. The sides of some rocks have been shaved clean, while others sport huge blisters as if they had been exposed to great heat.

Also near Lexington is Buffalo Lick, a huge boulder fifty feet high and located five feet from a steep cliff. It rests on a foundation of two stones, each a foot in circumference. Pioneers of the area said the rest of the base was licked away by animals, particularly buffalo, seeking salt. Another Buffalo Lick in Oglethorpe County was a large hollow on Dry Fork Creek, formed by animals exploiting its salt content.

In western McDuffie County, located just off an old Indian trail between the old George Granada place and the old Ray place, is a balance rock or "Indian throne" where "one large rock is perfectly balanced upon another, so that it rocks to and fro, upon being given a start, yet cannot be dislodged," according to a local history book. It somewhat resembles a throne, and local legend has Indian chiefs using it as such.

TOOT, TOOT—THE BOAT ROCK

A mile east of Owl Rock in Fulton County is Boat Rock Road, which is an immense boulder, shaped like the hull of a giant ocean liner, looming threateningly over a two-story house.

GROANING ROCK

The first settlers of Jackson County were frightened by ghastly moaning sounds that were heard on windy nights. After investigating, they were relieved to learn that the noise came not from the spirits of deceased Indians, but from a large sandstone rock with a hole in the center that emitted an eerie sound when the wind blew through it. The pioneers eventually named their first community Groaning Rock, but later residents changed it to the more sophisticated Commerce.

The rock is still there, just southeast of Commerce, but it is not accessible to the casual visitor. Also, the hollow is filled with leaf mold, so it has been a long time since the rock has groaned. Earline, Paul, and I endured a rocking tractor ride, courtesy of a kind farmer, followed by an invigorating hike to find it.

FROG ROCK

The famed Frog Rock is found at Lithia Springs, a distinguished old community that lies between Austell and Douglasville in Douglas County. It was a resort one hundred years ago, when the wealthy came to the medicinal springs to rest and recuperate. Those vacationers, and visitors ever since, have been intrigued by the rock. Located beside U.S. 78 near the remains of the resort is an enormous, fifteen-foot-high boulder that resembles a frog looking for all the world as if it is waiting for a petrified insect to zap with its stone tongue. Geologists believe the granite outcropping may be seven hundred million years old.

The famous Frog Rock in Lithia Springs. The Georgia Department of Transportation nearly sent the stone amphibian to extinction in a road-widening project.

The Frog still squats near the springs, although the Georgia Department of Transportation, which widened the highway, once threatened its habitat. Intervention by the Sweetwater Historical Society saved the formation, but perhaps Frog Rock should be declared an endangered species. We certainly wouldn't want this amphibian to croak, would we?

PULPIT ROCK

Beside GA 11 north of Monticello in Jasper County is a large boulder on which Rev. Lorenzo Dow preached when this area was sparsely populated.

Reverend Lorenzo Dow preached to the people of Jasper County from Pulpit Rock. In Screven County, Dow cursed Jacksonboro when the people rejected him. The community soon died out.

Brother Dow pronounced a curse on Jacksonboro in Screven County, and the community soon withered and died.

SANDS, MAN

SINGING SAND

When most sand is walked on, it makes no comment, but in a few rare locations sand being compressed emits a strange "singing" sound which is more accurately described as the crushing of newly fallen snow, or wet fingers being drawn across plastic wrap. Geologists say Georgia has four fine examples of this unusual phenomenon.

The most vocal of Georgia's "singing sands" is found near Thundering Springs, eight miles east of Woodbury in Meriwether County. The others are found near Groveland on sandbars in the Canoochee River, along the Ochlockonee River, and on the Alapaha River near Statenville.

Geologists continue to argue about what makes the sand sing. All they know for certain is that most of it is found in sandbars along small rivers. Some sand sings only when dry, some only when wet.

A number of sandhills across southern Georgia either were deposited by prehistoric wind patterns or the state's ancient beach line. These dunes near Albany mark Georgia's beachfront property eons ago.

SAND DUNES

This isn't about the beaches at Tybee or Jekyll but sand dunes where you wouldn't expect to find sand dunes, like the middle of the state. Actually, we find lost sand dunes in southwest and southeast Georgia.

A thirty-mile stretch of fossil sand dunes in the southwest extends along the Flint River and peaks just south of Albany. Geologists believe they are one million years old and marked the northern edge of the Gulf of Mexico at that time. The hills, twenty to thirty feet high, are composed of coarse, sharp, cream-colored grains. The dunes make an interesting recreational area for some, but unfortunately much of the sand is being mined for construction.

The Ohoopee Dunes are found in the southeast, along the Ohoopee and Canoochee Rivers, near Gordonia Altamaha State Park. These are small, prehistoric deserts that were located by scientists studying satellite photographs. They noticed unusual oval shapes, one and a half miles by four and a half miles, along the east banks of the two streams. Research indicates that the dunes were created in ancient times during a dry period when winds, blowing mainly from the west, picked up sand from the riverbeds and deposited it on the east banks of the rivers.

This part of the coastal plain was underwater for twenty million years during the Miocene era. Today the sand hills are inhabited by gopher tortoises, which tunnel thirty-five feet into the dunes to build their homes. The dunes resemble miniature deserts, where only small, twisted oak trees, tough shrubs, and lichens grow.

NATURAL WONDERS

WE NOW RETURN CONTROL OF YOUR CAR—MAGIC HILL

A mile west of Manchester, at the foot of Pine Mountain, was once a curiosity known as Magic Hill. For one hundred yards along a stretch of red clay road that extended across a spur of mountain, a car in neutral would appear to coast uphill. After passing over the apparent summit of the elevation, the vehicle then rolled to a halt on what looked like a downgrade. Water was similarly affected and seemed to defy the law of gravity by running uphill, and then flowing off the road and into a ditch instead of flowing on the downgrade.

Early settlers originally called the spot Ghost Hill because their wagons stalled going downhill, and ran away on the upslope. The enigma was pegged Magic Hill by journalists when it gained national prominence during the Great Depression. Newspapers picked up stories about the curious happenings there, and Robert L. Ripley made Magic Hill a "Believe It or Not" entry. It was featured as a short film at movie theaters,

Magic Hill has lost its charm. Graded and paved, it lives only in local lore near Manchester.

and picture postcards helped spread its fame. Local officials placed signs to the attraction to direct the people who arrived from a hundred miles around to determine if their cars would be affected. They invariably were. The ride was slow, but sure, and best of all, mysterious.

Surveyors solved the mystery over fifty years ago when they discovered that the ridge runs in a different direction from the road and the drainage ditch. That created an optical illusion that distorted a person's perception of the terrain. The phenomenon is fairly common and was often turned into tourist attractions. Others are found at Lake Wales, Florida; Magnetic Hill, Manitoba; Ayrshire, England; northern Portugal; and Cheju Do, an island off the coast of South Korea.

370

A "gravity hill" is located inside the Dalton Cemetery, where cars seem to be pushed up a slight rise, particularly at night with headlights extinguished.

TALLULAH GORGE

At one time north Georgia's Tallulah Gorge was the most famous natural landmark in America, transcending even Arizona's Grand Canyon, which a century ago was isolated and difficult to reach. Geologists tell us that Tallulah still beats the Grand Canyon in one respect—age. They claim that our own beloved gorge is the oldest in North America, about six hundred million years old, cut through the hard metamorphic rock of the Blue Ridge.

Vast Tallulah Gorge is three miles in length and reaches a depth of over one thousand feet and is about the same distance across. For 160 years it has attracted curious sightseers, scientists, daredevils, movie moguls, and an occasional eccentric mystic who expects something earthshaking to occur at this tear in terra firma.

Cherokee Indians, who inhabited the area until 150 years ago, feared the gorge and would not venture to its floor. They believed the canyon contained the entrance to hell, its gates guarded by a race of hostile pygmies who dwelled in caves. The Cherokee word *tallulah* translates to "terrible" in English. When the gold rush swept north Georgia in the 1830s, people prospected in the canyon. Although fabulous stories are told of a prospector named Weaver who found a nugget as big as a grindstone, no gold was thought to have been found here.

For many years Tallulah Falls was a major resort center. It was called both the "Grand Canyon of the East" and the "Niagara Falls of the South." Tallulah was a natural haven for honeymooners and wealthy coastal planters who fled the disease-infested lowlands during summers. A narrow-gauge railroad transported swarms of visitors into the scenic mountains, where they stayed at a number of large resort hotels. The best bands and orchestras performed, and fine restaurants prospered. For a time, Tallulah rivaled Niagara Falls in popularity.

When Georgia Power built the Tallulah Hydroelectric Station in 1913, they diverted the water and at the same time turned off the tourist tap. Now lacking the falls, this wonder was renamed Tallulah Gorge, which lacked the dramatic flair of a "falls." "Falls" is active; a "gorge" just sits there. Tourists stopped coming and the hotels closed. People went to nearby Toccoa for their falls, or further into the mountains, where waterfalls are plentiful.

In 1971 actor Jon Voight, as a character in the movie *Deliverance* (which, incidentally, did more for the reputation of backwoods Southerners than any number of *Beverly Hillbillies* or *Dukes of Hazzard* reruns ever could), scaled the gorge wall, long after daredevils started walking across the crevice on high wires.

Georgia Power has recently released water to the falls and Georgia has opened a state park at the site. Let the good times fall.

PROVIDENCE CANYONS

"Georgia's Little Grand Canyons," found near Lumpkin in Stewart County, are a recent geological landmark. It is truly amazing how quickly Providence Canyons, named for a church (built, apparently, on shifting sands) which it swallowed, formed so quickly. It took the Tallulah River six hundred million years to carve out Tallulah Gorge, but it only took a handful of Georgia farmers less than 150 years to produce Providence. That's progress.

Despite fanciful legends about what precipitated the formation of this great hole, severe erosion was the actual culprit. The action started in the 1820s; by 1850 there were four ditches, each about five feet deep and 150

Providence Canyon, Georgia's "Little Grand Canyon," is a series of glorified gullies cut over the past century by erosion.

feet long. It took a very short time to produce a number of astonishing gorges in the soft earth. Some of the canyons are now 150 feet deep, 400 feet wide, and half a mile long.

This is the coastal plain, where the soil, composed of loosely arranged sand and particles of clay, was deposited in colorful layers called *sediments*, beginning sixty-five to eighty-five million years ago. When settlers arrived in southwest Georgia in the early 1800s, they clear-cut the land and began farming, ignorant of modern conservation techniques such as contour plowing. Rainwater, unobstructed by vegetation, ran across plowed fields, carrying away the topsoil, carving gullies, called caves by locals, and running wild through the soft underlying sediments. Erosion continues at Providence Canyons. It is not unusual for twenty-five to fifty tons of soil to abruptly collapse, taking many trees down with it. A heavy rain can cause six feet of erosion in a single night.

GETTING OFF AT THE ROCKS

The Rocks are a curious geological formation found north of Broxton in northwestern Coffee County, across the state from Providence Canyons in southeastern Georgia. One-third of south Georgia, fifteen thousand square miles, sits atop a formation called the Altamaha Grit, sandstone laid down fifteen million years ago during the Miocene epoch. It is almost completely covered by later sediments that constitute the flat topography of the coastal plain.

At the Rocks, erosion caused by the swift waters of Rocky Creek has carved a dramatic, sandstone canyon that ends at the Ocmulgee River. The formation, twenty miles long, one mile wide, and sixty feet deep, was created in the past fifteen thousand years—recent by geological standards. It is the largest sandstone outcrop on the coastal plain of the southeastern United States.

The sculpting of the easily eroded sandstone has created a unique preserve for the region, which includes a ten-foot-high waterfall, rapids, and caves. The top of the cliff is fractured by a maze of crevices, or canyons, which are narrow at the top, from a few inches to several feet, but are deep and wide at the bottom. Local tradition attributes this to earthquakes, but simple water erosion is the true cause.

The site is not just geologically interesting, it also creates a unique ecology, home to 450 species of flora, sixty of them rarely found outside of northern Georgia, and several rare and endangered species. Additional species are frequently discovered. In the spring flowers that are seen nowhere else in the region blossom. Beneath the sandstone outcroppings are overhangs, cool, damp, and dark places that are home to a dozen species of orchids. There turkey buzzards nest, and gopher tortoises and endangered indigo snakes burrow. Lichens grow on the stone, softening it with acid and creating soil that nourishes vegetation. Trees sprout from the rock.

RINGS OF FIRE

On July 18, 1881, a unique tornado danced across Sumter County, according to landowner Z. T. Baisden, who described the phenomenon to the *Americus Republican* in an article widely reprinted. At noon the whirlwind, fairly small, five feet in diameter and up to one hundred feet in height, struck a twelve-acre cornfield.

"The body of it was perfectly black," the press report stated, "with fire in the centre and emitted a strong sulfurous vapor that could be smelt three hundred yards from it."

Periodically, the storm split into three parts and swept quickly across the field, "twisting up the cornstalks by the roots" and carrying them off with considerable dirt. "These three minor whirlwinds would then come together with a loud crash, crackling and burning and shoot high up into the heavens."

Three young ladies approached to a distance of 150 feet from the phenomenon, "but received such a shower of burning sand upon their faces and necks" that they raced for refuge in the house. Baisden's field hands were frightened by the bizarre event. Although the cyclone seemed to be a furnace, none of the corn, even that sucked up by the whirlwind, was burnt. Could the fire have been an illusion? Unlikely, for "its sulfurous vapor sickened and burnt all who got close enough to get a full breath of it."

On March 20, 1875, a terrible tornado tore across three states, entering Georgia from Alabama and raging through Harris, Talbot, Upson, Monroe, Jones, Baldwin, Hancock, Warren, McDuffie, and Columbia Counties before exiting into South Carolina. McDuffie County residents observed it from the north and it was described "as luminous, as flame with an unusual light," according to the county historian. "Black volumes of smoke, seemingly propelled by an Almighty Power, were ushered from the mouth of the awful-looking furnace."

Fiery tornadoes apparently love us, for the *Chicago Tribune* of January 7, 1892, reported "a black tornado filled with fire" which, according to Charles Fort in *LO!*, "shot across the state of Georgia" like a fiery blast tearing down the slopes of Vesuvius.

This phenomenon has been observed in Tennessee, England, France, India, and Spain. The modern master researcher of anomalies, William Corliss, finds these events to be larger than ball lightning but smaller than tornadoes and combining elements of both. He suggests it is an "electrical discharge phenomena."

GREAT BALLS OF FIRE

Corliss describes ball lightning as a luminous sphere that can vary from one inch to five feet in diameter and "moves freely in the atmosphere, descending from clouds and following tortuous paths in the open air, sometimes against the wind, and wending its way around rooms in buildings almost as if it were inspecting the premises." Colored yellow, red, blue-white, purple, and green, it can be "sharply defined, fuzzy, or surrounded" by a halo. "A hissing or buzzing sound" is often heard, and although materializes silently, disappears instantly with an explosion, leaving a smell of sulfur or ozone.

The most spectacular such event in Georgia occurred in 1952 when an aircraft from Moody Air Force Base in Valdosta collided with a large orange fireball. The encounter rocked the plane and fused a radio and a compass.

From Heard County, Owen C. Davis Sr. claimed several encounters with ball lightning, in both ball and a rare cylindrical version. During the summer of 1942 Davis was looking out a kitchen window at dusk as "the ball of fire came through my window but did not break the glass." Ten inches in diameter, it flew across the kitchen and entered a hall, then detoured into a bedroom and disappeared through another window.

At 11:00 P.M. on July 10, 1982, barking dogs directed Davis's attention to a window. "I thought a car had stopped and had its lights on," Davis said, "but then I saw it was not a car.

"I could see my garden and field just like day. I looked up the road and saw a log that looked like it was red hot traveling about a hundred feet above the ground. It was red all over, but I don't believe it was hot. It was about forty or fifty feet from my house." It traveled north to south at an altitude of six to eight feet, and measured twelve-feet long and twenty inches in diameter.

During the summer of 1919 two teachers, Dewey Davis and his brother-in-law Benjamin Franklin, were returning from a meeting in a buggy when they noticed "a ball of light the size of a basketball" exiting the gate of a cemetery. It approached them and attached itself to the lamppost on the wagon. Although terrified, they continued the journey for a mile. While crossing a bridge over Hillabahatchee Creek the ball left and followed the creek out of sight.

According to Davis's daughter, Dorothy Jean Davis Moore, the men "thought they had seen a ghost or a spirit" and "told the story . . . till the end of their lives."

A final Heard County account was made in February 1990 at 3:00 A.M. as a resident watched television. Looking out a window, she spotted a bright red ball moving beside the house for five minutes.

A Heard County history book noted that the area produces many heavy thunderstorms, the climatic conditions "just right for producing" ball lightning.

A FOGGY NIGHT IN GEORGIA

A spot where nature has conspired to create perfect conditions for the accumulation of fog is appropriately named "No Man's Friend Swamp." Unfortunately, a two-and-a-half-mile stretch of I-75, one of America's busiest highways, runs straight through it. Every day tens of thousands of vehicles race through the affected area. Too often fog suddenly drops visibility to near zero. That, combined with the practice of burning off fields in the area, was responsible for three spectacular pileups in the 1980s.

In 1981 four people were killed in a multivehicle wreck created by these peculiar conditions. On December 29, 1984, fifteen people were injured under similar circumstances. On November 18, 1985, one person was killed and seventeen hospitalized when five tractor-trailer trucks and eleven other vehicles piled up at 3:00 A.M. The fog-smoke fell quickly, "like a curtain coming down," one witness said. "You couldn't see nothing," another stated. A third commented, "All I could hear was fenders banging and people screaming."

To prevent these massive wrecks, local authorities were given the power to close the interstate when necessary. Georgia Tech also developed a two-million-dollar computerized system that would automatically detect dangerous conditions and alert officials.

FOR A FOGGY NIGHT (THANKS TO LARRY NIVEN)

Hurricane Hazel slammed into the South Carolina coast at 9:00 A.M. on October 15, 1954. Her 150-mile-per-hour winds and dangerous storm surge killed ninety-eight people and caused over $250 million in damages. She also destroyed a number of navigational devices, so several days later the Coast Guard buoy tender *Smilax* set out to repair or replace them.

The *Smilax*'s captain, Chief Warrant Officer Creech, left Brunswick and steamed north. In Ossabaw Sound near Savannah the crew entered extremely dense fog. Creech slowed the one-hundred-foot vessel to two knots and once each minute the vessel's foghorn sounded for five seconds.

Another foghorn sounded to their front and was approaching. Creech stopped the ship, but the other foghorn seemed to have also become stationary. The *Smilax* resumed its trip and the other horn moved behind it. Then a second foghorn blasted from their front, getting louder as the one behind diminished.

Creech stopped again. The crew had been studying their radar, but it indicated no other ships in the area, just a buoy and the shore.

Creech ordered Seaman Second Class Ike Levine to activate the ship's powerful carbon arc light, but the beam illuminated the fog for only a few yards before disappearing. Abruptly, a beam of light shown down on the *Smilax* from above. Again, the radar showed nothing. When Levine tilted his light up toward the other beam, the light disappeared.

A puzzled crew sailed out of the fog a few minutes later. After considerable thought, they believed the mystery solved. The foghorns belonged to fish-packing facilities that dotted the coast. They were stationary, while the ship moved. The light was probably their own, refracted in a variety of directions by the different layers and densities of the fog. *Maybe.*

BALD MOUNTAINS AND ROCK DOUGHNUTS

A number of Georgia's mountaintops are "balds," so eroded that only bare stone remains on the summits, allowing no opportunity for vegetation to flourish. Blood Mountain, the highest and most popular stretch of the Appalachian Trail in Georgia, is a bald, with extraordinary views of mountains and valleys. Another easily accessible bald is Black Rock Mountain, named for the dark granite that composes its bare shoulders, part of a state park in Rabun County. Brasstown Bald, Georgia's highest peak (4,748 feet), has a visitors center on the summit, from which four states may be seen.

On several of the bald mountains, particularly Stone Mountain, are a curious anomaly—shallow circular depressions, two to six feet in diameter, primarily ring-shaped with deeply etched rims, but with a protruding, hollow center. While this is generally credited to weathering, they are found just west of the Carolina Bays (discussed later in this chapter) and "may somehow be associated with the Bays," states one expert, say, through a common explanation in terms of meteorite impact.

LUMPKIN COUNTY'S ROCK HOUSES

For over half a century hikers on the Appalachian Trail and motorists who drive up to Neel's Gap on U.S. 19 have stopped at the Walasi-Yi Center and asked for the location of the "rock house." It is supposed to be located on the summit of 4,463-foot-high Blood Mountain, named for a vicious battle fought there three hundred years ago when the Cherokees defeated an invading force of Creeks. The rock house is alleged to extend up to fifty feet into the mountain through solid stone.

Known locally as Rock House, the opening is a small, cramped hole bored into the base of a steep cliff face. The front of the cliff is obscured by an artificial wall made of closely stacked rocks that are so old they are now covered by a layer of thick lichens. The cave, about seven feet high, is large enough to hold a number of people, the walls and ceiling covered by soot from many fires. In the center of the cave are heaps of ashes.

According to Cherokee legend, the interior of this majestic mountain is a subterranean home of the *Nunnehi*, or Immortals, a benevolent race of beings who live forever. They helped the Cherokees, particularly children, when they were lost or hurt in the mountain wilderness. The Yunwee Chuns Dee, or little people, a race of fairies whose music once drifted across the peaks, also traditionally inhabited the mountain. This rock house/cave/tunnel was supposedly an entrance to the Cherokee netherlands.

The story of the Rock House was apparently first published in *Georgia: A Guide to Its Towns and Countryside* (1940), a Great Depression project reprinted by the University of Georgia Press. The late Earnest Andrews featured a slightly different version in *Georgia's Fabulous Treasure Hoards.* According to him, a ranger found petroglyphs indicating that an Indian treasure was hidden in or near the cave, so he dynamited it, but no treasure was found.

Curiously, the depression tour guide mentioned a second rock house that was located on a branch path of the Appalachian Trail between Tenastee Gap and Neel's Gap, also in Lumpkin County. It was reached on the Enotah Trail from Chattahoochee Gap, and a mile off Enotah Trail on an unmarked path. Apparently, neither rock house ever existed.

Another natural curiosity is found in southwestern Pickens County, where Sharp Mountain and adjacent Talley Mountain form the shape of a sleeping woman. According to legend, the Cherokee returned here for their hidden treasure, perhaps in a now-sealed cave beneath Sharp Mountain that ran underground for several miles. The Cherokee also revered a "hot hole" from which steam occasionally escaped. The latter feature, also now sealed, yielded the fossilized teeth of saber-toothed tigers.

Caves are commonly found in northwest Georgia, but they are dangerous to enter without professional guides, and even then they can be treacherous. I had not heard from one college buddy for years until I was watching the news a few years back and saw that he was one of a party that nearly drowned from a flash flood while exploring one of those caverns.

SHELL BLUFF

Shell Bluff, which runs for miles along the Georgia side of the Savannah River, rises 150 feet above the water seven miles east of McBean, in Burke County. Composed of giant sea oyster shells from the Eocene age, the formation has long attracted renowned scientists. In 1765 famed naturalist John Bartram visited the site, followed by his son William in 1773, who said the shells had the "color and consistency of clear white marble" and marveled at their "incredible magnitude, generally fifteen or twenty inches in length, from six to eight inches wide, and two to four inches in thickness, and their hallows sufficient to receive an ordinary man's foot." They were "undoubtedly very ancient" and locals used them for lime in construction projects. The formation sits atop a foundation of soft white rock consisting of pulverized shells. Noted British geologist Sir Charles Cyell, who worked for three days collecting forty species of shells, first scientifically described the site in 1842. In 1834 A. T. Conrad had bestowed an official name on the shells—*ostrea georgiana.*

SHOW ME THE MONEY ROCKS
A jumble of curious rock formations and boulders are found on the south side of Money Rocks Road, near Gibson Road in Talbot County. Rumors persist that residents secreted currency, gold, and silver coins in the area during the Civil War. Federal troops passed through in early April 1865, in the closing days of the conflict. Nothing has ever been found, but treasure hunters still occasionally scour the area.

THAT SINKHOLE FEELING
South and northwest Georgia have problems with limestone sinkholes. Underground water slowly eats away the soft stone until a large section of

Portions of Berry College's beautiful campus have repeatedly been undermined by sinkholes.

land is undermined and caves in. Geologists report that sinkholes are also caused by "coids," underground stream paths that dry up, which is why so many sinkholes appear during summer. Some have swallowed houses and swimming pools, and the highway department occasionally issues warnings about pulling off the road in certain areas for fear that the earth will swallow unwary motorists. A sinkhole once threatened to engulf a museum in Albany, where the city has put twin lime sinks to good use as playing fields.

After Hurricane Alberto dumped two feet of rain on Albany in a single day, over three hundred sinkholes developed, literally overnight. They swallowed a large rescue truck and several homes, and created hazards in a number of streets. "It's Swiss cheese over there," said James Hyatt, an assistant professor of geology at Valdosta State University.

Berry College in Rome has had periodic problems with limestone sinkholes for over half a century. They probably result from aquifers beneath the campus, which dissolve the limestone. In the mid-1980s a campus landmark, Victory Lake, opened after World War I, was emptied by two sinkholes "like an open drain in a bathtub," said a college official. After two six-foot-deep holes were filled with clay, a third again emptied the lake. When a third repair job was defeated by a fourth hole, nature was awarded a win.

One of Georgia's many giant lime sinks located, appropriately enough, at Lakeland, in Lanier County.

In the late 1990s a series of sinks opened, swallowing a cow grazing in a pasture and a maintenance worker on a riding lawn mower. Man and beast were recovered, startled but unhurt.

Four sinkholes in Fairmount recently threatened a main rail line. Trains were required to travel at only sixty miles per hour and the rails were inspected before and after the passage of each. The company pumped cement beneath the rail bed to depths of fifty feet to stabilize the area, and reinforced an eighty-foot-long bridge. A forty-foot-deep sinkhole opened up near the city sewage treatment pond, forcing the town to build another plant. A year earlier, a sinkhole had dried up Satacoa Creek, the city's water supply.

Early historians were puzzled by the origin of numerous perfect ponds with stands of trees in them. White wrote of several that covered a total of six square miles. In 1827 he claimed that the earth in one place abruptly sank one hundred feet and eventually filled with water. He also noted that many streams in Lowndes County would disappear for miles, then reappear, usually in and out of caves.

Ten miles from Quitman, near Harmony Church, is the Devil's Hopper. A narrow ravine, two hundred yards long, thirty feet deep, and twenty-five feet wide, leads to a cave variously described as a narrow vortex, funnel, entrance, throat, or gullet, which has swallowed trees, animals, and tons of clay and limestone. For centuries people have clamored down or been lowered eight feet into the cave, which they report to be filled with large limestone blocks. Large rooms have been hollowed out of the soft material. The walls are made of clay and large masses fall from the ceilings. Many bones are found, left by animals that fell into the pit and could not scramble out. The cave begins high enough for a person to walk, but narrows. For a long time locals claimed that the bottom of the Hopper could not be determined, but a river can be heard rushing far below. A local newspaper columnist ventured down into the Hopper and discovered a crucifix sculptured from clay and the letters *I N R I*.

ROCK HOUSES

Rock House Cave (the depression formerly known as Hamilton Sink) is several miles east of Ashburn. It is seventy feet deep and five hundred feet in circumference, with perpendicular cliffs on all sides save one. Water occasionally escapes through a hole in the bottom.

A similar feature, on the west side of the Alapaha River, is a large depression or hole 300 feet long, 150 feet wide, and 200 feet deep. At the bottom is a rock house fifteen feet square, with carved stairs leading down to the water. Over the years many visitors have chiseled their names on the stone walls.

Twelve miles west of Quitman near Ozell in Brooks County is Dry Lake, which mysteriously drains every two to three years and becomes bone dry after the water slowly flows through two small, deep drains, or "suckholes" as they are locally called, into an underground stream that feeds the lake. As the last water drains, it makes a terrible roaring sound, which can be heard for some distance. During the water's retreat, people wade into the mud and gather large quantities of fish left by the receding water, which exposed a thirty-foot-deep basin with a smooth clay bottom.

The lake periodically fills and drains, according to local legend, every seventh year, and empties in a week. In truth the water recessional occurs at intervals of three to ten years, and requires three months to drain. At one time the owner attempted to stop the draining by making a great stopper of brush and baling wire, but the hole sucked the whole contraption away. During drainings the owner sold tickets for the collection of fish, but on one occasion he sold too many. There was a near riot as fisherpersons speared each other's feet.

Between Valdosta and Quitman are the Blue Springs, a popular picnic area. It has a pool filled with spring water, which occasionally runs dry.

Near Adel, in Cook County, is the Lime Suck. Small and surrounded by trees, it is a popular picnic site. This one never runs dry, and legend says no one has ever touched the bottom.

CRYSTAL LAKE

The original name of Crystal Lake, one of the most beautiful bodies of water in southern Georgia, was Bone Lake, named for its Civil War–era owner, Willie Bone. Because millers were exempted from military service, he purchased the land around the lake and hauled steam-powered milling machines through the forests to establish a gristmill. Bone, whatever his origin, certainly opposed slavery and the war, evaded the draft, and reportedly beat up an elderly resident. His character was held in low regard by the locals.

When an area slave named Tony, owned by Samuel M. Young, disappeared, rumor spread that Bone was hiding him until he could book passage north on the Underground Railroad. Jack Walker was dispatched to search for the runaway. In Bone's field he saw Tom's footprints, distinctive because of a missing toe on one foot. While tying up the slave, Walker laid down his gun. As Tony struggled, Bone either shot Walker with his own gun or killed him with a blow from a heavy rock. Bone buried Walker in a shallow grave beside the creek. His son, Philip, later claimed that his father also killed Tony and dumped him in the deepest portion of the lake. Two days after Walker disappeared, a posse arrived and discovered Walker's body. The vigilantes immediately hanged Bone from a handy tree. An alternate version of this tale has Bone giving refugee to several Union prisoners who escaped from Andersonville.

Since that time, stories have circulated about Tony's ghost being seen on the surface of the lake, Walker's ghost walking the sandy soil, and Bone's spirit hanging around the tree (pun intended).

In the 1920s investors renamed the one-hundred-acre body Crystal Lake and opened it as a recreational area with swimming, dancing, bowling, skating, and all manner of diversions for the young. One summer night a party on the beautiful white sand shore broke up in hysteria when revelers saw the devil rise up from the lake's depths (or so they say).

Crystal Lake, fifteen miles east of Ashburn, is still a popular recreational area. There are rumors that it is bottomless, which is not true, for past owners have attempted to cement the limestone drain that occasionally emptied the lake underground into the Alapaha River.

On the western side of the Alapaha River in Irwin County, Deep Creek flows into the river from Ross Lake, three-quarters of a mile long and one-quarter of a mile wide, which abounds with fish. On the east side is a 150-foot bluff, and at the foot of the bluff is an underground waterway twelve feet square at the top but smaller at the bottom where water enters.

Not far away is a similar, smaller lake, called Coleman Pond, which ran dry every three to seven years, when fish gathering was great sport and good eating.

Rev. George White mentioned this phenomenon in his *Historical Collections of Georgia*. His sink was located on the Little River, and most of the water was diverted into a subterranean stream. When the sulfuric water rushed out at a rate of ten thousand gallons a minute, it turned a mill wheel, which worked in low water and was submerged in high. The springs were five to thirty feet in diameter, and apparently bottomless.

Four miles from Thomasville, on the extensive Millpond Plantation, is a T-shaped limesink that is twenty to five hundred feet wide and more than forty feet deep. It runs dry every summer, and fills with water in the winter. Attempts to stop the water from running out failed.

CRISP COUNTY'S ROCK HOUSE

Crisp County has a Rock House Cave, located two miles east of I-75 and south of Cordele. It has several entrances, but the primary one is fourteen feet in diameter and descends to a depth of thirty-five feet. There are low spots where one must crawl, and narrow places that barely accommodate the human body. The formation has a number of rooms and corridors that extend in several directions. In the cave are waterfalls and deep lakes, the source of which has been difficult to determine. At spots candles and lanterns flickered out, indicating low oxygen levels. Parts of the grotto have yet to be explored.

Stories are told of mysterious noises and unusual scenes in the cave. It is said to be an Indian burial site, its most prominent inhabitant a Chief Hunting More (honest). Petrified bodies and Indian artifacts have been found there. It is considered a dangerous place to visit.

A CAVE THAT SUCKS AND BLOWS

A particular type of natural phenomenon are blowing wells. Our example, which sucks as well as blows, is found in Decatur County, located at the bottom of a thirty-foot-deep hole. "From the mouth of this cave issue strong currents of air," a scientific treatise on the topic reads, "with a continuous roar that is heard seventy yards off. At certain hours of the day, a hat . . . or other light object thrown at it, are blown six or seven feet high into the air, and at other hours of the day, with a suction relatively great, the mouth of the cave draws in any such article placed near it."

Scientists suggest that it has a diurnal cycle, its activity precipitated by changes in temperature. "Temperature differences between the air in the caves and the outside air can give rise to natural circulation," wrote William Corliss, dean of natural phenomenon research.

Many of these unique formations have silted over, but there is hope that the state will clean some out and establish a state park around them.

ROCK OVEN

The swampy, isolated Altamaha River swamp near Baxley in Appling County is eerily quiet and foreboding. It is devoid of habitants but often visited by those who hunt, fish, hike, picnic, and canoe, and the generally curious. The sluggish stream and lazy lagoons harbor quicksand, wildcats, bears, and poisonous snakes.

A strange limestone ridge, two hundred yards long, rises fifty to sixty feet above the morass. Discovered in 1818, there were once hundreds of names carved on its soft sides. A number of tunnels and caves pierced this peculiar geographic formation, in which charcoal from ancient fires and Indian artifacts have been found, dating back at least four thousand years. Many of the excavations have crumbled. The largest chamber, the Rock Oven, covered with soot on the inside, was originally much deeper and larger. Over time, rocks, some weighing tons, have fallen.

"There's something down there that's awful strange," said Benny Coursey, local resident for ninety years. "I've heard fellows tell me they've seen ghosts around those old caves and heard voices like babies crying or a woman screaming."

Others have seen strange green lights dancing over the lowlands and Indians, perhaps spirits of the native Tama, dancing before the entrances to the caves. Rumors circulate that Satan worshipers favor the eerie spot, and Spanish treasure is said to be secreted in the bottomlands.

SHAKE, RATTLE, AND ROLL

In 1811 and 1812 the most severe earthquakes ever recorded in North America occurred around New Madrid, Missouri. The quakes were so severe that the Mississippi River ran backward, yawning crevices opened and closed in the ground, and large areas of land rose and fell. The earth movement was so intense that it was plainly felt on the eastern seaboard. One quake on December 16, 1811, caused citizens of Savannah "to totter as if on shipboard," as did the residents of Athens. Continuing shocks during January 1812 caused an Augusta man to observe that "a large proportion of our inhabitants never lay down at night with feelings similar to those they experienced when going to bed during the past week."

An earthquake on February 7, 1812, cracked brick and stone buildings in Savannah and produced sounds described as thunder, carriages passing over paved roads, and heavy artillery. That month also produced sulfurous odors and earthquake lights over the city.

According to Indian legend, the great Shawnee chief Tecumseh, angry that some tribes would not agree to his plans for attacking settlers, stomped the ground and made the earth quake. Tecumseh's mother, Methoatagke, was reportedly a Georgia native.

Events of the year 1811 in Wilkes County brought predictions of doom after severe earth shocks frightened humans and animals alike, a "bright, broad, fan-tailed comet" passed across the sky, and a devastating storm of giant hailstones fell.

THE BIG ONE

At five minutes till 9:00 P.M. on Tuesday night, August 31, 1886, the strongest earthquake ever recorded east of the Mississippi River devastated Charleston, South Carolina, killing over a hundred people and inflicting devastating damage to the city. The quake was so powerful that it had a significant impact on large parts of Georgia, the first wave lasting from one to three minutes, with up to six aftershocks. Those who experienced it, even as children, retained vivid memories of the event their entire lives and frequently told the tales, often exaggerated and humorous. Across the state bricks and stones toppled from chimneys, plaster fell from ceilings and walls, tables and chairs danced across floors. Doors and cabinets opened and shut, floors creaked, brick walls cracked, clocks stopped ticking, and dishes rattled and fell off tables, shelves, and cupboards.

In Douglas County, the congregation of a small frame Methodist Church, located at Broad Street and Rose Avenue, had finished their final prayer and the choir director launched the congregation into a rousing chorus of "How Firm a Foundation." At that point the temple began to shake, "leading the multitude to realize that the foundation referred to in the hymn was not old mother earth," according to a county history book.

A number of people noticed peculiar behavior from their animals minutes before the quake struck. One woman watched the family cat drag her litter out of the house and bed them down in bushes several feet away. Other cats deserted the premises for several days. Horses and mules pawed open stable doors and escaped into the open, cattle bellowed, chickens left their roosts, and dogs barked urgently. Many people felt these were further signs that the world was ending. It has since been theorized that animals are receptive to electrically charged particles released from the ground just before the earth moves in a quake.

In Atlanta, the new *Constitution* building survived a severe shaking, but three downtown houses suffered damage to roofs and chimneys.

From the Methodist Church in Lawrenceville, where a religious revival was coming to a close, the *Constitution* reported, "When it was ascertained that the earth was melting beneath them the wildest confusion and consternation ensued. Most of the people were seized with an impulse to flee from the house, some did, but those of the assembly present less excited succeeded in calming the more excited and restless ones and order was for a short while resumed. Mr. Worley had just closed a most powerful appeal to the people to come to the altar and publicly renounce their sins and seek Christ. After appealing to them in the strongest terms possible only one came; and while he was again persuading them to come and telling them they knew not the day nor the hour when they would be summoned before the judgment seat to answer for their deeds in this world, the earth began to shake, the house trembled, and the people rose from their seats, some screaming and others praying, and still others rejoicing, exclaiming that they were glad of it; that it was a warning to the people to flee from the wrath to come before it was too late. In a short time the church was deserted."

THE ROD OF MOSES
Another effect was noticed in Gwinnett County where a productive spring on the Doc Harris place between Grayson and New Hope Church ceased to flow. However, the face of a flat rock nearby cracked "and from it gushed the stream of crystal clear water that had formally fed the old spring." A

neat basin was chiseled from the granite below the spring, which is report-edly still visible.

In Milledgeville the walls of the Darien Bank were so warped by severe shocks that extensive repairs were required. Several houses and the Old Capital were damaged as bricks tumbled from chimneys and plaster sepa-rated from walls. The ominous low rumbling emptied the McComb Hotel. At nearby Meriwether Station a farmer spent the entire night praying, and it was reported that a persistent Bible salesman trooping across the county the next day made record sales.

Mill hands in Surrency, our haunted spot in Appling County, were having a spirited night of poker when the first shock puzzled and alarmed them. Subsequent jolts sent them to a railroad embankment where poker gave way to prayer and gospel singing as water in the ditches splashed up around them.

When the shock hit McDuffie County praying was in progress at the Fountain Campground. In context, it seemed like a divine warning and many came forward to repent and rededicate their lives. Another religious revival was being conducted in a home in Thompson when the quake struck, shaking the home like a locomotive was thundering through.

Pine Log Methodist Church, in Bartow County, is one of Georgia's oldest surviving houses of worship. Built in 1842, it had seen service for over four decades when the quake struck. Reverend J. N. Sullivan was con-ducting campground meetings that night and had grown frustrated when the congregation did not respond as fervently as they might. Sullivan fell to his knees and prayed, "Lord, if it takes it to move the hearts of these people, shake the ground on which this old building stands."

"Almost before these words were out of the minister's mouth," Mrs. Eliza-beth Garrison recorded, "the building shook perceptibly. My aunt Lulu remembered opening her eyes and seeing the preacher's water glass and pitcher on the pulpit shaking."

The camp-meeting crowd surged toward the altar, joined by many in the community who abandoned their homes and raced for salvation, physi-cal and spiritual. Many were never convinced that an earthquake had caused the phenomenon, and records prove that attendance and contribu-tions increased dramatically afterward.

LIGHTNING STRIKES

William Corliss has collected sixteen documented cases of "lightning fig-ures," including one incident from Georgia. In Americus (see also flaming tornado) on July 12, 1875, lightning struck a tree, severing a limb, then passed into a house where its several inhabitants "were rendered insensible for a time—and on their recovery there were found impressed upon the bodies of them all more or less distinct images of this tree," particularly on the body of a child who had stood in the center of the room. A witness said, "The child is impressed upon its back and exactly opposite upon its stomach. The entire tree is plain, and perfect in toto: every limb, branch, and leaf, and even the severed part, is plainly perceptible."

Impressions of entire leaves were not left on the body, but the skeleton outline of each was. In time the figures faded away.

AGAIN AND AGAIN AND AGAIN AND AGAIN (LOU CHRISTIE)

It seems that vast stretches of concrete attracts lightning. During the spring and summer large strikes crater the runway at Hartsfield International Airport two or three times a week. In mid-April 1997, an unusually large crater, four feet across and nine inches deep, closed a runway for ninety minutes, causing thirty-five flights to be delayed.

METEORITES

Twenty-one recognized meteorites have been recovered in Georgia, composed predominately of iron and iron/nickel alloy, with only four classed as stony, an unusually small percentage. They range in weight from one-tenth of an ounce to nearly two thousand pounds. The thirteen-pound Twin City meteorite has an unusual shape—two large, irregular interlocking pieces. The Locust Grove meteorite resembles a jawbone.

Georgia lays claim to perhaps the oldest meteorite found in the nation, and it is also by far the largest discovered in Georgia. A farmer plowing his fields in 1940 in Jenkins County found the Sardis meteorite, weighing 1,764 pounds and measuring thirty-eight by twenty-eight by twelve inches.

The first meteorite to be seen falling from the sky in the United States impacted near Forsyth in Monroe County at 3:30 P.M. on May 8, 1829. Witnesses first saw a small black cloud that emitted two separate explosions, followed by a "tremendous rumbling or whizzing noise" that lasted two to five minutes. Several hours later slaves working a field one mile south of Forsyth discovered a thirty-six-pound meteorite embedded in the soil at a depth of nearly three feet. It was excavated within hours of impact.

A 516-pound meteorite barely missed B. F. Wilson, who was picking cotton four miles south of Thompson on October 15, 1880. On impact it penetrated six inches into the earth.

A number of people in Stewart County heard a commotion in the sky on October 6, 1869. According to a witness, over half a minute he heard "first a succession of about three explosions, followed by deep roaring for several seconds, and then by a rushing or whizzing sound of something rushing with great speed through the air nearby. The sound ceased suddenly." Two workmen saw the thirteen-ounce meteorite kick up dirt as it landed only twenty feet from them, leaving an eighteen-inch circle of loose soil on an otherwise bare, hard-packed yard.

Georgia's best-known meteorite was found in Social Circle in 1926. The 219-pound iron has been extensively studied, twice by the U.S. National Museum, because of an unusually uniform granular texture that extends throughout the entire body. This is thought to be the result of heating up before entering earth's atmosphere, perhaps by a close approach to the sun.

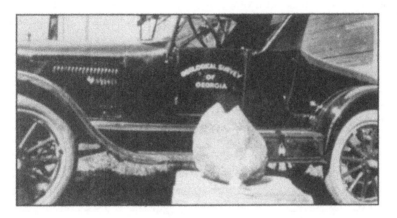

The Social Circle meteorite. Eleven hacksaw blades were ruined removing the triangular piece from the top. (Courtesy of Georgia Geological Survey)

One meteorite left off the list compiled by the Georgia Geological Survey fell in 1875 in Catoosa County, according to the county history. Men cutting wood on Roger Bowman's property broke for lunch, during which a brief but violent thunderstorm passed. Returning to the woods, they found a large hot rock deeply embedded in the soil—it had caused fallen leaves to ignite. Said to be iron-stone, it was reportedly left in place.

According to Athenaeum in 1836, in 1826 several persons were killed by a falling aerolite in Georgia, and in July 1829 an Indian named Alika was also killed. Additional information would be appreciated.

What was briefly thought to be an enormous meteorite near Blue Ridge was found to be something much more ordinary. In the spring of 1986 bulldozers grading a hill exposed an unusual formation composed of iron located fifteen feet beneath the surface. Awaiting an analysis by geologists, developers tried to protect the find while many people did their best to make off with keepsakes. The verdict: an unusually large iron geode, formed by groundwater depositing iron over millions of years around a cavity—in this case the size of a small car. Most geodes are no larger than a fist.

IT WOULD HAVE LOOKED LIKE ARMAGGEDON

The landscape of southern and eastern Georgia is dotted with giant shallow craters that may be the result of a comet explosion that occurred forty thousand years ago. They are called Carolina Bays because most are found in those states, but Georgia ranks third in number, with more than one thousand, and they cover an incredible quarter of a million acres.

These facts are known about the craters, according to state geologist Sam Pickering: They always occur in sandy soil, are always pointed in the same direction, and all are roughly oval or elliptical-shaped. Each has a pronounced rim of sand surrounding it, the rim lowest to the southeast, which indicates the direction from which the giant shotgun blast came, apparently at an angle of thirty-five to fifty-five degrees.

There are other, more mundane suggestions about their origin, but Pickering said: "The only theory I have not been able to destroy to my own satisfaction or the only one to which I have been able to give any serious consideration, is that they are very shallow meteor-impact craters, probably caused by a comet mass which broke up in the upper atmosphere sometime within the last several thousand years. Fragments of icy material from the comet came down through the atmosphere at very high speeds and the air blast ahead of the fragments blew out the craters in the surface sand.

"To most people, the term *crater* implies a hole blasted from solid rock, but that is not what Carolina Bays are. They would be better described as loose sand blown away by the shock waves of a meteor."

This is the only theory that accounts for the distinctive characteristics of the bays. Also, since all are equally eroded, they must have been formed at the same time.

There is no established pattern to their distribution. The bays are simply scattered at random from New Jersey down the Atlantic coast to extreme south Georgia. Most are located miles from the coast in a rough line from Augusta to Waycross. At some spots they appear like pellets from a cosmic shotgun blast—a dozen or more side by side. In other places there may be two or three bays co-joined, and still others are isolated miles from its nearest neighbor.

All the bays are swampy and contain year-round standing water. Dense cypress forests are found in each, and grass, plants, and ferns form a springy floor. It is impossible to estimate their original depth. The rims are covered by an interwoven network of bushes, grass, and briars that make a formidable hindrance to entrance. Snakes, alligators, bobcats, ducks, and, according to some, panthers occupy these. The bays seem to be migratory way stations for birds.

The bays have been recognized for about fifty years, but only with the advent of satellite and aerial photographs were their position, size, and sheer numbers calculated. They are immediately recognizable from above, but almost impossible to find on the ground unless guided by a geological survey map. Useless Bay in Clinch County was so named because, according to a local, "Hit's hard to git about in, and ain't fit fer nuthin'."

MOONSTRUCK

American astronauts brought back moon rocks in 1969, but Georgia has some that were delivered an estimated thirty-two million years ago. Called *tektites*, they are small, spherical, glassy globules found in a very few areas of the world called strewn fields, primarily in Texas, the Czech Republic and Slovakia, Indochina, and Africa's Ivory Coast. Scientists have estimated that eons ago giant meteors struck the moon (that's where those huge craters originated) with such force that pieces of the moon were blasted to earth a quarter-million miles away. They partially melted while falling through the atmosphere, which is where they acquired the glassy, teardrop look.

Georgiates, honestly, is the scientific name for Georgia tektites. Tektites are usually found in Pleistocene-era gravel. Most have been found in Australia, and Texas, but our own Dodge County has become famous for the number of tektites discovered there. Most were found around Plainfield, Empire, Eastman, Jay Bird Springs, Roddy, and Chester, and one came from the main intersection in Eastman. Over twelve hundred tektites, a total of about sixteen pounds, have been found, one thousand in Dodge and Bleckley Counties, but others have been located in Laurens, Pulaski, Wheeler, Washington, Irwin, and Houston Counties. Certainly many more have been gathered but remain unidentified, or rest ignored amid the gravel. Georgia's are the oldest and rarest tektites, about thirty-three million years old. The largest weighs a mere thirty-six grams and the longest measures only seven centimeters.

These stones are valuable in a monetary sense, but priceless from a scientific viewpoint. To find a glassy tektite is the ultimate discovery for any Georgia collector. Consider that few parts of the globe have been struck by pieces of the moon.

ALTERNATE THEORIES

The lunar theory of tektites is supported by their composition, which suggests they were formed in a vacuum, but detractors say that during their quarter-million-mile trip they could not have stayed grouped together to fall in a select number of locations. One idea, proposed in the *Science News Letter* by Dr. Carl W. Rufus of the University of Michigan, proposes "that the Pacific Ocean is a scar on the earth—created when the moon was torn away ten million years ago by a powerful tidal force." Tektites are material that lingered in space for a while from that event, then fell to earth.

An article by Henry Faul in the journal *Science* suggested the tektites were formed by meteorite or comet impacts at four different points in earth history. The youngest stones, found in Australia, Indochina, China, the Philippines, and Indonesia, are only seven hundred thousand years old. Those of the Ivory Coast are one and a half million years old. The Czech-Slovakian tektites are fifteen million years old. And Georgia's were created thirty-two million years ago. The site of impact for Georgia's edition of tektites is elusive—erosion on the coastal plain and the Gulf of Mexico would have erased traces of such a long-ago event.

FAIRY STONES (LET IT GO)

The mineral *staurolite* is known as the "Fairy Stone," a world-famous good-luck charm. Although the best known are from the Appalachians of Virginia, Georgia is proud to have the second-best-known examples in both quantity and quality.

Staurolite is composed of two individual crystals that interpenetrate and form geometric angles. There are two different types, crossings of sixty degrees, called Saint Andrew's Cross, and the smaller, rarer, ninety-degree Greek Crosses. The ones you buy on chains in tourist shops have been altered to perfection, but ones found in the raw are more intriguing.

Most of our fairy stones come from several locations in Cherokee County, particularly Ballground, but also near Sharp Mountain Creek and Fairview Church. Staurolite can also be found near Blue Ridge and Mineral Bluff in Fannin County, Gold Mine in Hart, the Dolly Cherry property in Upson, and Norwood in Warren. Consult *Minerals of Georgia* for specific information.

HARDER THAN ROCK

Considerable petrified wood has been found along the Chattahoochee River valley south of Columbus, particularly in the Fort Gaines area. Much of it is fifty to sixty million years old and was formed from trees knocked down by floodwaters and quickly covered by mud, so that they never decayed. Over time the fibers were mineralized, a process that perfectly preserved the wood as stone.

Georgia's petrified wood looks a lot like driftwood and is primarily dark brown in color. Most of it is found in small pieces in fields and ditches, but enormously heavy trunks have been found in the river and tributary streams. The Corps of Engineers at Fort Gaines has an impressive collection recovered during the building of Walter F. George Lake.

MULTIPLE-CHOICE QUESTION: A. SWAMP GAS, B. THE AURORA BOREALIS, C. CHEMICALS

Residents of several southeastern states from Memphis to the Atlantic Ocean reported a strange glow in the sky in late March 1991. Sheila Steverson was traveling with her family at 11:20 P.M. near Fort Gordon when she spotted a bizarre red cloud "at least six miles long" stretching across the sky. She reported driving through "a big white streak going up in the sky. There were red arches in the sky . . . at least one hundred yards apart." Truckers were discussing the unusual sight on their CB radios.

Explanations ranged from chemicals released by NASA as part of a scientific study (like those in October 1973) to the aurora borealis. The control tower at Montgomery's Dannelly Field suggested moonbeams that refracted across a substance similar to swamp gas in the air.

TOTAL ECLIPSE OF THE HEARTLAND

A total eclipse crossed Valdosta in the autumn of 1865. Surely it was seen by many diehard Confederates as the end of the world. Most residents were unaware of the event beforehand, and as chickens roosted, cows lowed, and dogs howled, many people prayed earnestly, fearful that Judgment Day had come.

A more-anticipated event occurred over central Georgia on May 28, 1900. Weeks earlier, scientists gathered atop Sugg's Hill just north of Thomaston to establish temporary observatories. That spot had been chosen as the highest point along the line of totality and weather service records predicted good weather for the event. Professors of astronomy arrived from Lick Observatory and the University of Pacific in California, Utrecht Observatory and Roual Observatory in Holland, Indiana University, and the Toronto Astronomical Society. Set up in Upson County were seven photographic telescopes, four photographic spectroscopes, and many other types of equipment. A four-foot telescope, the largest, had been used to survey eclipses in Chile in 1893 and Japan in 1896. Dozens of photographs were taken of the event.

Several decades ago a Ballground entrepreneur created a number of Stonehenge-like structures and formed mounds of mineral-rich earth for amateur rock hounds to paw through. The enterprise is now defunct.

The eclipse was also experienced in McDuffie County, where it was called the "Big Blackout." What most impressed witnesses was the sudden, unnatural stillness created when chickens roosted, birds stopped singing, and dogs ceased to bark. One woman heard farmhands "shouting and praying in fear."

PORTENTS OF WAR

In Pike County early one night in 1860 "a queer whizzing sound was heard in the air, and all at once the whole of the northern heavens was lighted up from horizon to zenith with a fiery aurora borealis." Such a scene had never been seen in the deep South, stated a county history. "Then it as mysteriously disappeared. All watched it with awe and shuddering thought—war!" Perhaps this was a meteor.

THE NIGHT THE STARS FELL

On November 12 and 13, 1833, a remarkable meteor shower was seen above Georgia, although the event was remembered as having occurred in different years across the state. Early Georgia historian Lucian Lamar Knight wrote that it gave rise to "a body of tradition, all of them more or less exaggerated" as the time "when the stars fell." The sky looked smoky for days, and the sun seemed on fire. Preachers warned of the imminent end of the earth.

Inhabitants of DeKalb County said so many stars fell that they had to dodge them. Witnesses in the woods claimed meteors seemed to fall through the branches of trees. When an alcoholic who passed out on the old Fayetteville Post Road awoke to the startling sight, he swore he had to jump over them to get to his horse. Athens remembered "the star fall—that memorable meteoric display which frightened hundreds of people who believed the day of judgment was at hand."

THE BLUE SKY RINSE

During the early afternoon of August 13, 1831, a blue tint settled over the face of the sun above Macon and remained until the sun set seven hours later. The good citizens of central Georgia quickly smoked glasses (cracking a number of lenses in the process) through which they watched the sun while thumbing frantically through almanacs. The phenomenon was apparently widespread, as some sources claim that in Virginia, Nat Turner saw it as a sign to incite slaves to rebellion. No satisfactory explanation for the event was ever offered.

STRANGE DAYS, DARK NIGHTS

Between April 1780 and June 1781, dark days descended upon Wilkes County, the worst occurring on May 19, 1780, according to Wilkes County historian Eliza Bowen. "At nine or ten o'clock in the morning, a singular, yellowish fog, or cloud, filled the air and by noon it had so obscured the sun that it was necessary to light the candles." While chickens and birds hit the roost for sleep, humans prayed on their knees or hid in cellars or beneath buildings.

On June 20, 1780, the morning again turned dark, but soon returned to normal. These events were presumed to be a result of debris belched into the sky by a volcanic eruption somewhere on earth.

A third dark day occurred in the late 1800s. Dr. Robert G. Stephens remembered elderly citizens dating occurrences in their lives by relating them to the dark day. The full eclipse of 1900 produced full churches the following Sunday.

COLD DAYS

Early inhabitants of Hart County remembered "the Cold Saturday," a day so unseasonably frigid that slaughtered hogs froze before farmers finished dressing them.

Jackson County had two bouts of extremely unusual weather, both occurring in 1785. In mid-May the temperature plummeted so low that it killed birds, animals, and trees. This event was followed by another strange day on November 24, when the sun, apparently shining normally, did not allow any light to fall on the area. Pioneers said it was like watching the moon through thick fog. Farmers trembled and cowered in their cabins.

Local Indians gathered at Yamacutah near their holy circle, where they remained through the day and that night. After the sun rose they completed a ceremony to the sun by walking sacred paths and left to the east. It was the last such service observed by Native Americans in the area.

ANGRY ROCKS

I suppose "mad stones" belong under natural phenomena (what else would they be?). In folklore, "mad stones" are used to prevent rabies from the bites of mad dogs and to remove poison from snakebites. We have two accounts. The first is from Mary Brett Ridley, whose family's mad stone originated from England, although supposedly from the maw of a buffalo (were there buffalo in England 150 years ago?). It was brought to America by her great-grandfather, and passed down to her grandfather and father. It was the size of "the end of the thumb" and oval-shaped. When a victim arrived, generally one to three times a week, the stone would be boiled in fresh sweet milk. It was taken out with a spoon and while warm would be applied to the wound. If the bite were rabid or poisonous the stone would stick like a magnet for up to three hours. When it fell off the stone was again boiled in milk, which would turn green, and reapplied until the stone no longer stuck. It apparently worked every time, even when the victims were already foaming at the mouth. Ridley found that although mad dogs were likely to occur at any time, they were mainly encountered in the spring.

Ridley's complaint was that an afflicted person would arrive from a number of surrounding counties at all hours in the company of their entire family, who would be fed and bedded down with her family. Although her father charged a ten-dollar fee for use of the stone, he used it for free on the poor, and the fee "just paid enough to pay for part of the food they would eat."

Possession of the stone was apparently a burden. When Ridley's father died, a half-brother offered her possession of it, but she replied: "I don't want that thing." It was used a few times by him in Carroll County, and at last report reposed in a safe deposit box.

James W. J. "Ruff" Jones, editor of the *Talbottom Register and Standard*, owned one in Talbot County. In 1884 it was described in the *Southern World* by a visitor: "We were especially struck with the appearance of a veritable madstone, taken more than a hundred years ago from the maw of a deer. It is roundly asserted that the stone has performed many miraculous cures. It is a curious, dark-looking substance, elliptical in shape, unlike any mineral specimen we had ever seen, and of considerable specific gravity."

It was "said to absorb every particle of the virus. This stone is held almost in superstitious veneration, all 'doubting Thomases to the contrary."

SQUIRRELY BEHAVIOR

Ah, the ups and downs of the animal kingdom. According to *Science News*, suddenly in the fall of 1968 there was a squirrel population explosion in northern Georgia and other parts of the country. The event was "quite sudden, with areas that a few days earlier were teeming with squirrels suddenly emptied and adjacent empty areas suddenly swarming." (The most troublesome aspect of this phenomenon is that we obviously paid people to keep track of abrupt squirrel movements.) Naturalists were puzzled because hunger did not figure in the migration. According to one game expert, roadkill squirrels were "well fed, nice and fat, in good shape."

The official explanation follows: 1967 produced a bumper crop of mast-acorns, walnuts, etc.—which allowed record numbers of squirrels to survive the winter and produce record numbers of squirrelettes. Unfortunately, a late frost in 1968 (the whole squirrel world's watching!) severely reduced nut production. The squirrels prospered during the bounty of summer, but come early fall the squirrel nation realized that there would not be enough nuts for the nonhibernating creatures to store away for winter. "Something akin to panic apparently set in," *Science News* noted.

Squirrels swarmed out of their home territory seeking storable nuts, producing "lemming-like determination to cross any obstacle" in their way, even large lakes, for which the animals were "completely unequipped." Apparently, large numbers of them met King Neptune.

THE RAINMAKER

Apparently, an argument over weather prognostication broke out in Elberton in late April 1949. Someone claimed that the absence of "the seven stars" would mean a lengthy drought. To prove this assertion wrong, the weatherman for the *Elberton Star* ventured into the woods and killed a black snake (a black snake is required), and hung it belly-up in a sassafras bush (other bushes would suffice, but this is the best). There were no visible clouds when this scientific process started, but soon thunderclouds boiled in with attendant thunder and a brisk storm erupted. Perhaps because the snake was too large, the storm also produced damaging wind and hail, which led the paper to state "that extreme caution is needed when meddling in the affairs of nature."

Other rainstorms occurred during the following week, and if precipitation continued to be excessive, plans were made for the removal of the snake.

EXPLODING PLAYGROUND (NOT A MONTY PYTHON SKIT OR TABLOID HEADLINE)

After school on January 18, 1999, second-grader Delores Norman joined her friends on the playground equipment at D. L. Stanton Park on Haygood Avenue in southeast Atlanta, an area known as Peoplestown.

As Delores started down a plastic spiral slide, an explosion rocked the park, followed by a hissing sound from beneath the slide. "The sliding board just popped up," Delores said, and she suffered second- and third-degree burns on her arms and legs. A second girl suffered slight injuries. They were rushed to Hughes Spalding Children's Hospital for treatment.

"When I looked at her arms I wondered how this could happen," said Delores's mother, Michelle Norman. She accused the city of withholding information. "They're not telling me everything. I want to know what happened."

The truth is that officials were just as puzzled by the incident. The only practical answer was an explosion of methane gas that had built up underground. The paramount mystery was what formed it—usually decomposing organic matter such as garbage and human and animal waste. City records indicated no formal dump or landfill on the site. However, residents claimed that it was a major illegal dump for restaurants, a chicken hatchery, and manufacturers. A little research revealed that during construction of a community center in the late 1960s, a methane gas explosion at the site killed two workers.

Another question was how the methane was concentrated enough outdoors to explode. "It's something I've never heard of in this scenario," said Christy Easter, a geologist with the Georgia Environmental Protection Division. Evidently, the gas was trapped beneath the solid, one-piece slide and ignited by the friction of children sliding.

Testing revealed that dangerous levels of methane gas remained in the park, which was closed off with plastic webbing and "Hazardous Area, Keep Out" tape. Residents feared that Stanton Elementary School and their homes might harbor the dangerous gas. State and city officials held neighborhood meetings in an attempt to calm residents' concerns and explain the measures being taken to deal with the problem.

Two months after the explosion the city confirmed the existence of a large landfill on the property before Atlanta purchased it and constructed the park. The methane problem was so extensive that the park was condemned and the recreation center demolished. It would require a year to remove the garbage and contaminated soil and build a new recreation center and park on new dirt and sod.

11

Assorted Fortean Files

I believe I have saved the best for last. This is very much a Fortean book, named for Charles Fort, who, during the earliest decades of the twentieth century, scoured libraries for strange events, including UFOs, odd occurrences in nature, and out-of-place artifacts. His groundbreaking *Book of the Damned* opened with the line, "A procession of the damned." A procession which I have chronicled for Georgia.

Our final chapter is quite a procession of damned incidents, beginning with Georgia's only documented case of spontaneous human combustion. Many weird things have fallen from our skies—alligators, angel hair, seeds, synthetic lines, massed flocks of birds, sky bergs, unique rains, and bizarre sunshine. Our atmosphere is frequently disrupted by strange booms, screams, whistles, and whines, some also heard from underground. The air often is permeated with mysterious illnesses that afflict schools, office buildings, courtrooms, jails, a medical school, and the Centers for Disease Control and Prevention (CDC), and in 1999 a MARTA car was attacked by a phantom gasser. In 1986 a phantom arsonist boldly torched seventy-five cars without detection. Finally, a man-made weirdness named the Guidestones was raised in mystery and left to generate its own mythology, which continues to grow. It offers wisdom to our posterity and attracts religious groups, witches, UFOs, and cows.

SPONTANEOUS HUMAN COMBUSTION

Don't laugh so hard. SHC is a serious subject to many researchers and certainly to every victim of what might be called a paranormal affliction, disease, or condition. Occasionally, a human being bursts into flame from no observable external physical cause. They apparently self-immolate from within, their bodies sometimes burning so violently that large portions of the body are cremated to ashes while other parts are left undamaged. Wait. The story gets weirder. External objects, clothing on the bed or chairs on which the victims were found, often bear no traces of being affected by heat.

The phenomenon is rare. Georgia has a single recorded incident of SHC, but it turns out to be the most important one ever investigated. Why? Because the victim survived!

His name, strangely enough, was Jack Angel. Late on November 12, 1974, he pulled his plush motor-home-rolling showroom into a hotel parking lot in Savannah. Sixty-six years old, he was in good health, had recently married, and ran a successful clothing-sales business. That night he called his wife, then turned in early, planning on meeting customers in the morning.

But that morning passed. And three more. On the fourth day Angel awoke to find both sides of his right hand charred from wrist to fingers, a frightening cavity in his chest, and assorted other burns. Remarkably, his pajamas, sheets, and bedcovers were untouched. Nothing in the motor home had been disturbed or marked by fire.

"It was just burned, blistered," Angel said of his hand. "And I had this big explosion in my chest. It left a hell of a hole. I was burned . . . on my ankle, and up and down my back, in spots."

Although his wounds throbbed, he felt no pain, but was disoriented by the long sleep.

Remarkably, Angel managed to shower and dress before walking toward the hotel to call his wife. Fainting in the parking lot, he woke up at Savannah Memorial Hospital.

Except for the obvious wounds, Angel was fine. There were no internal injuries or evidence of what had scorched him. The doctors "told me I was burned *internally*," Angel said.

It was a bizarre story.

Angel, certain there had been a problem in his motor home, asked his wife to investigate. Determined to find the cause of his serious injuries, they engaged an engineer consultant to take the motor home apart and hired lawyers to sue the manufacturer. After two days of exhaustive scrutiny, the vehicle was found to be sound. "(They) couldn't find a thing, not a thing," Angel revealed. "No burn spots on the clothing. No evidence of any fire in that bus." There were no faulty wires, no electrical problems. After two years of study, Angel still had no case. There was no evidence of problems in the motor home, no evidence of tampering with any part of the vehicle, and no evidence of criminal activity.

Angel's life was wrecked by the phenomenon. Infection forced the amputation of his right arm, and he suffered from psychological problems. His wife divorced him, and he experienced financial reverses. Angel became disabled and was confined to his house.

"Our own conclusion is that Jack burned himself inside," stated Larry E. Arnold, the foremost expert on SHC. According to Arnold, on occasion a

400

person's internal electrical system "appears to go haywire" and ignites internal gases in the human body. The fire burns the body to varying degrees, sometimes including total cremation.

Another psychic phenomenon that seems to originate from within humans is poltergeist activity. Michael Harrison, in his book *Fire From Heaven*, suggests that the agency resulting in objects being remotely manipulated without physical cause can also ignite people. In both phenomenons, those responsible have no idea that they are generating the results.

Whatever the cause might be, it was no relief for Jack Angel.

FALLS

Some things are supposed to fall from the sky—rain, snow, hail, meteorites, and the occasional life-scouring comet/asteroid—but not huge chunks of pure ice, unidentifiable strings, alligators, and seeds. But fall they do.

A FINE-FEATHERED FALL

An astounding fall consisting of fifty thousand birds rained down from the skies in October 1954, and onto the runways of Robins Air Force Base in Warner Robins. Whatever had struck these birds was nondiscriminatory, for representatives of fifty-three different species of birds were identified. Birds have fallen in many different places across the world, but never in such quantity.

WHAT'S MY LINE

The strangest thing in this category did not fall, and that was its most intriguing characteristic—it was suspended in the air.

Near dawn of June 5, 1972, Hut Wallace sat on the front porch of his Mattox Drive home in Elberton, enjoying the cool of the morning. In the early gray light he spotted something hanging in the sky.

"A shining line seemed to reach right up to the moon in front of his home and to stretch into infinity at the back," wrote newsman Herbert Wilcox, an old friend of Wallace's, who immediately responded when Wallace called.

Wilcox considered that perhaps the Skylab astronauts had left something in space that was unraveling. Whimsically, he then suggested it might be a kite string. "If so, it was about the longest and fanciest kite string anybody ever had around here. And there was no kite to be seen to hold it in the heavens."

That afternoon Wallace's son-in-law, Eddie Boswell, climbed atop the house, where the mystery line was closest to the ground, and pulled in many yards of the line, which was composed of two different types of material. The

*In 1972 Hut Wallace spotted a "shining line" hanging suspended without sup-
port in the sky over Elberton. Considerable amounts were reeled in without
exhausting the supply. (Courtesy of the* Elberton Star and Examiner)

string pulled down from the west "was a fluffy, shiny, white material. That
from the east was a tiny, hard-finished line. Both materials were unusually
strong." Boswell could not tell what supported the line in either direction.

Wilcox noted that local textile mills used similar material and that
some of it had been discarded, but he concluded "the mystery remains as to
how it was placed in the sky and what kept it up there."

A captioned photograph of Wallace holding some of the "shining line"
stated that the material "apparently came from the textile mill here." In
reality, the cosmic string could never be identified.

GATOR FALLS

On December 26, 1877, the *New York Times* reprinted a story from the *Aiken* (South Carolina) *Journal*. According to that article, Dr. J. L. Smith was opening a new turpentine mill on a sandy bluff about six miles from the Savannah River. While sitting outside his tent, he spotted something fall from the sky. The incident grew weird when he noticed the object start crawling toward him. The aerolite proved to be a lively alligator, about twelve inches in length. After seeing a second reptile drop, Dr. Smith examined the area closely. In a space of two hundred yards he counted six additional gators, all alive, active, and the same size. The supposition was that the creatures were "taken up in a water-spout at some distant locality, and dropped in the region where they were found."

That incident occurred in South Carolina, although mere miles from Georgia soil, but we have a similar occurrence nearly fifty years later in rural Bulloch County, three miles west of Statesboro. After a heavy rain, a young farmer found what the local newspaper described as "a saurian reptile which had very much the appearance of an alligator except the head was shaped more like a snake's." The man inquired whether "anyone had ever heard of alligators raining down." Well . . . yes.

CHARLOTTE'S SORDID AFFAIR

Bulloch County seems to have a history of producing hybrid creatures, although this one did not fall. Fifteen years before the arrival of the aerial alligator with the snake's head, during the summer of 1909, a Mr. Adams reported the birth of a litter of seven pigs. "Six of them had alligator heads and crawled around just like an alligator," a news report noted. "Their heads and mouths were so much like alligators, they couldn't suck the sow and soon died." A second sow then sired four offspring, two of them alligalets. Mr. Adams felt that their early demise was kind, "for the reason that should they live he wouldn't know just how to make pork out of them." Tastes just like . . . ?

ANGEL HAIR, OR INVASION OF THE MICROSCOPIC, HIGH-FLYING, PARA-CHUTING ARACHNIDS

Georgia's single encounter with angel hair occurred in three widely separated parts of the state on October 27, 1959, around Savannah, Washington, Rome, Atlanta, and other communities.

The first reports originated in Savannah, where the substance rained down on the roofs of the historic city. It was described as thousands of "fragile, silvery strands" resembling the tinsel used to decorate Christmas trees. The material drifted down from a nearly cloudless blue sky and draped itself over treetops, utility lines, television antennas (this *was*

B.C.—before cable), and rooftops, where it glittered in the bright autumn sunshine.

Scores of frightened, concerned, and merely intrigued citizens phoned the *Savannah News-Press* office, radio and TV stations, and the police department to report the alien strands and to inquire after its origin. The media and police watched the fall with similar fascination and lack of understanding. TV station WSAV captured some of the wispy threads and transported them to the state crime laboratory. The suspense was palatable while toxicologist Charles H. Sullenger examined the faux silk through a microscope and conducted several experiments on it. To the dissatisfaction of all, the expert admitted that he did not have a clue.

After someone suggested that the fibers had been cobwebs, woven on the wind by airborne, migrating spiders, a biology instructor at Armstrong College refuted the thesis when contacted by the *News-Press*. Rather than a biological origin, he felt the strands were some type of chemical substance. The teacher detected no evidence of spiders in the material he examined.

The "angel hair" also drifted to earth over large areas of Wilkes and Taliaferro Counties in northeast Georgia. Witnesses saw the material float down first upon the antebellum splendor of Washington before spreading to the neighboring communities of Crawfordville, Lexington, and Sharon. They described it as long strands of "disappearing spider webs" which seemed to come from the sun. Trees and rooftops were covered with the stuff, which stuck to whatever it hit. The ends of the strange material always pointed up to the sky. By morning it had disappeared.

The angel hair also gently descended on Rome and Atlanta. In Atlanta the threads accumulated on a two-hundred-foot television tower belonging to an auto company on Stewart Avenue, Southwest. It was easily visible against the bright blue sky, streaming to windward. One worker scaled the tower to collect some of the stuff, only to discover its fragile state.

"It just disappears when you touch it," he found. "But it does leave your hands sticky—sort of cotton candy stuff."

Leave it to the experts to accept this fall as a challenge. When the material draped itself across Athens, three University of Georgia professors, chemists William D. Jacobs and George E. Philbrook and entomologist Robert P. Hunter, gathered strands from a radio antenna at the airport. They then caught a spider they spotted twenty-five feet in the air that had apparently been caught in its own web. Hunter quickly identified the arachnids and shifted into lecture mode.

What plagued Georgia was one of a species commonly called "ballooning" spiders. Hunter explained that they occupy treetops and spin webs as long as fifty feet and use the material as a "parachute" (today it would more accurately be called a parasail) to soar away on the winds. Insect collectors in airplanes have captured the tiny creatures cruising along at ten thousand feet. The webs float thirty to forty feet ahead of the spiders, which surf the winds for hundreds of miles. After landing, the spider disembarks and the web balls up, creating the impression that many spiders were responsible, although they are limited to only one bug per strand.

The scientists announced that such web falls are "common in the fall usually on clear, sunny days when the winds are not too high." They can best be seen by standing in the shade and looking toward the sun. Few spiders are found because when the web hits the ground, the pilots scurry away.

Another UGA scientist, Dr. J. J. Paul, explained that there are several different types of arachnids in this species, but they are no danger to people or animals. The gray creatures are tiny—Paul had never encountered one larger than an eighth of an inch in diameter. The webs occur every year, but in 1959 climatic conditions apparently provided them with ideal temperatures and food supplies. The spiders flourished in record numbers and took to the winds to race across southern skies.

Following a two-day investigation at Robins Air Force Base, the air force semiconfidently, if not competently, concluded that the substance was probably silver halide, used to seed clouds and make rain. However, this was a wet period when additional rain was not particularly desired. The Atlanta Weather Bureau pleaded ignorance of the entire controversy and reported that it knew of no government agency or private company recently engaged in cloud seeding.

THE ICE CHUNKS COMETH, OR NON-BLUE ICE FOLLIES
At the same time that angel hair/spider webs were floating gently down on northeastern Georgia, large masses of ice were crashing into the same area. Also on October 27, 1959, a forty-pound piece of ice plunged from the sky into a flower garden in Toccoa. It shattered on impact but still managed to create a hole described as the size of a car wheel. Because the water was of such purity, with no traces of chlorine or other substances, it was not thought to have fallen from an aircraft. Speculation was that it had formed somewhere in space before falling to earth.

Two days later, on October 29, a fifty-pound chunk of frozen water impacted a farm at Martin, twelve miles from Carnesville in Franklin County, not far from Toccoa. Despite the insistence of witnesses who stoutly maintained that no airplanes were visible or audible in the clear sky, the air force and U.S. Weather Bureau insisted that the miniberg was "plain drinking water from a jet airliner" and dismissed the phenomenon.

If the official explanation was correct, then that plane with the defective plumbing was so consistent that the air force should have enlisted its pilots as bombardiers. Almost exactly one year later, on October 3, 1960, a similar mass, a piece of ice weighing fifty pounds, plummeted to earth in another cultivated field near Carnesville.

Willie Kirk and E. W. Norris were standing in Norris's yard at 5:10 on that Sunday afternoon when they heard a "whoosh from the sky" and saw the ice impact on the neighboring property of Hoke Wright. A third and independent witness was Ted Overman, a truck driver from Chamblee.

Overman immediately stopped and ran to the impact site. He found the ice in crystal form and described it as "like one of those big icicles." He wrapped several pieces in ice and hoped to reach his freezer at home before they melted.

For decades all reports of ice falls were dismissed as originating from airplanes. However, ten years after a new theory was met with universal derision, scientists were forced to accept the fact that every day aerial glaciers enter the earth's atmosphere. Forteans were *way* ahead of them.

SEED STORM

In February 1858 an unexplained shower of seeds mystified Savannah. Additional details are solicited from my knowledgeable readers.

JUNKYARD DOG

Adel was struck by two objects that crashed from the sky in two separate incidents about a year apart. In 1995 a chunk of bright blue ice, presumably but not demonstratively from a passing airliner (listen, if a phenomenon is really messing with us, why not throw down something that corresponds to a phenomenon we think we can explain), struck the parking lot of a car dealership. In mid-October 1996, a scorched piece of coarse metal, squarish in shape, five inches wide and one inch thick, crashed through the roof of the Talley-Corbett Box Company and dented an oak desk. It was presumed to be a piece of space junk, perhaps the remains of a satellite launched years ago by NASA or the Soviets.

A METEOR THAT ANNOUNCED ITS PRESENCE

A witness to a meteor should not be able to hear the object before it is seen, but on July 11, 1933, a father and son working their farm near Athens heard a strange singing or humming sound they described as "like an airplane flying high." The noise grew louder for five minutes before it became a whizzing noise, then a swish and thud announced the arrival of a nine-ounce meteorite near them.

A DISCRIMINATING SHOWER

A heavy, hour-long rain in September 1886 drenched Dawson, or at least the twenty-five-foot-diameter area where the downpour was confined.

THE PERPETUAL PIDDLE

Besides rain falling in one restricted area at one particular time, we had a spot with eternal rain. It was located in Gum Creek Swamp in Telfair County, five miles from McRae, where Telfair, Montgomery, Laurens, and Dodge Counties converge. Hundreds of local residents have visited the spot to examine the curious phenomenon and decide for themselves if more fanciful tales told of this magical locale are real or imagined.

Water fell continuously, night and day, in every season, in a spot measuring fifty by one hundred feet. Decades ago E. P. Whiddon and a companion trekked into the wilderness with a thermometer and a barometer. The temperature dropped precipitously as they approached the enchanted rain spot, where it was twenty degrees cooler. The barometer also "showed considerable agitation," Whiddon noted.

He observed that a "rain or mist" would fall through the leaves of a magnolia tree for ten seconds, then descend through the foliage of a great birch tree. The two investigators climbed to the top of the magnolia, surprised to find the bark and leaves generally dry—only an occasional drop of water was seen on a leaf "as if a heavy dew had fallen." A good view of the countryside was had from the treetop, but the sun was "considerably clouded by the spray."

The rain fell heaviest in this haunted place on hot days with a bright sun and high humidity. Less water materialized on cold or windy days, and the precipitation constantly shifted location. Water that accumulated in a glass tasted "barkish," Whiddon observed.

SUN SPOTS

Something nearly invisible fell upon Coffee County in August 1914. Perhaps it was a type of cosmic radiation. It was three o'clock in the afternoon, cloudless with no wind. W. H. Vickers, who farmed four miles south of Douglas, was standing under a shelter and watching the sky as farmers were wont to do before the advent of all weather cable channels. Suddenly, according to Warren P. Ward in his *History of Coffee County*, "The heavens seemed to light up as though a cloud had passed from under the sun, but the sun was shining all the time." In the "twinkling of an eye," Ward wrote, "hundreds of acres of cotton plants were wilted in the fields. The destruction was worst at Vickers's farm, but fields were affected in an irregular pattern across the county—some areas inexplicably spared."

Ward recorded that many cotton plants recovered and developed normally, "but many of the leaves twisted up and crimped around the edges and finally died."

AN ILL WIND

The *Baker County News* reported a strange sandstorm that swept over the area one Sunday afternoon in 1875. Church services and dinner had been concluded, and family and friends of John Harvey Coker, overseer of Primus Jones's plantation, had gathered on his extensive verandah to relax and chat. Someone noticed that the sky was turning red, the velocity of the wind was rapidly increasing, and sand was flying. The storm built quickly, coloring the sky red and casting a reddish tinge over the countryside. The assembled multitude retired hastily to a newly erected shelter they called a stockade. They had just reached its safety when all hell broke loose. Flying sand blotted out exterior views and the wind shook the timbers of the shelter. For long minutes children screamed, women wept, and men prayed earnestly. Abruptly, the storm lifted. There had been no injuries, but crops were considerably damaged. John's wife later commented to the local minister, "I bet there were more converted in my stockade last Sunday than were converted at your church."

These "red storms" are often blamed on violent windstorms that pick up red sand and carry it a considerable distance, sometimes across oceans.

SOME FALLS ARE EXPLAINABLE

On February 18, 1997, a dense hunk of metal half the size of a brick and weighing six pounds blasted through the roof and bedroom ceiling of John and Allison Cox's Dunwoody home and committed mayhem on their unoccupied bed. This thing did not look extraterrestrial—two sheered bolts protruded from it, and the object was speckled with good red Georgia clay. Although obviously of terrestrial origin, there remained a mystery regarding its source and how it rained down with such force on suburban Atlanta. Airplanes were a natural suspect.

"We had some pretty expert people examine it," said Kathleen Bergen, a spokesperson for the Federal Aviation Administration, "and it doesn't appear to be part of an airplane . . . one person here speculated it looked like part of a car," which would have made it an even greater mystery.

A television account of the curious incident brought the solution. Workers were clearing trees for home construction one hundred yards from the Cox's home and feeding the trunks into an industrial-strength chipper.

"The machine apparently rotates at a high speed and chews up trees," related insurance adjuster Chuck Moseler, "and a piece flew up in the air" and descended with great force.

MYSTERY MISSILE

On March 12, 1997, Atlanta was briefly excited over the appearance of a missilelike object found on a road. It was reported that a man who touched it suffered radiation burns and was hospitalized. Subsequent investigation revealed that a cone-shaped, hollow pipe had been found west of Dallas on Brushy Mountain Road off U.S. 278. A man who touched it did go to a hospital, which alerted the Paulding County Sheriff's Department. Firefighters, sheriff's deputies, and news crews descended on the spot and found an ordinary pipe and no evidence of radiation. It was revealed that the touchy man had a rash that was not connected in any way with the pipe.

THE BLOB

I don't even know what category this next report should be filed under. It didn't exactly fall, but rather oozed. In September 1996, engineers at the DeKalb County landfill located two separate areas of "blue running muck" that were fifty feet deep, covered an entire acre, and were every bit as treacherous as quicksand.

"It's kind of like a Tarzan movie," quipped county development director Tom Black. "If you walked on it, you'd be gone."

The blue gunk was thought to be a mixture of silt and sediment lying atop underground springs. Although the matter seems quirky, the county spent two and a half million dollars to pour stone into the pools until they were stabilized.

SONIC WEIRDNESS: THINGS THAT GO BOOM, WHINE, AND AIIIIII! IN THE NIGHT

THE PEACHTREE SCREAMER

One of Atlanta's eeriest places happens not to be an old, haunted house. In this case it's the seventh floor of Peachtree Center's South Tower, then one of the city's newest and most exclusive business addresses. The weirdness there started in the late 1970s. Somewhere on this floor was located "the Screamer." This thing that screamed had self-imposed restrictions—he, she, or it only bellowed once a week, and always on Mondays or Thursdays.

"It was the most bloodcurdling sound I've ever heard in my life," said one credible witness, who added that it "sounds exactly like someone being murdered." How did she know?

Ms. Artis Roderick, an employee of a seventh-floor business, added, "It has to be sick. The scream is so frantic and agonizing it absolutely freezes you and curls your toes." The blood-chilling scream lasted up to twelve seconds.

"It makes you really jumpy about working late here," added Roderick. "In the back of your mind you wonder what you might open a door to. At first it was kind of amusing. Then after a while it makes you angry. Whoever's doing it needs help."

Police were summoned when it first began, during the summer of 1979, but they found that a hoarse, disembodied voice was difficult to track.

This might be related to a story out of New York City in 1990, where a horrifying howl terrified a large section of the city for five weeks and drew hundreds of complaints. One local resident, Anthony Mazzola, editor in chief of *Harper's Bazaar*, hit the asphalt to locate the source.

"I've been all over the street trying to find the noise," Mazzola said. "You think you're in a loony bin. You can't get away from it."

An investigation launched by Ian Matthews of New York City's Department of Environmental Conservation located the culprit—the Cityspire building. Topping the seventy-second floor, eight hundred feet in the sky, was an eight-sided, louvered dome.

"With the right winds, it becomes a big whistle," Matthews said, and the noise reverberated through the street caverns created by soaring skyscrapers.

The building developer was issued a summons for violating noise control laws, which could bring a top fine of nearly one thousand dollars. The developer and architect said they were unaware of the problem, which seemed to strike them as somewhat humorous.

PHANTOM WHISTLERS AND WHINERS

Two different audible "things" popped up in Forsyth and Carrollton in the spring of 1980. For weeks a phantom "whistler" haunted the best neighborhoods in Forsyth and drove both residents and police to distraction. However, no culprits, either real or ethereal, were ever sighted, merely heard. Meanwhile, in Carrollton a shrill scream that penetrated every house in the city was heard at night. Its location could never be pinpointed because the sound seemed to emanate from everywhere.

THE WHINY HOUSE

For nearly nine years Wayne and Kitty LaFountain lived peacefully in their Warner Robins home. Then Kitty noticed a high-pitched whining noise inside the house. Three months later Wayne also heard it, and the couple were soon driven to distraction when the sound became perpetual. Wayne, who works with electronics at Robins Air Force Base, and Kitty, an instructor and interpreter for the deaf, systematically went about isolating the source of the noise and eliminating it. They turned off the electricity, gas, telephones, turbines on the roof, and cable television. They had the refrigerator worked on and replaced the TV. Nothing worked, suggesting that the phenomenon was not created within the house, although that is the only place it could be heard.

Wayne believes a distant engine or machine could create the noise, or, he speculates, perhaps the house is located at a spot where a sound wave meets the earth. Experts agree.

"Every object in nature has a harmonic frequency," stated Dr. Kenneth Walker, an ear, nose, and throat specialist. "If a house is hit with the right frequency, it will reverberate."

"Wind in itself blowing over a building can excite sound," suggested Eugene Patronis, a physicist at Georgia Tech. "All buildings can make sound."

In other words, the house may be vibrating like a guitar being strummed.

Unable to locate the source of the noise, the LaFountains have attempted to deal with the noise. It cannot be ignored, and earplugs and sound machines offer only partial or temporary relief. The couple have spent an occasional night in local hotels in order to get a good night's sleep. Awakened by the noise one morning at 3:00 A.M., Kitty reported that one ear "felt like I'd been at a rock concert. It seriously hurts." She has been known to sleep on the porch. "You could put me in a cardboard box and I'd be happy," she claimed.

After suffering in silence for months, in February 1996, the couple publicized their problem in hopes of locating someone who could find a solution. Calls came from as far away as Ohio, Missouri, and Washington, D.C.

"The majority of people are serious and trying to help," Kitty related. "Some of them are crazier. Some have suggested UFOs and ghosts," and after a local TV station suggested the house was haunted they started receiving calls from psychics.

"I'm sure they're well-intentioned," Kitty kindly continued, "but this is not a haunted house—it is a house with a problem."

THINGS THAT GO BOOM

The booms first surfaced in 1978 along the eastern seaboard from Nova Scotia to Charleston, South Carolina. Thousands of people called police stations reporting booms that rattled their homes. Supersonic airplanes, earthquakes, and even bubbles of natural gas rising from the sea floor and igniting were suggested as explanations, but none were proven.

On June 24, 1981, a house-shaking boom rattled coastal Georgia and both Carolinas. Scientists investigated and found no earthquakes, jets, or construction explosions. One theory is a great piece of the continental shelf broke loose and fell into the depths of the Atlantic Ocean.

Between 11:00 P.M. and 1:00 A.M. on January 7 and 8, 1987, residents along Macon's Vineville and Ingleside avenues were shaken awake by a series of three blasts. The first was heard at 11:15 P.M., the other two occurred in rapid succession at 12:45 A.M.

Thomas Clay was preparing for bed when the two explosions "rattled the windows. It sounded like a quarter stick of dynamite. We've been hearing them off and on" since Christmas, eight altogether, he said. "Usually, when you hear it once, you'll hear it again. Each time I jump. It's that loud."

A sensitive seismograph at Eatonton registered a ten-second incident at 12:45 A.M., said Dr. Tim Long, a Georgia Tech seismologist. However, it had an acoustic signal unlike earthquakes. "It's undoubtedly an atmospheric-type occurrence," Long said. "But we cannot identify its source."

Problems such as these in central Georgia always draw attention to Robins Air Force Base and F-15 Eagles, supersonic fighter jets that occasionally break the sound barriers near populated areas despite regulations.

"They damn sure don't do that at midnight," said spokesman Dale Brinkman, and only "over sparsely populated areas."

Georgia Power ruled out exploding transformers; Atlanta Gas Light eliminated methane gas explosions in sewers; the National Weather Service reported no unusual atmospheric disturbances; NORAD discounted reentering space debris; and local mining companies had not been blasting. The mystery remains.

During 1991 and 1992 a series of mysterious blasts rocked extreme southeastern Georgia, centered around Waycross. The most powerful boom originated on February 10, 1992, when they "shook my house," said Grace Kearson. She and a number of her neighbors believed the shocks originated from the Ware County landfill, located a mile away. However, the blasts were heard and felt in Pearson, Jamestown, and in neighboring Brantley and Pierce Counties.

Some blamed Moody Air Force Base in Valdosta, Jacksonville Naval Air Station, and Robins, but those installations had no planes up to account for the phenomenon.

Witnesses across the region believed the sound originated from different locations. The sheriff's office and police department received many reports from residents, but had no solution.

Virginia Thomas had been hearing the booms for two years, "at least three or four a month," if not more frequently. "Sometimes it'll happen right in the middle of the night," frightening her family. "It's scary."

At 4:03 P.M. on February 11 a Ware County man heard a boom that "rattled windows and reminded me of thunder . . . it didn't sound like a sonic boom," which is sharper than what he heard. The man happened to be reading a previous account of the booms when this occurred.

By February 13 Jim Wheeler, director of the local civil defense and coordinator of Ware County's emergency management, had grown concerned enough to fly over "the entire county to look for sinkholes or tree damage that may have occurred during the booms," he said after three additional booms occurred at 3:45 A.M., around noon, and at 2:44 P.M.

Myra Johns, city editor of the *Waycross Journal Herald*, had arrived at the primary Ware County fire station when the 2:44 double explosion rattled its windows and doors. She had just inspected the landfill, which many residents believed generated the booms, perhaps from methane gas that gathered in underground pockets and exploded. She had found no damage there, and Jimmy Cannon, executive operator of the dump, heard a boom near noon and thought it originated from a distance away from the landfill.

Wheeler investigated whether seismic activity could have accounted for the booms, but Dr. Long at Georgia Tech found no activity in southeastern Georgia, which had been quiet for months.

Anther popular theory was supersonic airplanes from Moody, Jacksonville, and Robins, but again all denied they had aircraft close enough to affect Ware County. One Waycross resident said "they are lying," and Long suggested the air force had been "fooled by the skip-distance phenomenon," which allows sonic booms over the ocean which might not be heard fifty miles away to "be heard very clearly at one hundred miles."

EARWITNESS NEWS

One Bacon County woman believed the booms traveled at or beneath ground level. She experienced a boom and called her mother, who lived five miles away.

"She said, 'Mama, did you hear that?'" the mother related, "and right then, as I opened my back door, I felt it. It jarred everything in the house. I'm convinced it took those few seconds to travel from her house to mine."

METRO ATLANTA REPORTS

Between 10:00 A.M. and noon on November 20, 1995, loud explosions rocked parts of DeKalb and Gwinnett Counties. After numerous reports were phoned into local authorities, DeKalb County sent a fire truck to Dunwoody, and Gwinnett County dispatched emergency personnel to six different locations, but nothing out of the ordinary was found. The booms rattled houses and set off dozens of fire and burglar alarms across the area.

SET AND MATCH

An explanation soon arrived but did not linger for long. The space shuttle *Atlantis*, returning from an eight-day docking mission with the Russian space station MIR, passed over the Atlanta area to land at Cape Canaveral, Florida. Shuttles reentering the atmosphere frequently generate loud sonic booms, and the Federal Aviation Administration office in Atlanta assured callers that was the cause of the booms. However, when the *Atlanta Constitution* asked spokeswoman Christy Williams of the FAA who had given her that information, she replied Lt. Col. Carol Ludwig of the air force. When contacted, Ludwig claimed that she had received the information from Williams. Back to Williams, who admitted, "We don't have any definitive information on what caused it." NASA estimated that the shuttle would have flown directly across the city between 11:35 and noon, far too late to be the origin of most reports.

RUMBLES IN LINCOLN COUNTY

At various times in Lincoln County's recorded history a great blast has rattled the region. One of the last episodes occurred on a cloudless Sunday evening in 1912. The incident was experienced by the author of a Lincoln County history and his father and sister, who were eating supper. "Suddenly, a deep roaring noise was heard," he wrote. "The house shook and the dishes rattled." Fearing that a chimney was collapsing, the family ran outside to see their neighbors also vacating their homes. No explosion was reported in the area, and no one outside Lincolnton had noticed a thing. Airplanes and space shuttles in 1912 could hardly be blamed.

Other residents recalled similar incidents, and George White's *Statistics of the State of Georgia*, written in 1849, stated that for the previous five years in Lincolnton "curious sounds, resembling those of distant thunder, have been heard. The noise has been so great as to produce a shaking of the glasses, fences, etc."

STRANGE DETONATIONS

Since about 1850 mystery noises, described by observers as the distant firing of cannon, have been heard emanating from Rabun Bald, one of Georgia's highest peaks, located near the North Carolina line. The distant "booms" have been heard by dozens of people at different points about the mountain in all kinds of weather and throughout the year. Long periods of time have passed without the guns being heard, even by those who camp out on the peak.

In November 1884 two gentlemen who spent the night atop the mountain heard a series of explosive sounds at 10:00 P.M. They thought at first they were the result of cannon firing at Walhalla, South Carolina, in celebration of the presidential election, "but soon the sounds were found to issue *from the ground* and from a ridge to the southwest of the mountain," reported the *Monthly Weather Review* in 1897. "The explosive sounds continued till late in the night. At times they seemed to proceed from the ground immediately under the observers."

There have been numerous local theories to explain the sounds. Many thought they were the ghostly activity of two men killed there in the 1860s, victims of bushwhackers, or the bushwhackers themselves hunted down by militia during the Civil War. An earlier hypothesis said the sounds originated when bears pushed small boulders off the mountainside in search of snails, worms, etc., but the explosions long outlived the bears. Some witnesses, apparently closer to the source of the explosions, said they sounded like trees falling.

Such underground explosions, which scientists generally speculate are seismic in nature, are heard in the Rocky Mountains, New York, and locations around the globe.

MYSTERY SMELLS

A strong and unidentified smell permeated Paulding County early on the morning of January 5, 1996, and was reported as far away as Stone Mountain. The pungent odor inspired dozens to call 911, concerned that it was a natural gas leak that might spark an explosion. Others believed the odor was sulfur. Two elementary schools delayed opening for half an hour while firemen and gas crews searched in vain for leaking lines.

"It was strong," stated one principal. "I could smell it with my car windows up."

Atlanta Gas Light Company immediately took samples of the air and announced that the smell was not natural gas.

A spokesman for the utility thought the dispersal pattern indicated a source that was heavier than air. Some callers were told the smell originated at a paper mill near the Alabama line west of Rome, but a paper mill employee in Paulding disputed that notion. "I know what a paper mill smells like," he asserted. "It wasn't a paper mill."

An employee of a pipeline company suggested it might be odorant, which is added to natural gas so it can be detected by smell. He was familiar with an earlier leak that was reported over two hundred miles away, but AGL had already dismissed the notion.

MYSTERY ILLNESSES

A fairly new phenomenon is mass illnesses that often have no discernible cause. These are particularly prevalent in schools, where emotional and easily influenced children are subject to panic attacks. One such illness occurred in

Atlanta's Fernbank Elementary School in early May 1983. After receiving reports of a gas leak in the school, police ordered it evacuated and sent sixty-four students to hospitals. The city's public safety director believed the incident began when several students were exposed to fumes that concentrated in a boiler room where a ventilation panel had been blocked. However, school officials said there was no gas leak or other detectable cause for the problem. The students complained of nausea and dizziness, but doctors at Grady Memorial Hospital found them suffering only from hyperventilation.

DISORDER IN THE COURT

The mass illness that swept Atlanta Municipal Traffic Court in late November 1992 had a physical, if still mysterious, origin. An unidentified man appeared to pay a traffic citation with two ten-dollar bills and a five-dollar bill, all of them "wet with some sort of chemical," the police report stated.

Court officials initially refused to accept the notes but relented. Within minutes fumes overcame a dozen people in the room. Rescue personnel were dispatched to the scene and twenty-five firemen searched the building after ordering it evacuated and cordoning off surrounding streets. Fifteen people were sent to the hospital complaining of irritation of the mouth, throat, and lungs. All were treated and released.

"The people we treated said it smelled like a strong pesticide, and they mostly had an irritation to the mouth and chest, and headaches and chest pains," said a doctor at Georgia Baptist Hospital.

The man responsible for the situation later called 911 to explain the problem. He had placed the ticket in the toolbox of his pickup truck, where it soaked up a lubricant used in car differentials. The substance was not toxic and had apparently never bothered anyone who worked with it.

ENVIRONMENTAL RACISM?

On May 19, 1995, a strong chemical odor sickened one hundred people in a six-block area of the Newtown section of Gainesville, sending twenty-five residents to the hospital. Victims reported nausea and shortness of breath. "You could smell it really strong," one local related. "I got dizzy and my stomach ached and my skin started jumping."

Investigation by the state Environmental Protection Division proved fruitless, as program director Bert Langley admitted two months later: "We have spent a lot of time and money investigating, and we can't find the source of the problem." The Environmental Protection Agency suggested that the symptoms were those of people suffering from pollen or automobile exhaust fumes.

Residents of the predominately black neighborhood believed this was a case of environmental racism related to industrial activity, which has been blamed for unusually high cancer rates in the area. A state investigation officially concluded five years earlier that the illnesses were caused by the lifestyles of the inhabitants.

The EPA focused on the use of the solvent hexane, which a local business used to extract oil from soybeans. The company had 375,000 pounds of hexane when the incident occurred, but they denied using the substance at that time, and hospital tests revealed no exposure to it. Despite this, five days after the incident the company offered to pay all hospital bills of local residents as a gesture of goodwill to the people of Newtown, the manager said. He hoped it would allay their suspicions of the factory.

PHYSICIANS, HEAL THYSELVES

Mystery illnesses are always serious, but when one breaks out at the Centers for Disease Control and Prevention (CDC) in Atlanta, it is particularly worrisome. Such an event occurred in late July 1996, when the occupants of Building 12, which contains the National Center for Prevention of HIV, STD, and Tuberculosis, and the National Immunization Program, suddenly complained of rapid heartbeat, nausea, diarrhea, and headache. The illness struck at 8:00 A.M., just as work began, and closed the structure for the day. Some victims were treated on the spot, while others were transported to hospitals. Whatever caused the attack, the workers had recovered late in the day. An emergency response team from the CDC immediately investigated the illness, but no cause was found.

The usual response was cited by spokesperson Barbara Reynolds. "The testing done to date didn't show any harmful substance in the building," she said, although the air would continue to be monitored.

Even when a site contains plenty of hazardous materials, the cause of an outbreak can still be mysterious. The Motorola Energy Products Division in Lawrenceville produces battery chargers. In mid-July 1996, thirteen people, including two firefighters, were hospitalized, and five hundred evacuated. The afflicted were treated for respiratory irritation and released later in the day. Hours after the incident, following inspections by the local fire department and federal environmental officers, the plant reopened. "We found absolutely nothing in that building," stated Gwinnett County fire officer Steve Rolader. His best guess was that someone's personal container of pepper gas or tear gas had gone off accidentally in the factory.

LET MY PEOPLE—NEVER MIND
A dozen fire engines were dispatched to the Atlanta Pretrial Detention Center on May 29, 1996, after inmates complained of strong smells that caused respiratory problems. Four prisoners and two guards were treated at Grady Memorial Hospital and released (not literally, at least not for the prisoners). Three of the jail's floors were evacuated outside or into an annex. The source of the problem was never identified.

GERM WARFARE
Anthrax scares became the bomb threats of the 1990s. By October and December 1998, seven threats were received in four states. Fortunately, all turned out to be hoaxes. Threatened were abortion clinics, offices of U.S. attorneys and other federal buildings, Catholic schools, and television and newspaper offices. The situation had become so serious that in 1999 the CDC received funding to prepare for bioterrorism. Much of the money was distributed to state and local agencies for help in fighting infectious diseases and spore-forming bacteria.

Anthrax, originally found in animals, can spread to humans and causes a mortality rate of 25 percent and higher, depending on the method of transport and prompt treatment with antibiotics. Once in the lungs, anthrax causes hemorrhaging, respiratory failure, and toxic shock.

In early 1999 a number of government agencies, health officials, and individuals were receiving plain white envelopes with typewritten notes claiming the receiver had just been exposed to anthrax. Some letters contained plastic sheets or bags containing a dark powder. On February 4 the NBC News bureau in Atlanta, the main post office in Columbus, and two places in Washington, D.C., received these envelopes.

In Atlanta the package arrived on the eleventh floor of a building at Colony Square at Fourteenth and Peachtree Streets. Police received the call at 11:40 A.M., and soon evacuated the building and a three-block area, closing Peachtree and West Peachtree from Tenth Street to Fourteenth Street. Adjacent buildings were also emptied.

An employee said a receptionist opened and read the letter, evacuated the room, and called the FBI, CDC, and Atlanta police and fire departments. Workers on the eleventh floor were not allowed to leave the building until the material was tested. The response was disjointed. Two policemen responded first to a bomb threat call, then firefighters started to evacuate the people in the office before changing their minds. "People in space suits came in and sprayed us head to toe with bleach," witnesses said.

They were taken down in a secure elevator and the first four were ordered to shower with their clothes on in the middle of Peachtree Street.

They then stripped behind makeshift curtains, entered a thirty-foot-long decontamination trailer and showered again. They received a bleach scrub before being wrapped in sheets in a warm room. At that point the procedure was stopped because it had been determined there was no real threat.

The note found in the Columbus post office read, "You have now been exposed to anthrax." The envelope, postmarked Independence, California, contained a small parcel of cinnamon-colored powder wrapped in plastic.

THE ALMOST-REAL THING

A highly disturbing incident occurred at 6:10 P.M. on February 11, 1999, when a man never identified stepped onto a southbound MARTA train stopped at the Oakland City Station and sprayed an unknown gas into a car. Coughing uncontrollably, the phantom gasser immediately exited the train as passengers fell violently ill. Twenty-one people had difficulty breathing, coughed spasmodically, felt tightness in their chests, and suffered nausea and eye irritation.

All were treated and released from Grady except for the worst case, a fourteen-year-old boy who had extreme difficulty breathing. His throat swelled shut and a tube was inserted into his lungs. The young man was monitored in pediatric intensive care, his condition listed as critical, but he rallied and was released several days later.

Because of a deadly gas attack in a Japanese subway and the envelopes allegedly containing anthrax mailed to organizations around the country, the Atlanta Fire Department reacted aggressively. Firemen hosed off the fully clothed victims with hoses, then they were wrapped in white sheets and hustled into ambulances at Lee Street. Some were breathing from oxygen bottles.

At Grady, plastic decontamination tents were hurriedly rigged. Hospital workers gave the victims a series of scrubbings and showers, with the wastewater collected in barrels instead of running into the sewer system. Clothing, sheets, towels, and other material were sealed in red hazardous waste bags.

Everyone who had contact with the victims, including police and fire personnel, EMTs, nurses, and doctors went through the same decontamination regimen.

Security guards sealed off the station, Lee Street, and the ambulance bay at Grady. The train and station were shut down, forcing MARTA to work around the blockage, transferring patrons by bus between West End and Lake stations, located on either side of Oak City, and reversing the trains along the tracks.

Fearing this was a terrorist attack, the incident was investigated by the FBI's domestic terrorist squad, the Bureau of Alcohol, Tobacco, and Firearms, the GBI, and local police agencies.

Descriptions of the attacker conflicted and security cameras did not help identify the culprit. "The entire picture is still unclear," stated MARTA police chief Gene Wilson. "I wish I knew why all of a sudden all those people got ill."

Thinking the mysterious agent of illness was pepper spray, air samples were taken in the train, but the gas was not captured in sufficient quantity to allow for identification. Police officers sprayed in training were certain it was not pepper spray. Neither the attacker nor the gas had been identified.

MED SCHOOL FOLLIES

Just before 9:00 A.M. on June 18, 1999, workers constructing a new visitors center at the Morehouse School of Medicine reported smelling a gas emanating from the second floor of the three-story structure. The Atlanta Fire Department immediately evacuated that building and another adjoining it. The gas affected forty-five people, and nine were stripped, decontaminated, taken to the hospital, and later released.

THE PHANTOM ARSONIST
Just the Facts, Madam

The metro–Atlanta area was terrorized by a phantom arsonist during the summer of 1986. His reign began suddenly on June 20 and extended through early August, when it stopped just as abruptly. During this period he/she/it torched at least seventy-five cars. Copycats probably burned up another ten or more cars. Another dozen vehicles were damaged when the set fires spread. The perpetrator worked largely in spurts, on June 20 and 26, July 2, 3, 9, and 11, and apparently set four small woods fires. The cars were torched in Atlanta as well DeKalb, Fulton, Cobb, and Gwinnett Counties.

The cars set ablaze were primarily General Motors vehicles, but several were Fords. Most were fairly new, although of different makes and years, and generally blue or gray. The pyro was an opportunist—every car had been unlocked or the windows rolled down, but he was no coward—the fires were nearly always located in crowded parking lots and along busy thoroughfares. The perp struck most often in the afternoon, between noon and 5:00 P.M., and primarily on the north side of Atlanta. Each vehicle was set ablaze with newspapers ignited on the front driver's side.

In the spree of June 26 ten cars were torched in three counties on one afternoon. On June 20 four cars in northwest Atlanta burned in thirty-five minutes. The brazen arsonist obviously had his own car and got around, but no one ever spotted him. Several cars in the GM parking lot at Doraville fell victim. The lot had security cameras, but the PA was not seen. The cameras had earlier been equipped with video recorders, which would have caught the criminal, assuming it was reality based, but union officials forced the company to remove the recorders for the privacy of workers—and, as it turned out, arsonists.

Metro arson investigators tend to be firefighters who receive police training. They investigated about 150 cases of car arson a year during the mid-1980s. Of that number half were found to be committed by owners to collect on insurance policies. It was feared that a number of copycats would take advantage of the arson spree to destroy their own cars for that purpose. Most of the imitators were easily identified because their accelerant of choice was petroleum products. One incident involving six cars damaged by fire at Lenox Square turned out to be the result of an overheated catalytic converter that set fire to pine straw beneath it and spread to other cars.

Investigators were stymied. They initially thought the arsonist's motive was hatred of GM, but that notion had been dismissed by early August. Sgt. Larry Herndon of the Cobb County Fire Department said, "We feel (the perpetrator) has some deep-seated psychological problems," an assumption reached primarily because they were unable to find "any other motives to the crime."

Investigators grew frustrated as time passed and no leads surfaced.

"We were hoping he'd brag about it to somebody and they'd call us," said Lt. J. E. Williams, also of the arson squad.

PAGING FOX MULDER

A psychological profile prepared for the brazen, wiley perp indicated the man was "a loner who doesn't function well with women, fairly intelligent and religious," one investigator said. On the latter point, the PA had removed Bibles from two or more vehicles before they were burned.

"Nobody in the country has ever had a situation like this, so it's difficult" to develop a psychological profile, complained Fulton County arson investigator Capt. Bill Dodd. He was expressing the frustration of every metro-arson cop when he said they would "like to catch this turkey. We're all scratching our heads trying to figure out what to do next."

Authorities seemed to catch a break on a day in early August when seven cars were torched. In Cobb County a woman at Akers Mill Shopping Center saw a man near a car that erupted in flames two minutes later. Officers were soon searching for a white male in his mid-twenties to thirties, "possibly a professional in occupation, and a meticulous dresser," announced

Cobb County fire investigator Larry Herndon. The man was tall and heavy, Herndon revealed, a "huge guy weighing three hundred pounds, maybe more, a big sucker. We're talking about one big guy here." The suspect was about six foot, three inches in height, with sandy-brown hair, light-colored eyes, and wire-frame glasses.

Investigators hoped to locate this man for questioning. They would ask if he had alibis for the times and locations of the earlier blazes. Of course, it was a moot point, for the suspect never materialized. A toll-free number and a twenty-five-hundred-dollar reward failed to garner any credible information. Anyone convicted of these crimes could have received ten years in jail and a twenty-five-thousand-dollar fine for each count—a hefty punishment.

Assuming for just a moment that we are dealing with a human criminal and not a phantom, a large portion of the problem with this investigation was institutional. City and county officials coordinated poorly. They met on several occasions, but no single investigator was placed in charge. The FBI offered help in assembling a psychological profile and their computers were capable of analyzing the locations of the fires, which could have narrowed down where the firebug lived. Unfortunately, no one accepted the responsibility of gathering the data from across five different jurisdictions and forwarding it to the feds.

Investigators had only one previous similar incident, almost certainly the work of the same person-entity. Two summers earlier, in 1984, twenty-two cars were torched in similar fashion in Cobb, DeKalb, and Gwinnett Counties. Again, no witnesses and no suspects.

A task force met monthly for a year and the files remain open. Officials waited for a recurrence of the crimes, but sixteen years later there have been none. Police and fire investigators were baffled by a crime that was truly Fortean in nature.

MR. CHRISTIAN!

Late on a Friday afternoon in May 1979, a man walked into the office of Joe Fendley Sr., president of Elberton Finishing Company, and introduced himself as R. C. Christian. He informed Fendley that he wanted to order a monument. Fendley, believing the man wanted a common gravestone, explained that his company was a wholesaler and not involved in individual orders.

"Then he told me what he wanted," Fendley told Boyd Lewis, a writer for *Brown's Guide to Georgia*. "The size, as he described it, was so large that it was unreal. There had never been a monument this large done in Elberton, and Elberton is the granite capital of the world."

Unknown persons erected Georgia's Stonehenge, the Guidestones, on a hilltop near Elberton. Inscribed on the stone slabs are ten "commandments" designed to help guide the future of humanity.

What Christian was asking for was a miniature Stonehenge that would be called the Guidestones.

When Fendley asked his motivation, Christian answered that it would be for the "conservation of the world, and to herald the coming of an age of reason." Fendley thought this was a prank orchestrated by a friend or perhaps the man was "some kind of kook." But it didn't turn out that way.

As the man left he said: "I ought to tell you that my name isn't Christian. It's just that I follow the teachings of Jesus Christ. And I represent a group of Americans who believe as I do, in God and country." He emphasized that they were patriots who lived outside of Georgia and stipulated that their organization would never be revealed.

"Then he said I'd never see him again, and I haven't. I don't expect to."

Fendley thought the mysterious stranger was in his fifties, well but casually dressed, and spoke with a Midwestern accent. He was obviously well educated.

Half an hour after Mr. Christian left Fendley, he visited Wyatt C. Martin, president of Granite City Bank. Martin soon phoned Fendley and revealed that Christian had made a large deposit in his bank to finance the monument. The sum was never revealed, but Fendley considered an estimate of $50,000 to be far too low.

Martin, the banker, required Christian to reveal his real name and his backing organization, but agreed that "I would never reveal their identity or where the money came from . . . I will carry this secret to my grave." Martin explained that by not revealing their identity, the message of the Guidestones would have a broader appeal. He was able to say that they were "a group of patriotic Americans who hope to present to mankind a message of reason and hope." They wanted the stones to be accessible, but removed from population centers. Georgia was selected because of its nearly diamond-hard granite, mild climate (although that could change after the coming pole shift), and the fact that Christian's great-grandmother was from Georgia.

A HEAVY MESSAGE

The message, which arrived in June, was divided into ten "guides," which some consider a New Age Ten Commandants. Introduced by "Let these be Guidestones to an age of reason," they read:

> "Maintain humanity under five hundred million in perpetual balance with nature."
> "Guide reproduction wisely, improving fitness and diversity."
> "Unite humanity with a living new language."
> "Rule passion-faith-tradition and all things with tempered reason."
> "Protect people and nations with fair laws and just courts."
> "Let all nations rule internally resolving external disputes in a world court."
> "Avoid petty laws and useless officials."
> "Balance personal rights with social duties."
> "Prize truth-beauty-love—seeking harmony with the infinite."
> "Be not a cancer on the earth—Leave room for nature—Leave room for nature."

These "guides" were nondenominational, Fendley said, because "if the nation was ever taken over by people that were atheistic or not God-fearing, that the monument would not be torn down. The sayings are designed not to offend anyone by being sectarian or religious." The careful wording and general morality was intended to appeal to all religious, cultural, and political groups.

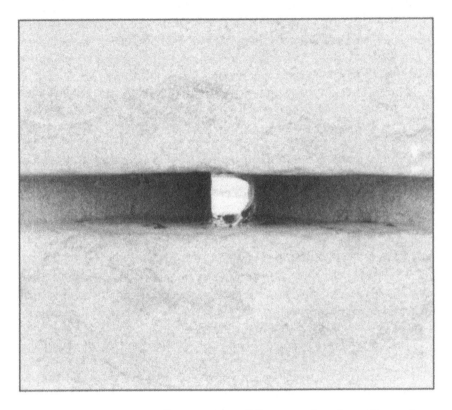

Holes drilled into the stones allow visitors to tell the time and track significant celestial events.

The guides would be sandblasted into the side of the granite monument in eight languages—English, Spanish, Chinese, Arabic, Hebrew, Russian, Swahili, and Hindi. Language experts at the University of Georgia and the New York Metropolitan Museum assisted in translating the guides. Those languages were chosen because they are spoken by the largest number of people in the world today.

Fendley, citing religious writings, including the Bible, believed the earth would be destroyed by fire. This granite monument should survive the fire and help direct the survivors of the worldwide cataclysm.

Lewis Boyd considered them "plucked from a Sierra Club mailing, stirred briskly with some of the United Nations' Charter, and sprinkled with . . . cosmic mysticism . . ." Journalist Bill Osinski called the messages a "generic combination of Malthusian eugenics," "moderate environmental activism," and "good old American laissez-faire democracy."

Christian returned once to see Martin, bearing a model of the Guidestones and specifications for the monument. Its resemblance to Stonehenge, England's famous four-thousand-year-old megalith, was no accident. Christian said he had visited it and was impressed by its astronomical alignments, which were incorporated into the Guidestones.

The stones were cut, appropriately, at Pyramid Quarry. Foreman Joe Davis said the unique shape of the stones and the fact that they were only nineteen inches wide, required a week of work to produce each. A number of early efforts were failures.

Fendley found it one of the most challenging endeavors of his career because of the magnitude of the project and its precise specifications.

High-pressure flame cutters powered by liquid oxygen and fuel oil cut the slabs from the four-hundred-million-year-old granite bed. Cranes then lifted the crude slabs from the 150-foot-deep quarry onto trucks that carried them to Oglesby Shed, where for nine months crews shaped the stones by hammering off four tons of granite from each.

Sandblaster Charlie Clamp did all the engraving, shooting pressurized abrasive black sand that gouged out over four thousand characters, each four inches high. Insulated by protective gear, he reported hearing disjointed music and voices during the process.

The ten guides were engraved on the eight sides of the slabs, while the capstone contained the following inscription, "Let these be Guides to An Age of Reason" in four archaic languages—Egyptian hieroglyphs, Babylonian cuneiform, Sanskrit, and Classical Greek.

Frank Coggins, a local quarry owner, purchased five acres of Wayne Mullinax's thirty-eight-acre cattle farm that occupies the highest hill in the county. He then donated the land to the county for the site of the Guidestones. The spot was chosen because of its commanding position with views to the east and west, the directions in which the stones are oriented, for the sunrises and sunsets on the summer and winter solstices. Workers excavating a foundation for the monument and those who erected it heard inexplicable sounds atop the windswept hill and complained of feeling dizzy or lightheaded during construction.

The finished stones were transported to their permanent location and laboriously hauled into position. After nine months of difficult, unique, and painstaking work, the monument was finished.

The erected monument measures nineteen feet, three inches in height, taller than Stonehenge. It contains 951 cubic feet of granite and weighs 119 tons. The four primary stones are each sixteen feet, four inches in height; six feet, six inches wide; and weigh 42,500 pounds. The capstone is nine feet, eight inches long; six feet, six inches wide; and weighs 25,000 pounds. A central pillar, officially called the Gnomen Stone, is nineteen inches thick and weighs 21,000 pounds. All are nineteen inches thick. The complex rests on a base of five support stones, four measuring seven feet, four inches in length; two feet in width; and sixteen inches in thickness. The fifth is smaller. The support stones weigh a combined 22,000 pounds.

Only one hundred people appeared for the March 1980 unveiling. William G. Hutton, president of the Monument Builders of North America, said, "The Guidestones are what may be one of the few lasting mementos of a civilization that some thousands of years hence may not exist." He speculated that in, say, A.D. 3586, people would decipher the stones and say, "I wonder what went wrong here?"

Several people lingered when the ceremony dispersed. One was a local minister who proclaimed that he and his congregation "don't think Mr. Christian is a Christian." He was upset by the world government idea. "That's where the Antichrist will unite the governments of the world under his power," he said, "the power of the devil."

The guides "seem so innocent in outward appearance," he continued, but noted that the Bible warns against "seducing spirits and doctrine of devils in the last days . . ." The preacher promised "to keep a close watch on this." He believes the monument was "for sun worshipers, for cult worship, and for devil worship."

Is That You, Samantha?

After the minister left the Guidestones, a young married couple lingered. The woman, Jodi, a self-proclaimed witch, stripped, then donned an embroidered purple velvet robe with a hood, picked up a walking stick with a two-foot blade, and drew a circle around the stones. With sandal water she twice drew pentagrams on each stone—the first to drive away negative forces, the second to invoke positive forces.

The man, John, also a witch, appreciated Mr. Christian's alignment of the monument. Sun and moon, solar and lunar reflect the "male and female principle of the Old Religion." He also believed the site was a convergence point of three energy paths running from a spring and "underground lines of magnetic energy, and track-lines used by animals." This concept, called ley lines, is widely known among the megaliths of Europe.

John, who had visited Stonehenge a number of times, said: "I feel the same energy here." He believed the stones contained a power that was amplified by the location and astronomical alignments. Witch John noted that Atlanta was a major player in the New Age movement and suggested that "North Georgia could be the center of the new world after the coming cataclysm."

Jodi agreed with John, saying the "Guidestones are to be a guide for humanity after the apocalypse, and it will probably be used as a gathering point for surviving factions."

LUCKY AS A SEVEN

These New Age cheerleaders were the first of many to recognize the relationship of this site with the number seven, the "magick" number and traditionally lucky (seventh son of a seventh son—any Johnny Rivers fans out there?). It sits on the Double 7 Ranch seven hundred feet from GA 77 on a hill just over seven hundred feet above sea level seven miles north of Elberton and seven miles south from Hartwell (more about that in a minute). This might be stretching the point (hey, this is derived from witches), but the upright stones measure five by two meters—you do the math—it adds up to . . . *seven*. Coincidence? Jodi and John think not. Let's take it to the fence. In Elbert County GA 77 crosses GA 17, and also in the area are highways 72, 79, and 172. Finally, and I noted this one myself, granite is a seventy-million-dollar-a-year industry in Elberton.

Seven is "very significant," Jodi droned on, "and the preponderance of sevens is even more so." It was the number of "the mystic, the initiate" and demonstrates "attainment of occult knowledge." We all know that "666" is the sign of the Antichrist, but "777" represents "God Supreme," and 17 indicates "guidance of a new era for mankind in the tarot."

Forget the occult as explanation for the Guidestones for a moment. A number of citizens suspected collusion between Fendley and Martin, a conspiracy to showcase the county's claim to fame and their craft. It would be a massive and perpetual publicity stunt and a tourist attraction in an area that traditionally draws few visitors. Both deny the charges, and their characters are attested to by all who have known them.

Mr. Christian sent two missives to Fendley and Martin while construction continued on the monument. The letters contained lengthy passages of New Age drivel—long-winded phrases such as "Make mankind more willing to accept the system of limited international law which will stress the responsibilities of individual nations in managing their internal affairs while assisting them collectively in regulating the international relationships"; "Eliminate war and make a beginning in establishing a conscien-

428

tious control by humanity over their destiny on earth"; and "Every one of us is a small but significant bit of the infinite . . . we must live in harmony with the infinite."

Someone has suggested that the name R. C. Christian might stand for Christian Rosencrantz, a nineteenth-century alchemist.

Have odd events occurred at the Guidestones? Oh, yes, beginning on September 12, 1982, when a round, brilliantly lighted UFO was seen hovering near the monument. It was twenty feet in diameter, encircled by green lights. Similar objects were seen at the same time across several neighboring counties.

A wide variety of people visit the Guidestones—witches, UFO buffs, and an assortment of granola (what isn't fruits or nuts are at least flakes) personalities. Many are drawn by the belief that the unique astronomical alignments to the sun and moon and the location combines to emit a powerful energy field. A former mayor admitted that there "have been some occult-type things going on out there, also tribal ritualistic dancing and nude dancing." But, he emphasized, "there have also been Christian activities there and even a wedding." The curious by the thousands visit every year from across the United States, Canada, and Europe.

On occasion vandals have sprayed the stones with graffiti claiming the site is evil, related to devil worship. A witch coven in Atlanta claimed that there "have been many rituals performed at this site. Witches, druids, ceremonial magicians, Native American, Christian, and Neo-Pagan groups have all made use of the site for their own purposes." It is no accident that the site is "located near a major geodetic alignment and over a Power Point," one claimed. The group feels the founders of the monument endowed it with a "mystical" feel by not putting their names to it.

Several groups find it interesting that Hebrew, used by only four million people, is included among the eight languages selected for the guides, which represent two-thirds of the world's population.

The site is even creating its own mythology. According to a prevalent legend, if you stretch out both arms toward the monument, with one palm up, the other down, a person becomes a "human antenna and will receive a message about the stones" (and if you look in the mirror and chant "Bloody Mary" . . .).

Early in 1997 a real "Christian" mystery man approached Carolyn Cann, editor of the *Elberton Star*. This anonymous gentleman desired to change the focus of the monument from mysteriously generic occult to a Christian-oriented prayer site. He funded a landscaping project, featuring evergreens and roses, at the stark site and established a trust to maintain it.

The man also paid for a full-page ad in the *Star* to proclaim his philosophy regarding the Guidestones.

"The place has a personality all its own," Cann wrote. "People are drawn there for a reason . . . It's a mystery, and I love a mystery." So do many others.

Several years after the Guidestones were dedicated, Atlanta astronomer John W. Burgess was called in to help orient a one-third scale model of the Guidestones, which was being prepared for Elberton's sister city in Japan, Jure. It was completed and dedicated at their city hall in 1984.

Burgess surveyed the site of the Guidestones and found "clever, if not ingenuous, astronomical alignments" incorporated into the placement of the monument. The astronomer visited the site several times to observe equinox and solstice sunrises, finding "sight lines to the extreme rising and setting points of the sun and moon, which was by season, as well as other astronomical phenomenon."

The alignment of the four Guidestones resembles "spokes or paddle wheels radiating from the center stone," Burgess wrote. Narrow openings are formed by the arrangement of those stones, some "aligned with the north-south extremes of the sun's rise along the eastern horizon from northeast to southeast."

Burgess found an unsuspected mystery incorporated into the monument. Mr. Christian's original plan called for alignments to determine the north celestial pole, actual noon and the time of year, and "the extreme rising point of the moon," a complex calculation, Burgess contends, because it varies over a nineteen-year cycle. However, as completed the stones not only accomplish all of these purposes, they also align with sunrise on the summer and winter solstices.

A MONUMENT OF BABBLE

The true meanings of the ten guides have been endlessly dissected. New Agers, represented by The Church of Y Tylwyth Teg, seem to accept the statements as benign suggestions for the long-range management of the human race, while Protestants and Catholics see the guides as stark evil. The first guide, for instance. A New Age organization sees it as the "human race at its climatic level for permanent balance with nature." Dr. David R. Reagan, with the conservative Lamb & Lion Ministries in Plano, Texas, interprets this to mean, "4.5 billion people will have to be eliminated!" A Catholic group finds this the "most frightening" of the guides, the "dreams of a world that has 90 percent fewer people. How is this proposed?" They suggest that the second guide implies "eugenics, forced sterilization, and abortion." The Protestants concur on the latter, citing "the Nazi concept of controlled reproduction of the species."

Both Christian groups are disturbed by number four, Catholics as "a possible control and interference in religion," while Protestants find "it clear that all true Christians would be a clear target of any elimination program, because Christians give primacy to faith."

Some Catholics see the eighth as suggesting "socialism and communism," and the ninth and tenth "very much resemble the values of the anti-Christian systems of Humanism, naturalism, pantheism, and paganism that are so prevalent today." One suggests that these anti-Christian systems "look upon Catholicism as cancer on the earth, leaving no room for fallen human nature. There is the evil of denying original sin, and looking upon corrupt human nature as being something 'good.' Such movements oppose the Will of the Creator and work to destroy human society rather than help it." Finally, it was suggested that the initials R. C. were meant to appeal to Roman Catholics.

Dr. Reagan sees two, five, seven, and eight as "cornerstones of centralized world government," and nine "an expression of the essence of most oriental mystical religions," with eight eliminating much of the Bill of Rights. The "infinite" is often interpreted as Satan or the false prophet, generally called the Antichrist. Reagan writes, "I can only conclude that the Georgia Guidestones may well contain the ten commandments of the Antichrist." Reagan is also upset that the astronomical alignments "are patterned after similar ancient pagan shrines in Europe."

R. C. Christian's group claimed to have planned the monument over a period of twenty years. One of their missives declared that "humanity now possesses the knowledge needed to establish an effective world government," and that knowledge "must be widely seeded in the consciousness of all mankind. Very soon the hearts of our human family must be touched and warmed so we will welcome a global rule of reason." Their philosophy, left on "a cluster of graven stones, would convey our ideas across time to other human beings" and would "merit increasing acceptance . . . through silent persistence" and "hasten in a small degree the coming Age of Reason."

A Radio Liberty Internet posting discussing the Guidestones claims that Yoko Ono, John Lennon's widow, said: "I want people to know about the stones—We're headed toward a world where we might blow ourselves up and maybe the globe will not exist—it's a nice time to reaffirm ourselves, knowing all the beautiful things that are in this country and the Georgia Stones symbolize that."

EARTH CENTRAL

Another mystery is located a few miles away. *Ah-Yek-A-Li-A-Lo-Hee*, a Cherokee phrase that means Center of the World, is located three miles southwest of Hartwell, on a plateau near the headwaters of four creeks. Historically, it was the intersection of numerous Indian trails that radiated out in all directions. Georgia's Native Americans used it as an assembly ground, where they traded with each other and Europeans settlers. It is here that the Cherokee met in council.

Not far from the Georgia Guide-stones is a spot the Cherokee believed was the center of the earth.

Some might find significance in the fact that it was a noted roost for passenger pigeons on their annual migration route. They roosted in such numbers that large tree limbs would break under their weight. Once the most numerous bird in the United States, the last passenger pigeon in the world died in 1914.

On October 25, 1923, the John Benson Chapter of the Daughters of the American Revolution unveiled a large monument of Elberton granite to commemorate the Cherokee Center of the World. A marker erected in 1954 by the Georgia Historical Commission reads: "Center of the World." This was *Al-Yek-lions-lo-Hee* (it has several different spellings), the Center of the World to the Cherokee Indians. To this assembly ground from which trails radiate in many directions, they came to hold their Councils, to dance and worship, which to them were related functions."

In the middle of the nineteenth century Hart County's residents split over choosing a location for their county seat. One faction favored the present site of Hartwell, while another figured that the spot the Cherokee considered to be the Center of the World was good enough for Americans. The latter group met there on May 27, 1854, and condemned the body that had "agreed and determined to locate the county site at a point ineligible, inconvenient, and destructive to the permanent interest of the people." Further, they protested "the improper, unjust and ill-advised action . . ."

The other group called this faction "malcontents," "senseless rebels," "miserable squad," and "small mob." It explained that the voters of the county had approved the alternate site, and that was that. It seems that even a century and a half ago people disagreed violently over a sacred spot.

Conclusion

People frequently ask me if I believe in UFOs, ghosts, bigfoot, sea serpents, and all the other phenomena explored in this book. "Yes," I reply, and as they start to agree or argue with that response I add, "but none of it is real." This usually draws a puzzled look. Let me explain.

I do not believe that UFOs are spaceships from other worlds or that their occupants are extraterrestrial biological entities, as the current phrase goes. I do not believe that ghosts are the spirits of the dearly departed or that poltergeists are acting out their frustrations on the living. I do not believe that bigfoot creatures are living throwbacks. These phenomena exist, but they are not real.

So, what are they? No one likes my reply. The truth is, I have no earthly (or unearthly) idea. But I have been convinced for twenty years that these seemingly disparate phenomena emanate from the same source. Call it the Miles Unified Theory of Weirdness. Let us briefly examine the characteristics of the various supernatural activities and identify similarities.

First, all of these events appear physically and even leave physical evidence—photos of UFOs, ghosts, bigfoot, etc.; UFO landing-gear impressions and bigfoot footprints; and even tape recordings of spectral sounds and voices of the dead—but all these phenomena remain elusive. Bigfoot is not in captivity; aliens and their craft are not in government hands (trust me on this one), and ghost busters have not sucked up protoplasmic specters. These phenomena are very physical when they manifest themselves, but when they vanish they are gone. In short, there is no known physical proof that these things exist in our reality. Some evidence, yes, but proof, no.

Second, the phenomena are too diverse. Hundreds of different types of UFOs have been sighted. Think about it. How many different kinds of aircraft do we produce? Not many, and they are easily classified by function—trainers, private, passenger, military, and cargo, in a few different sizes. How many different fighters and bombers does the air force fly? The resources needed to establish an aircraft assembly line is prohibitive. Now imagine the resources required to design and produce an interstellar (or interdimensional or intertemporal or whatever theory you subscribe to) ship. We will not be sending a variety of manned probes to Alpha Centauri and certainly not all at one time. The variety of UFO designs is too vast. In addition, the aliens encountered are similarly diverse. Before popular culture decreed that all aliens were Grays, there were a plethora of different aliens (which might explain the number of different spaceships, eh?). Select one representative from each species and you could create your own *Star Wars* cantina scene. I cannot believe that somewhere in the galaxy an entrepreneur has started a "Gray Lines Tour" (pun absolutely intended) which transports rubes from across the quadrant to "experience" Earth.

Third, and most importantly. Since recorded history humankind has experienced phenomena that assumes forms appropriate to the times. We see spaceships; in the late 1940s they saw rockets; in the late nineteenth-century people saw exotic dirigibles; in earlier times our ancestors saw flaming shields and swords. Same phenomena, different time. We see big-foot, they saw a hundred varieties of leprechauns who behaved suspiciously like current occupants of UFOs, constantly abducting humans and copulating with them. The phenomenon is old. It has developed with us.

What is the source of these phenomena? I know not, but there are plenty of suggestions:

1. Perhaps another dimension or dimensions occasionally intrude upon our reality. In turn we could be playing havoc with the reality of other dimensions. Just think, at this very moment you could be scaring the crap out of beings in the seventh dimension.

2. Perhaps these are materializations, conscious or unconscious, projected from the nether regions of our own minds. Consider the bizarre visions your dreams manifest.

3. Perhaps there is a cosmic "trickster," a term taken from American Indian lore and portrayed in the *Star Trek* universe as the mischievous "Q" being, which amuses itself at our expense. Some would even suggest that we were created for the entertainment of such an intelligence. If so, considering human nature, our ratings should be astronomical.

4. Perhaps it is the "dark side," Satan or a similar creature, whose purpose is to distract or mislead us—UFO contactees and abductees seem to return with an abundance of "instructions" for humankind that invariably turn out to be insipid rubbish.

5. Perhaps we are incapable of imagining the source of these phenomena. But, what do I know? Maybe Mars does need women, or the Watchers need snacks and ache to really serve mankind. Perhaps Ultra-Terrestrial teachers get bored and take field trips.

My advice? Allow yourself to be intrigued by these mysteries, but do not seek them out or become obsessed with them. Taking these enigmas too seriously can easily warp lives and ruin relationships.

On a final note, modern society has succumbed to several types of supernatural mania. Alien "Grays" infest the media and are spilling over onto bumper stickers. One survey places the number of abductees in the millions! The abundance of angel wings currently believed to be fluttering across the globe should cure global warming and whip up apoplectic hurricanes. Mysterious beings bearing ancient inscriptions that reveal the secrets to cure all of society's problems are legion. I will close with this. If your personal philosophy has to be spelled out to you by aliens, angels, self-proclaimed prophets, or a clown like me, you have a serious need to reevaluate your life.

A DISCLAIMER, OF SORTS

If I failed to gore your sacred cow, I apologize. If I did not offend your beliefs, it was not for wont of effort. I promise you I have attempted with great vigor to tread on all toes. On the other hand, I make no apologies for poking fun at your closely held convictions—perhaps you hold them too closely. Loosen up. Life is a joke, and the universe obviously has a sense of humor. Roll with it.

SEQUEL MADNESS!

Over the past twenty years I have logged tens of thousands of miles criss-crossing the state of Georgia while researching a number of topics. I have consulted thousands of books, and magazines, journals, and newspapers beyond counting. I have spoken with numerous people who have experienced eerie events. But my efforts have barely scratched the weird surface of Georgia, and I request the help of readers.

I earnestly request copies of your yellowed newspaper clippings and accounts of odd things witnessed by you or those that you trust. These accounts may be included in future books. If you so request, your identity will be withheld. Do not send your only copy of a photograph—they may get lost in the mail (oh, hell, let's be honest; I'm a slob, they could get lost in the Bermuda Triangle I call my desk). Photographs may be submitted for scientific testing, so, if possible, have duplicate copies of negatives made and send the original negatives.

Also, please send your ghostly manifestations for a future spectacular Ghost Blowout book.

For Further Study

If you enjoyed this book, here are a few suggestions for keeping up with developments in the various fields of weirdness or delving deeper into certain areas. While compiling sources to further your investigation of the paranormal, I realized that most of them were UFO or bigfoot related. I assume this is because those two areas attract the most interest.

Let's start with UFOs. There are two web sites to explore weekly, *Filer's Files* and *UFO Roundup*. My favorite is *Filer's Files*, edited by George A. Filer, eastern director for MUFON, which keeps well abreast of developments in Georgia. *UFO Roundup* is edited by Joseph Trainor, who seems to concentrate more on the world scene. It has an index dating back several years, and the past several years' worth of weekly reports are available from both sites. MUFON Georgia may yet develop a good site (MUFONGA@webtv.net).

To read really in-depth reports on UFO activity, primarily in the west central Georgia Troup-Heard Corridor, check in regularly with the International Society for UFO Research (ISUR) Database (ISUR@America.net), which consists of over 140 full-scale investigations put together by John Thompson and associates, who also cooperate with MUFON. It includes cases from other parts of Georgia, and a few from around the country and world. Particularly intriguing are a number of entity sightings and abduction reports. Be sure to read John Thompson's *Abductions: The Truth,* and check out the other material under *Articles and Archives.* The snail mail address is International Society for UFO Research, P.O. Box 52491, Atlanta, GA 30355. You may join ISUR and MUFON. The National UFO Reporting Center has an index of reports by state, including a sizeable number from Georgia. Try it at HYPERLINK http://WWW.UFOcenter.com.

The Okefenokee X-Files at Okefenokee.com, which is part of a tourism site, is off to a good start with true tales of regional ghosts, UFOs, and bigfoot.

The UFO Newsclipping Service, a classic since 1971 and still run by my old UFO buddy Lucius Farish, a legendary figure in UFO research, is a twenty-page, legal-sized monthly compilation of UFO reports from newspapers worldwide, and also features a Fortean section. In this modern age of free, weekly web sites, its $5.00 monthly cost (or $55 for a year) might be for the serious investigator. The address is UFO Newsclipping Service, #2 Caney Valley Drive, Plumerville, Arkansas 72127.

Published in late 1999 is *Georgia's Aerial Phenomenon 1947–1987,* a large-format, 102-page book by Michael D. Hitt, MUFON's Georgia historian. It is a digest of UFO sightings made over a forty-year period. Most of the reports were taken from state newspapers, but many originated from declassified government documents (Blue Book and other programs) and written statements by witnesses submitted to the UFO investigation organizations CUFOS and NICAP. The book has a county index (eighty-two of Georgia's 159 counties have had significant sightings). The cases are arranged chronologically by year, with sources listed under each of 220 separate accounts. To obtain a copy ($13, postage included) E-mail mufonga@webtv.net.

Georgia bigfoot reports can be found on the web site of the Bigfoot Field Researchers Organization (BFRO), which features a geographic database. Other Georgia bigfoot sightings are offered on the Gulf Coast Bigfoot Research Organization's (GCBRO) web site.

Altamaha-ha's chronicler is Ann Davis (HYPERLINK mailto:ann-davis@gate.net), who operates Sea Griffin Gallery & Books, P.O. Box 1415, Darien, Georgia 31305. Her web site contains a long article about the creature.

Weird magazines come and go, but *Fate* has been a constant since 1947. It investigates every realm under weirdness and contains several sections composed of eerie experiences submitted by readers. *Fate* is currently issuing a series of books featuring articles from its archives (including mine, although they pay nothing extra for the honor—sorry, just a common writer's complaint). Subscriptions are $24.95 for twelve monthly issues. Fate Magazine, P.O. Box 1940, 170 Future Way, Marion, Ohio 43305-1940, 1-800-728-2730.

The *Fortean Times* also does good work, but, being British, it tends to concentrate on Europe.

A number of UFO magazines come and go and exhibit varying degrees of quality. In the 1970s I wrote for half a dozen of them, but today I do not read a single one.

If you want to learn more about the phenomena explored in this book, read John A. Keel's *The Mothman Prophecies* (IllumiNet Press, P.O. Box 2808, Lilburn, Georgia 30226) and Jacques Vallee's *Passport to Magnolia* (Contemporary). For an understanding of UFO history, consider wading through Jerome Clark's *The UFO Book* (Visible Ink Press, 835 Penobscot Building, Detroit, Michigan 48226-4096), which is a seven-hundred-page condensation of his three-volume *The UFO Encyclopedia* (Visible Ink). Clark's *Unexplained!* (Visible Ink Press) is a good primer on every type of weirdness. To understand the origin of Fortean studies, read Charles Fort's *The Book of the Damned* (Prometheus Books) or go hogwild and tackle *The Complete Books of Charles Fort* (Dover Publications). There are hundreds, if not thousands, of books out there about UFOs, strange creatures, alternate archaeology, ghosts, and other weirdness. Be careful what you read and what you believe. Don't be too gullible, and enjoy yourself.

Index

438

Index

Avans, Robin, 58
Avera, James, police chief, 201
Aviation Weekly & Space Technology (magazine), 334, 341
Awehsa Untari (Native American word) 75

Bacon County, 413
Bailey, David, photographer, 100-101
Bainbridge, 239
Baisden, Z. T., 374
Baker County News (publication), 408
Baldwin, 374
Ballard, Danny, 27
Ballground, 203, 392
Barclay, W. A., 239
Barnes, Margaret Ann, author, 315
Barnesville, 27
Barreth, R. M., 83
Bartlett, Sgt. Gene, 86
Bartow County, 134, 223, 308, 387
Bartram, John, naturalist, 378
Bartram, William (John's son), 378
Bat Creek Stone, 149-150
Bates, Hank, UFO 88
Batesville, 133
Battle, Archibald, 297
Battle, John, editor, 6
Baxley, 67, 384
Bazemore, Linda, 99
Beall, Mrs. Hugh D., 93
Beasley, D. T., 75
Beavers, W. A., 28
Beck, Randy, murder victim, 325
Beechan, Dr., 249
Before Columbus (book), 146
Belden, Chris, game and fish specialist, 75
Bell, Alexander Graham, 298
Bell, Art, radio personality, 340
Bell, Debbie (Madam Bell's daughter), 319
Bell, Madam, (*aka* Judy Marks and Dina Adams), 318-320
Benjamin Hawkins, Camp, 32
Bennett, Jim Henry, 233
Benning, Fort, 282
Benson, John, Chapter of the Daughters of the American Revolution, 432
Benton, Dr. Julius, 196
Bergen, Kathleen, FAA, 408
Berlitz, Charles, author, 10
Berrien County, 71
Berry College, 122, 380
Beverly Hillbillies (TV show), 371
"Big Bird," 65

bigfoot, 29, 41-64
Big Mountain, 139
Billy Holler Bugger (creature nickname), 49
Bishop, Sanford, 202
Black, Penny, 92
Black, Tom, 409
Blackman, Harvey, 69
black panthers, etc., 74-78
Black Rock Mountain, 377
Blackshear, 241
Blackshear, David, 179
Blackshear Georgian (publication), 220
Blackshear's Ferry, 179
Blairsville, 208
Blakely, 182
Bleckley County, 391
Bledsoe, Virgil, sheriff, 235
Blitch, Rev. Benjamin, 216
Bloecher, Ted, UFO researcher, 17
Blood Mountain, 377
Blue Book, Project, 6, 7, 10, 11, 32, 110
Blue Ridge, 208
Blue Springs, 382
Bone Cave, 139
Bone Lake, 382
Bone, Willie, 382
Book of the Damned (book), xi, 164, 399
Borg, Bjorn, tennis star, 244
Boston (Georgia), 41
Boston, Philip, 194
Boston Transcript (newspaper), 304
Boswell, Eddie, 401
Bowen, Eliza, historian, 395
Bowen, Jim, forest ranger, 45
Bowens Mill, 161
Bowman, 28
Bowman, Alvin, 74
Bowman, Roger, 389
Boyd, Lewis, 426
Bradeen, Captain, "the Jumbo of Athens," 297
Bradley Observatory, 9
Bradley, Roy, 260
Bramlett, Delaney and Bonnie, musicians, 262
Branham, Levi, author and former slave, 231
Brantley County, 412
Brantley, John B., 297
Brasstown Bald, 377
Brenau University, ix, 177
Briar Patch, 75
Brinkman, Dale, 412
Broach, Keith, policeman, 88
Bronwood, 41, 45, 79

Index

Index

Index

Index